The Failure of Modern Civilization and the Struggle for a "Deep" Alternative

BEITRÄGE ZUR DISSIDENZ

Herausgegeben von Claudia von Werlhof

Band 26

Frankfurt am Main · Berlin · Bern · Bruxelles · New York · Oxford · Wien

Claudia von Werlhof

The Failure of Modern Civilization and the Struggle for a "Deep" Alternative

On "Critical Theory of Patriarchy" as a New Paradigm

PETER LANG
Internationaler Verlag der Wissenschaften

Bibliographic Information published by the Deutsche Nationalbibliothek
The Deutsche Nationalbibliothek lists this publication in the Deutsche Nationalbibliografie; detailed bibliographic data is available in the internet at http://dnb.d-nb.de.

ISSN 0949-1120
ISBN 978-3-631-61552-2
© Peter Lang GmbH
Internationaler Verlag der Wissenschaften
Frankfurt am Main 2011
All rights reserved.

All parts of this publication are protected by copyright. Any utilisation outside the strict limits of the copyright law, without the permission of the publisher, is forbidden and liable to prosecution. This applies in particular to reproductions, translations, microfilming, and storage and processing in electronic retrieval systems.

www.peterlang.de

Claudia von Werlhof is one the most creative activist scholars I know. As feminists we have worked together since the seventies when we discovered, that the main source of capital accumulation was not the exploitation of the male proletarian but that of housewives, small peasants and Nature, in short, the exploitation of subsistence producers. Following from this she developed the theory, that capitalism needed patriarchy and that both needed warfare to develop what still today is called "progress". Without this system of warfare against women, children, and Mother Earth no economic "growth" would be possible. She discovered that the method used in the development of capitalist patriarchy was basically the same which alchemists had used in earlier times, namely to devalue and destroy Nature, and to produce something supposedly "higher", and more "valuable". They tried to create gold – and thus money. This male fantasy of production as a "creative destruction" is still the guiding principle for modern science and technology.

These insights Claudia von Werlhof did not gain in academic conferences but in taking part in a number of social movements which try to change the status quo. However, this combination of practice and theory did not bring her much applause from the academic establishment. Yet her passion and compassion for Mother Earth and all her children is the reason why she continues to struggle for a "deep alternative" to the present destructive system.

Maria Mies – Prof.em., Cologne, Germany

At last we have in English a clear and complete presentation of the critical theory of patriarchy, expounded by one of its leading theorists. This is a book worth pondering carefully by all persons working in the worldwide alter-globalization movements.

Immanuel Wallerstein – Yale University, USA

In many ways 2010 plus is a period in world history of dynamic conflict and change, arising from very different underlying world views! This differs from the past mostly in rapidity and scale. I believe that in such a situation the voices which analyze the phenomenon from different angles contribute a great gift to the common understanding and clarity in our human way forward. After all there is only one world and a common future! The voice of Claudia von Werlhof and her understanding of deep ecology, patriarchy and militarism are important and a must-read for scholars, women and those who are attempting to lead others without a full understanding of the high stakes risks for our Earth habitat!

Rosalie Bertell – Ph.D., USA/Canada

Half a century of struggles, in theory and practice, are condensed here. These struggles come from far away and today are more relevant than ever. The time of Mother Earth is also the time for a radical change in our perceptions and attitudes - as Claudia von Werlhof, at her best, presents in this book.

Gustavo Esteva – Universidad de la Tierra, Oaxaca, Mexico

Von Werlhof courageously moves the barycenter of critique away from the individual and towards the systemic biopathic aspects of Patriarchy and Capitalism. In her breakthrough analysis, von Werlhof shows that one cannot be an authentic anti-Patriarchal feminist without at the same time being against Capitalism, and she explains how the desire to take over and eliminate maternal creativity, while replacing it with its own death dealing devices is motivating the system to cause planetary destruction. Capitalist Patriarchal technology has now made it possible for a very few to create havoc for all creatures. Von Werlhof gives us hope by showing how egalitarian Matriarchal societies offer the values for a viable alternative. This is an important book for those who love the Earth and all her species.

Genevieve Vaughan – Texas/Rome, author *For Giving. A Feminist Critique of Exchange*

"The Failure of Modern Civilization and the Struggle for a 'Deep' Alternative" is Claudia von Werlhof's magnum opus and a major contribution to political theory and action. In it Werlhof reflects on and synthesizes all the major themes of her life's work from her critique of capitalist patriarchy to her reinterpretation of alchemy, to provide not only a searing indictment of the present world order but also a visionary proposal for a Movement for Mother Earth. This is a book that anyone concerned with the fate of feminism and the struggles grass-root movements worldwide are making to end the capitalist destruction of the planet need to read and discuss.

Silvia Federici – New York, author *Caliban and the Witch*

Claudia von Werlhof's work is basic: she gives a deep and radical analysis of "patriarchy", which is the best in this field. It is urgently needed as well as for theoretical conceptualizing as for political activism in this destructive time.

Heide Goettner-Abendroth

Table of contents

Introduction:
The Failure of Modern Civilization and the
"Critical Theory of Patriarchy" 9

A. Capitalism as "Globalization": TINA - There Is No Alternative?

1. The Globalization of Neo-Liberalism, its Consequences and some of its Basic Alternatives 27

2. "Globalization" and the "Permanent" Process of "Primitive" Accumulation: The Example of the Multilateral Agreement on Investment, MAI 65

3. Self-appointed Saviors Propagate Globalization. Opponents of Globalization versus Members of the World Economic Forum . . 85

4. The New will only arise from the Bottom! "Our" University? Social Movements, Society, Education, and Science today 95

B. From "Patriarchy" to "Capitalist Patriarchy"

5. No Critique of Capitalism without a Critique of Patriarchy! Why the Left is no Alternative 115

6. Patriarchy as Negation of Matriarchy. The Perspective of a Delusion 137

7. Loosing Faith in Progress? Capitalist Patriarchy as an "Alchemical System" 153

8. The Utopia of a Motherless World – Patriarchy as "War-System" . 185

C. The Globalization of Capitalist Patriarchy and the Alternatives

9. Globalization, Patriarchy and Women's Movements 207

10. Capitalist Patriarchy and the Re-emergence of Matriarchy – The Struggle for a "Deep" Alternative 221

11. Upheaval from the Depth: The "Zapatistas", the Indigenous Civilization, the Question of Matriarchy and the West 231

12. The Interconnectedness of all Being. A new Spirituality for a new Civilization 259

D. The Latest Challenge: "Military Alchemy" as a Dystopia for Planet Earth

13. Call for a "Planetary Movement for Mother Earth" 269

14. What is Man Doing – What Mother Nature?
Planet Earth in Growing Distress 285

15. Public Appeal to Social Movements Worldwide 297

Introduction

The Failure of Modern Civilization and the "Critical Theory of Patriarchy"*

A new paradigm emerging

The "Critical Theory of Patriarchy" has developed into a new and potentially all-embracing trans-disciplinary paradigm (Projektgruppe 2009, von Werlhof 2010), which recently has also been explored philosophically (Behmann 2009; von Werlhof/Behmann 2010).

In contrast to most existing theoretical approaches, Critical Theory of Patriarchy is able to explain the crisis of the West – modern civilization or the "modern world system" – as the logical failure of the development of patriarchal civilization up to modernity as "capitalist patriarchy"; a failure that could not be understood as long as patriarchy was banned to the collective unconsciousness, wrongly defined, a "blind spot" and the apparently unspeakable "secret" of the "Modern World System".

The new theoretical approach is also able to consider the existence of patriarchy and make us aware of the historical depth of the present global crisis and the strong interconnectedness of its different dimensions.

It is further able to discuss the logic for the alternatives to 500 years of modern civilization and 5000 years of different forms of pre-modern patriarchy; and it is able to explain the tremendous difficulties, if not the impossibility, of a general conscious and peaceful global change towards post-capitalist-patriarchal social relations and a totally different civilization, so urgently needed now.

Origins and potential of the new paradigm

The Critical Theory of Patriarchy has been developed in the last 20 years.
- It is based on the earlier feminist analysis of global capitalism/socialism as the modern world system of "capitalist patriarchy", which showed that instead of proletarian wage labor it is the worldwide "housewifeization" of women and their systematically low or completely unpaid labor in private and public that has been and is the human pre-condition for capitalist accumulation since the end of the witch-hunts (cf. Mies 1986; Mies, Bennholdt-Thomsen, von Werlhof 1988; later Federici 2004).

---

* Translation from German by Dr. Gabriel Kuhn

- It is further based on "eco-feminism" as it defines the relationship between society, women, nature and "mother earth", shows the fundamental importance of nature in general and gives a new definition of it as a living organism instead of supposedly "dead matter"; whereby the latter has been suggested by the modern sciences which are responsible for the "death of nature" (Merchant) since the 17th century, and even a theoretically possible death of "mother earth", a "Terracide" today (Bertell 2000 and 2010) – following the death of women as "witches" (cf. Daly 1978, Merchant 1980; Mies, Shiva 1993).
- It is also based on the historical analysis of "patriarchy" as the "deep structure" of modern civilization itself; whereby patriarchy is no longer defined as a merely "traditional" remnant of male domination that will sooner or later be abolished by modernity – a position held by most analysts, "gender" studies and the left (von Werlhof 2007a).
- And it is based on a different definition of "civilization", comparing the original and in many parts of the world still existing matriarchal civilizations to the patriarchal one(s) that developed later against the matriarchal ones. We thus reject the false image of patriarchy as the first or general form of organization of human society and/or its first form of "high civilization" and the simultaneous wrong definition of matriarchy and matriarchal civilization as women's or mothers "rule and domination", or their denial all together – like that of pre-modern indigenous cultures/civilizations. Matriarchy – *mater arché* – means "in the beginning the mother" and is based on the evidence of the origins of life in the mother (cf. discussion in Göttner-Abendroth 1988; Derungs 1993, Genth 2009, von Werlhof 2009a).
- Finally, the new paradigm is based on an analysis of techniques (cf. Greek "techné", meaning ruse, trick), as a means to develop patriarchy as a social utopia opposing the world of mothers and of matriarchal civilizations, of nature and today even of Gaia as our planet Earth. We therefore reject the idea that these techniques developed by patriarchy are "neutral" and the presumably necessary and inevitable "evolutionary progress" of humanity (cf. Mumford 1977; Wagner 1970, Genth 2002; Bertell 2000, 2010; von Werlhof 1997a, 2001, 2007b, 2010c).

Critical Theory of Patriarchy has identified the struggles of the Left for a new socialism as a project of industrial society and thus of patriarchy and modern civilization in general. The Left cannot present alternatives to the crises of today. We have worked together with Immanuel Wallerstein, the founder of the modern world system-theory, a cooperation which began in the 1980s (cf. last time, von Werlhof 2004). However, our concept of patriarchy, capitalist patriarchy and the critique of modern technology as the so-called "development of the productive forces", and of "progress" as "patriarchal" have not yet been discussed by most theorists. André Gunder Frank as an early leading theorist, for example, did not want to consider the category of patriarchy, even if it had enriched his unusual and far-reaching intent to understand not only 500 but 5000 years of "world systems" (cf. Frank, Gills 1999).

We do not see how alternatives to the modern world system can emerge from it as the Modern Capitalist World System of Patriarchy. We are more related to indigenous alternatives in the global South that stem from pre-colonial, mostly matriarchal civilizations, which are still or again practiced worldwide (by the Zapatistas, cf. von Werlhof 1997b, the Bolivian "Rights for Mother Earth" or "Pachamama" movement, the Indian "Earth Democracy" movement, cf. Shiva 2005, or Brazilian liberation theology, cf. Boff 2010). These alternatives can also be found in the pre-patriarchal "indigenous" history of the global North (cf. Gimbutas 1991; Eisler 1987; Derungs 1993).

Concepts:

Modern civilization as a failed utopia -
the definition of patriarchy as an opposition to matriarchy -
the technological project of patriarchy as an opposition to nature and the planet itself

Western modernity, the modern world system of capitalist patriarchy, can be characterized as a civilization that tries by all means to materialize the utopia of a supposedly "better" and "higher" life. Today, with the "globalization" of neo-liberalism as the most advanced form of capitalist/modern world patriarchy, war, economy and technology, it is evident that this project has failed. Instead of a supposed heaven, we are facing hell on earth, already experienced by masses of people in the global South (Chossudovsky/Marshall 2010).

There exists, nevertheless, no explanation for this "development of underdevelopment" (Frank 1967). The confusion can first be met by using a "larger telescope" (Mies 2003). This means to compare the two central forms of civilization in human history – on the one hand the egalitarian and co-operative matriarchal civilization in tune with nature and life, and on the other hand the hierarchical patriarchal one trying to dominate nature and life. The approximately 5000-year-old patriarchal society has reached its climax of material realization with modernity. Nearly all of the relationships of the original matriarchal civilizations of the world, including growing parts of nature itself, have been "replaced" by a "progressive" counter-world and counter-nature in form of "capital" (the commodity, modern money, machinery, systems of domination). This destructive transformation that could not have been realized with "tools", but is based on continuous wars, processes of "primitive accumulation" – e.g. different forms of colonialism – inside and outside of Europe, and the development of the "natural" sciences, paradoxically has been glorified as "peaceful", "civilized", "productive", "humane" and "creative". It defines "capitalist patriarchy" as the modern world system, including "socialism". It is futuristic and utopian as it proclaims the possibility to construct a better alternative to life, matter, mothers, nature and ultimately to the suppressed matriarchies, being based on processes of "creation by destruction" (cf. von Werlhof 2001, 2004).

The failure of western civilization as the Modern World System can be observed today on a global level as well as on all levels of human, animal and plant existence, including the elements themselves, though this is of course not really recognized "officially" and much less "explained", neither by political and social groups and institutions nor by the sciences in general. On the contrary, in spite of the planetary crises in all aspects of life, and even of the planet itself, which are developing their synergetic effects and may even lead to a general collapse of the fundamental conditions for the maintenance of life on earth as such, nearly all of those who comment on this system(atical) crisis still maintain the idea of infinite progress and development, of industrial society as the best form of civilization in history and of rationality as the highest form of intelligence (critics by Jaeger 2008; von Werlhof 2008; Projektgruppe 2009; Bertell 2010; O'Leary 2010).

In view of this paradox, we can use our new and newly defined theoretical concepts that are mutually interrelated and can explain the overall "logic" of the failure of modern civilization as a "necessary" one: in the long run, the "war logic" of destruction cannot be a success (cf. von Werlhof 2009a).

Our approach is based on a new and much broader as well as more complex and detailed concept of "patriarchy" that brings a new, "technical", definition and "periodization" of it into the debate. This definition exceeds by far the usual understanding of patriarchy as the domination of the father or the man in the family, society and/or the state, and it leads to a new understanding of industrial society and modern civilization by linking it to the much longer global historical development of patriarchy.

By doing this, the patriarchal "project" – or delusion – of constructing a new world, which is opposed to the existing one, could be identified. This is the reason why patriarchy is so much occupied with techniques that would help in this respect only, doing away with all the other techniques of the past and present that would lead into a different direction.

The utopian "New and Better World"-Project that directly and deeply opposes the former matriarchal world and absorbs the whole of nature and Earth itself in the course of its development as a form of "divide, transform and rule!" has been propagated since the beginnings of patriarchy. Its main characteristic is: "alchemy"!

This was my main "discovery", when I tried to find out which category would define the transformation process from the patriarchal past into capitalism as the patriarchal present (von Werlhof 1997a, 2001, 2004, 2009b).

"Alchemy" as the link between the past patriarchy and the present, "capitalist" one: the modern world system as a patriarchal "civilization of alchemists" and a "system of war"

In Critical Theory of Patriarchy, "alchemy" is understood as a world view and an "interdisciplinary science", technique, ideology, religion and "psychology" in form of a quest for patriarchal male identity and "individuation". Alchemy – one of its translations being "black mud of the Nile" – has its origins in the matriarchal garden-civilizations of the so called Paradise (the Persian word for garden). After their conquest by war, the method of the beginnings of patriarchy as a societal order (Eisler 1987, Dieckvoss 2003), the alchemical tradition is passed over to patriarchs and experiences big changes and total perversions. The purpose of alchemy under more or less patriarchal conditions is no longer related to a cooperation with nature and a good life of the community, but defined by trying to realize the "Gnostic" utopia of a "male creation" that is supposed to be higher, better and more divine than the natural or female, matriarchal one.

The new, alchemical idea of a creation under male control, or even as an independent male "creation", is based on the negation, transformation, destruction and "replacement" of the female creation, of nature in general and ultimately of the human being and even Mother Earth herself! This way, destruction is becoming the pre-condition of "creation" or "production" and of "control" and "domination" – a conscious deterioration of the pre-condition for a supposed "improvement"!

Starting in the wars of conquest of matriarchal civilizations and in the laboratories of single alchemists, the idea of a male "creation by destruction" was developed, using the warriors experience and justification, his techniques, the enrichment as a result of war as plunder and experiments on the basis of still pre-patriarchal knowledge. Alchemical experiments were in the beginning very much related to those of shamans, blacksmiths and metallurgy in service of war (cf. Eliade 1980). These experiments have been meditative and immaterial as well as material and practical. In any case, they are systematically separating and dissolving living matter, trying to overcome time by speed and generally aiming at surmounting nature and her cycles, life and death. Alchemy under patriarchy intends to become independent from mothers and nature in bringing death to life/matter – "mortification" – as well as in "creating" life, and in becoming active in transforming the origins and "Gestalt" of existing matter by re-combining separate matters in the alchemist's final "Opus Magnum" – "Solve et Coagula" (Schütt 2000). The result of the procedure is supposed to be the "philosopher's stone", a symbol of ultimate power over nature as a whole (cf. von Werlhof man. in process).

Alchemy, however, is starting its general and global career only with modernity, embracing in the end the whole world and finally our planet. Most of the literature on alchemy argues that alchemy was a failure already in antiquity, not to speak of the "Latin" middle ages, as it did never succeed in producing gold and life and has therefore allegedly been abolished until the end of the 18th century. My concept of alchemy as a violent patriarchal technique and general method of an artificial male creation, however, proves not only its ongoing existence but also its final "success" insofar as it has become the ideological, religious, psychological and practical basis of modern technology (machinery), science and "progress", and of capitalism in general, extending to a sort of economic, social and political alchemy as well (von Werlhof 2001, 2010c and man. in process).

In the texts and justifications of modern progress, it is argued that all matter/life has to be appropriated, brought to the laboratory, cut into pieces (called "analysis"), put together with other materials and be transformed into something supposedly higher, better and more civilized. This is nothing else than the alchemical form of destruction – "mortification" in Latin alchemy – which, as we have seen, is followed by the intended "Opus Magnum" of a new, now male creation of matter/life, which is not necessarily born but made – today through machine technology – and which is supposed to be much "higher" than the supposedly "low", bad and uncivilized, if not sinful, creations of mothers, mother Nature and planet Earth!

This generalization of modern alchemy does not mean, however, it has not failed at the same time. The project of controlling and dominating living nature as a whole, on a micro- as well as on a macro-level, its exploitation, dissection and transformation into "dead matter" and ultimately into dead "capital", and the intents to replace it by a "second nature" (Bruiger 2006) of a "new life" or "industrial society" and generally of capital, cannot work. The times of "ostrich policies" are over as the effects have become planetary in their dimensions.

All this has become obvious to many people who have started a search for an alternative world and relationship to nature, also on a technical level. But, as they do generally not have a theoretical concept of alchemy from the point of view of patriarchy, they even think of pre-modern alchemy as an alternative to modern science and technology! (cf. Wilson, Bamford, Townley 2007). Such illusions have to be stopped. They do not lead out of our dilemma.

The belief in alchemical principles is obviously very old and a religious one, based on the patriarchal idea of the "Creator" as a male God beyond nature, mothers, the Goddess and Earth. From then on (Assmann 2003) it was apparently only this God who was able to "make" matter and life exist, and this not only in the beginning, but also after it as well: from the perspective of progress, Man thinks it his calling to improve creation in a supposedly divine manner as if He could act like God on Earth. This is what alchemy and science or progress are about, the alchemists/scientists/capitalists trying to become divine creators on Earth, godly "Fathers" of a new, "pure" and better matter – like gold – and of a new and better life – a "new" human being, or today even a "post-human" one (Weizenbaum 1976; Rifkin 1983; Schirrmacher 2001; von Werlhof 2009a and 2010a).

Patriarchy as a utopia can be materially realized only via a successful male "creation by destruction". From this perspective, modern civilization with industrial society was and is the huge worldwide intent spreading from Europe by means of colonialism, imperialism, war and "globalization", in order to develop such a "pure" patriarchy without any matriarchal remnants and dependencies, be they related to women, mothers or Mother Nature and the planet itself.

I therefore call the developed modern world system of today the "civilization of alchemists", since nearly everybody has become a part of this indeed "Great Transformation" (Polanyi 1978) of the world into a machine for the globally growing "creation" by destruction: commodity production, modern money, machinery and command – "capital". Capital, as the most important result of modern alchemy, is indeed regarded to be the new gold (cf. Binswanger 1985) and – paradoxically – even "life". This way a concept of life has emerged that does not relate to real life – which has never been defined by the sciences anyway – but calls life what is the result of the alchemical Opus Magnum, namely the death of life and its new assembly to the fetish of the commodity or other forms of capital (cf. 2010, genetic engineer C. Venter spoke of "life", pretending to have created it himself in form of a new bacterium). This perversion is related to the fact that the alchemical production process, not to mention its most modern forms, is not peaceful at all, though the system tries by all means to hide its systematic violence.

Hence I call it a "system of war". This war is occurring every day and does not have to be "declared". "Life", nevertheless, can principally not be created by alchemy, neither in earlier times nor today. On the contrary, under the regime of alchemy, real life is dying out. This shows that it is possible to kill life, but not to bring it into being artificially. In alchemical terms: mortification is working, but the Opus Magnum is not, and the idea of the philosopher's stone in reality is vanishing into the nowhere!

The West's failure is due to the "alchemical" destruction of the world and the so-called natural "resources"; a destruction that is thought of, theologically proclaimed and fetishized as "creation" (cf. Vatican 2010). Wherever and whatever alchemy is used for, it is applied by following the same principles. But the counter-productivity of the patriarchal project's "necessary" violence cannot be recognized and given up neither by its "elites", nor by most of the men and always more women in this world. It would mean to renounce patriarchy and patriarchal civilization, and not only 500 but 5000 years of it! The utopian dream of modern civilization to be or become finally detached from history, nature, the planet itself and the female part of the species, will not become true.

Critical Theory of Patriarchy helps to leave behind the confusion, ideologies, illusions, belief systems and propaganda about "The West" and the modern world system. It allows for a completely new insight into the real, long-term character of modern civilization at the very moment of its failure, and it is therefore necessary for all those who want and have to move forward to real, "deep" alternatives. Patriarchy or – real – Life! This has become the question of today.

The War System as a planetary one: a new "Military Alchemy" and the threat for planet Earth: the whole planet as weapon?

Mostly unnoticed by the public and academics, the latest developments in military technology since World War II (Bertell 2000) show that the Modern World System of Patriarchy has reached its ultimate goal: the intent to subject, change and control not only nature and (wo)man, but also the planet itself. The Military tries to convert it from a living "mother Earth" into a "system" – as artificial "life" – that can be switched on and off like a machine (von Werlhof 2010b). The Earth as a whole is irresponsibly and criminally put at risk by the purposeful use of technologies that are transforming the planet itself into a weapon of mass-destruction: instead of nuclear armament – "nuclear alchemy" (Wagner 1970, Bertell 1985) – the new non-nuclear one is working with "plasma weapons, weather wars and geo-engineering" (Bertell 2010, Hamilton 2010).

It seems as if the biblical, lightning-and-thunder-throwing God Jahwe has become incarnated! In "Slowly Wrecking our Planet", Bertell describes the negative effects on the organization of life of planet Earth which can be identified in the partly destruction of the atmosphere and atmospheric layers, the ozone hole, a wobbling of the planets course and the dangerous interferences in its magnetic field inside as well as outside of it (Bertell 2010).

Most of these realities that we experience as climate change and -chaos or natural catastrophes, for instance, are already undermining the oldest belief of (wo)mankind: our deep confidence in mother Nature. Is this loss occurring in any ones interest? For Europeans this has happened already once, namely at the beginnings of modern society, when nature – like woman – was presented to the people as a bad and violent, demonic and dangerous stepmother instead of a caring, peaceful and nurturing mother of all beings (Merchant 1980).

In fact, the program to dominate nature by modern science was developed at the same time. The realities we are facing today, on the other side, cannot simply be explained as a "revenge" of nature to CO^2 carbon emissions, though in the climate change debate they are presented as such. They are instead to an unknown percentage produced by the use of artificially created super-powerful electromagnetic waves through "ionospheric heaters" (!) in installations like HAARP in Alaska, "Woodpecker" in Russia, EISKAT in Tromsö, Norway, Arecibo in Puerto Rico and in about six to eight further places on the globe, known originally as Nicola Tesla's (1856-1943) inventions (Tesla 1997).

They were the result of a rather alternative view of the earth and the solar system as a living – "electro-magnetic" – interconnectedness, and opposed to the mainstream of scientists who since the 16th century have had a mechanistic understanding of the earth and the planetary system as a sort of dead mechanism. Instead of using the peaceful potential of Tesla's inventions for the urgently needed alternatives (O'Leary 2010), the military in the East and the West took over – in the US as Eastlund patents – and used them for the opposite. They seem unable to imagine anything else than seizing power as if "might is right" (Bertell), destroying life and appropriating the "global commons", establishing control over everything by violent transformation, now of the planet itself – and propagating this procedure as a "progress" in the control, domination and "improvement" of nature and Earth herself!

The entire scale of the negative effects of these experiments is not known at all, at least not to the public, which is not allowed to know. This ignorance is leading the public again to the wrong conclusion, namely that even more control and domination of nature is needed! What is at stake is the ultimate step to gain power over humankind, the totality of the planet and its "alchemical" transformation into a "better" one, which means, into a destroyed one.

Today the military and related economic, academic and political interest groups are on the way to establish a literal "system of war" – the totalitarian "New World Order" – as the last outcome of the modern "civilization of alchemists".

At this point of an apparent "success" of the powerful, which is still hiding the catastrophes that are already under way and will be accumulated further on if not stopped in time, the general failure of western civilization as the modern capitalist and patriarchal world system can be observed on a new and last dimension, the planetary level. The unimaginable mega-crimes to which the Earth and all living creatures on it are more and more exposed, for instance by a steadily growing number of experiments with the planet and their cumulative effects or "collateral damages", could even lead to an overall "Omnicide" (Bertell 1986) or "Terracide" (Hoags 2010). Who can speak of "success" in face of these incredible dangers?

Founding the "Planetary Movement for Mother Earth"

We, hundreds of women and a minority of men founded the "Planetary Movement for Mother Earth" in Germany in May 2010 (von Werlhof 2010b). We have to do something about the situation of our planet and we will – together with other already existing social movements – try to inform and mobilize as many people as possible worldwide! (www.pbme-online.org)

I do not know if any other theoretical approach exists that is able to explain the unimaginable horror and megalomania of the new "Military Alchemy". For Critical Theory of Patriarchy it is "easy", but we do not consider this to be a triumph. We would rather like to be wrong! (cf. Klein 2007).

Our approach has widened the analysis and added something to it, which was necessary in order to fully understand the crisis of today and the alternatives to it that need to be discussed and practiced. The crucial difference between our approach and other theories and approaches from right to left is our critique of modernity as "patriarchal", which is why we do not believe in the capacity of all sorts of progressive and modernizing theories to lead to the needed alternative.

On the contrary, we are looking for remnants of our matriarchal past and present as a "second culture" (Genth 1996) underneath patriarchy. These are the "indigenous" sources of our endeavor for today and the future. And we will look for alternatives from the point of view of this knowledge.

The book and its contents

In relation to this development of Critical Theory of Patriarchy, the book is organized around four parts:

A. *Capitalism as "Globalization"*
   contains a discussion and critique of neo-liberalism as a process of neo-colonialism and a new worldwide phase of "primitive accumulation" and war that comprises the North as well – a development which is not yet understood by the people of Europe and the US, as it leads to the final plunder and under-development of the entire world.

B. *From "Patriarchy" to "Capitalist Patriarchy"*
   confronts the narrow definitions of capitalism used by the Left, with the patriarchal "deep" structure of modern civilization and its "alchemical" transformation into a "war-system" of "progress" and "creation by destruction"/destruction through "creation". Furthermore, this is discussed from the still larger perspective of matriarchal civilizations and their colonization by developing patriarchies. This way the roots of the present world-crisis of modern civilization and its "necessary" failure can be traced back to their origins.

C. *The Globalization of Capitalist Patriarchy and the Alternatives*
   discusses the re-emergence of matriarchies as the struggle to establish a "deep" alternative to capitalist patriarchy, and presents a view on the Western women's movement, which is actually split into patriarchy-critical feminism and neo-liberal "gender"-movements. Seen in comparison with indigenous movements like the one of the Mexican "Zapatistas", we learn about the huge gap that divides the movements in the global South from most of those in the global North. This part of the book ends with a rather indigenous look on a "new spirituality" for a "new civilization".

D. *The Latest Challenge: "Military Alchemy" as a Dystopia for Planet Earth*
   presents the first papers of the recently founded "Planetary Movement for Mother Earth". They inform about the incredible assaults that have been committed against our planet already, hidden behind our backs. Critical Theory of Patriarchy seems to be the only approach capable of explaining the "unthinkable" new technologies that transform the planet itself into a huge weapon. Finally, social movements around the world are called to action in favor of Mother Earth.

I am thankful to all the women and men who accompanied this travel over decades with their critique, co-operation and advice, especially Maria Mies, Veronika Bennholdt-Thomsen, Renate Genth, Immanuel Wallerstein, Heide Göttner-Abendroth, Gustavo Esteva, Vandana Shiva, Michel Chossudovsky, Silvia Federici, Pierre Franzen, Genevieve Vaughan, and ultimately Rosalie Bertell.

I am dedicating the book to indigenous-, subsistence perspective-, diverse women for diversity-, gift-economy- and matriarchal studies-groups worldwide, and, last but not least, to the recently founded "Planetary Movement for Mother Earth".

Claudia von Werlhof, Innsbruck, December 2010

Bibliography

Assmann, J. (2003) *Die Mosaische Unterscheidung oder Der Preis des Monotheismus*, München: Hanser

Behmann, M. (2009) *Idee und Programm einer Matriarchalen Natur- und Patriarchatskritischen Geschichtsphilosophie. Zur Grundlegung der Kritischen Patriarchatstheorie angesichts der ‚Krise der allgemeinsten Lebensbedingungen'*, in Projektgruppe „Zivilisationspolitik", 107-177

Bertell, R. (1985) *No Immediate Danger? Prognosis for a Radioactive Earth*, London: The Women's Press

Bertell, R. (2000) *Planet Earth. The Latest Weapon of War*, London: The Women's Press

Bertell, R. (2010) 'Slowly Wrecking our Planet', Epilog for "*Planet Earth*", German edition in preparation

Binswanger, H. C. (1985) *Geld und Magie*, Stuttgart: Edition Weitbrecht

Boff, L. (2010) *Die Erde ist uns anvertraut. Eine ökologische Spiritualität*, Kevelaer: Butzon & Bercker

Bruiger, D. (2006) *Second Nature. The Man-made World of Idealism, Technology and Power*, Victoria: Leftfieldpress

Chossudovsky, M. and Marshall, A. G. (eds.) (2010) *The Global Economic Crisis. The Great Depression of the XXI Century*, Montréal: Global Research Publishers

Daly, M. (1978) *Gyn/ecology: A Metaethics of Radical Feminism*, Boston: Beacon Press

Derungs, K. (2003) ‚Die Natur der Göttin', in E.O. James *Der Kult der Großen Göttin*, Bern: Amalia, 12-55

Dieckvoss, G. (2003) *Wie kam Krieg in die Welt? Ein archäologisch-mythologischer Streifzug*, Hamburg: Konkret Literatur

Eisler, R. (1987) *The Chalice and the Blade. Our history, our future*, San Francisco: Harper

Eliade, M. (1980) *Schmiede und Alchemisten*, Stuttgart: Klett-Cotta

Federici, S. (2004) *Caliban and the Witch. Women, the Body and Primitive Accumulation*, New York: Autonomedia

Frank, A. G. (1967) *Capitalism and Underdevelopment in Latin America*, New York: Monthly Press

Frank, A. G. and Gills, B. K. (1999) *The World System: Five Hundred Years or Five Thousand?* London: Routledge

Genth, R. (1996) ‚Matrirchat als zweite Kultur', in C. von Werlhof, A. Schweighofer and W. Ernst (eds.) *Herren-Los: Herrschaft-Erkenntnis-Lebensform*, Frankfurt a. M.: Peter Lang, 17-38

Genth, R. (2002) *Über Maschinisierung und Mimesis. Erfindungsgeist und mimetische Begabung im Widerstreit und ihre Bedeutung für das Mensch-Maschine-Verhältnis*, Frankfurt a. M.: Peter Lang

Genth, R. (2009) ‚Zivilisationskrise und Zivilisationspolitik', in Projektgruppe „Zivilisationspolitik", 31-57

Gimbutas, M. (1991) *The Civilization of the Goddess. The World of Old Europe*, San Francisco: Harper

Göttner-Abendroth, H. (1988) *Das Matriarchat I. Die Geschichte seiner Erforschung*, Stuttgart: Klett Cotta

Hamilton, C. (2010) The Return of Dr. Strangelove. The politics of climate engineering as a response to global warming, in *Requiem for a Species: Why we resist the truth about climate change*, London/Washington DC: Earthscan and Allen & Unwin, Australia

Hoags, Bonnie (2010) email 23rd of August, The Bonnefire Coalition website accessible at www.agriculturedefensecoalition.org

Jaeger, M. (2008) *Global Player Faust oder Das Verschwinden der Gegenwart. Zur Aktualität Goethes*, Berlin: wjs

Klein, N. (2007) *The Shock Doctrine. The Rise of Disaster Capitalism*, New York, Toronto: Metropolitan Books, Knopf Canada

Merchant, C. (1980) *The Death of Nature. Women, Ecology and the Scientific Revolution*, San Francisco: Harper & Row

Mies, M. (1986) *Patriarchy and Accumulation on a World Scale. Women in the International Division of Labour*, London: Zed Books

Mies, M. (2003) ‚Über die Notwendigkeit, Europa zu entkolonisieren', in C. von Werlhof, V. Bennholdt-Thomsen und N. Faraclas (eds.) *Subsistenz und Widerstand. Alternativen zur Globalisierung*, Wien: Promedia, 19-40

Mies, M., Bennholdt-Thomsen, V., von Werlhof, C. (1988) *Women, the Last Colony*, London: Zed-Books; New Delhi: Kali

Mies, M. and Shiva, V. (1993) *Ecofeminism*, London: Zed Books

Mumford, L. (1977) *Mythos der Maschine*, Frankfurt a. M.: Fischer

O'Leary, Brian (2010) *The Turquoise Revolution. Innovation and Sustainable Solutions – an urgent appeal to Scientists, Environmentalists and Progressives*, http://drbiranoleary@wordpress.com, June 14

Polanyi, K. (1978) *The Great Transformation*, Frankfurt a. M.: Suhrkamp

Projektgruppe "Zivilisationspolitik" (2009) *Aufbruch aus dem Patriarchat – Wege in eine neue Zivilisation?*, Frankfurt a. M.: Peter Lang

Rifkin, J. (1983) *Algeny*, New York: Viking

Schirrmacher, Frank (ed.) (2001) *Die Darwin AG. Wie Nanotechnologie, Biotechnologie und Computer den neuen Menschen träumen*, Köln: Kiepenheuer & Witsch

Schütt, H. W. (2000) *Auf der Suche nach dem Stein der Weisen. Die Geschichte der Alchemie,* München: CH Beck

Shiva, V. (2005) *Earth Democracy,* Cambridge: South End Press

Tesla, N. (1997) *Seine Werke. Edition Nikola Tesla,* Peiting: Michaels Verlag

Vatican (2010) The Pontifical Academy of Sciences, Declaration on Genetic Engineering. Outlook by Richard L. Tomasch: ‚Der Vatikan sagt Ja zur „Grünen Gentechnik"!

‚Päpstliche Akademie der Wissenschaften plädiert für gentechnischen Fortschritt in der Landwirtschaft', in: *Pro Leben, antiGENtechnik Plattform Österreich,* 3.12.2010

Venter, Craig (2010) ‚Genpapst Craig Venter schafft Bakterium mit künstlichem Erbgut', in: *Handelsblatt,* 21.5.2010

von Werlhof, C. (1997a) ‚Ökonomie, die praktische Seite der Religion. Wirtschaft als Gottesbeweis und die Methode der Alchemie', in Ernst, U., Gubitzer, L. and Schmidt, A. (eds.): *Ökonomie M(m)acht Angst. Zum Verhältnis von Ökonomie und Religion,* Frankfurt a. M.: Peter Lang, 95-121

von Werlhof, C. (1997b) 'Upheaval from the Depth. The „Zapatistas", the Indigenous Civilization, the Question of Matriarchy and the West', *International Journal of Comparative Sociology,* Issue „Injustice and Inequality from Comparative Perspectives", 106-130; last time in Kumar, C. (ed.) (2007) *Asking, we walk. The south as new political imaginary,* Bangalore: Streelekha, Vol. 2, 249-268.

von Werlhof, C. (2001) 'Losing Faith in Progress? Capitalist Patriarchy as an „Alchemical System"', in Bennholdt-Thomsen, V. Faraclas, N. and von Werlhof, C. (eds.): *There is an Alternative: Subsistence and Worldwide Resistance to Corporate Globalization,* London: Zed Books, 15-40

von Werlhof, C. (2004) 'Using, Producing, and Replacing Life? Alchemy as Theory and Practice in Capitalism', in Wallerstein, I. (ed.) *The Modern World-System in the Longue Durée,* Boulder/London: Paradigm, 65-78

von Werlhof, C. (2007a) 'Capitalist Patriarchy and the Negation of Matriarchy. The Struggle for a „Deep" Alternative', in Vaughan, G. (ed.) *Women and the Gift-Economy. A Radically Different World View is Possible.* Toronto: Inanna, 139-153

von Werlhof, C. (2007b) 'No Critique of Capitalism without Critique of Patriarchy! Why the Left is No Alternative', in *CNS – Capitalism Nature Socialism,* Vol. 18, Nr.1, March, New York/London: Routledge, 13-27

von Werlhof, C. (2008) 'The Globalization of Neoliberalism, its Consequences, and Some of its Basic Alternatives', in CNS – *Capitalism-Nature-Socialism,* Vol. 19, Issue 3, September, London/New York: Routledge, 94-117; and in Chossudovsky, M. and Marshall, A. G. (2010), 116-144 von Werlhof, C. (2009a) 'The Utopia of a Motherless World. Patriarchy as War-System', in Göttner-Abendroth, H. (ed.): *Societies of Peace, matriarchies past present and future,* Toronto: Inanna, 29-44

von Werlhof, C. (2009b) „Das Patriarchat: "Befreiung" von Mutter (und) Natur?', in Projektgruppe „Zivilisationspolitik", 59-103

von Werlhof, C. (2010) *West-End. Das Scheitern der Moderne als „kapitalistisches Patriarchat" und die Logik der Alternativen,* Köln: PapyRossa

von Werlhof, C. (2010a) *Vom Diesseits der Utopie zum Jenseits der Gewalt. Feministisch-patriarchatskritische Analysen – Blicke in die Zukunft?,* Freiburg: Centaurus

von Werlhof, C. (2010b) 'Call for a "Planetary Movement for Mother Earth"', speech at the *International Goddess-Conference "Politics and Spirituality",* Hambach, Germany, 29 May

von Werlhof, C. (2010c) What is Man doing – what Mother Earth? The Planet in growing distress..., www.pbme-online.org

von Werlhof, C. *Die Zivilisation der Alchemisten,* manuscript in process

von Werlhof, C. and Behmann, M. (2010) *Teoría Crítica del Patriarcado. Hacia una Ciencia y un Mundo ya no Capitalistas ni Patriarcales,* Frankfurt a. M.: Peter Lang

Wagner, F. (1970) *Weg und Abweg der Naturwissenschaft,* München: CH Beck

Wallerstein, I. (1974) 'The Rise and future Demise of the World Capitalist System: Concepts for Comparative Analysis', *Comparative Studies in Society and History,* Vol. 16, Noi.4, 387-415

Weizenbaum, J. (1976): *Computer Power and Human Reason. From Judgement to Calculation,* New York: W. H. Freeman & Company.

Wilson, P. L., Bamford, C. and Townley, K. (2007) *Green Hermeticism. Alchemy and Ecology,* Great Barrington: Lindisfarne Books

A

Capitalism as "Globalization": TINA - There Is No Alternative?

1. The Globalization of Neoliberalism, its Consequences, and some of its Basic Alternatives*

> Elaboration on a lecture given at a panel discussion with Ferdinand Lacina, Austrian Ex-Minister of Finance and Ewald Nowotny, President of the BAWAG-Bank during the "Dallinger Conference", AK Wien, November 21, 2005. Original German Title: "Alternativen zur neoliberalen Globalisierung, oder: Die Globalisierung des Neoliberalismus und seine Folgen", Wien, Picus 2007
>
> (Shortened version in: CNS – Capitalism, Nature, Socialism, Vol. 19, Nr. 3, September 2008, Routledge, pp 94-117, and in: Michel Chossudovsky and Gavin Marshall (Eds.): The Global Economic Crisis. The Great Depression of the XXI Century, Montréal, Global research Publ., 2010, pp.116-144)

Preliminary remark 2010

After the financial crash in 2008 and in the midst of a worldwide economic crisis that is still increasing in severity, the following considerations should be regarded as outdated, part of a past that could now be recognized as erroneous, dangerous, suicidal and criminal. But this is not happening. On the contrary, trillions of Dollars and Euros from the tax payers have been spent to save the global, neo-liberal speculators. This means that their crisis was stopped and a new growth is being proclaimed. It is a growth for them only. We, therefore, have to ask: Was the crisis produced in order to transform virtual and vanished money into real money, rewarding the speculators instead of punishing them?

By this logic the next crisis has to follow as the nation states start to go bankrupt, one by one, for giving the money they control to the speculators, banks and corporations. The national governments therefore have to take more and more money from the people directly nowadays: they empty their pockets and take their wages, pensions, savings and social security away – and ultimately sacrifice their future.

This phase of the crisis has now started in Europe, concretely in Greece and Ireland. It is declared that the money which the EU as a whole is able to mobilize can save these and more countries if necessary – and it will be necessary. This is ensured by the ongoing speculation with the Euro. Consequently, the EU Commission has now agreed upon en even permanent "security mechanism", ensuring that this process is not going to stop in 2013 as was planned earlier.

---

* Translation from German by Dr. Gabriel Kuhn

Once again the actual tranche of trillions of Euros is not going to save countries like Greece and Ireland at all, especially not their citizens. This money goes once more directly to the banks and corporations, for example to the German defense industry with which the Greek government is indebted. The Greek people, nevertheless, will not see a single Euro of this money, on the contrary – *they will have to pay the bill*!

In other words: The national European governments are now defined as nothing else than money collectors for the banks and corporations. Under the umbrella of the EU this is going to function like a common liability facing the "creditors", the banks and corporations. It resembles somehow what Mohammad Yunus is doing with poor women in Bangladesh: They get the credit only when a whole group of them is guaranteeing the repayment of every single one.

The European governments thus have to organize a growth which is generated by expropriation, including the last commons, creating new and even violent forms of primitive accumulation, like privatization, and they have to guarantee the safe transfer of the booty.

The North has become a colony of the corporations. The organized plunder of Europe has begun.

Having surrounded the globe, the politics of the "Go West" and "Go to loot the colonies!", is coming back from where it had started 500 years ago. Today this means: "West-end", the end of the west. In this final phase of the crisis (and) of globalization, the policy of neo-liberalism finally succeeds in getting things done. Its ultimate logical perspective is "militarism, the last executor of capital accumulation" (Rosa Luxemburg 1922).

Or is there anyone who can stop this process? And why does almost nobody – besides the perpetrators – even understand what is happening? Most people in the North still believe in the propaganda of modernity which is said to mean progress, peace, growing wellbeing and development for everybody.

Brainwashed and accomplices over centuries, the people of the North are now facing a count-down for which they are totally unprepared.

Opening

Is there an alternative to plundering the earth?
Is there an alternative to making war?
Is there an alternative to destroying the planet?

No one asks these questions because they seem absurd. Yet, no one can escape them either. They have to be asked. Ultimate absurdity has taken hold of our lives. We are not only headed towards the world's annihilation – we are headed towards it with ever increasing speed. The reason is the "globalization" of so-called "neoliberalism". Its motto is TINA: "There Is No Alternative!" It is the deal of deals, the big feast, the final battle – Armageddon.

Wrong? Exaggerated?

Let us first clarify what globalization and neoliberalism are, where they come from, who they are directed by, what they claim, what they do, why their effects are so fatal, why they will fail, and why people nonetheless cling to them. Then, let us look at the responses of those who are not – or will not – be able to live with the consequences they cause.

1. What Is "Neoliberal Globalization"?

1.1   TINA – Supposedly without Alternative

Before talking about the topic of today – alternatives to neoliberal globalization, or: the globalization of neoliberalism – one has to acknowledge that there is indeed a problem here. And not only that: One also has to define what the problem is exactly.

This is where the difficulties begin. For a good twenty years now we have been told that there is no alternative to neoliberal globalization/the globalization of neoliberalism, and that, in fact, no such alternative is needed either. Over and over again, we have been confronted with the TINA-concept: "There Is No Alternative!" The "iron lady", Margaret Thatcher, was one of those who reiterated this belief without end – it is an embarrassment to women when one of their own displays such a politics of callousness once she has gained power.

The TINA-concept prohibits all thought. It follows the rationale that there is no point in analyzing and discussing neoliberalism and so-called globalization because they are inevitable. Whether we condone what is happening or not does not matter, it is happening anyway. There is no point in trying to understand. Hence: Go with it! Kill or be killed!

Some go as far as suggesting that neoliberalism and its globalization – meaning, a specific economic system that developed within specific socio-historical circumstances – is nothing less but a law of nature. In turn, "human nature" is supposedly reflected by the character of the system's economic subjects: egotistical, ruthless, greedy and cold. This, we are told, works towards everyone's benefit.

The question remains, of course, why Adam Smith's "invisible hand" (which supposedly guides the economic process towards the common good, even if this remains imperceptible to the individual, Binswanger 1998) has become a "visible fist"? While a tiny minority reaps enormous benefits of today's economic liberalism (none of which will remain, of course), the vast majority of the earth's population, yes the earth itself, suffer hardship to an extent that puts their very survival at risk. The damage done seems irreversible.

All over the world media outlets – especially television stations – avoid addressing the problem. A common excuse is that it cannot be explained (Mies/Werlhof 2003, p. 23ff, 36ff). The true reason is, of course, the media's corporate control. Neoliberalism means corporate politics.

Unfortunately, this still evades the public. In most Western countries – as, for example, in Austria – "neoliberalism" is not even commonly accepted as a term, and even "globalization" struggles to find recognition (Salmutter 1998, Dimmel/Schmee 2005). In the Austrian example, a curious provincialism reigns that pretends the country was somehow excluded from everything happening around it. If one listened to former chancellor Schüssel, it sounded like Austria knew no problems at all. The logic seems that if there is no term, there is no problem either. Unnamable, unspeakable, unthinkable: non-existing. Felix Austria.

Although Austria's decision to join the European Union in 1995 bore the same consequences that neoliberalism bears everywhere, the connections remain ignored. This despite the fact that the European Union is – next to, and partly even ahead of the US – the main driving force behind neoliberalism and its globalization. But let us take one step at a time...

1.2. What Does the "Neo" in Neoliberalism Stand for?

Neoliberalism as an economic politics began in Chile in 1973. Its inauguration consisted of a US-organized coup against a democratically elected socialist president and the installment of a bloody military dictatorship notorious for systematic torture. This was the only way to turn the neoliberal model of the so-called "Chicago Boys" under the leadership of Milton Friedman – a student of Austrian-born Friedrich von Hayek – into reality. The predecessor of the neoliberal model is the economic liberalism of the 18th and 19th century and its notion of "free trade". Goethe's assessment at the time was: "Free trade, piracy, war – an inseparable three!" (Faust 2)

At the center of both old and new economic liberalism lies "self-interest and individualism; segregation of ethical principles and economic affairs, in other words: a process of 'de-bedding' economy from society; economic rationality as a mere cost-benefit calculation and profit maximization; competition as the essential driving force for growth and progress; specialization and the replacement of a subsistence economy with profit-oriented foreign trade ('comparative cost advantage'); and the proscription of public (state) interference with market forces" (Mies 2005, p. 34).

Where the new economic liberalism outdoes the old is in its global claim. Today's economic liberalism functions as a model for each and everyone, all parts of the economy, all sectors of society, yes, of life/nature itself. As a consequence, the once "de-bedded" economy now claims to "im-bed" everything, including political power. Furthermore, a new, twisted "economic ethics" (and with it a certain idea of "human nature") emerges that mocks everything from so-called "do-gooders" to altruism to selfless help to care for others to a notion of responsibility (Gruen 1997).

This goes as far as claiming that the common good depends entirely on the uncontrolled egoism of the individual and, especially, on the prosperity of transnational corporations. The allegedly necessary "freedom" of the economy – which, paradoxically, only means the freedom of corporations – hence consists of a freedom *from* responsibility and commitment to society. In turn, the rational cost-benefit calculation aiming at maximized profit not only serves as a model for corporate production and the associated service industry and trade, but also for the public sector that has so far been exempted from such demands (in fact, it has historically been defined by this exemption). The same goes for the sector of reproduction, especially the household.

The maximization of profit itself must occur within the shortest possible time; this means, preferably, through speculation and "shareholder value". It must meet as few obstacles as possible. Today, global economic interests outweigh not only extra-economic concerns but also national economic considerations since corporations today see themselves beyond both community and nation (Sassen 2000). A "level playing field" is created that offers the global players the best possible conditions. This playing field knows of no legal, social, ecological, cultural or national "barriers" (Mies/Werlhof 2003, p. 24). As a result, economic competition plays out on a market that is free of all non-market, extra-economic or "protectionist" influences – unless they serve the interests of the "big players" (the corporations), of course. The corporations' interests – their maximal "growth" and "progress" – take on complete priority. This is rationalized by alleging that their well-being means the well-being of small enterprises and workshops as well.

The difference between the new and the old economic liberalism can first be articulated in quantitative terms: After capitalism went through a series of ruptures and challenges – caused by the "competition of systems", the crisis of capitalism, post-war "Keynesianism" with its social and welfare state tendencies, internal mass consumer demand (so-called "Fordism"), and the objective of full employment in the North – the liberal economic goals of the past are now not only euphorically resurrected but they are also "globalized". The main reason is indeed that the "competition of systems" is gone. However, to conclude that this confirms the victory of "capitalism" and the "golden West" over "dark socialism" is only one possible interpretation. Another – opposing – interpretation is to see the "modern world system" (which contains both capitalism and socialism, Wallerstein 1979, 2004) as having hit a general crisis which causes total and merciless competition over global resources while leveling the way for "investment" opportunities, i.e. the valorization of capital.

The ongoing globalization of neoliberalism demonstrates which interpretation is right. Not least, because the differences between the old and the new economic liberalism can not only be articulated in quantitative terms but in qualitative ones too. What we are witnessing are completely new phenomena: Instead of a democratic "complete competition" between many small enterprises enjoying the "freedom of the market", only the big corporations win. In turn, they create new market oligopolies and monopolies of previously unknown dimensions. The market hence only remains free for them, while it is rendered "unfree" for all others who are condemned to an existence of dependency (as enforced producers, workers and consumers) or excluded from the market altogether (if they have neither anything to sell or buy). About 50% of the world's population fall into this group today, and the percentage is rising (George 2001).

Anti-trust laws have lost all power since the transnational corporations set the norms. It is the corporations – not "the market" as an anonymous mechanism or "invisible hand" – that determine today's rules of trade, for example prices and legal regulations. This happens outside any political control. Speculation with an average 20% profit margin (Altvater 2005) edges out honest producers who become "unprofitable". Money becomes too precious for comparatively non-profitable, long-term projects, or projects that "only" – how audacious! – serve *a good life*. Money instead "travels upwards" and disappears. Financial capital determines more and more what the markets are and do (Altvater/Mahnkopf 1996). In fact, it has by now – through Nixon's separation of the dollar from the gold standard in 1971 – "emancipated" from productive capital und forms its own "fiscal bubble" multiplying the money volume that is covered by the production of the many (Lietaer 2006, Kennedy 1990). Moreover, these days most of us are – exactly like all governments – in debt. It is financial capital that has all the money – we have none (Creutz 1995).

The consequences of neoliberalism are:

Small, medium, even some bigger enterprises are pushed out of the market, forced to fold or swallowed by transnational corporations because their performances are "below average" in comparison to speculation – rather: *spookulation* – wins. The public sector, which has historically been defined as a sector of not-for-profit economy and administration, is "slimmed" and its "profitable" parts ("gems") handed to corporations ("privatized"). As a consequence, social services that are necessary for our existence disappear. Small and medium private businesses – which, until recently, employed 80% of the workforce and provided "normal working conditions" – are affected by these developments as well. The alleged correlation between economic growth and secure employment is false. Where economic growth only means the fusion of businesses, jobs are lost (Mies/Werlhof 2003, p. 7ff);

If there are any new jobs, most are "precarious", meaning that they are only available temporarily and badly paid. One job is usually not enough to make a living (Ehrenreich 2001). This means that the working conditions in the North become akin to those in the South and the working conditions of men akin to those of women – a trend diametrically opposed to what we have always been told. Corporations now leave for the South (or East) to use cheap – and particularly female – labor without "union affiliation". This has already been happening since the 1970s in the "Free Production Zones" (FPZs, "world market factories" or "maquiladoras"), where most of the world's computer chips, sneakers, clothes and electronic goods are produced (Fröbel/Heinrichs/Kreye 1977). The FPZs lie in areas where century-old colonial-capitalist and authoritarian-patriarchal conditions guarantee the availability of the cheap labor needed (Bennholdt-Thomsen/Mies/Werlhof 1988). The recent shift of business opportunities from consumer goods to armaments is a particularly troubling development (Chossudovsky 2003).

It is not only commodity production that is "outsourced" and located in the FPZs, but service industries as well. This is a result of the so-called "Third Industrial Revolution", meaning the development of new information and communication technologies. Many jobs have disappeared entirely due to computerization, also in administrative fields (Fröbel et al. 1977). The combination of the principles of "high tech" and "low wage"/"no wage" (always denied by "progress" enthusiasts) guarantees a "comparative cost advantage" in foreign trade. This will eventually lead to "Chinese salaries" in the West. A potential loss of Western consumers is not seen as a threat. A corporate economy does not care whether consumers are European, Chinese or Indian.

The means of production become concentrated in fewer and fewer hands, especially since finance capital – rendered precarious itself – controls asset value ever more aggressively. New forms of private property are created, not least through the "clearance" of public property and the transformation of formerly public and small-scale private services and industries to a corporate business sector. This concerns primarily fields that have long been (at least partly) excluded from the logics of profit – e.g. education, health, energy, or water supply/disposal. New forms of so-called "enclosures" emerge from today's total commercialization of formerly small-scale private or public industries and services, of the "commons", and of natural resources like oceans, rain forests, regions of genetic diversity or geopolitical interest (e.g. potential pipeline routes), etc. (Isla 2005). As far as the new virtual spaces and communication networks go, we are witnessing frantic efforts to bring these under private control as well (Hepburn 2005).

All these new forms of private property are essentially created by (more or less) predatory forms of appropriation. In this sense, they are a modified continuation of the history of so-called "original accumulation" (Werlhof 1991, 2003a) which has expanded globally following to the motto: "Growth through expropriation!"

Most people have less and less access to the means of production, and so the dependence on scarce and underpaid work increases. The destruction of the welfare state also destroys the notion that individuals can rely on the community to provide for them in times of need. Our existence relies exclusively on private, i.e. expensive, services that are often of much worse quality and much less reliable than public services. (It is a myth that the private always outdoes the public.) What we are experiencing is undersupply formerly only known by the colonial South. The old claim that the South will eventually develop into the North is proven wrong. It is the North that increasingly develops into the South. We are witnessing the latest form of "development": namely, a world system of underdevelopment (Frank 1969). Development and underdevelopment go hand in hand (Mies 2005). This might even dawn on "development aid" workers soon.

It is usually women who are called upon to counterbalance underdevelopment through increased work ("service provisions") in the household. As a result, the workload and underpay of women takes on horrendous dimensions: they do unpaid work inside their homes and poorly paid "housewifized" work outside (Bennholdt-Thomsen et al. 1988). Yet, commercialization does not stop in front of the home's doors either. Even housework becomes commercially co-opted ("new maid question"), with hardly any financial benefits for the women who do the work (Werlhof 2004).

Not least because of this, women are increasingly coerced into prostitution (Isla 2003, 2005), one of today's biggest global industries. This illustrates two things: a) how little the "emancipation" of women actually leads to "equal terms" with men; and b) that "capitalist development" does not imply increased "freedom" in wage labor relations, as the Left has claimed for a long time

(Wallerstein 1979). If the latter was the case, then neoliberalism would mean the voluntary end of capitalism once it reaches its furthest extension. This, however, does not appear likely.

Today, hundreds of millions of quasi-slaves, more than ever before, exist in the "world system" (Bales 2001). The authoritarian model of the "Free Production Zones" is conquering the East and threatening the North. The redistribution of wealth runs ever more – and with ever accelerated speed – from the bottom to the top. The gap between the rich and the poor has never been wider. The middle classes disappear. This is the situation we are facing.

It becomes obvious that neoliberalism marks not the end of colonialism but, to the contrary, the colonization of the North. This new "colonization of the world" (Mies 2005) points back to the beginnings of the "modern world system" in the "long 16th century" (Wallerstein 1979, Frank 2005, Mies 1986), when the conquering of the Americas, their exploitation and colonial transformation, allowed for the rise and "development" of Europe. The so-called "children's diseases" of modernity keep on haunting it, even in old age. They are, in fact, the main feature of modernity's latest stage. They are expanding instead of disappearing.

Where there is no South, there is no North; where there is no periphery, there is no center; where there is no colony, there is no – in any case no "Western" – civilization (Werlhof 2007a).

Austria is part of the world system too. It is increasingly becoming a corporate colony (particularly of German corporations). This, however, does not keep it from being an active colonizer itself, especially in the East (Hofbauer 2003, Salzburger 2006).

Social, cultural, traditional and ecological considerations are abandoned and give way to a mentality of plundering. All global resources that we still have – natural resources, forests, water, genetic pools – have turned into objects of "utilization". Rapid ecological destruction through depletion is the consequence. If one makes more profit by cutting down trees than by planting them, then there is no reason not to cut them (Lietaer 2006). Neither the public nor the state interferes, despite global warming and the obvious fact that the clearing of the few remaining rain forests will irreversibly destroy the earth's climate – not to even speak of the many other negative effects of such action (Raggam 2004). Climate, animal, plants, human and general ecological rights are worth nothing compared to the interests of the corporations – no matter that the rain forest is no renewable resource and that the entire earth's ecosystem depends on it. If greed – and the rationalism with which it is economically enforced – really was an inherent anthropological trait, we would have never even reached this day.

The commander of the Space Shuttle that circled the earth in 2005 remarked that "the center of Africa was burning". She meant the Congo, in which the last great rain forest of the continent is located. Without it there will be no more rain clouds above the sources of the Nile. However, it needs to disappear in order for corporations to gain free access to the Congo's natural resources that are the reason for the wars that plague the region today. After all, one needs petrol, diamonds, and coltan for mobile phones.

The forests of Asia have been burning for many years too, and in late 2005 the Brazilian parliament has approved the clearing of 50% of the remaining Amazon. Meanwhile, rumors abound that Brazil and Venezuela have already sold their rights to the earth's biggest remaining rain forest – not to the US-Americans, but to the supposedly "left" Chinese who suffer from chronic wood shortage and cannot sustain their enormous economic growth and economic superpower ambitions without securing global resources.

Given today's race for the earth's last resources, one wonders what the representatives of the World Trade Organization (WTO) thought when they accepted China as a new member in 2001. They probably had the giant Chinese market in mind but not the giant Chinese competition. After all, a quarter of the world's population lives in China. Of course it has long been established that a further expansion of the Western lifestyle will lead to global ecological collapse – the faster, the sooner (Sarkar 2001).

Today, everything on earth is turned into commodities, i.e. everything becomes an object of "trade" and commercialization (which truly means "liquidation": the transformation of all into liquid money). In its neoliberal stage it is not enough for capitalism to globally pursue less cost-intensive and preferably "wageless" commodity production. The objective is to transform *everyone* and *everything* into commodities (Wallerstein 1979), including life itself. We are racing blindly towards the violent and absolute conclusion of this "mode of production", namely total capitalization/liquidation by "monetarization" (Genth 2006).

We are not only witnessing perpetual praise of the market – we are witnessing what can be described as "market fundamentalism". People believe in the market as if it was a god. There seems to be a sense that nothing could ever happen without it. Total global maximized accumulation of money/capital as abstract wealth becomes the sole purpose of economic activity. A "free" world market for everything has to be established – a world market that functions according to the interests of the corporations and capitalist money. The installment of such a market proceeds with dazzling speed. It creates new profit possibilities where they have not existed before, e.g. in Iraq, Eastern Europe or China.

One thing remains generally overlooked: The abstract wealth created for accumulation implies the destruction of nature as concrete wealth. The result is a "hole in the ground" (Galtung), and next to it a garbage dump with used commodities, outdated machinery, and money without value. However, once all concrete wealth (which today consists mainly of the last natural resources) will be gone, abstract wealth will disappear as well. It will, in Marx' words, "evaporate". The fact that abstract wealth is not real wealth will become obvious, and so will the answer to the question which wealth modern economic activity has really created. In the end it is nothing but monetary wealth (and even this mainly exists virtually or on accounts) that constitutes a "monoculture" controlled by a tiny minority. Diversity is suffocated and millions of people are left wondering how to survive. And really: how *do* you survive with neither resources nor means of production nor money?

The nihilism of our economic system is evident. The whole world will be transformed into money – and then it will "disappear". After all, money cannot be eaten. What no one seems to consider is the fact that it is impossible to *re-transform* commodities, money, capital and machinery into nature or concrete wealth. It seems that underlying all economic "development" is the assumption that "resources", the "sources of wealth" (Marx), are renewable and everlasting – just like the "growth" they create (Werlhof 2001 a). The treachery of this assumption becomes harder and harder to deny. For example, the "peak" in oil production has just been passed – meaning we are beyond exploiting 50% of all there is.

Ironically though, it seems like the prospect of some resources coming to an end only accelerates the economic race. Everything natural is commercialized in dimensions not seen before, with unprecedented speed and by means of ever more advanced technology. The ultimate goal remains to create new possibilities of investment and profit, in other words: new possibilities of growth able to create new accumulation possibilities – future ones included. The material limits of such a politics become clearer day by day: the global ecological, economic, monetary, social, and political collapse (Diamond 2005) it inevitably leads to has already begun: "Global West End".

How else can we understand the fact that in times when civilization has reached its alleged zenith, a human being starves every second (Ziegler 2004)? How can such a politics be taken seriously? It is in every sense a crime. Unfortunately, the facade of trivial "rationality" – what Hannah Arendt called the "banality of evil" – behind which it operates, still makes it invisible to many. People do not recognize its true character. This is a result of the enormous crisis of spirit and soul that accompanies the material crisis that many of us remain unaware of; namely, the annihilation of matter through its transformation into commodity, which we, in delusion, call "materialism" (I call it "patriarchy", Werlhof 2001 a). The original richness of mat(t)er ("mother earth") is now giving way to a barren wasteland that will remain unrecognized by many as long as their belief in "progress" will block their views. The last phase of patriarchy and capitalism is not only without sense but it will soon be without life as well: *kaputalism*.

It seems impossible not to ask oneself how the entire economy came to follow one motive only: the monism of making money. Especially since this does not only apply to the economy, but also to politics, science, arts and even our social relations.

The notion that capitalism and democracy are one is proven a myth by neoliberalism and its "monetary totalitarianism" (Genth 2006). The primacy of politics over economy has been lost. Politicians of all parties have abandoned it. It is the corporations that dictate politics. Where corporate interests are concerned, there is no place for democratic convention or community control. Public space disappears. The "res publica" turns into a "res privata", or – as we could say today – a "res privata transnationale" (in its original Latin meaning, "privare" means "to deprive"). Only those in power still have rights. They give themselves the licenses they need, from the "license to plunder" to the "license to kill" (Mies/Werlhof 2003, Mies 2005). Those who get in their way or challenge their "rights" are vilified, criminalized and to an increasing degree defined as "terrorists", or, in the case of defiant governments, as "rogue states" – a label that usually implies threatened or actual military attack, as we can see in the cases of Yugoslavia, Afghanistan and Iraq, and maybe Syria and Iran in the near future. US President Bush has even spoken of the possibility of "preemptive" nuclear strikes should the US feel endangered by weapons of mass destruction (Chossudovsky 2005). The European Union did not object (Chossudovsky 2006).

Neoliberalism and war are two sides of the same coin (Altvater/Chossudovsky/Roy/Serfati 2003, Mies 2005). Free trade, piracy, and war are still "an inseparable three" – today maybe more so than ever. War is not only "good for the economy" (Hendersen 1996), but is indeed its driving force and can be understood as the "continuation of economy with other means". War and economy have become almost indistinguishable (Werlhof 2005 b). Wars about resources (Klare 2001) – especially oil and water – have already begun. The Gulf Wars are the most obvious examples. Militarism once again appears as the "executor of capital accumulation" (Luxemburg 1970) – potentially everywhere and enduringly.

Human rights and rights of sovereignty have been transferred from people, communities and governments to corporations (Clarke 1998). The notion of the people as a sovereign body has practically been abolished. We have witnessed a coup of sorts. The political systems of the West and the nation state as guarantees for and expression of the international division of labor in the modern world system are increasingly dissolving (Sassen 2000). Nation states are developing into "periphery states" according to the inferior role they play in the proto-despotic "New World Order" (Hardt/Negri 2001, Chomsky 2003). Democracy appears outdated. After all, it "hinders business" (Werlhof 2005 a).

The "New World Order" implies a new division of labor that does no longer distinguish between North and South, East and West – today, everywhere is South. An according International Law is established which effectively functions from top to bottom ("top-down") and eliminates all local and regional communal rights. And not only that: many such rights are rendered invalid both retroactively and for the future (cf. the "roll back" and "stand still" clauses in the WTO agreements, Mies/Werlhof 2003).

The logic of neoliberalism as a sort of totalitarian neo-mercantilism is that all resources, all markets, all money, all profits, all means of production, all "investment opportunities", all rights, and all power belong to the corporations only. To paraphrase Richard Sennett (2005): "Everything to the Corporations!" One might add: "Now!"

The corporations are free to do whatever they please with what they get. Nobody is allowed to interfere. Ironically, we are expected to rely on them to find a way out of the crisis we are in. This puts the entire globe at risk since responsibility is something the corporations do not have or know. The times of social contracts are gone (Werlhof 2003 a). In fact, pointing out the crisis alone has become a crime and all critique will soon be defined as "terror" and persecuted as such (Chossudovsky 2005).

1.3. Neoliberal Politics in Action

The logic of neoliberalism does not remain in the economic sphere alone. Instead, it enters and transforms politics and hence – since the events in Chile in 1973 – creates global injustice. The injustice's executors are Western governments, corporate entities (like the International Chamber of Commerce, ICC, the European Round Table of Industrialists, ERT, the Organization for Economic Cooperation and Development, OECD, the European Services Network, ESN, the US Coalition of Service Industries, USCSI, etc.), and the post-WW-II Bretton-Woods institutions like the World Bank (WB) the International Monetary Fond (IMF), and the World Trade Organization (WTO – the continuation of the General Agreement on Tariffs and Trade, GATT, abolished in 1994) (Perkins 2004).

The theory of capitalism embodying a "natural law" receives massive support in the neoliberal era. This helps not only to globalize capitalism's power, but also to accelerate the globalization of neoliberalism. "Speed kills" is the obscene slogan used to describe this development by many Western politicians. This confirms that they are aware of what is going on and of what they are doing. The slogan hints at the fact that once neoliberal "reforms" (which actually "deform") gain a certain momentum, it becomes impossible for the people affected to keep up with what is happening – the reforms are decided above their heads and implemented behind their backs. Once the consequences kick in – which usually happens with a short delay – those responsible are long gone and/or there is no legal way to "rectify" anything (Werlhof 2005 a). Due to such foul play, protest and resistance are always late. Once they arise, everything has already become irrevocable reality – it appears as if a "natural" catastrophe has taken place.

It is the same politicians who tell us that there is no stopping globalization and that their "reform politics" are the solution and not the problem, and who have, in fact, introduced and enforced the global neoliberalism they describe as an inescapable part of history. They have done this within nation state policies as well as through participation in the bodies of the EU and the WTO, the World Bank and the IMF. Of course we have never heard any proper explanation as to why they have done this (and, in fact, continue to do so). This goes seemingly for all political parties – without exception (?) – ,which retain some kind of power or nestle in its proximity (Dimmel/Schmee 2005). Some of them even appear to have forgotten that just a short while ago they still knew alternatives and held opposite views. What has happened to them? Were they bought? Threatened? Extorted? "Brainwashed"?

One thing is clear: The politicians do not suffer from the misery they create and justify every day. They act as employees of corporations and take care of the everyday political business the corporations cannot or do not want to take care of themselves. But again, let us take one step at a time...

Since the 1980s, it is mainly the Structural Adjustment Programs, SAPs, of the World Bank and the IMF that act as the enforcers of neoliberalism. These programs are levied against the countries of the South which can be extorted due to their debts. Meanwhile, numerous military interventions and wars help to take possession of the assets that still remain, secure resources, install neoliberalism as the global economic politics, crush resistance movements (which are cynically labeled as "IMF uprisings"), and facilitate the lucrative business of reconstruction (Chossudovsky 2002, Mies 2005, Bennholdt-Thomsen/ Faraclas/Werlhof 2001).

In the 1980s, Ronald Reagan and Margaret Thatcher introduced neoliberalism in Anglo-America. In 1989, the so-called "Washington

Consensus" was formulated. It claimed to lead to global freedom, prosperity and economic growth through "deregulation, liberalization and privatization". This has become the credo and promise of all neoliberals. Today we know that the promise has come true for the corporations only – not for anybody else.

In the Middle East, the Western support for Saddam Hussein in the war between Iraq and Iran in the 1980s, and the Gulf War of the early 1990s, announced the permanent US presence in the world's most contested oil region.

In continental Europe, neoliberalism began with the crisis in Yugoslavia caused by the SAPs of the World Bank and the IMF. The country was heavily exploited, fell apart, and finally beset by a civil war over its last remaining resources (Chossudovsky 2002). Since the NATO war in 1999 (Richter/Schmähling/Spoo 2000), the Balkans are fragmented, occupied and geopolitically under neoliberal control. The region is of main strategic interest for future oil and gas transport from the Caucasus to the West (for example the "Nabucco" gas pipeline that is supposed to start operating from the Caspian Sea through Turkey and the Balkans by 2011, Lietaer 2006). The reconstruction of the Balkans is exclusively in the hands of Western corporations.

Many European Union contracts – for example those of Maastricht and Amsterdam – are blatantly neoliberal (Boulboullé 2003). They declare Europe a neoliberal zone and leave no alternative. All governments, whether left, right, liberal or green, accept this. There is no analysis of the connection between the politics of neoliberalism, its history, its background and its effects on Europe and other parts of the world. Likewise, there is no analysis of its connection to the new militarism.

If we take the example of Austria, approximately 66% of its population voted for joining the EU in 1995 without having received any information about what this actually meant. As a consequence, we first had the so-called "austerity package", an SAP equivalent, that started the redistribution of wealth from the bottom to the top. Then tax reforms followed, privatizations, the reform of the pension system. Finally, the Euro caused an inflation of more than 30% and an according loss of income overnight (a fact that is still officially denied). Today, the unemployment rates are rising and working conditions deteriorate across the country (Sozialministerium 2005). 80% of all laws regulating life in Austria are passed in Brussels. The Austrian government's actual power is minimal and it has practically given up its responsibility for the population. However, more than ten years after joining the EU, there is still no public debate on what neoliberalism has to do with the EU, or what Austria has to do with Chile or the Congo.

When the WTO was founded in 1995, the EU member states adapted all WTO agreements on neoliberal enforcement unanimously. These agreements included: the Multilateral Agreement on Investments (MAI), the General Agreement on Trade in Services (GATS), the Agreement on Trade-Related Aspects of Intellectual Property Rights (TRIPS), and the Agreement on Agriculture (AoA) which has meanwhile been supplemented by the Agreement on Non-Agricultural-Market Access (NAMA). All these agreements aim at a rapid global implementation of corporate rule.

The MAI, for example, demanded at a total liberation of all corporate activities (defined as "investments"). These activities were to be freed of all interference, legal bindings or state regulations. This should have first applied to all 29 OECD member countries, and then be extended to all 150 countries assembled in the WTO (Mies/Werlhof 2003). It actually proved impossible to implement the agreement in the form it was planned. Most of its contents, however, have later been implemented by other means (see II).

Never before, not even in colonial times, have those in power so completely been "freed" from all responsibility for their actions. No wonder the MAI negotiations had been kept secret for years. However, the trade unions knew, since they were part of the negotiations through the Trade Union Advisory Committee (TUAC) that took part at the OECD conferences in Paris when the MAI was discussed.

Information about the MAI was leaked to the public in 1997. Still, even then many political bodies, like the Austrian Ministry for Economy, simply tried to play it down and accuse its critics of "cowardice" (since they were supposedly afraid of "something new"), "xenophobia" (towards the multinationals!) and "conspiracy theories". No one ever spoke of "theories", though: the contents of the MAI – which truly transcend the wildest imaginations – are no theories but the praxis of neoliberalism. And no one spoke of "conspiracies" either – because there were none: governments were part of the agreement, certain NGOs were, of course corporations, and even trade unions. Then again, if all representatives of power can form their own conspiracy, then this truly was one. In any case, the people of this planet, who bear the agreement's weight, were not informed – leave alone invited to participate.

To a large degree, the contents of the MAI have become reality through bilateral treaties and the North American Free Trade Agreement, NAFTA, signed by the US, Canada and Mexico in 1994. The attempt to turn all of the Americas into a Free Trade Zone, the FTAA, has so far failed, due to the resistance of most Latin American governments – this, without doubt, provides hope.

Negotiations of the GATS, the so-called General Agreement on Trade in Services, have also been kept secret since the late 1990s. The GATS stands for total corporate "privatization" and "commercialization" of life, and for the transformation of all of life's dimensions into "trade-related", meaning:

"commercial", services or commodities (Mies/Werlhof 2003, p. 7ff). The GATS can be understood as a global process of successive "liberalization" of services. Suggestions are collected from all WTO member countries and according demands directed back at them. It often enough proves impossible to gain insight into what these demands actually contain. "Sensitive" areas like education, health or water supply are reputedly excluded from the negotiations, which is a proven lie. In Austria, for example, the foundation of medical universities is a clear indication for the privatization of health services, and the University Law of 2002, the UG02, is an indication of the privatization of education at the tertiary level (Werlhof 2005a). Such privatizations have already been happening internationally for years. Many in Austria saw the development as an expression of the conservative-right "black-blue"[1] coalition government and not of neoliberal politics – as if we could have expected anything else from a "red-green"[2] government. In any case, consequences were, among others, the abolition of free university access, democratic student rights, and tenure jobs. Instead, university fees and authoritarian corporate structures were introduced – the latter demonstrating a well hidden neoliberal absolutism. Funding for the humanities was cut and an academic "evaluation" system modeled after private business criteria implemented (Progress 2002-2004). The re-organization und economization of academic research and teaching in the name of higher investment possibilities and the profitability of the transnational education industry are in full swing. The rationale that has entered our universities is that good research is research that brings money. This is truly a declaration of intellectual bankruptcy (Werlhof 2003 b).

Privatization has been a main feature in Austrian politics for many years now, especially concerning the country's infrastructure. The development is exemplified in the Cross-Border Leasing (CBL) contracts which have been signed between many Austrian towns and US investors (Rügemer 2004, Oberhöller 2006). The contracts gave the towns the so-called "Barwertvorteil" ("present value advantage"), an immediate payment the US investors provided as a cut from their tax exemptions for direct foreign investment – in return, parts of the towns' infrastructure were "leased" to them. However, these parts were immediately "leased back" because it was still the towns that were expected to maintain the infrastructure – but now for foreign proprietors. Whatever happened with the payments, no one knows. What one does know is that the

---

1 In Austrian party politics, the color "black" stands for the conservative Austrian People's Party, "blue" for the extreme right-wing Freedom Party. (GK)
2 "Red" stands for the Social Democratic Party of Austria, "green" for the Green Alternative. (GK)

loophole in the US tax law that made them possible has been closed and that all CBL contracts have retroactively been declared illegal in early 2004 (Der Standard 2005). It seems fair to assume that many more such deals will eventually be revealed. Austrians then might finally get to know about all the silverware that has been sold, as well as about the extent and forms of corruption involved – a characteristic feature in privatizations (Barlow/Clarke 2003, Shiva 2003).

In the GATS, services are defined as "everything that cannot fall on your foot", as someone once remarked ironically. This means that they are no longer reduced to traditional services, but now extend to human thoughts, feelings and actions as well. Even the elements – air, water, earth, fire (energy) – are increasingly turned into commodities (in some places this process is already completed) in order to make profit from the fact that we have to breathe, drink, stand and move (Barlow 2001, Isla 2003).

In Nicaragua, there exist water privatization plans that include fines of up to ten months' salary if one was to hand a bucket of water to a thirsty neighbor who cannot afford her own water connection (Südwind 2003). If it was up to the water corporations – the biggest of which are French and German (Vivendi Universal, Suez, RWE), which means that the privatization of water is mainly a European business – then the neighbor was rather to die of thirst. After all, compassion only upsets business.

In India, whole rivers have been sold. Stories tell of women who came to the river banks with buffalos, children and their laundry, as they had done for generations, only to be called "water thieves" and chased away by the police. There are even plans to sell the "holy mother Ganges" (Shiva 2003).

Fresh water (just about 2% of the earth's water reserves) is as such neither renewable nor increasable and of such essential importance to local ecosystems that it seems utterly absurd to treat it is a commodity that can be traded away (Barlow/Clarke 2003, Shiva 2003). Nonetheless, this is already happening. The effects, of course, are horrendous. Coca-Cola has left parts of the southern Indian state of Kerala a virtual desert by exploiting their entire ground water reserves. According to the intentionally "weak" corporate definition of the term, even "investments" can nowadays count as "services". There is, for example, much talk about "financial services" – which also means that the MAI has basically been incorporated into the GATS. The GATS is, so to speak, the MAI for the whole world. (There are also current attempts to reintroduce the MAI on the OECD level.)

The so-called "Bolkestein Directive" (named after the former EU Commissioner Bolkestein, cf. Dräger 2005) can be seen as one of the GATS' latest versions. It aims at a sort of privatization of salaries within the EU. This means that migrant workers in the EU are paid according to the salaries of their countries of origin, irrespective of the salary standards of the countries they work in. Once this directive is in effect, all obstacles to "Chinese labor conditions" are gone, and European trade unions will basically be rendered obsolete. This makes the fact that they have shown so little resistance against neoliberalism ever more curious.

The GATS can be considered the most radical expression of militant neoliberalism so far because it formulates its ultimate ambition in a way it has not been formulated before; namely, that no social, cultural, public or natural sectors should remain outside of economic control and exploitation – without exception. The GATS has hence to be understood as the attempt to turn absolutely everything in this world into "commodities" or commercial "services" in order to extract profit. This applies to all of nature (animals and plants as much as natural elements and landscapes), the entire human being (including its skin, hair, etc.) and all aspects of human life: work and leisure, sexuality and pregnancy, birth and death, sickness and distress, peace and war, desire and will, spirit and soul (Frauennetz Attac 2003).

What will happen when there are no non-commercial areas left? What if the division between "life with value" and "life without value" becomes normal social praxis? (This division was first heralded in National Socialism as a quasi futuristic concept, Ruault 2006. No backwardness here!) What if the way to deal with humans as so-called "human capital" starts to define everyday life? What will happen when everything has become a commodity? Is this even possible?

If it is, then life would essentially stop. Nothing could be turned into commodities anymore and the commodified world would collapse and decease – including us humans. This would mean general death – a death without new life to follow. Since the commodity has no life of its own but is only "life that once was", it cannot produce new life (Werlhof 2006).

It is only because of thousands of years of patriarchal "alchemical" thought (Werlhof 2001 a) that the (allegedly "creative") transformation of nature and living creatures into (partly or completely) artificial things is not conceived as the destruction it is. Instead, it is understood as producing something "higher", "more noble", "better". Due to its global and potentially complete enforcement, the latest stage of this transformation, namely modern commodity production, reveals how most people did indeed fall for this "alchemical belief in miracles" and its so-called "progress". It is a form of religious belief that we are describing here – one that has been able to prevent many from recognizing the violence that is an imminent part of the process it supports. Hence, we have been unable to stop it. Let us take the GATS as an example: not even completely implemented yet, it is already responsible for enormous – and partly irreparable – damage done to the earth and all of us. The TRIPS overlaps with the GATS insofar as it tries to co-opt the thought and experience of thousand-year old cultures, meaning: their spiritual legacy. The goal, of course, is to get paid. Formerly persecuted cultures now become interesting as a source of corporate profit. Ironically, "trade-related" intellectual property rights are established not to protect these cultures' legacies but their corporate exploitation. And not only that: The same intellectual property rights are also used to force Western thought and experience onto others – if necessary, by violence.

Patent rights are used to protect all related interests. So-called "patents for life" take on special meaning in this context as they go hand in hand with the rapid development of genetic engineering (Shiva 2004). What happens is that once a genetic manipulation has occurred, something "new" has been invented that someone can lay a legal claim on. Sometimes, however, one does not even deem this necessary. The genes of plants, animals, even humans, are sometimes stolen, claimed as "discovered" and made one's own legal "property". This "bio piracy" (Thaler 2004) exploits the profit potentials of all resources by charging others monopoly prices for using them. There is now a patent on "Basmati" rice. A patent claim to the Indian Neem tree did almost pass.

The best known example for a company selling its "inventions" is the case of Monsanto. Monsanto tries to make all peasants and farmers of the planet dependent on its genetically modified seeds that are, intentionally, only fertile once ("terminator seeds"). This means that the farmers have to buy new seeds from the company every year. This is already happening in most parts of India where many thousands of peasants have been forced to give up farming which, in turn, led to a shocking number of suicides (Shiva 2004). The Indian physicist, ecologist and globalization critic Vandana Shiva calls this process "trading our lives away" (Shiva 1995). In Korea, "WTO kills farmers!" has become a popular slogan amongst many farming communities.

The transnational agro-industrial corporations now even discuss a general prohibition of "traditional" farming methods (arte 2005). Iraqi farmers have already been forced to burn all their seeds since the US invasion and use "terminator seeds" instead – this in Mesopotamia, the "cradle of agriculture" (Junge Welt 2004). What these developments make clear is that genetic engineering is not about a better life but about installing global monopolies. This becomes most obvious in the current attempts to implement monopoly control on basic products and services which each human being's life depends on. Now we understand the meaning of the rally cries "Agrobusiness is the Biggest Business!" or "Wheat Becomes a Weapon!" (Krieg 1980).

Meanwhile, problems with genetically modified organisms, GMOs, are on the increase everywhere. Genetically modified seeds, for example, are expensive, vulnerable and of poor quality (Grössler 2005). They constantly need more – instead of less – pesticides. They also "pollute", which means that they destroy the non-modified species (while not being able to reproduce themselves – or only partially, Verhaag 2004). It becomes harder and harder to deny that GMOs cause irreversible destruction of a still unknown part of flora and – depending on how they are used – fauna. A new infertility enters the world instead of a new creation. The consequence is an artificially created death – a death with no life to follow. No one seems to know how to prevent this (Werlhof 2006).

All this sounds like a nightmare. Unfortunately, it is reality. For example, there is no more natural rapeseed in Canada. In Argentina and China, millions of hectares are sown with GMO seeds. Emergency deliveries to regions affected by famine consist almost exclusively of such seeds. In Germany, cows that were fed with GMO feed died a horrible death after two-and-a-half years (Glöckner 2005). Even in Austria, where people take pride in being environmentally conscious, no GMO free animal feed remains on the market, and GMO rapeseed is being planted despite all negative experiences (Karg 2005).

It is hard to grasp what is happening. Food is produced that kills – yet people are forced to eat it. And not only that: they have to pay a lot of money for it too! A grosser distortion of life is hardly imaginable. Amongst the most ludicrous examples is the idea to distribute contraceptive GMO corn, developed by the Swiss company Syngenta, in regions that suffer from so-called "overpopulation" (Reiter 2005). This means *gen*ocide, murder and business, all in one!

The idea of a technological progress that follows the notion of a machine technology can never offer any prospects – even when people mean to do good instead of kill. The destruction of life cycles and the manipulation of some of their components can never create a substitute for non-manipulated life – in any case, none that would be superior (Werlhof 1997). Characteristically, the cows that died in Germany died of different forms of circulatory collapse. They had, in a sense, lost the bodily (and spiritual?) cycles on which their existence is based (we may also think of the symptoms of BSE, the so-called "mad cow disease"). What confused their owner most, however, was that neither politicians nor scientists were interested in what had happened.

Meanwhile, the US have achieved that the EU can be forced to introduce and use GMO products (Felber 2005). Certain politicians, like the current German Minister of Agriculture; Seehofer; already work hard on implementing these demands (Alt 2005). By doing so, they simply ignore the fact that the majority of European consumers have so far clearly rejected GMO "food" (Greenpeace 2004).

The AoA, the WTO's Agreement on Agriculture, is a prime example for how "free trade" sure does not mean the same for everyone. On the one hand, it allows the North to force its agricultural surplus onto the South by means of highly subsidized dumping prices, thereby destroying the national markets and sale opportunities for local farmers; on the other hand, products from the South are kept from Northern markets by tax barriers. Since three billion of the world's people still work as small farmers (Amin 2004), the AoA threatens the survival of more than half the world's population. This not only because the AoA changes the markets in favor of the agricultural corporations; the AoA also erodes – in combination with the TRIPS – the existential basis of the world's farmers by other means. To begin with, much of their land is – ever more rapidly – acquired by foreign companies. These implement their new seeds, and often only focus on luxury goods (such as shrimps and flowers) for the markets of the wealthy without giving any consideration to local needs (Widerspruch 2004). The reality resembles that of colonial times, only that the damage done now is worse, since subsistence production itself falls victim to neo-colonial destruction (Bennholdt-Thomsen/Mies/Werlhof 1988). After all, no profit is to be made with subsistence production. As a consequence, more and more farmers turn to commodity production for the world market. However, this does not help them either. The profit is always made by others (Shiva 2004).

The NAMA negotiations featured strongly at the WTO Summit in Hong Kong in December 2005. In line with all other WTO agreements, every nature-related activity was defined as economically exploitable even when it did not immediately relate to agriculture, but, for example, fishery, forestry, or even the control of oxygen (Isla 2005). In short, total commercialization was proclaimed. One of the most immediate consequences was the loss of living space for indigenous people. Meanwhile, their resistance was criminalized and they were accused of trying to "expropriate" corporations and of "violating" their rights (Goldman 1998).

It is safe to call all WTO agreements malicious. They are all exclusively based on corporate interests. They have no regard for life. Life exists only for exploitation and annihilation.

When they concern corporate interests (investment, service, intellectual property), all WTO regulations are vague, widely accommodating and open to interpretation – when they concern challenges to these interests ("obstacles" of whatever sort, or "creeping expropriation"), they become very definite and unbendable.

Branding people who take the corporations to task as "expropriators" is of course only cynical. In reality, it is the corporations that expropriate the people. On top of this, the only safeguards the corporations are concerned about are their own. In any other case, safeguards are deemed "protectionism" and harshly condemned. The same goes for customs duties or subsidies. The corporations' "liberalism" consists of expecting others to drop all guards. There is no liberalism outside the one that serves corporate interests.

Today, the rights of corporations are better protected than those of human individuals. We might even say that "human rights" only apply to corporations. After all, individuals will always claim their rights in conflicts with corporations in vain. Only corporations have the power to effectively sue everyone who jeopardizes their interests.

The WTO itself demonstrates how to prevail against resistance by such means. It contains the so-called "Dispute Settlement Mechanism", a kind of international court that allows to enforce its agreements and resolutions, when necessary by means of harsh punishment, especially financially. At this court – which, exactly like the WTO as a whole, has no democratic legitimacy – corporations and their representatives can claim the "rights" that the WTO agreements grant them against state governments and other national or communal bodies. They usually win. Reverse procedures are impossible: no state government or other national body – not to even mention communities not defined by a nation state – even have the right to sue corporations. So, essentially, this means that no rights other than those of the corporations even exist any longer – not even on paper (Werlhof 2003 a).

How can one explain such a politics to people and have them agree with it? Not at all, of course. This is why nothing ever is explained. Neoliberalism does not bother with ideology. Neoliberalism is a conscious betrayal of the interests of 99% of the people on this planet. It justifies robbery and pillage. It is, both in intention and effect, a true "weapon of mass destruction" – even when no immediate wars are fought. How many lives are sacrificed to neoliberalism? Some estimate that the numbers already go into hundreds of millions (Ziegler 2004, Widerspruch 2004).

Paradoxically, the WTO and its agreements are anchored in international law while they rob and pillage the people whose rights are supposed to be protected by this law. Violations against the WTO agreements count hence as violations against a law that stands above all national and regional regulations. As a consequence, legal cases challenging the compatibility of WTO (or EU) law with national constitutions have repeatedly been rejected – in Austria as recently as in 2005.

The WTO and its agreements act effectively as a global oligarchic constitution. They are the first attempt at installing neo-totalitarian "global corporate governance" – or even a "global corporate government". It feels like despotism is establishing itself again, but this time globally. What we are witnessing might be dubbed a new kind of "AMP", the so-called former "Asiatic Mode of Production" – only that its origins are now American instead of Asiatic. I think a more accurate name for the WTO would be WWO: "World War Order". Or, alternatively, W.K.O.: "World Knock Out". In any case, the organization sweeps across the globe like a tsunami, taking everything with it that promises profit.

1.4. European Union: Neoliberalism and Militarism

On a European level, the EU functions as the continental equivalent to the WTO. The EU constitution treaty – a legal basis for a centralized European government – follows standard neoliberal principles. It is, in fact, the first constitution treaty that includes a legal commitment to a specific economic order – the neoliberal – as well as to engagement in armament and military operations (Oberansmayr 2004).

Once again, neoliberalism and militarism appear as Siamese twins (Lechthaler 2005). Economy is understood as a kind of war (both internally and externally), and military "defense" as part of the economy. This applies, in the words of the former German Minister of Defense, Struck, "even to the Hindu Kush". Not that we should be surprised...

The draft of the EU constitution promises to be part of an effort to secure peace. This follows a peculiar logic, namely one that refers to acts of war as "humanitarian intervention" (or, alternatively, as "acts of defense" – even if there has never been an aggression), allows to claim that wars like the NATO war against Yugoslavia were none, and is able to portray the EU as an "order of peace" (Attac EU-AG Stuttgart und Region 2005). All this to be seen against the background, that there will soon be deployable nuclear weapons in Europe (Galtung 1993, p. 145, Oberansmayr 2004, p. 114ff). Meanwhile, any resistance at government levels against harboring nuclear weapons has subsided, especially in France, but also in Germany. Austria keeps silent too. Politicians everywhere have given up a notion that was once sacrosanct (Guernica 2006).

A particularly shocking example for the European way of blending neoliberalism with war was exposed in the documentary film "Darwin's Nightmare" (Sauper 2005). The film depicts the development of a modern fishing industry – financed by the EU – at Lake Victoria in Tanzania.

The Nile perch, a fish growing to the size of a human being, was released into the lake in the 1950s. By now, it has all but extinguished the lake's other species, and it is only a question of time when the world's largest tropical lake will be dead. The majority of local fisher folk are without work and income. Women are forced into prostitution, HIV and AIDS are rampant, and youths organize in gangs. Pilots from the regions of the former Soviet Union fly the factory-packaged fish filets to their European consumers in huge Ilyushin planes. When they return, they bring weapons that are smuggled into the Congo and other African regions rattled by military conflict – forget about so-called "tribal wars"!

The deceiving self-portrayal of the EU as an "order of peace" has curious implications. It allows, for example, the Austrian government to pretend that Austria is still a neutral country. In fact, the 50th anniversary of the country's neutrality was celebrated in 2005. This despite the fact that already in 1998, §23f was added to the Austrian constitution: a paragraph assuring Austria's commitment to contribute soldiers to military action carried out by the EU (some call it the "war authorization paragraph", Oberansmayr 2004, p. 46f). The public hardly took notice of this. The Eurofighters[3] are played down as a mere means to protect Austrian airspace, while the prospect of future Austrian engagement in wars all across the globe is described as a commitment to "peace missions" (carried out, ironically, by so-called EU "battle troops"). Military expenses in Austria have grown by 30% between 2004 and 2007 (Werkstatt Frieden und Solidarität 2005). At least in this case it is hard to argue that a lot of money has been made. However, it means that Austria contributes significantly (in fact, since 2001) to making the EADS, the European Aeronautic Defence and Space Company, a European armament giant and a huge power player on the continent (Oberansmayr 2004, p. 126ff). It seems like the common trick here is to simply claim the opposite of what is true. The meanings of words are turned upside down.

The draft of the EU constitution also contains references to citizen's "basic rights". How these can be claimed against the constitution's cornerstones – neoliberalism and militarism – remains unclear, however, to say the least. Hence, listing these rights appears as little more than a facade ("tinsel") that tries to win public approval for what happens behind it and no one really knows about. Otherwise, an approval would be very hard to come by. The idea seems to make a curse appear like a blessing so that even the cursed will consent.

Of course no one seems to have an answer to what will happen if the neoliberal economic politics fail since no one even has ever thought about an alternative. What though, if, for example, the military will be used internally?

The rejection of the EU constitution by the people of France and the Netherlands is all the more remarkable considering the fact that the EU prevents all general critical discussion and has always played down the constitution's

---

3 In 2003, the Austrian government signed a controversial contract to purchase 18 Typhoon Eurofighters from the Eurofighter Jagdflugzeug GmbH. (GK)

significance. In Austria or Germany, the people's opinion has not even been asked. One wonders what the results in these countries would have been. In any case, the EU's 2007 Lisbon Declaration decided to turn the declaration into European law anyway – approved by the national parliaments only.

Why an Austrian constitution that has long been rendered ineffective still needs to be "reformed", is another question that remains unanswered. The idea probably is to hide its actual ineffectiveness by adapting it to EU and WTO principles.

How deep is the crisis of the EU? Can its neoliberal politics reach its limits (Widerspruch 2005)? How many more than 30 million unemployed can it handle? How many more than 70 million who live below the poverty line (Armutskonferenz)? And how many more failures of privatization, like the one of the British railway system, can be saved by a so-called "Public Private Partnerships" (PPPs) that channel tax money into corporations? What will happen once the assets of all nations have been sold? How far can the EU go with its destruction of the middle classes? How is it going to deal with the frustrated young men who have lost all perspective – even when they are white? Do the 2005 revolts in the French suburbs mean that the civil war in the European North has already begun? How is the EU going to approach the danger of the extreme Right? What is the EU going to do when oil and gas prices explode? What is it going to do when oil and (as is already the case in Southern Europe due to global warming) drinking water become rare? What it is going to do when neither industry nor agriculture, neither transport nor nuclear power stations can be maintained any longer, especially as long as solar power remains no viable solution to the energy crisis (Sarkar 2001)? How will the EU, given its proclaimed "ethical values", explain possible military action not only outside but within the union? Will it have to justify its own politics by terror (Chossudovsky 2003)? The EU is not unaware of all these pending problems. At the European Security Conference 2005, it already discussed scenarios of poor people's revolts (Genth 2006).

Today, we are facing a threat no smaller than a possible nuclear war of the West against Iran (Chossudovsky 2006, Petras 2006). This war would be fought to gain Western corporate control over the oil and gas reserves of Central Asia – a control that is today not only challenged by Russia, but India and especially China as well.

How long will it be possible to appease the population while imposing one's interests upon it behind closed curtains?

II. Alternatives to the Gobalization of Neoliberalism

It seems ironic that the magistrate of Vienna invites us in November 2005 to discuss "Alternatives to Neoliberal Globalization" when no one has even officially acknowledged a problem yet. Unsurprisingly, the discussions do not go very far, even though the 300 people assembled here would have sure been interested in hearing heartening ideas. They experience in their daily lives what neoliberal politics mean, they search for an explanation and hope for change. None of this will come from those "at the top", however. So much is clear. Nothing positive ever comes from those "at the top".

The real debate about alternatives to neoliberal globalization began on the 1st of January 1994 with the uprising of well organized Indios of the Southern Mexican jungle (Topitas 1994). Men, women and children of the so-called "Zapatista National Liberation Army", named after the Mexican peasant and successful leader of the Mexican Revolution of 1910, Emiliano Zapata, occupied without force some central areas of the state of Chiapas. They declared to fight Mexico's integration into the neoliberal NAFTA, the North American Free Trade Agreement, alongside the USA and Canada. NAFTA was inaugurated the same day. One of the movement's speakers, the now world famous "Subcommandante Marcos", declared that neoliberalism was a "world war waged by financial power against humanity" and an expression of the worldwide crisis of capitalism, not its success. The Indios had decided not to be part of this. They chose to resist. Their idea of an alternative life was clear and they practiced it despite the hostility they received from the government and the military (Rodriguez 2005). Their resistance was based on an indigenous version of "good governance": direct democracy, egalitarianism and a non-exploitative subsistence economy entrenched in local independence and a respect for every individual's dignity (Werlhof 2007 a) – a concept derived from pre-colonial experience, from the so-called "deep Mexico", a cultural and spiritual heritage maintained throughout centuries.

In the North, it was not before 1997/98 that the social movement against neoliberalism gathered momentum with the struggle against the ratification of the MAI. The movement's first success was the failure of the MAI due to France's refusal to ratify it.

The movement then spread wide and fast across the globe and mobilized a total of up to 15 million people for protests against the wars in Yugoslavia, Afghanistan, and Iraq. In 2002 and 2003, the struggle focused on the "Stop GATS!" campaign, led by international groups like Attac. Support was widespread. "Social Forums" began to be organized and every year individuals, groups and organizations critical of neoliberal globalization met regionally, nationally, continentally, and globally. The "World Social Forums" gathered up to 100.000 people and more from all over the world under the motto: "Another world is possible!"

Activists also came together regularly at the summits of the WTO, the WEF (World Economic Forum), the G8 or the World Bank. They managed to cause two WTO conferences, in Seattle and Cancún, to fail, which dealt a strong blow to the organization (Shiva 2005).

Still, euphoria would be out of place. An alternative to neoliberalism is not created through analysis and protest alone. An alternative to neoliberalism has to be practiced. Opinions on how to do this differ. Some discuss "alternatives" that are none: a reform of the WTO; a "control" of globalization through NGOs; a return to Keynesianism; a restoration of "social market economy"; or even a revival of socialism. Such ideas ignore reality and trivialize the problem. Much more is at stake – neoliberalism shows this every day.

Neoliberalism is an apocalypse, a "revelation". There is no way to deny this any longer. It is impossible for neoliberalism to justify itself by the reality it creates. No one can be fooled anymore by calling the corporations harmless "players" either. Things have become serious. There is no ambiguity. As a consequence, the perpetrators of neoliberal politics simply lie about what is happening.

In a way, we can say that the only good thing about neoliberalism is that it reveals the truth about "Western civilization" and "European values". This means that people now have the chance to draw the right conclusions about what is really needed.

What is really needed, of course, is nothing less than a different civilization. A different economy alone, or a different society or culture will not suffice. We need a civilization that is the exact opposite of neoliberalism and the patriarchal capitalist world system it is rooted in. The logic of our alternative must be one that completely undermines the logic of neoliberalism (Werlhof 2007 b). Neoliberalism has turned everything that would ensure a good life for all beings on this planet upside down. Many people still have a hard time understanding that the horror we are experiencing is indeed a reality – a reality willingly produced, maintained and justified by "our" politicians. But even if the alternative got half-way on its feet – no more plundering, exploitation, destruction, violence, war, coercion, mercilessness, accumulation, greed, corruption – we would still be left with all the damage that the earth has already suffered.

The earth is not the paradise it was (at least in many places) 500 years ago, 200 years ago or even 100 years ago. The devastation has been incredible: large parts of our drinking water are disappearing mainly due to the melting of the glaciers and polar caps; our climate has changed dramatically, causing turbulences and catastrophes; our atmosphere is no longer protected against ultraviolet radiation ("ozone layer problem"); many species of our fauna and flora are extinguished; most cultures and their knowledge are destroyed; most natural resources exhausted. And all this happened within what only comes to a nanosecond of the earth's history.

We have to establish a new economy and a new technology; a new relationship with nature; a new relationship between men and women that will finally be defined by mutual respect; a new relationship between the generations that reaches even further than to the "seventh"; and a new political understanding based on egalitarianism and the acknowledgment of the dignity of each individual. But even once we have achieved all this, we will still need to establish an appropriate "spirituality" with regard to the earth (Werlhof 2007 c). The dominant religions cannot help us here. They have failed miserably.

We have to atone for at least some of the harm and violence that has been done against the earth. Nobody knows to what degree, and if at all, this is even possible. What is certain, however, is that if we want to have any chance to succeed, we need a completely new "cultura" for this: a "caring" relationship with the earth based on emotional qualities that have been suppressed and destroyed in the name of commodity production and "progress". We need to regain the ability to feel, to endure pain, to lose fear and to love in ways that seem inconceivable today (Anders 1994, Vaughan 1997). If this happens then a new life on and with our earth might really be possible. In any case, it is the only earth we have.

Fortunately, there are signs pointing in the right direction. In many regions in the South, indigenous movements have arisen following in the footsteps of the Zapatistas (Esteva 2001). Especially the indigenous people in Latin America have returned (or, at the same time, "advanced") to ways of agriculture and subsistence that had been practiced for millions of years and produced a diversity of concrete wealth. Indigenous people have also established mini-markets to trade products they themselves do not need. By doing this, they secure both the social and ecological survival of their immediate (and extended) environment (Bennholdt-Thomsen/Mies 1999, Bennholdt-Thomsen/Holzer/ Müller 1999). The global peasants' movement "Via Campesina" defends the rights of small farmers all across the world. It counts millions of members today. The "localization" (Norberg-Hodge 2001) of politics and economy is on the rise everywhere. New communities, as well as new "commons" and new cooperatives, are being formed. Local councils organize and network regionally. In India, this is called "living democracy" – a democracy that includes the earth and that we can hence call an "earth democracy" as well (Shiva in Werlhof 2001 b). In the North, thousands of local networks exist in which "free money" replaces money that comes with interest, accumulates value and serves as a means for speculation rather than trade (Lietaer 1999). A "solidarity economy" and a "green economy" expand globally and challenge the prevailing "profit economy" (Milani 2000). In the North as well as in the South, people experiment with so-called "participatory budgets" in which the inhabitants of neighborhoods or whole towns decide on how to use tax money. Even the concept of an economy of gift-giving in a post-capitalist and post-patriarchal society is discussed (Vaughan 2004, 2006). In any case, fundamentally new communal experiences beyond egoism are sought. Communities are being created in which people support each other, allowing every individual to think, feel and act differently.

No alternatives have ever come from "the top". Alternatives arise where people, alone or in groups, decide to take initiative in order to control their destiny (Korten 1996). From the bottom of society (Mies 2001), a new feeling of life, a new energy and a new solidarity spread and strengthen each and every one involved. As a result, people are able to free themselves from a notion of "individuality" that reduces them to "sentient commodities" or, even worse, "functioning machines".

The mentioned examples of resistance and alternatives do truly undermine neoliberalism and its globalization. People who are engaged in them reach a completely different way of thinking. They have lost faith in "development" and have seen through the game. To them, "development" has become an affront or an object of ridicule. Politicians are expected to "get lost", as we have recently seen in Argentina: "Que se vayan todos!" It has become clear that no one wants to have anything to do with conventional politics and politicians anymore. People have realized that politics as a "system" never serves but betrays and divides them. Some people have developed almost allergic reactions to conventional politics. They have experienced long enough that domination inevitably negates life.

Of course there are alternatives to plundering the earth, to making war and to destroying the planet. Once we realize this, something different already begins to take shape. It is mandatory to let it emerge before the hubris' boomerang finds us all.

Bibliography

Alt, Franz, 2005, CDU/CSU setzen sich bei Gentechnik durch, in Sonnenseite, 13.11.

Altvater, Elmar, 2005, Das Ende des Kapitalismus, wie wir ihn kennen, Münster, Westfälisches Dampfboot

Altvater, Elmar und Mahnkopf, Birgit, 1996, Grenzen der Globalisierung. Ökonomie, Ökologie und Politik in der Weltgesellschaft, Münster, Westfälisches Dampfboot

Altvater / Chossudovsky / Roy / Serfati, 2003, Globalisierung und Krieg, in Sand im Getriebe 17, Internationaler deutschsprachiger Rundbrief der ATTAC- Bewegung, Sonderausgabe zu den Anti-Kriegs-Demonstrationen am 15.2.

Amin, Samir, 2004, Die neue Agrarfrage. Drei Milliarden Bäuerinnen und Bauern sind bedroht, in Widerspruch 47, p. 25-30

Anders, Günther, 1994, Die Antiquiertheit des Menschen, Bd.1: Über die Seele im Zeitalter der zweiten industriellen Revolution, München, Beck

arte – Sender, 2005, US-Firmen patentieren Nutzpflanzen und wollen traditionellen Anbau verbieten, 15.11.

Attac EU-AG Stuttgart und Region (Hg), 2005, EU global – fatal? Ergebnisse der Europa-Konferenz, Stuttgart

Bales, Kevin, 2001, Die neue Sklaverei. München, Kunstmann

Barlow, Maude, 2001, The Last Frontier, in The Ecologist, Februar, London

Barlow, Maude und Clarke, Tony, 2003, Blaues Gold. Das globale Geschäft mit dem Wasser, München, Kunstmann

Bennholdt-Thomsen, Veronika, Mies, Maria und Werlhof, Claudia von, 1988, Women, the Last Colony, London/ New Delhi, Zed Books

Bennholdt-Thomsen, Veronika, Holzer, Brigitte und Müller, Christa (Hg), 1999, Das Subsistenzhandbuch. Widerstandskulturen in Europa, Asien und Lateinamerika, Wien, Promedia

Bennholdt-Thomsen, Veronika and Mies, Maria, 1999, The Subsistence Perspective. Beyond the Globalised Economy, London, Zed Books

Bennholdt-Thomsen, Veronika, Mies, Maria and Werlhof, Claudia von (Eds.): There is an Alternative. Subsistence and Worldwide Resistance to Corporate Globalization, London, Zed Books

Binswanger, Hans Christoph, 1998, Die Glaubensgemeinschaft der Ökonomen; München, Gerling Akademie Verlag

Boulboullé, Carla, 2003, Das MAI vor dem Hintergrund der Maastrichter und Amsterdamer Verträge, in Mies / Werlhof; p. 108-115

Chomsky, Noam, 2003, Hybris. Die endgültige Sicherstellung der globalen –

Vormachtstellung der USA, Hamburg-Wien, Europaverlag
Chossudovsky, Michel, 2005, Americas „War on Terrorism", Ottawa
Chossudovsky, Michel, 2002, Global Brutal. Der entfesselte Welthandel, die Armut, der Krieg, Frankfurt, Zweitausendeins
Chossudovsky, Michel, 2003, War and Globalization - The Truth behind September 11th, Ottawa
Chossudovsky, Michel, 2006, Nuclear War against Iran, in: Global Research.ca, Center for Research on Globalization, Ottawa 13.1.
Clarke, Tony, 2003, Der Angriff auf demokratische Rechte und Freiheiten, in Mies/Werlhof, p. 80-94
Creutz, Helmut, 1995, Das Geldsyndrom. Wege zur krisenfreien Marktwirtschaft, Frankfurt, Ullstein
Der Standard, 2005, Tirol: Zittern um Cross- Border- Leasing-Verträge, 5.3.
Diamond, Jared, 2005, Kollaps. Warum Gesellschaften überleben oder untergehen, Frankfurt, Fischer
Dimmel, Nikolaus und Schmee, Josef (Hg), 2005, Politische Kultur in Österreich 2000-2005, Wien, Promedia
Dräger, Klaus, 2005, Bolkesteins Hammer. Projekt Dienstleistungsbinnenmarkt 2010, in Infobrief gegen Konzernherrschaft und neoliberale Politik, 19: Täter EU – Raubzüge in Ost und West, Köln, p. 17-22
Ehrenreich, Barbara, 2001, Arbeit poor. Unterwegs in der Dienstleistungsgesellschaft, München, Kunstmann
Esteva, Gustavo, 2001, Mexico: Creating Your Own Path at the Grassroots, in: Bennholdt-Thomsen/ Faraclas/Werlhof, p. 155-166
Felber, Christian, 2005, WTO-Entscheidung im Gentech- Streit. USA besiegen EU, Kurier, Wien 29.11.
Frank, Andre Gunder, 1969, Die Entwicklung der Unterentwicklung, in ders. u.a.: Kritik des bürgerlichen Antiimperialismus, Berlin, Wagenbach
Frank, Andre Gunder, 2005, Orientierung im Weltsystem. Von der Neuen Welt zum Reich der Mitte, Wien, Promedia
Frauennetz Attac (Hg), 2003, Dienste ohne Grenzen? GATS, Privatisierung und die Folgen für Frauen, Dokumentation des Internationalen Kongresses, 9.-11.5.03 in Köln, Frankfurt
Fröbel, Folker, Heinrichs, Jürgen und Kreye, Otto, 1977, Die neue internationale Arbeitsteilung. Strukturelle Arbeitslosigkeit in den Industrieländern und die Industrialisierung der Entwicklungsländer, Reinbek, Rowohlt
Galtung, Johan;1993, Eurotopia. Die Zukunft eines Kontinents, Wien, Promedia
Genth, Renate, 2006, Die Bedrohung der Demokratie durch die Ökonomisierung der Politik, feature für den Saarländischen Rundfunk am 4.3.

George, Susan, 2001, im Vortrag, Treffen von Gegnern und Befürwortern der Globalisierung im Rahmen der Tagung des WEF (World Economic Forum), Salzburg

Glöckner, Gottfried, 2005, Der Genmais und das große Rindersterben, in Grössler, p. 25-37

Goldman, Michael, 1998, Privatizing Nature. Poitical Struggles for the Global Commons, London, Pluto Press

Greenpeace, 2004, Kein Markt für umstrittenen Gentech- Mais, in Begegnungszentrum für aktive Gewaltlosigkeit, 113. Rundbrief, Bad Ischl, p. 15

Grössler, Manfred (Hg), 2005, Gefahr Gentechnik. Irrweg und Ausweg. Experten klären auf, Graz; Concord

Gruen, Arno, 1997, Der Verlust des Mitgefühls. Über die Politik der Gleichgültigkeit, München, dtv

guernica, Zeitung für Frieden und Solidarität, Neutralität und EU-Opposition, 2006, Nr.1 (Linz)

Hardt, Michael und Negri, Antonio, 2001, Empire, Cambridge, Harvard Univ. Press

Hendersen, Hazel, 1996, Building a Win-Win World. Life Beyond Global Economic Warfare, San Francisco

Hepburn John, 2005, Die Rückeroberung von Allmenden – von alten und von neuen, übers. Vortrag bei „Other Worlds Conference"; Univ.of Pennsylvania; 28./29.4.; verbreitet von greenhouse@jpberlin, 14.11.

Hofbauer, Hannes, 2003, Osterweiterung. Vom Drang nach Osten zur peripheren EU-Integration, Wien, Promedia

Isla, Ana; 2003, Women and Biodiversity as Capital Accumulation: An Eco-Feminist View, in Socialist Bulletin, Vol. 69, Winter, p. 21-34

Isla, Ana, 2005, The Tragedy of the Enclosures: An Eco-Feminist Perspective on Selling Oxygen and Prostitution in Costa Rica , Man., Brock Univ., Sociology Dpt.., St. Catherines, Ontario, Canada

Junge Welt, 2004, Die grüne Kriegsfront. USA verordnen dem von ihrem Militär besetzten Irak den Anbau von genmanipuliertem Getreide. Millionen Kleinbauern droht der Ruin, 29.11.

Karg, Jens, 2005, Trügerische Schönheit, in Global News. Das Umweltmagazin von global 2000, p. 7

Kennedy, Margrit, 1990, Geld ohne Zinsen und Inflation, Steyerberg, Permakultur

Klare, Michael T., 2001, Resource Wars. The New Landscape of Global Conflict, New York, Henry Holt and Company

Korten, David, 1996, When Corporations Rule the World, San Francisco, Berret-Koehler
Krieg, Peter, 1980, Septemberweizen, Film, Freiburg
Lechthaler, Boris, 2005, Friedensvolksbegehren und EU-Verfassung, in Attac EU-AG Stuttgart, p. 30-34
Lietaer, Bernard, 1999, Das Geld der Zukunft. Über die destruktive Wirkung des existierenden Geldsystems und die Entwicklung von Komplementärwährungen, München, Riemann
Lietaer, Bernard, 2006, Jenseits von Gier und Knappheit, Interview mit Sarah van Gelder, www.transaction.net/press/interviews/Lietaer0497.html
Luxemburg, Rosa, 1970, Die Akkumulation des Kapitals, Frankfurt
Mies, Maria, 1986, Patriarchy and Accumulation on a World Scale - Women in the International Division of Labour, London, Zed Books
Mies, Maria, 2001, Globalisierung von unten. Der Kampf gegen die Herrschaft der Konzerne, Hamburg, Rotbuch
Mies, Maria, 2005, Krieg ohne Grenzen. Die neue Kolonisierung der Welt, Köln, PapyRossa
Mies, Maria und Werlhof, Claudia von (Hg), 2003 (1998); Lizenz zum Plündern. Das Multilaterale Abkommen über Investitionen „MAI". Globalisierung der Konzernherrschaft - und was wir dagegen tun können, Hamburg, EVA
Milani, Brian, 2000, Designing the Green Economy. The Postindustrial Alternative to Corporate Globalization, Lanham, Rowman & Littlefield
Norberg-Hodge, Helena, 2001, Local Lifeline: Rejecting Globalization – Embracing Localization, in: Bennholdt-Thomsen/Faraclas/Werlhof, p. 178-188
Oberansmayr, Gerald; 2004, Auf dem Weg zur Supermacht. Die Militarisierung der europäischen Union, Wien, Promedia
Oberhöller, Verena, 2006, Wasserlos in Tirol. Gemein – öffentlich –privatisiert?, Frankfurt – New York, Peter Lang Verlag
Perkins, John, 2004, Confessions of an Economic Hit Man, San Francisco, Berret-Koehler
Petras, James, 2006, Israel's War Deadline: Iran in the Crosshairs, in Global Research. Ca, Center for Research on Globalization, Ottawa, 13.1.
Progress, 2002-2004, Zeitschrift der Österreichischen Hochschülerschaft, Wien
Raggam, August 2004, Klimawandel. Biomasse als Chance gegen Klimakollaps und globale Erwärmung, Graz, Gerhard Erker
Reiter, Gerhard, 2005, GEN OZID, Flugblatt der bioBauern Schärding, ProLeben Oberösterreich, November
Richter, Wolfgang, Schmähling, Elmar und Spoo, Eckart (Hg), 2000, Die Wahrheit über den NATO-Krieg gegen Jugoslawien, Schkeuditz,

Schkeuditzer Buchverlag

Richter, Wolfgang, Schmähling, Elmar und Spoo, Eckart (Hg), 2000, Die deutsche Verantwortung für den NATO-Krieg gegen Jugoslawien, Schkeuditz, Schkeuditzer Buchverlag

Rodriguez, Sergio, interviewt von Miguel Romero, 2005, The Zapatista Approach to Politics, in Viento Sur, Nr. 83, online: http://auto_sol.tao.ca/node/view/1649

Ruault, Franco, 2006, „Neuschöpfer des deutschen Volkes": Julius Streicher im Kampf gegen „Rassenschande"; Frankfurt- New York, Peter Lang Verlag

Rügemer, Werner, 2004, Cross Border Leasing. Ein Lehrstück zur globalen Enteignung der Städte, Münster, Westfälisches Dampfboot

Salmutter, Hans (Hg); 1998, Wie viel Globalisierung verträgt unser Land? Zwänge und Alternativen, Wien, ÖGB Verlag

Salzburger, Andrea, 2006, Zurück in die Zukunft des Kapitalismus. Kommerz und Verelendung in Polen, Frankfurt- New York, Peter Lang Verlag

Sarkar, Sharal, 2001, Sustainable Development: Rescue Operation for a Dying Illusion, in: Bennholdt-Thomsen/Faraclas/Werlhof, p. 41-54

Sassen Saskia, 2000, Machtbeben. Wohin führt die Globalisierung?, Stuttgart-München, DVA

Sauper, Hubert, 2005, Darwin's Nightmare, Film

Sennett, Richard, zit. In Einladung zu den Wiener Vorlesungen, 21.11.2005: Alternativen zur neoliberalen Globalisierung

Shiva, Vandana, 1995, Trading our Lives Away. An Ecological and Gender Analysis of "Free Trade" and the WTO, New Delhi, Research Foundation for Science, -technology and Natural Resource Policy

Shiva, Vandana, 2003, Der Kampf um das blaue Gold. Ursachen und Folgen der Wasserverknappung, Zürich, Rotpunktverlag

Shiva, Vandana, 2004, Geraubte Ernte. Biodiversität und Ernährungspolitik, Zürich, Rotpunktverlag

Shiva, Vandana, 2005, From Doha to Hong Kong via Cancún. Will WTO Shrink or Sink? web-mail2.uibk.ac.at/horde/imp/message.php?index=22627

Sozialministerium, 2005, Armutsbericht, Wien

Südwind, 2003, Nicaragua: Ausverkauf auf Kosten der Menschen, Flugblatt, 12.11.

Thaler, Barbara, 2004, Biopiraterie und indigener Widerstand, Frankfurt, New York., Peter Lang Verlag

Topitas (Hg) 1994, „Ya basta!" Der Aufstand der Zapatistas, Hamburg, Libertäre Assoziation

Vaughan, Genevieve; 1997, For-Giving - A Feminist Criticism of Exchange, Austin, Anomaly Press

Vaughan, Genevieve (Hg), 2004,The Gift, *Il Donno*, Athanor; Anno XV, nuova serie, n.8

Vaughan, Genevieve (Hg), 2006, A Radically Different World View is Posssible. The Gift Economy Inside and Outside Patriarchal Capitalism, Inanna Press (Frühjahr)

Verhaag, 2004, Leben außer Kontrolle, München, Denkmalfilm

Wallerstein, Immanuel, 1979, Aufstieg und künftiger Niedergang des kapitalistischen Weltsystems, in Senghaas, Dieter: Kapitalistische Weltökonomie. Kontroversen über ihren Ursprung und ihre Entwicklungsdynamik, Frankfurt, Suhrkamp

Wallerstein, Immanuel (Hg), 2004, The Modern World-System in the *Longue Durée,* Boulder/ London; Paradigm Publishers

Werkstatt Frieden und Solidarität, 2005, Brief zum Vereinsjahr 2004-2005, Linz

Werlhof, Claudia von, 1991, Was haben die Hühner mit dem Dollar zu tun? Frauen und Ökonomie; München, Frauenoffensive

Werlhof, Claudia von, 1997, Schöpfung aus Zerstörung? Die Gentechnik als moderne Alchemie und ihre ethisch-religiöse Rechtfertigung, in Baier, Wilhelm (Ed.), Genetik. Einführung und Kontroverse, Graz, pp. 79-115

Werlhof, Claudia von, 2001 a, Loosing Faith in Progress: Capitalist Patriarchy as an 'Alchemical System', in: Bennholdt-Thomsen et.al. (Eds.): There is an Alternative, pp. 15-40

Werlhof, Claudia von, 2001 b, Globale Kriegswirtschaft oder Earth Democracy?, in Grüne Bildungswerkstatt (Ed.) Die Gewalt des Zusammenhangs. Neoliberalismus – Militarismus – Rechtsextremismus, Wien, Promedia, pp. 125-142

Werlhof, Claudia von, 2003 a, MAInopoly: Aus Spiel wird Ernst, in Mies/Werlhof, pp. 148-192

Werlhof, Claudia von, 2003 b, GATS und Bildung, in Frauennetzwerk, pp. 42-45

Werlhof, Claudia von, 2004, Frauen und Ökonomie. Reden, Vorträge ...2002-2004, Themen GATS, Globalisierung.., Mechernich, Gerda-Weiler-Stiftung

Werlhof, Claudia von, 2005 a, „Speed kills!", in Dimmel/Schmee, 2005, pp. 284-292

Werlhof, Claudia von 2005 b, Vom Wirtschaftskrieg zur Kriegswirtschaft. Die Waffen der „Neuen-Welt-Ordnung", in Mies 2005, pp. 40-48

Werlhof, Claudia von, 2005 c, Wider die Vernichtung unserer Existenzgrundlagen, in Dietl, Claudia und Krondorfer, Birge (Eds.), Widerstand – quo vadis? Wien; AUFedition, pp. 48-52

Werlhof, Claudia von, 2006, The Utopia of a Motherless World - Patriarchy as "War-System", in Göttner-Abendroth, Heide (Ed.): Societies of Peace – matriarchies pat present and future, Toronto, Inanna (appeared in 2009, pp.29-44)

Werlhof, Claudia von, 2007a, Questions to Ramona, in: Corinne Kumar (Ed.): Asking, we walk. The south as new political imaginary, Vol. 2, Bangalore, Streelekha, pp.2149-268

Werlhof, Claudia von, 2007b, Capitalist Patriarchy and the Negation of Matriarchy: The Struggle for a "Deep" Alternative, in: Genevieve Vaughan (Ed.): Women and the Gift Economy, a radically different world view is possible, Toronto, Inanna, pp. 139-153

Werlhof, Claudia von, 2007c, The Interconnectedness of All Being: A New Spirituality for a New Civilization, in: Corinne Kumar (Ed.): Asking, we walk. The south as new political imaginary, Vol.2, Bangalore, Streelekha, pp. 379-386

Widerspruch, Beiträge zu sozialistischer Politik, 47/ 2004, Agrobusiness – Hunger und Recht auf Nahrung, Zürich

Widerspruch, Beiträge zu sozialistischer Politik, 48/ 2005, Europa Sozial, Zürich

Ziegler, Jean, 2004, Das tägliche Massaker des Hungers, in Widersrpuch 47, pp. 19-24

2. "Globalization" and the "Permanent" Process of "Primitive" Accumulation: The example of the Multilateral Agreement on Investment, MAI[*]

in Journal of World- Systems Research, VI, 3, Fall/Winter 2000, pp 728-747
Special issue: Festschrift for Immanuel Wallerstein – Part II, ISSN 1076-156x

Preliminary Remark 2010:

The WTO Agreement MAI was the one which started the critic of globalization and the anti-globalization movement internationally. Tony Clarke from Canada was the first person who alarmed the public about it. Actually – and finally – the MAI was never agreed upon and was never applied as such. This was considered as a victory of the anti-globalization movement. However, another WTO Agreement replaced the MAI: the GATS, General Agreement on Trade in Services. Its purpose is to reach MAIs original goals and it therefore has its own paragraphs regarding "financial services". By this means the MAI was not necessary any more.

The Political Economy of "Globalization": The MAI

The MAI is a draft text of an agreement which, since 1995, has been negotiated in Paris by the 29 largest industrial states organized in the OECD (Organization of Economic Co-operation and Development), without the public being informed at all. Only two years later, in 1997, the draft was leaked to the public on account of deliberate indiscretion and it reached the world public through the analyses of Tony Clarke from Canada and Martin Khor from Malaysia (T. Clarke 1997, T. Clarke/M. Barlow 1997, 1998; M. Khor). Since then international resistance to signing the draft agreement, which had to be postponed several times, has been growing constantly. Thousands of environment, women's, third world, church and other groups of "civil society" (D. Korten 1998) in OECD countries as well as an increasing number of groups of the South are engaged in opposing the MAI. The last round of negotiations in Paris, in October 1998, was paralysed by the French Prime Minister, Jospin,

---

[*] Translation from German by Dr. Ursula Ernst

declaring that his country was to move out of the negotiations after he had seen an expertise on the consequences of the application of the MAI (TAZ 15.10.1998). At present speculations are going on as to whether the MAI is dead on account of this last round of negotiations, whether it should be put back onto the level of the WTO (World Trade Organization) where it originally came from, or if it will come up again in different international contexts such as the IMF (International Monetary Fund), the so-called "Transatlantic Economic Market Place", or different other institutions that would have to be established. For there is one thing the MAI has, in the meantime, made clear: The interests behind it still exist and push towards realization. The effort to formulate an "agreement on investment protection" which has nothing less than the character of a new political world constitution could hardly be explained otherwise. For the MAI does not, as it seems, regulate investment activities, it regulates politics which should be the basis of such "de-regulated", "free" investment activities. The MAI is a "Licence to Loot" (M. Mies/C. v. Werlhof 1998), for big business at the expense of the rest of humankind and nature. It is the final consequence of neo-liberal globalization, and the permanent codification of the reversal of everything else that has so far been claimed to be the aim of economy and politics, such as democracy, prosperity, freedom, self-realization, human rights and a future for everybody. Without any explanation, let alone any apology, the MAI finishes off with these illusions.

The historical background

The MAI – according to my understanding – formulates the new Political Economy which is required by the main actors of the world economy under circumstances of monopolistic conditions and a new "industrial revolution". In the decades after World War Two, and particularly since the seventies, new average conditions of production and politics most favorable for capital have emerged which are on the brink of being globally pushed through as norm or standard. These new conditions include certain kinds of use and organic composition of capital as well as the orientation towards a certain profit level, which, historically seen, is very high today, because it is adjusted to something like an "average" speculation-profit. In order to achieve this, it is important to establish an adequate global political constitution, which produces the "necessary" prerequisites for the evolvement of such a phase of the world-economy, including adaquate sanctions, that is, the use of violence in "deviating" situations. As a result, the MAI has been negotiated by the nation-states governments, which seems paradoxical because the MAI is doing away with large parts of national sovereignty. It is these governments that, since the beginning of the contemporary world-economy, the "Capitalist World System", have been concerned with producing it and its means of sanctioning. The nation-state and international division of labor have, from the very start, worked together, so that not only today, but all along, the nation-state can be explained not by itself but only from an international and colonial perspective (I. Wallerstein 1974a, 1980, 1989; M. Mies 1986; M. Mies/ V. Shiva 1993). The same is true today: It has always been the "world system" and not the nation-state, which forms the analytic entity that informs us about our present situation (I. Wallerstein 1974b).

Since the world economic conditions have changed in the meantime, the nation-state constitution should or must be adjusted to the new development. This is what from the point of view of monopoly-capital, the MAI has formulated.

So much for the political side of political economy. Let us now look at its economic side.

Seen historically, changes in the world Political Economy are nothing new. The economy of modern history, capitalism, starts out right from the beginning as a worldwide process, namely as colonization by Europe and within Europe ("external" and "internal" colonization). The process was termed by Karl Marx (K. Marx 1974) a process of "separating the producers from their means of production" or a process of so-called "original" or "primitive" accumulation. This process was considered to be the historical prerequisite for the subsequent process of "capital accumulation proper". Rosa Luxemburg (R. Luxemburg 1971) applied this analysis to the entire world. For not only in Europe but also in the colonies peasants and craftsmen, the producers in those days, were "separated" from their opportunities, means, and traditions of production which, if they were not destroyed in the course of this process, they had to hand over to the new masters, the colonial rulers or land owners.

Feminist research has extended this analysis and included into this process women, who, by witch hunts in Europe and by colonization outside Europe, were the first to be separated from their work and production means, their culture, their knowledge, and their skills, and from control over their own labor force and even their bodies because of their reproductive capacities. Thus, in a very special way, women too, lost control over their immediate living conditions, and even themselves as living beings, having been transformed into "housewives". Since this process is still taking place today and, in order to be effective, "must" be forced anew upon every new generation, we have coined the term of worldwide "permanent" primitive accumulation (Werlhof 1978; M. Mies 1986 is calling it "ongoing" process of primitive accumulation). The extension of the term shall help to recognize the extent to which modern Political Economy up to the present time builds upon the producers', men's and even more so women's, permanent worldwide expropriation and deprivation of power. They have not only historically, that is once, been robbed by "original accumulation", they are being robbed again and again. The process of capital accumulation still depends on "primitive accumulation", which, therefore, cannot only – as Marx did – be understood as earlier or preceding accumulation, but must always and simultaneously be seen as a necessary part of accumulation as a whole. Thus, original accumulation is not only chronologically but also logically an integral part of accumulation and possesses a clearly capitalist and not a "pre-capitalist" or "non-capitalist" (A.G. Frank) character. In other words, capitalist accumulation is always "original accumulation", too, and thus "responsible" for its effects.

For the first time in history, since the beginning of processes of original accumulation, the immediate producers are not fundamentally producing to mutually provide for themselves and for each other locally or regionally – a form of economy based on so called "subsistence production" –, but are used (exploited) as raw material(producers) of the entire process of capital utilization and accumulation. This does not happen in the same way and all over the world to an equal extent, but, there is the tendency to do so, and it has become the principle of economic and political behavior. Only in this way, the Political Economy of the "capitalist world system", has come about: Africa has produced the mass of the labor force that then as slaves, as "raw material" of labor, produced the raw material of colonial commodities in America, especially in the form of agricultural and mining products which, in turn, served as material for European industrialization on the basis of proletarian wage labor. The latter includes the most-forgotten "inner" colony of "housewives" (s. Bennholdt-Thomsen/Mies/Werlhof 1988), who during their lifetime had - so to speak, according to the "African model" – to work without wage for the "production" of the next generation of labor force and the reproduction thereof.

After original accumulation had robbed many people off their culture and especially of their means of production, the process continued by trying to subsequently separate them from their labour and even their bodies. Those who, after the first phase of original accumulation, were at least paid for their labor, often forget that such payment is based upon the twofold expropriation of those who, at the lower end of the accumulation process, until today bear the full brunt of "permanent" primitive accumulation. This is the reason why trade unions have never tried to organize "precarious" employees, such as foreigners and women, to say nothing of housewives. And for the same reason left-wing theory has only considered wage labor as contributing to accumulation and as "value producing", and left-wing politics has only had an eye on "free wage laborers", the (industrial) "proletariate", especially those in the centers, according to the – false – motto: Everything else is part of the past, it belongs to the historical phase of original accumulation, and will be overcome very soon, since progress would consist in universalization, that is general expansion of free wage labor conditions over the entire globe (C. v. Werlhof 1984).

In this context, "housewifeization" (Hausfrauisierung, see M. Mies, V. Bennholdt-Thomsen, C. v. Werlhof 1988) of women subsequent to witch hunts shows, for the first time, how "international" conditions return on a "national" level or, to say it differently, how already in the initial stage of the world system the same things occur in microeconomics as in macroeconomics. It is exactly this "de-geographization" of conditions which generally characterizes the present "globalization". Compared to the international division of labor until now, globalization means that the north-south-difference disappears, not to make room for supposedly "civilized" conditions everywhere, on the contrary, it disappears geographically, but as a principle it survives and prospers and as such it is celebrating its universal "globalization". Now it can be anywhere and is not connected with continents or countries. Globalization, therefore, does not mean universalization of wage labor and abolishment of slavery and unpaid labor – such as housework – on the contrary, it means global extension of colonial conditions, namely slavery and unpaid labor or, to put it differently, it is the "housewifeization", including men's labor, all over the world, and for one reason only: to lower labor costs and to increase profits.

The new Political Economy, announced by the MAI, is still based upon the same foundations that have been laid during colonial times, but this fact is rarely seen or discussed. With the new expansion of "permanent" processes of original accumulation, the principally and not only initially violent character of our world-economy is again coming forth with increased force in the centers, too. For throughout history, the immediate producers have never parted voluntarily with their culture, their means of production, their labor power, let alone control over their own bodies. Such violence, as the immediate, political, and direct method of original accumulation, was called by Karl Marx its "secret". This secret is shared by the globalized economy of today. It was no coincidence that the MAI originated in the cellar of a building in Paris, and that it was to be kept a strict secret. And it is no coincidence as well that globalized violence is expressing itself in new wars around the globe whose causes are kept secret, too. But, from the perspective of MAI-politics it can easily be seen that these wars are invented to put under control world wide ressources, like the Caspian oil. This way re-colonization-politics become a normal investment project (see M. Chossudovsky).

The globalized war-economy affects women most deeply, as they are the producers as well as reproducers of human life and basic living conditions.

The MAI-"Economy" or: Where (un-)freedom is limitless
"Investor" and "investment" as the one and only standard of civil action

"Investor" and "investment" are the central economic concepts in the MAI (C. v. Werlhof 1998). Everything revolves around their practically limitless freedom, their possibly absolute protection, and their possibly 100 percent security: "safer investment". Reading the relevant passages in the MAI, one does not suspect anything bad, as long as one does not know the scope of the definition of investment and the extent to which investment activities are considered to be an almost absolute, the one and only standard for the entire social life. The MAI defines investment as "every kind of asset owned or controlled, directly or indirectly, by an investor". Such an investment need not necessarily create jobs, nor does it have to have anything to do with job creation. It does not refer to useful activities to supply the needs of a population, nor does it refer to the protection of resources or to any of the things the average person may have in mind when thinking of investment. In the MAI, "investment" is everything done by an investor, and be it simply the increase of the investor's property and his control over resources. It does not matter, whether he speculates or deals with drugs, arms and women or is "laundering money", whether he penetrates or monopolizes existing markets, or creates new markets to put them under his control; whether he exploits the local mineral resources, and gets hold of the land to build up new agricultural industries, or whether he for himself takes a patent out of local "intellectual property", the so-called TRIPS, *the Trade Related Intellectual Property Rights (*V. Shiva 1995*).* The MAI wants to give the investor free access to everywhere and anything and is not at all restricted to so-called "virtual" spheres. His main interest seems to be in land, such as nature reserves for electrical industries or tourism. This kind of investment is not investment in the best or narrower sense of the word, it is the acquisition of available opportunities for profit maximization. In this sense the Canadians, for example, have, after four years of NAFTA (North American Free Trade Association, called the "little MAI"), learned that investment activities consisted mainly in buying up or pushing out of the market other business companies, and to dismiss employees to "reduce costs" (T. Clarke/M. Barlow 1997). Thus the promise of NAFTA-advocates to create 200.000 new jobs has not only not been kept, on the contrary, 400.000 jobs were abolished in the U. S. A. only (L. Wallach/R. Naiman 1998).

The market structure reveals itself as power structure: Monopolies, oligopolies, and cartels dominate. "Mega-enterprises" erode the order of competition (C. Noé 1998). National cartel offices have no objections to "companies getting bigger and bigger... since the others are doing the same" (ibid.). "We are in danger of putting ourselves at the mercy of a steadily decreasing number of private power centers and their globally acting managers who call themselves, full of self-confidence, ‚Global Players'" (W. Kartte, former president of the cartels office, quoted in Noé, ibid). Such "looting associations" (C. Noé) are seldom criticized these days, even though Adam Smith, founder of modern economic liberalism, explicitly warned of the formation of monopolies: Free trade were only possible, if enterprises were owned locally and had their roots in the communities (A. Smith 1976). This, however, is, to an increasing extent, no longer the case. The investor the MAI has in mind must rather be compared to the "absentee landlord", and investment looks more like the colonial "enclave", run anonymously and set up in the country like an alien property whose owner cannot be got hold of and sometimes disappeares over night together with his "business", a practice made possible by capital-"flexibility" under present technological circumstances. In any case, such owners will not be afflicted by damages done locally, and, as is known from experience, in case of doubt do not feel responsible for such damages (s. f. ex. Seveso in Italy and Bhopal in India; D. Korten 1996).

It is no coincidence that the history of the agrarian sector resembles the MAI-investor, since the principles of "permanent" original accumulation have always come out most clearly in agriculture. This phenomenon is still mistaken as "feudalism" or Third World "traditionalism", whereas, in reality, these processes are the most profitable ones of modern economy and were since colonialism invented by it (C. v. Werlhof 1985; C. v. Werlhof/H.P. Neuhoff 1982).

So-called "investment" is already leading to the death of local business enterprises all over the world, a process which, with the MAI, will increase in the future and will, paradoxically, threaten "free enterprise" as such. Those entrepreneurs or business people who expect to be protected by the MAI in their function of investors do not seem to understand this process. But why should big international corporations let smaller investors have their profits? The crux of the matter is exactly the fact that the investor sees himself as a (legal) person or institution characterized by one and only one interest, namely to make the biggest profits as quickly as possible and thus to be absolutey doing what he wants to do or not be doing what he does not want to do – he is already trying to avoid taxes and he is more and more successful in doing so. Thus he will export his profits rather than leave them in the country where he made them, if this is to his advantage (R. Engels et al. 1998). Such "de-regulation" and "debureaucratization" of investment activities are considered to be particularly positive aspects of the MAI. Therefore, "the temptation for business companies" is increasing, "to become so gigantic that they present themselves as duchies for strategic market arrangements. When these arrangements are successful ... competition is dictated by *capitalist* dukes and prince electors and takes place at the expense of the many nationally and regionally limited, so-called middle-class producers and services that look for credits." (C. Noé, s. a.; "capitalist" added by C. v. W.) At present the 500 biggest companies control 80 percent of the world's investment activities.

Nevertheless, the investor's activity is not only given highest economic priority, it is also given top social priority. "The investors' gains are the highest human value. Everything else is of second order." (President of United Technologies, Gray, according to N. Chomsky 1995, p.18) The protection of this species is, therefore, seen as free trade (ibid) and not as protectionism, which, with respect to the rest of the market participants, is ridiculed as anachronistic. "Investment protection", within the MAI, does not mean protection of labor, environment, and nature or perhaps human rights and vital interests of the people (B. Mark-Ungericht 1998), it stands exclusively for the protection of the investor-monoculture. The protection of others besides the investor, count as restriction of the investor's freedom.

Present troubles of capital valorization, which are primarily due to the enormous increase of no longer "productively" covered finance- and speculation- capital and oversized profit expectations, apparently are so deep (Third World Resurgence 1998) that right at the time, when "the limits of growth" on the planet and its exploitation and devastation are being seen as "ecological question", and when people are searching for a "sustainable", even "subsistence oriented" economy (V. Bennholdt-Thomsen/M. Mies 1997), the MAI wants to establish a radically opposite way as universal model and world constitution. Globalization, the race for the last resources of the globe, has entered its final ruthless phase.

Globalization is not the fulfilment of the illusions of "progress", on the contrary, it is the rapid and brutal disposal of the social achievements since the beginning of the industrial revolution. There are already 18 Million people unemployed in Europe, child labor amounts to 1.5 Million, and in England the decrease of the state of labor conditions and wages or wage differences are back to figures of 1886 (S. Halimi). It seems that the MAI provisions for investment can, principally and to a large extent, do without free wage labor. The best example for this are the "free production zones", "world market factories" or "maquiladoras" of the South, where chips, electronics, and textiles are produced for the corporations, using cheapest female labor force under conditions of forced labor (M. Mies 1986; L. Gabriel 1998). This colonial treatment of labor is spreading right at the time of a new technological development, or a so-called third industrial revolution which makes such colonization possible. The new technologies on the basis of computerization make it possible to reduce labor on a large scale – estimates count with about 80% (H. P. Martin, H. Schumann 1996) – and to use the cheapest form of untrained labor in high technology areas. High tech combines with low wage. A new form of slavery, home workers, and housework are all back in high tech outfits. Now "real" subsumption of labor under capital in the sense of free wage labor is being replaced by "marginal" subsumption of labor, which, if at all, is only marginally paid (V. Bennholdt-Thomsen 1980), and it is "unfree" insofar as it no longer faces capital as a "free" and "equal" contractual partner.

Critics of modern technologies are dismissed as mere "Luddites". (D. Noble 1985. Ned Ludd from Nottingham, England, was the first to attack machine production and automatization in the early decades of the 19th century). Apparently technology and progress are still euphorically accepted, though even in the old industrial countries they have not kept what they had promised. Thus, for instance, "the end of labor" must be understood as the end of wage.

It is, therefore, not surprising to see what in the MAI is seen as "most-favoured nation-principle", "non-discrimination", and "equal treatment" of investors and investments. Nothing must be in the way of investor and investment, no matter what their objectives are, and it must be secured that those unequal competitors, namely corporations and smaller investors, are globally considered to be "equal". They are given the globally most favorable conditions, which is nothing but systematic "positive discrimination" of the great and the duplication of their competition and power advantages. The same result will be achieved by the fact that according to the MAI certain branches, business firms, areas or regions will no longer be publically supported or given subsidies, because the equal treatment or non-discrimination clause implies that any other investor has the same right to the support measure. Since, of course, the means for such "limitless" support are not available, the support mechanism as such breaks down and the survival chances of those who had been supported earlier will also be reduced to zero, until finally the welfare state elements that is, provisions in health, pensions and education, will also be abolished.

Within such a Political Economy of monopoly-capital, which with the MAI would have only rights and neither duties nor responsibilities, there can no longer be any talk of the best possible provision of people and households in the "market economy". The "Ford-model" of paying wages which enables the workers to afford a Ford (J. Hirsch, R. Roth) is no longer necessary within a globalized economy, because the markets are, from a global perspective, always big enough to absorb any production (H. P. Martin/ H. Schumann 1996) at least as long as there is no depression. Therefore, the trade unions strategy of "re-distribution" will, on the whole, have no big chance of success, apart from the fact that such strategy does not question the conditions of production as such, namely, so-called investment, and is thus prepared to accept looting and exploitation.

The MAI-Politics or: The world as colony of corporations
So-called "expropriation" as the one and only standard of political action

That the MAI economy serves "investors" is only possible, if this process is supported by policies which correspond to permanent "primitive accumulation". If primitive accumulation is understood as creating the prerequisites for "accumulation proper" by concentrating the relevant means of production in the hands of those who, on this basis, are able to accumulate, then, especially today, it becomes obvious why this process has not come to a historical conclusion, as Marx had still believed. On the contrary, particularly under the MAI, politics is clearly defined in such a way that "primitive" accumulation is again and globally carried out on a comprehensive scale under modern conditions. Such politics and policies want to enforce severe re-distribution from bottom to top and in all areas of the economy and by all means, violence and even military intervention (Europäisches Parlament 1996) not excluded, as we can see it most clearly since the war of aggression against Yugoslawia. This political process, which is also part of the prerequisites of so-called globalization in general, has to be expected particularly under the MAI-regime:

- Separation of small, medium-sized and even larger firms or investors from their capital: an increasing number of firms are collapsing, "unfree" enterprise (for instance, new forms of sub-enterprises), credit-induced "contractual" production, new quasi self-employed people such as homeworkers, "alternative" businesses, a general trend towards a "lumpenbourgeoisie" (A. G. Frank 1968; V. Bennholdt-Thomsen 1988; C. v. Werlhof 1983).
- Renewed separation of farmers from their land: expulsion of farmers, abolishment of agricultural reform laws – as presently in Mexico -; coercive introduction of genetic and new reproduction technologies in agriculture, animal raising and plant growing; patenting of life forms; robbery of "intellectual property" of indigenous producers (V. Shiva 1998; M. Mies, V. Shiva 1993; Forum on Land, Food Security and Agriculture 1998).

- The technological separation of women from their bodies: coercive introduction of genetic and reproductive technologies for eugenic purposes, generally further reduction of women's control over their own bodies and continued experiments to break women's child-bearing "monopoly" (A. Bergmann 1992; C. v. Werlhof 1997a).
- Separation of workers – men and women – from their work place, their wages, and their labor power as such: "wageless commodity production", generally precarious employment conditions such as part time work, 620-DM-jobs (DM is short for German Marks), "flexibilization" of work; work paid below the existence level; exploitation of unpaid work according to the model of a housewife's work in the form of expansion of "housewifeization" of employment conditions; general "marginalization" of labor force or "lumpenproletarianization" and general reduction of people to mere and simply potentially usable "raw material", which, according to demand, can be utilized or destroyed (G. Anders 1980; V. Bennholdt-Thomsen 1979).
- Separation of the public hand (local communities, states, central governments) from its property: "privatization" in favor of private monopolies, sale of land, buildings, public enterprises, community property, the "commons" (T. Clarke 1997).

"Expropriation" is, next to "investment", the central category of the MAI and it is equally widely understood as well as equally perverted. "Expropriation" in the MAI is a collective term for circumstances that are to be avoided, because they are considered detrimental or obstructive to investment activities. The term is not only used in the classical sense of nationalization or socialization or even "socialist expropriation". According to the MAI, the term of expropriation even includes "indirect" ("creeping") expropriation which is already the case when expected profits do not happen or happen only partly, for instance, on account of the validity of existing laws, common law, or because of disturbances. Therefore, the MAI provides that all laws and regulations which at some time and some place could hinder the investor's freedom and would thus not conform to the MAI would have to be abolished retroactively ("roll-back" clause). Of course, no such new laws and regulations must be introduced for the 20 years time of the contract ("stand still" clause), which would make any policies of non-conformism with the MAI impossible. Finally, any investor who feels hindered can at any time resort to the MAI dispute settlement mechanism to enforce his interests before an international court of arbitration which puts itself out of reach of any democratic control. The investor may sue for damages any local community, any country, any government and any other investor because of "expropriation", if, in his eyes, he is hindered by the defendant in realizing his freedom of investment. As we know, the MAI arbitral tribunal is constructed in such a way that it will, in any case, support the "requesting" investor, for otherwise he could resort to the relevant local or national courts. Furthermore, there have been precedents in Canada and Mexico in which it has been argued that the investor's rights have precedence over potential health hazards to the population affected (s. the case of the U. S. Ethyl Corporation in Canada, in which the company has won against the Canadian State; Toronto Star 1998).

As for the MAI's dealing with the term of expropriation, the following consequences must be mentioned:

"Expropriation" does not really refer to the threat of expropriation of the investor, but to the investor threatening others with expropriation. In fact, non-investors as well as smaller and medium-sized investors are expropriated in favor of large investors. This is the classical case of robbery in the sense of primitive accumulation which, however, with the MAI, becomes a legal procedure if not the legal standard. The MAI thus affirms and legalizes a tendency which so far has been growing ruthlessly, but has always been treated by the judiciary ambivalently. With the MAI the world is, indeed, seen exclusively through the eyes of the "investor". As a result, those who make attempts at fighting that their health, their nutrition, their welfare and vital interests shall not be sacrificed to potential investor-interests must risk to be considered potential criminals according to the MAI. This would eventually lead to a special criminalization of women who simply try to fulfill the needs of their children and families.

The MAI is, in the eyes of its advocates, not only a "political" contract, but almost like the materialization of a "natural law". From this angle, the MAI is a long "necessary" act to enable globally pure capital utilization, liberated from any natural and social restrictions. It is "the level playing field", cleared off any and all obstacles and bumps, the "operating theatre", the purified battlefield. The MAI defines anew what is "Nature" and what is "Culture". In addition to women, peasants, and colonized people, everybody else is defined out of culture and back into "nature", except for a tiny minority who exclusively claim the achievements of culture, "civilization" and human rights for themselves. As "nature" as such is seen as having no "value", the labor and lives of "naturalized" people seem to have no value, too (C. v. Werlhof 1988) – just like women. Such politics of "naturalization" would therefore mean a sort of "feminization" of most people in the world.

The MAI would be the basis of a new political world order or world constitution and of a new nation-state, the MAI-state. It defines the fundamental conditions of legal and political actions - the "mono-pol-itics" - for the next twenty years. With the MAI, governments on all levels are not simply divested of their sovereignty, as is often complained (T. Clarke/M. Barlow 1997; 1998), but by signing the agreement they are trying to rob the people of their sovereignty or to "separate" them from their sovereignty, which, according to the idea of democratic constitutions, is impossible. At the same time signatory governments lose much of their sovereignty by allowing investors not only a status equal to the standing of the nation-state but of even greater power and higher order: in dispute settlements with private investors they can be the losers. Governments also reduce their economic power by allowing the privatization of public property which already is being sold to private investors not only to fill up the state treasury or public purse but also to partly enrich corporations. With the MAI, governments even allow the order of competition and their legal cartel regulations or antitrust laws to be sacrificed to private monopolies by considering the political order problem of monopolies (or oligopolies) only in the area of public or state monopolies and not as referring to private monopolies. According to the MAI only state and not private monopolies have a negative connotation.

The state shall, however, not be abolished. It will always have to take care of the investor's primitive accumulation (as well as its own). In this sense, the state turns into the "pimp" for its own population and for more "resources", which he has to offer to investors at globally most favorable conditions. "Poverty is the criterion for securing the location of investment" (A. Zumach 1996). Since force and violence (must) dominate at that level, the state progressively turns into a police state, a military state (s. the Tindemans-Report of the European Parliament 1966). It will (have to) "educate" (S. Halimi) its population as far as possible to identify with the investors' interests and to internalize these interests to the extent that civil disturbances, which might get the state into the trouble of being sued for damages by an investor, are repressed even preventively. In case this education – which could form the basis of a new educational system in MAI-states – does not do its job, the MAI does not restrict the state in establishing law and order. On the contrary, the areas of "inner security" are the only areas that are explicitly excluded by the MAI.

The "MAI-revolution", therefore, implies that the modern nation-state of the center, turns into a ("semi-)peripherical" colonial state to guarantee that inside it primitive accumulation can take place on a large scale, whereas corporations turn into "nation-states" of central importance, forming the top of the new global pyramide of the "capitalist world system".

The MAI proves that capitalism and democracy appear and stay together only as long as the colonial regime or primitive accumulation has not yet been established everywhere for everybody. It also proves that its starting point is a contradiction between "investments" and human rights or vital interests of the population (s. the Harvard study quoted by E. Drake et al. 1998). The Zapatista movement in Mexico, which started with the NAFTA (C. v. Werlhof 1997b), calls this development a "New World War" and speaks of a "war against all peoples, against human beings, culture, history ... Neo-liberalism (is) a process of renewed conquest of the land ... the conquerors are the same as 500 years ago ... they tell us that we are an obstacle, we are not only dispensable, we are an obstacle to progress" (Marcos 1995). Since then, the Mexican government is said to have been asked by the Chase-Manhattan-Bank in the U. S. A. to liquidate the Zapatista movement by military force, since it is a threat not to the state as such but to the investor's belief in political stability in Mexico (Pérez 1998).

With the MAI a similar development may occur in North America and Europe.

The term of "permanent" primitive accumulation is an analytical instrument to explain the political consequences of the MAI and to understand its logic of the "necessity" of permanent political violence. In this kind of "expanded" primitive accumulation the state is given a new order in which there is a tendency to abolish the traditional division of powers and in which its power no longer "comes from the people" but is rather systematically turned against the people. This tendency is also growing in the "centers". Real political power is, with the MAI, "legally" taken from the people and given to big corporations, thus creating a new "corporatism", a new form of co-operation between state and capital, which particularly characterizes modern dictatorship (Boulboullé/Schuster).

Conclusion

The discussions, disputes and struggles which we may expect for the near future will, therefore, not only concern the "distribution of the loot" from the process of (primitive) accumulation, nor will it be about extended "participation" in a changing political order, it will primarily have to deal with the abolition of "permanent" primitive accumulation and insofar it will also deal with the secret basis of the entire process of accumulation: In the final analysis we will no longer be concerned about participating in the capitalist "productive" property which has for quite some time now turned out to be "destructive" property. This is why property and "prosperity" exist not for more and more, but for fewer and fewer people. A world-"economy" looting the planet, cannot last for ever. Therefore, we will have to desert from the "TINA" - There Is No Alternative - "syndrome" (V Shiva 1993) and will have to reconquer the true means (of subsistence) which we need for our daily lives.

The universal quasi-religious belief in the technological progress, economic "growth", corporate "rationality", and its outcome: money, will increasingly contradict reality (H.C. Binswanger 1998). "Greed does not feed" (S. Prakash/J. Mourin 1998).The global economic crisis can no longer be "triggered" by "financial warfare" (M. Chossudovsky 1998). Finally, the pre-condition of western confidence in the "capitalist world-system", the old patriarchal utopia of being able to replace the "bad world" by a man-made "brave new world" will soon be recognized as a lethal fraud. The "globalization of poverty" (M. Chossudovsky), the "housewifeization" of labor, and the irreversible destruction of the natural environment cannot be declared the pre-requisites for a happy future of human kind any longer.

Therefore, the main problem – with and without the MAI – will consist in finding again a "real" economy, put back from its head to its feet: an economy which is not organized around profit, competition and colonization of people and nature. Women worldwide, especially in the south, are already starting to practice this new economy as a "moral economy" (M. Mies) which has finished with the counterproductive eploitative relationship with life (see the movement for a "nayakrishi andolon" – for a happy life – in Bangladesh and the international movement "diverse women for diversity").

At the end of progress we will have to approach the end of violence and to reconquer a culture built on co-operation and co-existence (s. I. Wallerstein 1991). For that purpose we need what capitalism and patriarchy have tried to "separate" us from: a "dissident" mind, based on the radical acceptance of live. "Deep feminism" is needed.

Bibliography

Anders, Günther (1980): Die Antiquiertheit des Menschen, II. Über die Zerstörung des Lebens im Zeitalter der 3. Industriellen Revolution, München

Bennholdt-Thomsen, Veronika (1979): Marginalität in Lateinamerika - Eine Theoriekritik, in: Lateinamerika, Analysen und Berichte 3, Berlin, pp. 45-85

Bennholdt-Thomsen, Veronika (1980): Towards a Class Analysis of Agrarian Sectors: Mexiko, in: Latin American Perspectives, Vol. VII, Nr. 4, pp. 100-114

Bennholdt-Thomsen, Veronika (1988): "Investment in the Poor": an Analysis of Worldbank Policy, in: Mies, Maria/Bennholdt-Thomsen, Veronika/von Werlhof, Claudia: Women, the last Colony, London, pp.51-63

Bennholdt-Thomsen, Veronika/Mies, Maria (1997): Eine Kuh für Hillary. Die Subsistenzperspektive, München

Bergmann, Anna (1992): Die verhütete Sexualität. Die Anfänge der modernen Geburtenkontrolle, Hamburg

Binswanger, Hans-Christoph (1998): Die Glaubensgemeinschaft der Ökonomen. Essays zur Kultur der Wirtschaft, München

Boulboullé, Carla/Schuster, H.W. (1998): Mit den Verträgen von Maastricht und Amsterdam und der Einheitswährung "EURO" bahnen die Regierungen der EU dem MAI-Vertrag den Weg, in: Soziale Politik & Demokratie, Sondernummer zum MAI-Vertrag, 21.4.

Clarke, Tony/Barlow, Maude (1998): The MAI and the Threat to American Freedom, Toronto

Chomsky, Noam (1995): Wirtschaft und Gewalt. Vom Kolonialismis zur neuen Weltordnung, München; in english language (1993): Year 501. The Conquest Continues, Boston

Chossudovsky, Michel (1998): "Financial Warfare triggers Global Economic Crisis", in: Third World Resurgence, Nr. 98, October (Penang), pp. 5-10

Clarke, Tony (1997): Silent Coup. Confronting the Big Business Takeover of Canada, Toronto

Clarke, Tony/Barlow, Maude (1997): MAI: The Multilateral Agreement on Investment and the Threat to Canadian Sovereignty, Toronto

Drake, Elizabeth/Benygar, Laura/Ewing, Michael et al. (1998): The Multilateral Agreement on Investment: A Step backward in International Human Rights, Harvard Law School, Human Rights Clinical Project Program/The Robert F. Kennedy Memorial Center for Human Rights, Cambridge, 19.5.

Engels, Rainer/Martens, Jens/Wahl, Peter et al. (1998): Alles neu macht das MAI. Das Multilaterale Investitionsabkommen. Informationen, Hintergründe, Kritik (WEED/Germanwatch), Bonn, (März)

Europäisches Parlament (1996): Entwurf eines Berichts über eine Sicherheits- und Verteidigungspolitik für die Europäische Union, Ausschuß für Auswärtige Angelegenheiten, Sicherheit und Verteidigungspolitik, Berichterstatter: Leo Tindemans, Brüssel, 11.6.

Forum on Land, Food Security and Agriculture (1998): Statement, International Conference on "Confronting Globalization. Asserting our Right to Food", Kuala Lumpur (Malaysia), 11.-12.November

Frank, André Gunder (1968): Kapitalismus und Unterentwicklung in Lateinamerika, Frankfurt

Frank, André Gunder (1976): On so-called Primitive Accumulation, in: Frank, André Gunder: World Accumulation, 1492-1789, New York

Gabriel, Leo (1998): Die globale Vereinnahmung und der Widerstand in Lateinamerika, Wien

Halimi, Serge (1996): Schlank und flexibel hinein in die Armut, in: Le Monde Diplomatique, (Juli)

Hirsch, Joachim/Roth, R. (1986): Das neue Gesicht des Kapitalismus. Vom Fordismus zum Postfordismus, Hamburg

Khor, Martin (1998): Die Folgen für den Süden, in: M. Mies/C. v. Werlhof (eds.) (1998): Lizenz zum Plündern. Das Multilaterale Abkommen über Investitionen - MAI - Globalisierung der Konzernherrschaft - und was wir dagegen tun können, Hamburg, pp. 79-91

Kommittee Widerstand gegen das MAI (1998): MAI, der Gipfel der Globalisierung, Reader zum Kongreß, Bonn

Korten, David (1996): When Corporations Rule the World, Westhardford/San Francisco

Korten, David (1998): Globalizing Civil Society. Reclaiming our Right to Power, New York

Luxemburg, Rosa (1971): The Accumulation of Capital, London

Mark-Ungericht, Bernhard (1998): Der Staat, die Politik und der Widerstand gegen das MAI, Manuscript, Graz

Martin, Hans-Peter/Schumann, Hans (1996): Die Globalisierungsfalle, Reinbek

Marx, Karl (1974): Die sogenannte ursprüngliche Akkumulation, in: Marx, Karl/Engels, Friedrich: Werke Band 23, pp. 741-791, Berlin

Mies, Maria (1986, 1999): Patriarchy and Accumulation on a World Scale. Women in the International Division of Labor, London

Mies, Maria/Bennholdt-Thomsen, Veronika/von Werlhof, Claudia (1988): Women, the Last Colony, London

Mies, Maria/Shiva, Vandana (1993): Ecofeminism, London

Mies, Maria/von Werlhof, Claudia (eds.) (1998): Lizenz zum Plündern. Das Multilaterale Abkommen über Investitionen - MAI - Globalisierung der

Konzernherrschaft - und was wir dagegen tun können, Hamburg

Noble, David (1985): Automation: Progress without People, San Pedro, California

Noé, Claus (1998): Warten auf das Weltkartellamt, in: Die Zeit, Nr. 11, 5.3.

OECD (Organization of Economic Co-operation and Development) (1997, 1998): The Multilateral Agreement on Investment, the MAI Negotiating Text. Directorate for Financal, Fiscal and Enterprise Affairs, Paris

Prakash, Suria/Mourin, Jennifer (1998): Hey TNCs! You can't feed the world on greed, report from PANasia Pacific, Listserver of Diverse Women for Diversity, New Delhi

Shiva, Vandana (1993): Monocultures of the Mind, Penang, (Introduction)

Shiva, Vandana (1995): Trading our Lives away. An Ecological and Gender Analysis of "Free Trade" and WTO, Penang/New Delhi

Shiva, Vandana (1998): Listserver of Diverse Women for Diversity, various numbers, New Delhi

Smith, Adam (1776): An Enquiry into the Nature and Causes of the Wealth of Nations, London

TAZ (Die Tageszeitung) (1998): 15.10.

Third World Reseurgence (1998): (Penang), October

Toronto Star (1998): 21.7.

Wallach, Lori/Naiman, Robert (1998): NAFTA. Four and a half Years later, in: The Ecologist, Vol. 28, Nr. 3, Mai/Juni

Wallerstein, Immanuel (1974a): The Modern World-System, New York

Wallerstein, Immanuel (1974b): The Rise and Future Demise of the World Capitalist System: Concepts for Comparative Analysis: in: Comparative Studies in Society and History 16 (4), pp. 387-415

Wallerstein, Immanuel (1980): The Modern World-System II: Mercantilism and the Consolidation of the European World-Economy, 1600-1750, San Diego/London

Wallerstein, Immanuel (1989): The Modern World-System III: The Second Area of Great Expansion of the Capitalist World-Economy, 1730-1840, San Diego/London

Wallerstein, Immanuel (1991): Unthinking Social Science. The Limits of 90th-Century Paradigms, Cambridge

Werlhof, Claudia von (1978): Frauenarbeit: Der "blinde Fleck" in der Kritik der Politischen Ökonomie, in: Beiträge zur feministischen Therorie und Praxis, I: Erste Orientierungen, Köln, in English language: Women's work: The blind spot in the critique of political economy, in: Mies, Maria/Bennholdt-Thomsen, Veronika/von Werlhof, Claudia (1988): Women, the last Colony, London, pp. 13-26

Werlhof, Claudia von (1983): Production Relations without Wage Labor and Labor Division by Sex, in: Review, Vol. VII, Nr. 2, (fall), pp.315-359

Werlhof, Claudia von (1984): The Proletarian is dead; long live the Housewife?, in: Smith, Joan/Wallerstein, Immanuel/Evers, Hans-Dieter (Eds.): Households and the World-Economy, Berverly Hills, London, New Delhi, pp. 131-147

Werlhof, Claudia von (1985): Wenn die Bauern wieder kommen. Frauen, Arbeit und Agrobusiness in Venezuela, Bremen

Werlhof, Claudia von (1985): Why Peasants and Housewives do not disappear in the Capitalist World-System, working paper Nr. 68, Sociology of Development Research Center, University of Bielefeld, Bielefeld

Werlhof, Claudia von (1991): Teile und Herrsche. Warum Bauern und Hausfrauen im kapitalistischen Weltsystem nicht verschwinden, in: Was haben die Hühner die mit dem Dollar zu tun? Frauen und Ökonomie, München, pp. 83-113

Werlhof, Claudia von (1988): On the Concept of Nature and Society in Capitalism, in: Mies, Maria/Bennholdt-Thomsen, Veronika/von Werlhof, Claudia: Women, the Last Colony, London, pp. 96-112

Werlhof, Claudia von (1997a): Schöpfung aus Zerstörung? Die Gentechnik als moderne Alchemie und ihre ethisch-religiöse Rechtfertigung, in: Baier, Wilhelm (ed.): Genetik. Einführung und Kontroverse, Graz, pp. 79-115

Werlhof, Claudia von (1997b): Upheavel from the Depth. The "Zapatistas", the Indigenous Zivilisation, the Question of Matriarchy and the West, in: International Journal of Comparative Sociology, Vol. XXXVIII/Nr. 1-2, June: Justice in Controversy: A Comparative Analysis of Injustice and Inequality, pp. 106-130

Werlhof, Claudia von (1998): MAInopoly: Aus Spiel wird Ernst, in: Mies, Maria/von Werlhof, Claudia (eds.): Lizenz zum Plündern. Das Multilaterale Abkommen über Investitionen - MAI - Globalisierung der Konzernherrschaft - und was wir dagegen tun können, Hamburg, pp. 131-176

Werlhof, Claudia von/Neuhoff, Hanns-Peter (1982): The Combination of Different Production Relations on the Basis of Non-Proletarianization: Agrarian Production in Yaracuy, Venezuela, in: Latin American Perspectives, Issue 34, summer, Vol. IX, Nr. 3: Rural Class Relations (Part I, Social Classes in Latin America), pp. 79-103

Zumach, Andreas (1996): Armut ist das Kriterium, das den Standort sichert, in: TAZ (Die Tageszeitung), Nr. 5099, Berlin 9.12.

3. Self appointed Saviors Propagate Globalization
Opponents of globalization versus members of the World Economic Forum, WEF[*]

in Annette Lyn Williams, Karen Nelson Villanueva and Lucia Chiavola Birnbaum (Eds.): She is Everywhere! Vol.2. An anthology of writings in womanist/feminist spirituality, Bloomington, IN 2009, iUniverse, Inc., pp. 71-80

In the first (and last) public confrontation between proponents and opponents of globalization in Austria in 2001, I participated on the side of opponents. In the following, I would like to reflect on this experience with the following notes:

1. The arguments of opponents and proponents, once presented, were left largely un-discussed. The main reason for this was that the proponents did not relate criticisms to themselves in any way at all.

2. Instead, the proponents tried to co-opt the criticisms by presenting themselves as critics in their own right, according to the motto, "We see problems too, but we're working at solutions". From this side, obviously, there was no questioning of globalization *as such*. One proponent, the "global player" Percy Barnevik, actually went so far as to claim that the problems related to globalization arise from the fact that instead of there being too much of it, there is too little.

What disturbed me particularly about this discussion were the lily-white consciences of the proponents of globalization.

How is it possible for one Percy Barnevik to say that he makes no apologies for being entirely profit-oriented, and for defining globalization as "the freedom for my group of companies …, to invest where and when it wants to, to produce whatever it wants to, to buy and sell wherever it wants to and to support the lowest possible restrictions resulting from labor laws and social contracts"[1] – without regarding this as scandalous, like everyone else did?

Barnevik's answer is that globalization has purportedly rescued around one thousand million people, one third of them Chinese, from absolute poverty. What is a claim of this nature based on? It rests entirely on one measurement alone: that of money. The moment someone has access to money, even if to the tiniest amounts, he or she is no longer regarded as living in "absolute poverty." The problem with this type of calculation is that the flip side of the coin is ignored: the fact that monetarization almost always entails the loss (of control)

---

[*]   Translation from German by Patricia Skorge

of the means of production and of subsistence in general that have hitherto made these people's existence possible. Barnevik would thus have to explain why he regards a relatively moneyless life as "absolute poverty" and the miniscule income of someone robbed of his means of production and subsistence as a liberation from such poverty. If questioned, the answers of those affected would be quite clear. But Barnevik isn't interested in them, since he only thinks about money. Whatever else happens as a consequence of introducing money is meaningless for him.

But that doesn't let him off the hook. Because only when people lose (control of) their means of production and subsistence can Barnevik & Co. use them or have them used for their own interests – for the re-implementation of large-scale land-holdings, for the spread of commodity production and to ensure "the market" is a world market, everywhere. Barnevik sees no harm in this, since only in this way can he make money himself, lots of it. And in any case the people can now (allegedly) buy on the market what they used to produce themselves – or whatever Barnevik & Co. are going to offer them instead.

There is only one snag: it isn't true. Susan George, who was also on the side opposed to globalization, pointed out that a growing number of people are unable to participate in market activities at all. Now it is already 50% (and in 20 years' time 70% of people) says George, are excluded from the market: not "still," but *"already."* In other words, absolute poverty is created by globalization in the first place. It is the state, in which people have neither the means of production, nor of subsistence, nor else a money income that is anywhere near sufficient. Their money income is so limited, that they are in no position to really have "demands" on the market.

What would Barnevik say if confronted with these conditions, which he bracketed out? Presumably he would say that *in the long run*, globalization will raise income and employment levels. Not that he could prove this. On the contrary, at present the global players' corporations employ only 1-2% of all waged employees, whilst constantly destroying millions of small and medium-sized enterprises – precisely those which have up to now provided the most employment opportunities. And it is the plantations, sweatshops, brothels, and "free production zones" that produce for the big corporations that pay wages of less than 1-2 US$ a day; not "still," but rather, they *no longer* pay more than this. This means that not only in the countries of the South, but in others – e.g. in the USA itself – one can speak of a "new slavery", affecting hundreds of millions of people throughout the world[2]. This is where Barnevik's argument ends; after all, he is himself in favor of "the lowest possible restrictions resulting from labor laws and social contracts." This means that he sees to it himself that things won't be able to get any better in the future. On the contrary, the globalizers went to the South first, to exploit the low labor costs there – the only remaining "comparative cost benefits" world-wide – subsequently achieving a gradual but drastic reduction of labor costs in the North too.

The empirically observable *simultaneity* of globalization on the one hand and impoverishment, war, and destruction of democracy on the other can thus be explained. Mr. Barnevik's "argumentation" and his good conscience are based on the fact that he does not take cognizance of the actual causes and effects. As a result, he can also behave as if he were completely "un-ideological" – unlike the critics of globalization, naturally. He puts his faith completely and utterly in money, in "the market." Only, there is a theory behind this faith – monetarism. The monetarism of Milton Friedman, Friedrich von Hayek, and the "Chicago Boys," whose first act in ushering in global neo-liberalism in the 70s was to install the dictator Augusto Pinochet in Chile. This economic theory underlies globalization policies. With the violence with which it is carried through politically, its totalitarian character, and its effects (in the form of its creation of wealth for some and poverty for nearly everyone else), it is of benefit to the global players, but not to the majority of human beings, also not in the long run. Of this there can no longer be any doubt. And so Mr. Barnevik has to act as if he didn't have any theory at all, so as not to be confronted with the preconditions for and consequences of his thinking. That, incidentally, includes deliberately leaving out historical comparisons, so making it possible not to recognize how closely globalization, colonialism, and imperialism resemble one another, except to the extent that globalization, this world economy, doesn't leave out anything or anyone anymore – not even its own inventors, the Western/Northern industrial countries. They too become "colonies of the corporations," because globalization means exactly what Mr. Barnevik understands it to be.

One basis for removing the premises on which this argumentation is built, together with this "good conscience," would therefore be knowledge and information. At the same time, proof of the deliberate ill-intent of the globalization project could be provided. For example, it was no coincidence that the notorious MAI, Multilateral Agreement on Investment was negotiated in secret and not supposed to reach the public eye at all. This happened because the MAI (which subsequently failed as a result of a veto from France and protests from the world-wide, civil-society based, anti-globalization movement, then in its infancy) in fact provided for the legalization of a campaign of exploitation conducted throughout the world by the big corporations. In addition, it would have been a kind of "authorization" in the form of a totalitarian world constitution[3]. Nor can the policies of the OECD, WTO, IMF, and World Bank, which have led to the collapse of entire national economies and to millions of deaths – especially those of children, as UNICEF has established – through poverty, hunger, and war throughout the world, be attributed to naivety or error[4]. Besides, the long-term planning and conduct of armed conflicts throughout the world, or the destruction of Yugoslavia and the war in the Balkans, a new war in the middle of Europe, cannot be seen as being for the good of humanity, although (or for which reason) they were presented as exactly that: as "humanitarian interventions."[5] Business hand in hand with militarism and speculation instead of investment – "investment" is really just more fusion – cannot really be regarded as "economic activity" in any positive sense. In addition, there are the increasingly open attacks on those democracies that still exist. It is not new that the Americans for example are not necessarily among the friends of democracy in countries of the South. Lately, democracy in the North has also been called "outmoded" by the WTO for example; and Margaret Thatcher's chief advisor, John Gray, stated that "global free trade and democracy are like fire and water."[6] In Austria too, in the context of neo-liberal University reform, which belongs to the domain of the privatization of services related to the GATS negotiations of the WTO, there is now talk of democracy in the universities hampering their "business potential."[7] The foreign affairs advisor to the American government in the post-war era, George Kennan, warned as early as 1948 against spreading illusions about growing wealth and democracy[8]. In a TV broadcast approximately two years ago, a member of the EU Commission of that time said: "If people knew what we really negotiate about, they would chase us away!" (Censorship evidently wasn't working normally in this case.)

It is possible to show by now when this project known as globalization will necessarily come to an end; at the latest when the non-renewable resources of the planet have been used up, which will mean that technological progress will come to an end as well. What is clear in any case, and undeniably so, is that Western lifestyles are utterly impossible to impose on a global scale. Ecological collapse would be the immediate result. *Why, then, do people continue to pretend that there is "no alternative" to the spread of the Western way of life?* We need to ask what a desirable society would be like, and whether the Western society, even in its centers, would have a place in it at all? Are we happy, are we healthy, do we relate to one another in caring ways, are we free enough not to have to worry about money and power for once? Are we people capable of deep feeling, do we have a good relationship to plants and animals, are we wise, open-hearted, and tolerant, do we know "friendship", have we managed to defeat crime, violence, and poverty?

On the back cover of the journal "The Ecologist"[9] there is a photograph of a girl of the Jarava people, who have lived on a group of islands in the Indian Ocean for thousands of years. The Jarava are now to be resettled by the Indian government. The girl in the picture is laughing gaily, still covered in water

droplets after bathing in the ocean, and her hair is decorated with skillfully arranged shells. The text to the picture runs: "What choice does she have in civilization?" The answer is: She will become:
- Untouchable
- Prostitute
- Beggar
- Servant
- Addict or
- Corpse.

Who has the right to inflict Western "civilization" on this girl?

Pamela Hartigan, my counterpart in the debate with the WEF, manager of the Schwab Foundation, which founded the WEF in the 70s, began her contribution with the following words:

"The birth of a new world is upon us!" What she meant was the globalized world, and she spoke with pathos. How can she do so, in spite of what we (could) know? And how can Mr. Barnevik still say, "They need our technology!"?

However, to put an end to the good consciences of the culprits, we need to take something more than just information, thinking in terms of cause and effect, and the leaving out of consequences into account. We need to consider belief. Because, the nihilism of the globalization – project is clearly accompanied by a message of salvation as well. Could it not be said that the constant, worldwide large-scale assemblies of representatives of corporations and heads of government are in fact *propaganda meetings of self-appointed saviors, whose mission it is to convince the public that what is good for capital is also good for humankind?* – This, incidentally, was done in the Nazi period. Are smooth global players like Barnevik a "better alternative" to elected politicians, and is the WEF summit in fact conceived as an alternative to democracy? The brainwashing only works as long as people believe in it. After all, we know:
- that violence and war cannot be good deeds;
- that it was a lie to say that the neoliberal policy of globalization would bring more wealth and democracy for all;
- that measures to reduce public spending are fraudulent; just like Structural Adjustment Programs (SAPs) in the South, all they mean is a redistribution from bottom to top, and they serve only speculators and the military arms buildup;
- that reactionary policies are not "reforms";
- that the "privatization" of public assets represents uncompensated expropriation and theft from the population;
- that it is a travesty when, what is labeled "racism" and "xenophobia", are no

longer worldwide neocolonialism or deaths as a result of deportation practices, but instead criticism of the piracy of large global corporations;
- that opponents of globalization are condemned as being adherents of "protectionism," while the corporations themselves are products of subsidies and of protectionism in their own interests;
- and not least, that opponents of globalization are now being systematically criminalized, because they heretically refuse to believe in the "good" (and godly?) of globalization; with the result that, right in the middle of Europe, some of them are being quite deliberately shot at (Göteborg, Genoa) – as if not just economically but also politically banana-republic methods were a feature of the most progressive achievements of global modernization.

The total turn-around of the hitherto (purportedly) valid view of the world is indicated by the macabre cynicism of the globalizers. Their propaganda of salvation however stands and falls with the idea of mission. What was promised in earlier times by Western Christianity is now promised by the "free market," even if it has disappeared behind monopolies by now – if it ever existed at all.

The idea of mission, like Pamela Hartigan's fantasy about the birth of a new world, is the core of the problem of the good conscience. What this means today, is that where there is no McDonald's, there is nothing to eat. Away with the roadside food vendor! Today's missionary assumes that McDonald's is the best for everyone, and he wouldn't dream of asking those concerned what they think. If he notices that someone has a different opinion, then he "educates" him – if need be, by the force of the facts that he fabricates. The puzzle about the secret of the good conscience is this: *the demolition of what already exists is not regarded as violence or destruction, but merely as a necessary prerequisite to the brave new world of Western lifestyles,* or to be more precise*: the American way of life*[10]. For Percy Barnevik and Pamela Hartigan it is inconceivable that anyone could have anything against this. Or if they do, this is interpreted as being way behind the times, and just too inflexible.

The central question to Barnevik and Hartigan and the other proponents of globalization is thus: How is it that they have no respect for that which other people have made; that they can in fact destroy it – and at the same time view this as legitimate, even as a good thing? That is the only question which they would, in the final analysis, not have been able to answer. The thinking of pro-globalizationists assumes a common religion, with a quasi-god (the market and money), in which scenario they themselves are a team of cleaners sent to cleanse the world of non-conformists and heretics. They are the heroes who sweep away the filth and set up shiny, clean McDonald's, full of light and air, everywhere. But anyone who talks about "them" needing our technology has failed to even recognize that "they" already have their own, and that it usually works a lot better for them. These shiny, happy global prophets of a clean new world would probably be nauseated if they even tried a roadside vendor's food. On an emotional level, too, they wouldn't know what to do with food that wasn't from McDonald's. Apparently, it seems dangerous to them, maybe even deadly. And since they regard food prepared at the roadside as a threat to life, they impose their own McDonald's on those who have been eating roadside food up to now, without dying from it in the slightest; except that McDonald's really is a threat to life. Without the roadside food vendor, but with McDonald's, many people will starve, and many already have. Not only because McDonald's food is bad, but also because most people can't afford it, and now have no alternative. McDonald's creates a void – and so does modern technology and money, which is oriented towards the world market and profit – not only at the scene of the crime, but also elsewhere, for example in the Amazon rainforests, where deforestation takes place for McDonald's: so that cattle can graze there for a few years and then be made into hamburgers, before the grazing lands turn in due course into barren steppes and deserts. This is what moved José Bové, a French farmer, to "dismantle" a branch of McDonald's under construction in his neighborhood[11].

The religion of progress embraced by the proponents of globalization is a belief in miracles and alchemy; according to this faith, the constant annihilation of life, the dramatic destruction of nature and the ever-faster devastation of other cultures (or what remains of them) are not crimes, indeed, they don't even matter; they should be greeted with jubilation by those affected, because what has been destroyed will be replaced with a wonderful new world of technical and other kinds of progress. This superstition is still found everywhere, even amongst opponents of globalization. After all, it is several hundred years old and, since colonial times, has evidently been the essence of our Western identity[12]. The difference to earlier times is only that now, at last, an end will be made once and for all to the last remnants of non-Western civilization and any impertinent attempts at revival on their part.

The Salzburg dispute in fact brought to light the actual dilemma of the globalization debate, even if it could not be formulated there and then. I doubt whether there are many people here in the West who can really prove that their "civilization" is the "better" one. Nevertheless, most people probably believe that it is. And as long as that is the case, the proponents' "charm offensive" and their strategy of "embracing" certain groups in critical civil society may lead to a rift in the latter, instead of the contra movement embarking *together* on the desperately needed discussion of fundamental alternatives[13] – these being possible alternatives to Western civilization itself.

My conclusion from the Salzburg experience is that the critique of globalization will only be safe from co-option and resistant to being turned into its opposite if it is not conducted under the premise of unreserved faith in Western civilization and its mission to play benefactor to the world.

The way forward is clear. It is also based on a feeling, only a completely different one. It is a feeling of responsibility for and empathy with those people negatively affected by colonization and globalization, and for all other creatures worldwide, and for the planet itself. This feeling tells us that what we want at last, for the whole world, is a non-violent, caring, egalitarian, cooperative civilization, and this is what we will probably need to survive globalization, possibly the last and most radical phase of Western civilization, at all. Because there is one thing that both opponents and proponents of globalization can be assumed to know, or that they could know if they wanted to: the globalization project is not one of long duration. It is already coming up against the material, intellectual, spiritual limits of the world. It is already in a crisis, and will inevitably fail. Neo-liberalism is the capitalist world system's answer to the crisis of profitable capital valorization, i.e. that of supposedly endless growth in the face of the finiteness of the world and its resources.

If the MAI was to last 20 years, then that is presumably the kind of time-span global players think in. But we, the other 99.9% of the world's population, cannot afford to have this kind of "then it's someone else's problem" mentality. We have to become oriented to life once more, and begin to think and act in ways that are both long-term and free of dominance.

Notes:

1. Susan George: at the debate, as well as *Tagesanzeiger*, 15.1.2001
2. Bales, Kevin: Die neue Sklaverei, Munich: Kunstmann 2001; english original: Disposable People, New Slavery in the Global Economy, California University Press 2000; Arlacchi, Pino: Ware Mensch. Der Skandal des modernen Sklavenhandels, Munich: Piper 2000.
3. Mies, Maria/von Werlhof, Claudia (Eds.) Lizenz zum Plündern. Das multilaterale Abkommen über Investitionen, MAI- Globalisierung der Konzernherrschaft und was wir dagegen tun können, Hamburg: Rotbuch 1998
4. Chossudovsky, Michel: The Globalization of Poverty, London: Zed Books 1998; Netzwerk gegen Konzernherrschaft und neoliberale Politik, German edition of: The International Forum on Globalization (IFG): Die Welthandelsorganisation (WTO): Unsichtbare Regierung für die Welt des neuen Jahrtausends? Eine Einführung, Analyse und Kritik, Cologne 2001; Soros, George: Die Krise des globalen Kapitalismus. Offene Gesellschaft in Gefahr, Berlin: Alexander Fest 1998; english original: The Crisis of Global Capitalism. Open Society Endangered, New York: public affairs, 1998
5. Chossudovsky, Michel: see 5 above, as well as, by the same author, Washington hinter den terroristischen Anschlägen in Mazedonien, 23.7.2001 (English original: http://emperors-clothes.com/articles/choss/behind.htm); Federici, Silvia: War, Globalization and Reproduction in: Bennholdt-Thomsen, V. /Faraclas, N./von Werlhof, C. (Eds.): There is an Alternative. Subsistence and Worldwide Resistance to Corporate Globalization, London: Zed Books 2001, pp. 133-145
6. Gray, John. Die falsche Verheißung. Der globale Kapitalismus und seine Folgen, Berlin: Alexander Fest 1999; English original: False Dawn. The Delusions of Global Capitalism, London: Granta Books, 1998
7. cf. von Werlhof, Claudia: Hochschulreform als neoliberaler "Putsch?", paper presented at the 29th German *Evangelischen Kirchentag* 2001 in Frankfurt/Main
8. cf. Chomsky, Noam: Profit over People. Neoliberalismus und globale Weltordnung, Hamburg/Vienna: Europaverlag 1999, p. 24; English original: Profit over People. Neoliberalism and Global Order, New York: Seven Stories Press, 1999
9. The Ecologist, Vol 31, No. 6, July/August 2001
10. Galtung, Johan: Die Welt in der Krise, in: Galtung et al.: Die Gewalt des Zusammenhangs. Neoliberalismus-Militarismus-Rechtsextremismus, Vienna: Promedia 2001, pp. 53-82
11. Bové, José/Dufour, Francois: Die Welt ist keine Ware. Bauern gegen Agromultis, Zürich: Rotpunkt 2001
12. Lapham, Lewis: Die Agonie des Mammon - Die Herrscher des Geldes tagen in Davos und erklären sich die Welt, Hamburg: EVA 1999
13. Mies, Maria: Globalisierung von unten. Die Kampf gegen die Herrschaft der Konzerne, Hamburg: Rotpunkt 2001; Bennholdt-Thomsen, Veronika/Faraclas, Nick/von Werlhof, Claudia (Eds.): There is an Alternative. Subsistence and Worldwide Resistance to Corporate Globalization, London: Zed Books 2001

4. The New will only arise from the Bottom! "Our" University? Social movements, society, education and science today[*]

- unpublished -

Preliminary remark 2010

To the surprise of the Austrian public a student movement broke out in October 2009. It started at the University for Applied Arts in Vienna, spread to other Austrian universities and reached Germany and all of Europe. During autumn and winter the students of about 60 universities from all over Europe participated in the movement. The movement occupied the main assembly halls of their universities, stayed there uninterruptedly for 2 months, organized a sort of communal life and prepared their protest activities from there. At my university in Innsbruck, the movement started on the 29th of October with the occupation of the so called "SoWiMax", the assembly hall of the Departments of the Social and Economic Sciences.

Personally, I had expected that the students would "mobilize" earlier because of the neo-liberal reform of the universities in Austria, which had started in 2002 already. Since the reform and its neo-liberal international background were not analyzed correctly and the effects of the reform had to be felt in practice, the students needed years to mobilize against it. But the movement broke up after the first weeks and lost most of its enthusiasm in the course of the semester. As I participated in its debates, defended it in various public discussions and was invited to give my classes in the occupied SoWiMax (what I accepted), I was able to observe the whole process also from within.

The following article is the elaboration of a so called "autonomous lecture" which I held there 2 days after the occupation. Looking back I must say that only a minority of the students really disposed of a concrete analysis of the societal conditions under which they were acting, so that most of them had no idea of the "objective" importance of their upheaval.

---

[*] Translated from German: Hanna Pallua and Gianluca Crepaldi, Innsbruck, December 2009

"Autonomous lecture", occupied SoWiMax on 31th Oct 2009, 2 pm, University of Innsbruck, Austria

After you had occupied the SoWiMax, I came to visit you two days ago and all I could say was "At last!" Finally I have the chance to witness a student movement once before I will have to quit university. By now I can see that you have made a good deal of experiences in terms of self organization on the foundation of basic democratic principles. For sure, you will need these experiences again at a later point in time.

I am going to address four issues today:
1. What is a social movement, what kind of social movement is yours?
2. What does the societal situation look like today and how does it affect education and science?
3. What does this mean for your study conditions at the university?
4. What to do?

1. What is a social movement, what kind of social movement is yours?

Since I have taken an active part in several social movements up to now, I dare to provide a definition for it, consisting of four theses:

Thesis a)
In the end, a social movement is in all its depths a declaration of love:
- *to life*
- *to the search of truth and*
- *to the self-evidence of domination-free existence*

However, these three theses lack several aspects nowadays:
- Life resembles a laboratory stay
- The search of truth does not take place, but it rather is a squeezing in of pieces of "information", above all the ones concerning mere procedural questions ("education")
- The self-evidence of domination-free existence gets transformed into subordination to increasing totalitarian "matter-necessities" and hierarchies of domination as well as into a radical heteronomy within the "mega-machine" (Mumford) of science, economy and society.

Thesis b)
Obviously, these conditions do not fit into the principle of being-human and into other human traditions that are re-appearing at the moment: as a memory, as a possibility, as an experience, as a vision and as a real – well, indeed a realistic –

perspective. This is about the revival of the *egalitarian heritage* from our basic-democratic, life-friendly and cooperative past, from the world of *matriarchal civilization*. It is obviously the still-existing model of the self-organization you are working on so naturally!

Due to this historic connection, social movements *cannot be made, but have to be born*. Therefore, they are in stark contrast to everything that is made: war, domination, commodity production, money, the machinery and the obedience towards them. Social movements generally refuse the suppressed condition of being human. The social community thus gets pregnant with those movements until they crowd out in an irrefutable, inevitable, so to speak in a "volcanical" way.

Social movements arise absolutely *against* the will and the intention of the rulers, the makers, and their "creations" and they thus induce them with a feeling of deep anxiety! Such movements are basically anti-domination and egalitarian...

Thesis c)
Every social movement is a mystery because of the impossibility of its manufacture.

Since the movement puts domination into question, it is alarming for the rulers. As a new born movement it is still like a child. The child primarily has to be kept alive, has to get to know itself bit by bit, to grow, to gain experiences and to try to fathom its own depth, height, broadness and how they can be expanded and further developed.

Above all, the young social movement has to learn how to protect itself against threats. These threats consist of attempts of "patriarchalization", hence the attempt to functionalize it for alien purposes, namely the ones serving authorities and "politics", and thus being forced to return to "normality". Things like these always end in its splitting.

Should your movement be a declaration of love, then certainly not one to money – or is it? I have heard about your demands for money, but I do not believe that this is your "mystery". Then it would not be one. So, you could ask: What do we really want?

For instance, I am sure that you too want, as every human being does, to be loved and to be needed, to be meant and to be wanted by this society, actually on a very personal basis. This means: You want to find or to create conditions for *a life in dignity*, wherever this may not be the case. And indeed, it is not the case now! In present times of neo-liberalism, dignity is not longer understood. However, without dignity, the principle of freedom and self-determination becomes useless; furthermore it results in the freedom of the powerful to define themselves through the victory over the weak. Thus, dignity means *to be appreciated and hence accepted* in terms of what someone is and desires and also to appreciate and accept others in the same manner.

Thesis d)
The thesis I have drawn from my time as a professor at Innsbruck University is that *in our times* a student movement can evolve at the latest when people start to realize that:
- They have *no future,* even as academics. This thesis has turned out to be right. Now it is important to examine this thesis.
- By now, even in schools a certain discomfort has evolved, and still, when you enter university, no changes of positive nature are taking place. How come?
- So you have already felt for a while that *something is not right there*, and that if you adapt, once again, this will be of no use for you. Therefore, you want your *freedom* at first, namely the freedom to look around, to gather experiences and to orientate yourself before taking long-term decisions. But exactly this freedom is (no longer) granted. Why?

The question is therefore how a humane life in dignity would look like for you and under which conditions such a life should take place.

Are such conditions in our current society still achievable, – even if they are not intended?
- Does the willingness to adaptation suffice these days? It does obviously not.
- Is your anxiety about the future justified these days? Yes, obviously it is.
- Thus you need a movement, unchained from the principles of adaptation and from anxiety, in order to work out, what kind of changes are possible to start a better future. Probably this is what your movement is about.

In the end it has to be found out to what extent something like *"different"* education, university, science and even society will be essential for it!

These questions are needed to be asked. Since your movement resulted from the collective social conditions, your movement is an answer to that and retroacts to them.

In one word: You are confronted with your *coming of age*, namely the decision about how and by which kind of education you want to arrange your life.

2. *How does the societal situation look like today and how does it affect education and science?*

Up to now, all analyses of the entire societal situation and of the miseries within education and university are defective and incomplete. At the utmost, the economic aspect is seen – keyword *"education=commodity"* or "(re)-commodification" and "commercialization" of education. In one word: "Education is not for sale!" (Krautz, Kellermann, Sambale).

But at the same time the result – "commodity" – is not asked about the conditions of its *production*. What does it mean to transform education into a commodity? How has this commodity arisen? How, from whom, why, for whom and what was it made from? In which ways does education-transformed-into-a-commodity differ from education that is not a commodity?

A commodity is something produced out of something that once has been alive and now encounters us as a "past", "congealed" life, as something that was *killed*, or rather something *dead* (Marx), a form of capital. The commodity is made out of a process of destruction-and-re-arrangement, namely the process of modern (machine) technology that was brought about in the course of industrialization and mechanization. I entitle this as the product of a *"creation through destruction"* (Werlhof 03, cf. Schumpeter).

The fact that commodity is not by accident "cadaver-like" (Bloch) gets veiled by its "value", i.e. the price that is paid for it, and which at the same time is used to manifest the "preciousness", the alleged "better" and "higher" character of it in comparison to a non-commodity.

On the contrary, education which is not a commodity would be *alive* and "born", the kind of education you are demanding for: an education organized around your needs and not around the needs of capital and accumulation. Not an education that is destroyed and destroying, but an education founded on *quality*, allegedly claimed to be valueless, but which is actually *priceless!* – In fact the kind of education you require and you are demanding for. This would be an education freed from exploiting interests and methods of destruction.

Therefore, the transformation of education into a commodity is scandalous, and it is not only scandalous because three billion dollars a year, one of the biggest assets in international economic scenery, will be used to make education a part of the commodification and the profit-making-process.

However, the essential problem resulting from education that gets transformed into a commodity is not frequently mentioned, namely a *technique* that constantly and thoroughly *destroys* the *quality of education* from behind. A global profitable bargain can only be achieved through standardized, quantified and *"canned-education"*. This is a kind of education that does not even deserve its name, as it is only a commodity that corresponds with the accumulation interests of the educational industry. For this reason, the WTO's General Agreement on Trade in Services (GATS) was enforced in 1995, which tries to achieve these goals on the basis of the neoliberal politics of *liberalization, globalization and privatization* of all services, including education

(Mies/Werlhof 1998). At the same time the concrete lively interests in education are ignored. Obviously, no one of the profiteers or politicians is interested in knowing how education gets transformed into its own caricature. Why?

For an answer we have to go further beyond.

The techniques of the transformation of things or creatures into commodities derive from science and therefore from university, from *"our university"*. This has been the most *"highbred"* product since modern age. Generally speaking, its *method* consists of the domination over and the exploitation of nature that goes ahead with the segmentation, quantification, intermixture and the new-composition of nature/matter/life-forms. Nature involved in this process is not understood as being alive, but as a dead "matter" and for this reason it does not get noticed from outside; this is a process of destruction. Only a person that is directly concerned with this process gets confronted with the violent character of modern sciences.

And *you are aware* of it, because now it concerns you, *it hits you*, but you do not know how, what and why.

This means that modern science and technology systematically began to include education as well as people to turn within their wheelwork. Since their existence they have started to destroy the world and have gradually expanded commodity production, the "realization of value" and the formation as well as the accumulation of capital to always larger sectors and territories. This is the reason why nowadays the "formation of education" ("Bildung") gets in fact turned into a formation of capital ("Kapital-Bildung"). In other words: Do you want to be free human beings or do you want to be transformed into "capital", actually into "human capital", like commodities and machines?

In the scientific-technical civilization of modern age, criticism on technology is seen as a taboo par excellence. It is seen as an offence to mention that economy and modern sciences have been turned into a *war*, if not into a "war system", against nature and human beings.

It already started with the inquisition. Its *method* had been adapted by the natural sciences and then gradually by almost all other sciences, above all by the medical one. This method has remained the same up to this day – it is an experiment: hence, the segmentation and fragmentation, thus the damage and/or destruction of the discrete animate forms – human being, animal, plant, element and mineral – and their intermixture and new-composition with other matters and so-called "raw materials" to commodities, machineries – "system" – and "capital" (Collard/Contrucci).

European *inquisition*, lasting for 600 years, set the beginning, namely with "shaping" *human beings* and especially, from the second half of the 15th century onwards, with shaping *women* as "witches" (Federici). At this time, inquisition developed methods to break human will and resistance, to make people obedient to the project and system of modern rule and to their repression and exploitation in favor of the modern nation state (Bodin, cf. Opitz-Belakhal), colonialism and the modern international economy of capitalism as a "world system" (Wallerstein) that is based on it. Likewise, the integration of women and the colonized as unpaid workers ("housewifeization of work", New Slavery; cf. Mies), the "domination of nature" in terms of exploitation of nature and its transformation in the name of progress (Merchant) as well as modern warfare (Heidelberger/Thiessen) are part of this system.

Are we now going to face a kind of second inquisition?

Yes, even more than that. Modern science has resulted in an industrial-military complex and in the power of corporations (Chossudovsky) as well as in the boomerang that now falls on our heads: the beginning apocalypse initiated by the climate catastrophe (Gore) that still can neither be understood nor stopped. This would only be possible if the military-industrial project (Bertell) that has triggered off this catastrophe would be immediately abandoned. Since the consequences of lethal sciences have by now become globally visible, *all of us* are aware that we find ourselves – without exception – among the victims.

This means that the *end of modern era* has begun (Werlhof 2007, Projektgruppe 2009). The rule to rather ignore than to identify the world-destroying character of modern civilization does not prevent the currently all over perceivable effects from making their appearance in form of crises in all sectors: in the economy, as for the value of money, the markets, especially the labor market and consequently the production of commodities. This also involves the so-called "resources" that are running short, the ecological problems that are the result of our relationship with nature, and the problems in the field of human ecology, namely the human condition. After all, the crisis also involves policies that are per definitionem not only up to the crisis' depth, but have indeed contributed so much to its development.

Thus, we have to turn away from the *promises of the modern era,* including the socialistic one saying that if the scheme of technical scientific progress is maintained, then progress, advance, peace, democracy and welfare will be open for an increasing amount of people. However, the exact opposite is occurring and we already know the reason for it.

The utopia of progress to create a paradise on earth has turned into the complete opposite: a dystopia of a *hell* on earth is about to arise.

This is exactly the sensation you get when you think about your *future*!

The extinction of species, the drying of fresh-water resources, the rise of the sea-level and the collapse of the climate demonstrate that beside the disappearing of natural resources, actually the *disappearing of the world* (Jaeger

08), science has a *wrong understanding of nature*. Indeed, the modern age's promise to control nature has led, totally unexpectedly, to a *nature out of control*. Our science is thus a *lethal science* (cf. part D.).

This is the kind of science you are becoming familiar with, right her at the University. *Do you really want this kind of science?*

Science has led, next to economy and to war – its "other sides" – to an actual crisis of civilization. This happens because the *utopia of an artificial "re-creation of the world" through its very extinction* is being realized. We now entitle this project "*capitalist patriarchy*" (Werlhof 03). It is the "patriarchal" project of a modern "second creation" of the world and not the matriarchal one that arises from co-operation with "Mother Nature".

By now, this project has met its limits and can be considered as being not only a failure, but also a terrible threat for life and the planet as a whole. But since society is rigidly adhering to it as long as it seems somehow possible, the system withdraws more and more from democratic rules and leans towards *totalitarianism*, which corresponds to a concept of "system" as "machinery", to the new "mega-machine" (Mumford). The machine and accordingly the system that has been formed upon the machine's patterns are – like military and corporations – incapable of democracy.

The masculine-patriarchal obsession with "creation" as *competition* with "Mother Nature" has been existent since antiquity and accordingly since the beginning of patriarchy, and it actually destroys life on earth. The technological progress that since modern times is trying to achieve the realization of the utopia of patriarchy is neither an innocent project of human curiosity nor an act on behalf of a supposed nature-"telos", but does deliberately create an *anti-nature* and an anti-world that is not in line with the earth and its living conditions.

We have to draw conclusions from it, whether we want to or not. The complete re-creation of the world on the basis of systematic industrialization, capitalism, mechanization and commodification does not only destroy the globe but also human beings, in other words, *you*. As modern times have begun with a complete re-modeling of human beings, they are also going to end with it. This means that now you are as well involved. You are supposed to become "*human capital*" or even "*post-human*" capital (Schirrmacher).

A perspective of enlightenment (Habermas, Ribolits, Liessmann, Menasse) does not suffice here, as it has itself always created, propagated and defended the conditions for such a kind of progress (Mumford, Sieferle, Noble, Wagner).

It is time to disclose the "*secret" of modernity*: to be aware of its secular nihilism towards life and the broadly applied, quasi-religiously legitimized "sacrifice" of life in the name of an alleged progress.

3. What does this mean for your study conditions at the university?

Now we have come to your personal situation and the study conditions that are depressing you. They are a direct consequence of current social changes that move towards a broad inclusion of the whole world in all its dimensions: the so-called "globalization". It forces human beings into a *process of technical control, appropriation, transformation and exploitation of everything that is alive, for the purpose of re-creating it in the shape of commodity/capital/machinery and*, in the end, *to profitably dispose of it.*

In comparison, slavery was presumably a naive endeavor. You are thought to become an object of this process, not only with neck and crop, but also with your emotions and your intellect. You would be downgraded to objects; you are actually forced to even become *"active objects"* (Genth), intended co-delinquents in terms of your own submission and adjustment to the modern "mega-machine" that is expanding progressively.

Science wants to make *customers* out of you, who are consuming education like a commodity; moreover, you will be trained to be producers of a commodity called "science", a kind of science that in truth is "capital" and which is deliberately destroying the world and you, the people, as well.

In particular the *ability to think* seems to disrupt the process; but be aware that thinking is the last resort of freedom. You are supposed to think only in a compliant manner that is corresponding to the logic of money, machines, orders or, in general, of capital; and you are not at all supposed to think different or even beyond the system (Werlhof 08). The computer serves as a model, as a "thinking-machine" (Genth). You should emulate it in its binary way of thinking: zero or one, one or zero? It is like a quiz show – scientific thinking degenerates to a quiz. "I *don't* think, therefore I am"!? By now, artificial limbs for thinking and thinking-substitutes are proclaimed as proper thinking.

"Heads? – Off!" – This is apparently the *secret curriculum of Bologna*, which is barely discussed in public with critical views on it. This kind of "guillotine" will rob your intellectual potential, an ability that is specifically human. Instead, you become a brainwashed or even brainless *raw material of the education industry* on a global "level playing field", just now prepared by politics. You will be downgraded to a *"pass through of capital"* that is – with the remaining "residual risk" – easily adjustable to the "mega-transformation-profit-machine": brain death, step by step! The „*homo oeconomicus-maquina-vacuus*" (Greco) faces his invention, though not his birth, the *"femina"* already included. In times of "gender" and in times when the "mother" is supposed to be replaced by genetic engineering and biotechnology, a more accurate differentiation is no more provided.

As a result you will not make your career, but rather be labeled with "*employability*", which is just a verification of your "usability" in terms of the system. Hierarchy and competition between you as well as violence and compulsion from above come along with it, because they belong to the essence of "machine-systems" (Genth). You even have to learn to love them, as Orwell says, and you have to become an intrinsic part of them by mimetically adapting to them (Genth). This is because the machine is the actual ideal of this civilization, an ideal that human beings have to match as well – becoming *human machines*. This kind of thinking may reach back to Descartes, but only nowadays it is in fact going to be implemented and allegedly proven.

This is the kind of *futurism* that the university reform process is based on. We should more precisely say: the de-form process. You shall *not* take notice! And how many of you already believe that the attempted abolition of thinking and its substitution by "computer literacy" has really got to do with "excellence"?!

You should dissociate yourselves from arts and humanities, the last reservoirs where thinking is still possible. Anyway, these areas melt down like glaciers in times of climate change. Instead you are supposed to feed yourselves with the so-called "*big science*", namely management- and natural sciences (Werlhof 05). In the light of a machine-like logic, this will be preached as rational and right choice. In contrast, I plead for the occupation of animal research laboratories and the liberation of those animals, which in fact would really be a reasonable and forward-looking action.

Since education is going to be organized as a huge system – as if it were an *education-machine* (Dreßen) – that is based on the systematic production of commodities, it is drawn into the overall destruction-process that comes from industrial transformation. As a result, education becomes destructive itself, which does affect all of you! All allegedly logical and rational justifications for this destruction can thus be ascribed to the "banality of evil" (Arendt), as it turns out nowadays.

This adds nothing to the kind of education you would need – far from it! Rather it could be compared to a straitjacket that pushes you into modules and schemes, into Anglicism and e-learning units of "canned education" that shape your study-programs today. At the end of the day, this type of education will "disburden" universities from teachers and supervising tutors, from co-operative ways of working and studying, even from books and, last but not least, from the remaining freedom and leftovers of democracy.

As a result, you will always more resemble inmates of the "*university-clink*", instead of becoming autonomous, free, self-determined, curious, young people that are in search for themselves and their place in the world. The latter is a *necessity* in order to learn to shape this world and its future. However, first of all the world as such will have to be preserved! Even if some of you do not see it yet: there will be soon – and partly there already is – a focus on academics and scientists that carry on with a *new, non-destructive, co-operative, life-friendly, intelligent science, which is democratically organized and free from interests of others*. Such tendencies already exist and (or, depending on your point of view) still exist. Where they do not, they have to be built up!

If you want it or not, if you take notice or not: *the duty that objectively lies upon you as a social movement* is to shed light on the "not yet understood powers" (Dutschke 1968). And far beyond that you need to claim, to launch, to practice and to implement a *fundamentally different science* – wherever you are inside the education-system, whether you work in research or practice.

Or would you rather continue with the crimes that science committed and is committing against human beings and nature? Would you like to be complicit and add blindly to the final and global collapse of this civilization and the life on earth?

4. What to do?

You are the generation that will face the burden of solving the crises of the 21st century. This will not work by the same means that have lead to the crisis (Orr). Therefore, you can claim that conditions and contents of your study-programs will be rechecked, revised, changed and founded on a new basis or even completely revolved by you and with you, since you are the generation in charge with a huge responsibility.

Time is limited, so let no grass grow under your feet. In the light of crises, that are accumulating themselves more and more, there will not be much time left for you to experiment and orientate yourself in a free manner, even under changed and more unrestricted conditions. You have to mature earlier than generations before you.

Hence, it is clear that without a free way of (re)searching and deciding, you will not find a way out of the dilemma of modern science. Therefore, you must fight for this in the first place. *Only free studies enable free science – a science free from alien influences – and vice versa: only such a free science wants a free study.*

This kind of freedom does not mean: being free from responsibility and being free in serving the interests of others. This freedom is a freedom towards responsibility and in this respect a freedom that is able to exclude those kinds of "third-party" interests. Such interests should be defined clearly: Those, which damage life further on and deny the co-operation with the human race and with nature should not be able to come to effect anymore. I know that this does implicate a scientific revolution, *a revolutionizing of science*, the university and the concept of "education". *Objectively*, nothing less is demanded from you, if you like it or not.

In this respect you must prepare yourselves also *subjectively*. This is what you want to achieve anyway by filing a suit for your freedom and your autonomy. Without it, nothing will be possible. The times of adaptation have already passed! Indeed the near future will demand complete different things from you. Therefore: Do not waste your time and your energy by investing it in your adjustment to the machine; refuse obedience by pointing at the responsibility that will hit us all. Adjustment is myopic. You were not given heads to get nice haircuts. So get them used, before you get rid of them.

It is right to demand money: but you have to say what you want the money for and what you *do not* want it for (anymore)! In any case: money alone is too little, since you have to prepare nothing less than a new civilization, its universities and sciences.

What kind of abilities and skills, what kind of knowledge, what kind of methods and what kind of insights do you need? How can in this respect the collapse of modernity be intercepted, endured and answered?

Your future is not a reduced life-form as "machine-human" (Bammé et al.), but rather beyond the machine. Such a life must be prepared, inspected and claimed. For this purpose, you have to be as much *uninjured, "unusable" and incorruptible as possible – and you have to be equipped with all senses, especially with appreciation, empathy, curiosity and openness.*

You will not get somewhere, where life is worth living, by obeying to competition and even more adjustment to something that allegedly has no "outside" and what we call the "mega-machine". That is the *new realism*! Autonomy today should be seen as the departure from modern patriarchy as well as the leaving-behind of its genuine obsession, whose essence is "creation by destruction"!

Hence, the following should be claimed: a type of education that corresponds to the needs of our time, and not to its excruciating abyss; a type of education that has contrary characteristics compared to those that led to the crisis of our civilization today.

Education in terms of "the machine" has to be refused, because it is a life-threatening imposition. Appreciation for the responsibility of science must be demanded. The idea of man that derives from neo-liberalism, namely the "homo oeconomicus-maquina-vacuus", has to be declined, because it is an obscene idea.

Education has to enable emancipation again, instead of enslaving everybody. Your reasoning powers have to take center-stage again. They are the main tool of survival and culture. *The spirit should blow through universities again – it has left them long ago.*

For that purpose we have to leave behind the "frozen desert of abstraction" (Benjamin) that shapes modern science. We have to reenter everyday life and everyday questions again. There is so much to do – *you shall take notice!*

It is clear that these things will only be achievable if the university will become (again) a place that is democratically organized; and a place where everybody will be able to start a dialogue on how to proceed, what to check, what to know and what to do – provided that everyone is aware of the *seriousness of the situation*. This seriousness has to be claimed for a start. Departments and lectors have to be confronted that you all need a new and a different science as well as a different education. In this respect, criteria must be established and inspected.

With regard to such a project, it should precisely be investigated what is required in terms of content, literature, methodology and what kind of lectors would be needed for such a purpose.

Vacancies have to be filled with appropriate people; research has to be carried out in new directions, which should be encouraged; curriculums have to be revised and become open to everyone; team-taught lecture series concerning important subjects should be organized; a call for international conferences on all these matters should be initiated.

The opening-process within universities after 1968 had already brought up a bunch of alternative views on science that built the kick off to an enormous spate of new theories and methodologies. It is possible to tie in with that again. Despite neo-liberalism, the growing criticism of globalization since the 1990ies also advanced new ways of scientific work and knowledge.

Nowadays, there are new approaches in every single discipline all over the world. All of them must be collected and be looked through. The borderlines between every single scientific discipline have to be annulated, because the situation today can not adequately be understood in the light of *disciplinary* thinking alone.

Maybe you should set up work-groups that at the beginning look for alternatives in their own disciplines, until they reach their particular borders. After that you should go through the material that the work-groups bring up and draw your own conclusions from that; then you meet up with other groups to exchange your findings. Doing so, something new will emerge quite soon.

And above all: you do not need to wait concerning all these questions; you do not need to wait until someone will conform to your requirements; *you can and you should immediately get active yourselves* – this is the most important point. Nothing and nobody can stop you, if you approach contents and questions of a new science which is not damaging the world anymore and which is not based on destruction, but rather on reparation and on co-operation with nature and the world.

May the "alma mater" rise up again and may the spirit blow through universities!

In the end: if you begin to understand the "mega-machine", it will become clear to you, who in this society is occupying which position inside the machine and how your own interests correspond to or differ from other groups and social classes within the society. This will help you in increasing solidarity with your objectives; and by doing that, you should be fully conscious of the extraordinary significance for the society of everything you intend to achieve.

There is nothing good to expect from politics at the moment. Politics have not failed, as some people assume; politics have rather become the lackeys of corporations, which have built up the "mega-machine" in order to control it and to functionalize it in the name of their own interests.

Thus, anything new will only arise from the bottom – it has to be done by you, or no one.

Bibliography

Arendt, Hannah, 2003, Über das Böse. Eine Vorlesung zu Fragen der Ethik, München/Zürich (Piper)
Bammé, Arno u.a., 1983, Maschinen-Menschen – Mensch-Maschinen. Grundrisse einer sozialen Beziehung, Reinbek (Rowohlt)
Behmann, Mathias, 2009, Idee und Programm einer Matriarchalen Natur- und Patriarchatskritischen Geschichtsphilosophie. Zur Grundlegung der Kritischen Patriarchatstheorie angesichts der ‚Krise der allgemeinsten Lebensbedingungen', in: Projektgruppe „Zivilisationspolitik", pp. 107-177
Benjamin, Walter, 1970, in: Adorno, Theodor W: Über Walter Benjamin. Aufsätze, Artikel, Briefe, Frankfurt a. M. (Suhrkamp), p. 39
Bertell, Rosalie, 2000, Planet Earth. The Latest Weapon of War, London (The Womens Press)
Chossudovsky, Michel, 2002, Global Brutal. Der entfesselte Welthandel, die Armut, der Krieg, Frankfurt a. M. (Zweitausendeins)
Collard, Renée und Contrucci, Joyce, 1989, Die Mörder der Göttin leben noch – Rape of the Wild –, München (Frauenoffensive)
Dressen, Wolfgang, 1982, Die pädagogische Maschine, Frankfurt a. M. (Ullstein)
Dutschke, Rudi, 1968, quoted in: grauzone: Student*Innen Flugblatt, verteilt bei der Demonstration in Innsbruck, 29.10.2009
Federici, Silvia, 2004, Caliban and the Witch - Women, the Body and Primitive Accumulation, New York (Autonomedia)
Genth, Renate, 2002, Über Maschinisierung und Mimesis. Erfindungsgeist und mimetische Begabung im Widerstreit und ihre Bedeutung für das Mensch-Maschine-Verhältnis, Frankfurt a. M. (Peter Lang)
Gore, Al, 2006, Eine unbequeme Wahrheit. Der drohende Klimawandel und was wir dagegen tun können, München (Riemann)
Greco, Monica, 2000, Homo Vacuus. Alexithymie und das neoliberale Gebot des Selbsteins, in: Bröckling, Ulrich/Krasmann, Susanne/Lemke, Thomas (Eds.): Gouvernementalität in der Gegenwart. Studien zur Ökonomisierung des Sozialen, Frankfurt a. M. Suhrkamp), pp. 265-285
Habermas, Jürgen, 2003, Bildung als Selbstbildung. Zur Kritik postmoderner Vorstellungen von der Bildung des Subjekts, Hamburg (Verlag Dr. Kovac)
Heidelberger, Michael und Thiessen, Sigrun, 1981: Natur und Erfahrung. Von der mittelalterlichen zur neuzeitlichen Naturwissenschaft, Reinbek (Rowohlt)
Jaeger, Michael, 2008, Gobal Player Faust oder Das Verschwinden der Gegenwart. Zur Aktualität Goethes, Berlin (wjs)
Kellermann, Paul/Boni, Manfred/Meyer-Renschhausen, Elisabeth (Eds.), 2009,

Zur Kritik europäischer Hochschulpolitik. Forschung und Lehre unter Kuratel betriebswirtschaftlicher Denkmuster, Wiesbaden (vs)

Krautz, Jochen, 2007, Ware Bildung. Schule und Universität unter dem Diktat der Ökonomie, Kreuzlingen (Hugendubel/Reihe Diederichs)

Liessmann, Konrad Paul, 2006, Theorie der Unbildung. Dir Irrtümer der Wissensgesellschaft, Wien (Paul Zsolnay)

Marx, Karl, 1974, Das Kapital 1, in: MEW, Vol. 23, Berlin (Dietz)

Menasse, Robert, 2009, Vortrag zu den Bildungsprotesten, besetzter HS 381, Kultur- und Gesellschaftswissenschaftliche Fakultät, Universität Salzburg

Merchant, Carolyn, 1987, Der Tod er Natur. Ökologie, Frauen und neuzeitliche Naturwissenschaft, München (Beck)

Mies, Maria, 1988, Kapital und Patriarchat. Frauen in der internationalen Arbeitsteilung, Zürich (Rotpunkt)

Mies, Maria und Werlhof, Claudia von (Eds.), 1998 (2003), Lizenz zum Plündern. Das Multilaterale Abkommen über Investitionen – MAI – Globalisierung der Konzernherrschaft und was wir dagegen tun können, Hamburg (Rotbuch/EVA)

Mumford, Lewis, 1977, Mythos der Maschine. Kultur, Technik und Macht, Frankfurt a. M. (Fischer)

Noble, David F., 1999, The Religion of Technology. The Divinity of Man and the Spirit of Invention, London (Pengiun Books)

Opitz-Belakhal, Claudia, 2006, Das Universum des Jean Bodin. Staatsbildung, Macht und Geschlecht im 16. Jahrhundert, Frankfurt a. M. (Campus)

Orr, David, 1991, What is Education For? Six myths about the foundations of modern education, and six new principles to replace them, in: The Learning Revolution, In Context No. 27, winter. pp. 52-58

Projektgruppe „Zivilisationspolitik", 2009, Aufbruch aus dem Patriarchat – Wege in eine neue Zivilisation?, Frankfurt a. M. (Peter Lang)

Ribolits, Erich, 2002, Wieso sollte eigentlich gerade Bildung nicht zur Ware werden? In: Österreichische Hochschülerschaft. ÖH (Ed.): Education not Profit, Wien, pp. 35-40

Sambale, Jens, Eick, Volker, Walk, Heike (Eds): Das Elend der Universitäten. Neoliberalisierung deutscher Hochschulpolitik, Münster (Westfälisches Dampfboot)

Schirrmacher, Frank (Ed.), 2001, Die Darwin AG. Wie Nanotechnologie, Biotechnologie und Computer den neuen Menschen träumen, Köln (Kiepenheuer & Witsch)

Schumpeter, Joseph A., 1962, Capitalism, Socialism and Democracy, New York (Harper Torchbooks)

Sieferle, Rolf, 1984, Fortschrittsfeinde? Opposition gegen Technik und Industrie von der Romantik bis zur Gegenwart, München (Beck)

Wagner, Friedrich, 1970, Weg und Abweg der Naturwissenschaft, München (Beck)

Wallerstein, Immanuel, 1979, Aufstieg und künftiger Niedergang des kapitalistischen Weltsystems, in: Senghaas, Dieter (Ed.): Kapitalistische Weltökonomie. Kontroversen über ihren Ursprung und ihre Entwicklungsdynamik, Frankfurt a. M. (Suhrkamp), pp. 31-67

Werlhof, Claudia von, 2003, Fortschrittsglaube am Ende? Das Kapitalistische Patriarchat als „Alchemistisches System", in: dies., Bennholdt-Thosmen, Veronika und Faraclas, Nicholas (Eds.): Subsistenz und Widerstand. Alternativen zur Globalisierung, Wien (Promedia), pp. 41-68

Werlhof, Claudia von, 2005, „Speed kills!" Hochschulreform als neoliberaler „Putsch"?, in: Dimmel, Nikolaus und Schmee, Josef (Eds.): Politische Kultur in Österreich 2000 – 2005, Wien (Promedia), pp. 284-292

Werlhof, Claudia von, 2007, Alternativen zur neoliberalen Globalisierung oder Die Globalisierung des Neoliberalismus und seine Folgen, Wien (Picus)

Werlhof, Claudia von, 2008, Kopf? – Ab! Die GATS- Guillotine. Realsatire zur neoliberalen Bildungsoffensive, in: Sambale, Jens, Eick, Volker, Walk, Heike (Eds.): Das Elend der Universitäten. Neoliberalisierung deutscher Hochschulpolitik, Münster (Westfälisches Dampfboot), pp. 205-223

Werlhof, Claudia von, 2009, Das Patriarchat: „Befreiung" von Mutter (und) Natur?, in: Projektgruppe „Zivilisationspolitik", pp. 59-103 (cf. Werlhof, Claudia von y Behmann, Mathias: Teoría Crítica del Patriarcado. Hacia una Ciencia y un Mundo ya no Capitlistas ni Patriarcales, Frankfurt a.M. 2010 (Peter Lang)

B

From "Patriarchy" to "Capitalist Patriarchy"

5. No Critique of Capitalism without a Critique of Patriarchy! Why the Left Is No Alternative[*/1]

in CNS – Capitalism – Nature – Socialism, Vol. 18, Nr. 1, New York/London (Routledge), March 2007, pp. 13-27

Preliminary remark 2010

Taking into account what is slowly but irrefutably coming to light today – a new "Military Alchemy" that uses the planet itself as a weapon of mass-destruction (cf. introduction and part D.) – the urgent need for a radical critique of modern technologies cannot be postponed or even refused any longer. The Left seems to be unprepared for such a critique, although the broad debate about machine-technology in general was prominent especially in German speaking countries in the 70s, 80s and part of the 90s. Since then, the advance of neo-liberalism has more or less undermined or repressed this type of public discussion. This went parallel to the suppression of radical feminism as a trans-disciplinary approach that criticizes capitalist patriarchy. Instead, a "domesticated" Left and a pro-neo-liberal "gender"-approach have risen to public awareness – but for how long?

The following article shows the theoretical development of the "Critical Theory of Patriarchy" starting from the so called "Bielefeld School", developing the concept of "capitalist patriarchy", and resulting in a more systematic critique of "technological" progress as patriarchal and destructive.

Feminist Research and the Left

Since the second half of the 1970s, a unique political understanding emerged within the new women's movement; one that not only questioned the foundations of Right-wing politics, but also those of the Left, and even the basis of modern science. In Germany, this work of a new and profound critique of capitalism and patriarchy was led by Maria Mies, Veronika Bennholdt-Thomsen, and myself Claudia von Werlhof – known as the Bielefeld School and later as a

---

[*] Translation from German: Dr. Gabriel Kuhn
[1] Article adapted from Claudia von Werlhof, "Keine Kapitalismus-Kritik ohne Patriarchatskritik! Warum die Linke keine Alternative ist," *Widerspruch. Beiträge zu sozialistischer Politik*, Nr. 50: Alternativen!, 26.Jg./1. Halbjahr 2006, Zürich, pp. 99-111

part of ecofeminism.[2] It did not take long, however, before the women's movement at large was beset by the fate of most social movements and became divided: in this case, into "Left-wing" women on the one side, and "feminist" women, on the other.[3] In the 1980s, feminist research began to be replaced almost exclusively by "gender studies" imported from the US. The result was a de-politicization of the feminist movement and of women's studies. This did not mean that women were now less present in science or in politics. In fact, the opposite was the case. However, the edge and radicalism of women's studies all but disappeared.[4]

What is called "globalization" has caused such a rapid deterioration of the living conditions of most people on this planet that it seems inexplicable why science and politics – including most women involved in both – seem to stubbornly ignore the issue.[5] This must strike us as particularly peculiar, since the right questions had long been asked, and an understanding had been reached to a degree that not only made proper analyses possible, but also opened up discussions about real alternatives. It has to be assumed, though, that it was exactly this achievement that caused the well orchestrated drives from the Left as much as the Right, to undermine the women's movement and feminist research. That episode in political history is too complex to be described here. Rather, this essay will examine the tension between feminism and the Left. As will become clear, it is the contention of the Bielefeld School that, despite its rhetoric, the Left does not – and cannot – pursue an alternative to the system we are living in.

---

2   Maria Mies, „Methodische Postulate zur Frauenforschung – dargestellt am Beispiel der Gewalt gegen Frauen", *Beiträge zur feministischen Theorie und Praxis*, Nr. 1: Erste Orientierungen, München, pp. 41-63. Maria Mies, *Patriarchy and Accumulation on a World Scale: Women in the International Division of Labour* (London: zedpress, 1986). Claudia v. Werlhof, Veronika Bennholdt-Thomsen and Maria Mies, *Frauen, die letzte Kolonie* (Reinbek: Rowohlt, 1983), in English, *Women, the Last Colony* (London: zedpress, 1988). Claudia v. Werlhof, „Frauenarbeit: der blinde Fleck in der Kritik der politischen Ökonomie", *Beiträge zur feministischen Theorie und Praxis*, Nr.1, München 1978, pp.18-32. Claudia v. Werlhof, *Wenn die Bauern wiederkommen. Frauen, Arbeit und Agrobusiness in Venezuela* (Bremen: periferia/CON, 1985). Ariel Salleh, *Ecofeminism as Politics: Nature, Marx and the Postmodern* (London: zedpress, 1997)
3   Claudia v. Werlhof, „Lohn hat einen „Wert", Leben nicht? Auseinandersetzung mit einer „linken" Frau", *Prokla*, Nr. 50: Marx und der Marxismus, Berlin 1983, pp.38-58
4   Diane Bell and Renate Klein (Eds.), *Radically Speaking. Feminism Reclaimed* (London: zedpress, 1996). Claudia v. Werlhof, „(Haus)Frauen, „Gender" und die Schein-Macht des Patriarchats", *Widerspruch*, Nr. 44, 23. Jg./1. Halbjahr 2003, Zürich, pp.173-189
5   Maria Mies, Claudia v. Werlhof (Eds.), *Lizenz zum Plündern - Das Multilaterale Abkommen über Investitionen – MAI – Globalisierung der Konzernherrschaft, und was wir dagegen tun können* (Hamburg: Rotbuch, 1998)

What does Capitalism Really Mean?

Amongst the first issues the new women's movement and its research focused on, were violence against women and unpaid domestic labor. The "woman question" was addressed as a part of the wider social and ecological context. The intent was to explain how these phenomena could exist in the midst of alleged peace and democracy, a capitalist regime of wage labor, and allegedly ever increasing standards of living within industrialized nations – what passes for "western civilization". However, a look beyond the confines of the so-called "First World" expanded the question further: How was it possible that, despite its incorporation under "progress" and "development", the so-called "Third World" remained characterized by underdevelopment and a lack of wage labor – not to mention dictatorship, war, and violence? And how was it possible that the supposedly anti-capitalist "socialism" of the so-called "Second World" (apparently engaged in a "competition of systems" with the West) did not even allow pseudo-democratic political conditions and never reached its "plan target"?

Following deliberation on all these matters, socio-economical research by Mies, Bennholdt-Thomsen, and myself, focused significantly on the so-called "Third part" of the world. The result was theorization of *a new, extended notion of capitalism.*[6] What follows is a summary statement of that theoretical position.

On Capitalist "Relations of Production"

- The main contradiction in capitalism is not that between wage labor and capital but that between all labor – life – and capital.
- Capitalist economy is not understood by those who understand wage labor, but by those who understand unpaid labor, especially modern domestic la-

---

6   For an account of the Bielefeld School see Arbeitsgruppe Bielefelder Entwicklungssoziologen (Ed.), *Subsistenzproduktion und Akkumulation* (Saarbrücken: Breitenbach, 1979). Veronika Bennholdt-Thomsen, „Marginalität in Lateinamerika. Eine Theoriekritik", *Lateinamerika. Analysen und Berichte,* 3: Verelendungsprozesse und Widerstandsformen (Berlin: Olle & Wolter, 1980), pp.45-85. Veronika Bennholdt-Thomsen, „Subsistenzproduktion und erweiterte Reproduktion. Ein Beitrag zur Produktionsweisendiskussion", *Gesellschaft. Beiträge zur Marxschen Theorie,* Nr. 14, Frankfurt 1981, pp.30-51. Veronika Bennholdt-Thomsen, *Bauern in Mexiko zwischen Subsistenz- und Warenproduktion* (Frankfurt/New York: Campus, 1982). Claudia v. Werlhof, Veronika Bennholdt-Thomsen and Maria Mies 1983, *ibid.;* Maria Mies, 1986, *ibid.* Claudia v. Werlhof, 1985, *op.cit.* Claudia v. Werlhof, *Was haben die Hühner mit dem Dollar zu tun? Frauen und Ökonomie* (München: Frauenoffensive, 1991)

bor/"house work". Capitalism follows the credo that labor – just as natural resources or house work – should be as free and "fruitful" as possible.
- It is not the proletarianization but the "housewifization" of labor (including always more the labor of white men) which characterizes capitalist development.
- Tendencies for the normal wage labor system to disappear do not mean a disappearance of capitalism, but, to the contrary, its deepening and expansion.
- Even more than the wage labor system, it is the forms of unpaid labor (or at least forms of non-regular wage labor) that define capitalism: domestic labor; new forms of slavery, forced labor, and serfdom; "marginality" and various hybrid forms of these "precarious" relations of production (and we are not only talking of commodity production, but of subsistence production as well).[7] None of these relations of production are to be misunderstood as pre-capitalist – they are all inherently capitalist! Capitalism is not about wage labor, but about the cheapest possible forms of commodity production.
- Capitalism has created the modern "sexual division of labor". This division is its foundation and is reproduced in the international division of labor within the capitalist world system. Peasants and colonial labor forces take on the role of women. No real value is attached to their labor and so it does nearly not have to be remunerated.

On the "Accumulation of Capital"

- The aim of capitalism is not the transformation of all labor into wage labor but the transformation of all labor, all life, and of the planet itself into capital, in other words: into money, commodity, machinery, and the "command over labor" (Marx).[8] The accumulation of capital does not only happen by exploiting wage labor, but by exploiting all labor, as well as nature and life itself. It is not the "socialization" of labor by "free contract" that allows devaluating labor and life and hence accumulating more capital, but it is labor's and life's "naturalization" and its transformation into a "natural resource" for exploitation/extraction (its "natural-resourcization") that do so.[9]
- So-called "original" or "primitive" accumulation (the separation of the producers from the means of production) does not only play a role in capitalisms

---

7 Veronika Bennholdt-Thomsen 1980, *ibid.*
8 Karl Marx in MEW (Marx-Engels-Werke), vol. 23, Das Kapital 1 (Berlin 1974: Dietz), pp. 168, 381, 391, 400, 424, 447
9 Claudia v. Werlhof 1991 *op.cit.*, Günther Anders, *Die Antiquiertheit des Menschen,* 2 volumes (München: Beck, 1989)

beginnings. It finds itself constantly reproduced in capitalism and is hence not pre- or non-capitalist, but an integral part of capitalism.[10]
- "Continued" original accumulation consists of theft. It is accumulation by expropriation. Those who are expropriated are predominantly women who are – anew with every generation and in an organized manner – separated from the control over their bodies as their "means of production", from the results of their labor, from their children, and from their vital powers.
- Each aspect of original accumulation are characterized by systems of violence. This "secret" (Marx) of original accumulation explains the permanent violence against women, nature and the colonized. What we are facing here is a perpetual war.[11]

On the Capitalist "Mode of Production"

- Capitalism as a mode of production is based on an array of different relations of production often misunderstood as separate "intertwined modes of production".[12] Capitalism is a global mode of appropriation and expropriation, and an equally violent mode of transformation and destruction. War is no exceptional state; it has always been a necessary and permanent aspect of capitalism's economy as a political one.
- War in capitalism does not only mean war of conquest, colonial war, or war of aggression. The capitalist mode of production itself always means both, war against humanity and war between humanity and nature.
- Capitalist mode of production has – contrary to common perception – an ongoing colonial character. Methods of internal and external colonization are its typical characteristics. This is precisely what defines its "modernity", "progress", and "civilization".[13]
- Intrinsically connected to the capitalist mode of production are not only imperialistic but also imperial tendencies that are based on the modern world system and that demand totalitarian world domination. Democratic political conditions are only a temporary expression of the capitalist mode of production and are by no means necessarily linked to it.[14]

---

10 Rosa Luxemburg, *The Accumulation of Capital* (1913) (London: Routledge, 1967). André Gunder Frank, On so-called Primitive Accumulation, *Dialectical Anthropology*, No. 2, 1977, pp. 87-106; Claudia v. Werlhof 1978, *op.cit.*
11 Karl Marx, 1974, *op.cit.*, pp. 741-744
12 Veronika Bennholdt-Thomsen, 1981, *op.cit.*
13 Maria Mies, 1986, *op.cit.*.
14 Claudia v. Werlhof, 1991, *op.cit.*, Claudia v. Werlhof, *Männliche Natur und künstliches Geschlecht. Texte zur Erkenntniskrise der Moderne* (Wien: Frauenverlag, 1991b)

- Capitalism as a "mode of production" – truly: of destruction - has always been based on the whole of the globe. This is why – reversing the common notion – it is the entire world that has to be the "unit of analysis" (Wallerstein) – not a "First", "Second", or "Third" World; or an individual nation state[15], since the nation state is only a consequence and perpetuation of the international division of labor/the world order. This is what we call "the illusion of the nation state".

Since the shock caused by the Chernobyl nuclear disaster in 1986 – which marked the beginning of the Soviet Union's downfall – some of us have focused increasingly on a critique of the so-called "development of the productive forces", in other words: on a critique of technology in capitalism.[16] This happened parallel to an intensified critique of patriarchy. It soon became apparent that the latter was in fact a precondition of the former.

---

15 Immanuel Wallerstein, "The Rise and Future Demise of the World Capitalist System: Concepts for Comparative Analysis", *Comparative Studies in Society and History,* Vol. 16, No. 4, 1974, pp.387-415.

16 Claudia v. Werlhof, „Wir werden das Leben unserer Kinder nicht dem Fortschritt opfern", in Gambaroff, Marina et. al., *Tschernobyl hat unser Leben verändert. Vom Ausstieg der Frauen* (Reinbek: Rowohlt, 1986), pp.8-24; Maria Mies, 1986, *op.cit.,* Maria Mies, *Wider die Industrialisierung des Lebens* (Pfaffenweiler: Centaurus, 1992). Maria Mies and Vandana Shiva, *Ecofeminism* (London: zedpress, 1993). Renate Genth, *Über Maschinisierung und Mimesis. Erfindungsgeist und mimetische Begabung im Widerstreit und ihre Bedeutung für das Mensch-Maschine-Verhältnis* (Frankfurt/Paris/New York: Peter Lang, 2002). Claudia v. Werlhof, „Ökonomie, die praktische Seite der Religion. Zum Zusammenhang von Patriarchat, Kapitalismus und Christentum", in Ulla Ernst et.al. (Eds.), *Ökonomie(M)macht Angst. Zum Verhältnis von Ökonomie und Religion* (Frankfurt/Paris/New York: Peter Lang, 1997), pp.95-121. Claudia v. Werlhof, „Patriarchat als "Alchemistisches System". Die (Z)ErSetzung des Lebendigen", in Maria Wolf (Ed.), *Optimierung und Zerstörung. Intertheoretische Analysen zum menschlich Lebendigen* (Innsbruck: STUDIA, 2000), pp.13-31. Claudia v. Werlhof, „Losing Faith in Progress: Capitalist Patriarchy as an Alchemical System", in Veronika Bennholdt-Thomsen, Nicholas Faraclas and Claudia v. Werlhof (Eds.), *There is an Alternative. Subsistence and Worldwide Resistance to Corporate Globalization* (London: zedpress, 2001), pp.15-40. Claudia v. Werlhof, "Using, Producing and Replacing Life?: Alchemy as Theory and Practice in Capitalism", in Immanuel Wallerstein (Ed.), *The Modern World System in the Longue Durée* (Boulder: paradigm, 2004b), pp. 65-78. Claudia v. Werlhof, "Natur, Maschine, Mimesis. Zur Kritik patriarchalischer Naturkonzepte", *Widerspruch,* Nr. 47, 24. Jg./2. Halbjahr 2004, Zürich, pp.155-171

- The development of the productive forces has always been tied to the needs of war, hence to the needs of inherently destructive forces.
- Labor that corresponds to these technologies has to be "war-like" or "soldier-like". It has to enter both obedient and aggressive relations with its "enemy", the object of labor. No "humanization" or "democratization" can be expected from such technologies.
- The factory is modeled according to the military camp. Its technology is not that of the artisan, but that of a machine geared for war. There is nothing "neutral" about such a technology.
- Contrary to artisanship, the technology of the machine is based on the notion of *divide and conquer*. It thereby follows the logic of the "alchemical" tradition, which, unnoticed by most, has always implied the principle of the machine.[17] Today, the technology of the machine is alchemy's modern and total implementation. Nonetheless, alchemy has so far failed in its ambition to separate productivity and creation from nature and women as part of its quest for world domination.
- First, the machine is a "closed system". It is like a total(itarian) institution. It has nothing to do with "artisanship" as a general technique anymore.[18] As an objective, anonymous, impersonal factual constraint, the machine is "congealed domination" and "congealed war".
- The output of the machine: the commodity, is (as capital/money is in general) "congealed, past life" (Marx), hence "corpse-like" (Bloch) – not only in the sense of being dead, but also in the sense of having been killed.[19] The commodity serves the accumulation of capital and not the satisfaction of human needs. This satisfaction has therefore little to do with the consumption of commodities.
- Today's "new" technologies are particularly harmful to women and mothers, the creation of life, and to life itself. Nowadays "machinization" – the transformation of life into machines – violently penetrates the bodies of women, men, and nature.
- It is the modern scientific notion of nature that provides with the foundation for the development of the productive forces. Within this notion, nature is re-

---

17 Claudia v. Werlhof, 1997, *op.cit.* Claudia v. Werlhof, 2000, *op.cit.* Claudia v. Werlhof, 2001, *op.cit.*
18 Renate Genth, 2002, *op.cit.*
19 Karl Marx, 1974, *op.cit.*, pp.247, 209, 271, 446. Ernst Bloch, *Naturrecht und menschliche Würde (*Frankfurt: Suhrkamp, 1991)

duced to a dead object, to lifeless material and spiritless matter. It is seen as an incessantly exploitable resource.[20] Treated like this, nature finally becomes what it was always supposed to be within the logic of an unrestricted human "productivity" that aims at dominating it: namely, a socially constructed "second nature" instead of a self-creative "first (wild) nature". This self-fulfilling prophecy denies of course the violence and destruction this process means for nature as a living – and therefore precisely not incessantly exploitable but destructible and finite – entity.

- Seen as a system, nature appears as a mechanism, a machine. Finally, the machine itself is seen as nature and manages to pretend to have really taken first nature's place.[21]
- Women have been seen as a part of this "machine nature" since the Enlightenment. Only male labor is regarded as "productive", especially when applying machines (and women – as part of the machine). Female labor – for example, the "production of human life" – is denied any value. The same goes for any non-machine related activity and the productivity of nature itself.[22]
- It is not surprising that the reasons for today's ecological disaster, which is also a human disaster, cannot really be understood. They are rooted in the fact that the truly productive forces: those of life ("first nature") have essentially been destroyed by their transformation through capitalist "production". Yet, instead of recognizing this, it is still nature that is made responsible for the ecological question and even for bringing further measures of its oppression upon itself – as if it was nature that is threatening man rather than man destroying nature.
- True male productivity could only arise where it was not bound to the machine. Currently, however, man is working on fortifying the machine using a sort of alchemical "vitalization": be it in form of a robot (artificial intelligence), or as a bio-machine of reproduction ("reproductive technologies", cyborgs, GMOs, nanotechnology).[23] Life becomes "programmed" into the

---

20 Carolyn Merchant, *The Death of Nature - Women, Ecology and the Scientific Revolution* (San Francisco: Harper & Row, 1983). Maria Mies, Vandana Shiva, 1993, *op. cit.*, Claudia v. Werlhof, 2004, *op.cit.*
21 Genth, Renate, 2002, *op.cit.*
22 Maria Mies, 1986, *op.cit.*
23 Janice Raymond, *Women as Wombs - Reproductive Technologies and the Battle over Women's Freedom* (San Francisco/Melbourne: Spinifex, 1994). Renate Klein, "Globalized Bodies in the Twenty-first Century: The Final Patriarchal Takeover?" in Veronika Bennholdt-Thomsen, Nicholas Faraclas and Claudia v. Werlhof (Eds.) 2001, *op.cit.*, pp. 91-105; Joseph Weizenbaum, *Computer Power and Human Reason: From Judgement to Calculation* (San Francisco: W.H. Freeman & Company, 1976). Jeremy Rifkin, *Algeny*

machine, or – seen the other way round – the machine is "forced on to" life. The intention is to coerce life into sustaining the machine and to make both inseparable so that finally the machine itself can appear as truly "productive" and "creative". This way, the machine becomes an "open system", and is no longer "under" but "out of" control. Nonetheless, it is supposed to reproduce itself as an allegedly highly superior substitute for mothers and nature.

Feminist Research: Globalization and Full Capitalization

This analysis of capitalism replaces the reductionism of both the natural sciences and of political economy (and the "critique" thereof). It thereby sees much further than the Left. The Left does not even want to see the true contradictions of real existing capitalism. Our analysis, on the other hand, puts capitalism "from its head on its feet". Seen from "below" and from "the outside", capitalism looks very different (at times even antithetical) to what it has so far been presented and criticized as – also by the Left. From this perspective, notions that long served as guidelines for a better future lose their meaning: - the proletariat, the unions, Left politics, technological progress, the "development" of industrialized nations, the leading role of the North, the superiority of men over women. If we were to follow these notions, nothing would await us but a dead-end road.

Since capitalism is an inherently global enterprise, it comprises the "Second World" and "Third World" rather than embodying an alternative to the allegedly "feudal" South or the "red" East. Capitalism, or the "First World", seems to have emerged as the sole winner of the last 30 years of "globalization". "Socialism", understood as a "post-capitalist" world, has almost entirely vanished. However, since 1989, the victorious West/North faces a crisis ("illusion of the welfare state") into which it has maneuvered also itself by plundering and destroying the world. The so-called "battle of production" proves to be much more battle than production. It has become impossible for anyone with open eyes to ignore the parasitic and counter-productive character of the capitalist world system.

Hence, the collapse of the real socialist state system did not mean the end of any "competition of systems," it merely marked the collapse of one part of the capitalist world system. Other parts can be expected to follow. The South is already caught in a downward spiral. And in the North, due to "reform politics" and the growing "precarity" of working conditions, many of the system's pillars

---

(New York: Viking, 1983). Frank Schirrmacher (Ed.), *Die Darwin AG. Wie Nanotechnologie, Biotechnologie und Computer den neuen Menschen träumen* (Köln: Kiepenheuer & Witsch, 2001)

begin to unravel: the bourgeois institutions, the wage labor system, the loyalty of the masses.[24] Rather than liberating people from suffering, capitalism is what makes people suffer in the first place. "Development" for some inevitably means underdevelopment for others. Instead of creating prosperity for all, capitalism exploits and destroys the riches of the earth ("privatization"). "Progress" means nothing but the improvement of violent methods of appropriation, expropriation, and destruction. "Growth" means war on all levels.[25]

The consequences drawn from this analysis of capitalism have to be uncompromising. What is at stake is how to stop the capitalist world system and its development from reaching its logical conclusion as a global war system. This implies leaving commodity production behind and reviving a subsistence economy that has long been oppressed and largely destroyed. This goes for both the North and the South. As developed by Bennholdt-Thomsen, Mies, Shiva, myself and others in our international debates, the *subsistence perspective* formulates the possibilities of a successive liberation of subsistence, life, existence, work, gender relations, politics, nature, and culture. It means liberation from the permanent war against humanity and nature waged by commodity production and the continued original accumulation.[26] The subsistence perspective has long been practiced and discussed as a viable alternative in the South, and is increasingly so in the North as well.[27]

What has to be pursued is a politics of "the self-evidence of an existence without domination", which means the re-creation of egalitarian social rela-

---

24 *Widerspruch*; Nr. 49, 25. Jg./2. Halbjahr 2005, Prekäre Arbeitsgesellschaft, Zürich. See also: http://en.wikipedia.org/wiki/Precarity
25 Maria Mies, *Krieg ohne Grenzen. Die neue Kolonisierung der Welt* (Köln: PapyRossa, 2004)
26 Veronika Bennholdt-Thomsen, 1981, *op.cit.*, Veronika Bennholdt-Thomsen, 1982, *op.cit.*, Veronika Bennholdt-Thomsen, *Juchitán – Stadt der Frauen. Vom Leben im Matriarchat* (Reinbek: Rowohlt, 1994). Veronika Bennholdt-Thomsen, Brigitte Holzer and Christa Müller (Eds.), *Das Subsistenzhandbuch. Widerstandskulturen in Europa, Asien und Lateinamerika* (Wien: Promedia, 1999). Veronika Bennholdt-Thomsen and Maria Mies, *Eine Kuh für Hillary. Die Subsistenzperspektive* (München: Frauenoffensive, 1995), in English, *The Subsistence Perspective. Beyond the Globalized Ecobnomy* (London: zedpress, 1999). Maria Mies, 1986, *op. cit.*, Maria Mies, Vandana Shiva, 1993, *op. cit.* Claudia v. Werlhof, 1985, *op. cit.*, Claudia v. Werlhof 1991, *op.cit,.* Claudia v. Werlhof, Veronika Bennholdt-Thomsen and Maria Mies, 1983, *op. cit;* Veronika Bennholdt-Thomsen, Nicholas Faraclas and Claudia v. Werlhof (Eds.), *There is an Alternatrive. Subsistence and Worldwide Resistance to Corporate Globalization* (London:zedpress, 2001)
27 Maria Mies, *Globalisierung von unten* (Hamburg: Rotbuch, 2001). Veronika Bennholdt-Thomsen, Nicholas Faraclas, Claudia v. Werlhof (Eds.) 2001, *op.cit.*

tions.[28] Our proposals have always been provocative for the Left. The concept of "subsistence" was seen as nothing but a regress to "traditionalism" and "underdevelopment" and regarded as unworthy of discussion – despite the obvious fact that it is precisely modern commodity production that causes *real* underdevelopment. The ecofeminist perspective of a different relation to nature struck the Left as "romantic" since nature was deemed violent and man had to allegedly control and dominate it. Yet, the natural catastrophes that we are witnessing today are nothing but the result of this so-called "domination of nature" – instead of reflecting nature's violence they reflect the violence of those trying to dominate it. As far as alternative gender relations are concerned, the male Left could not even conceive of any; and when it tried, it always saw itself instantly overpowered by women (instead of feeling overwhelmed by women's contributions!)

The critique of the machine seemed to be an outright affront and was decidedly rejected – as if "Man" loses his identity without his machine world. Finally (and strangely enough, it would seem), our vision of social relations without domination seemed to cause fear within the Left. Our critique of domination was seen as a critique without a theory – as "anarchy". What a betrayal! Does theory have to establish and maintain domination in order to be considered "scientific" or "political"; or to be "relevant"? Does "Man" base his identity solely on his role as one who dominates? It seems to be so. However, true feminists can never be included in a state project as the state has been invented for domination.

It has not only been the experience of the Bielefeld School that the Left is not interested in real alternatives. The alternatives proposed by the Left are indeed none. They are all reduced to one agenda: the mere redistribution of capital = command, money and commodities. The Left's only question has always been: How do we come to power? The goal was never to topple the system (maybe to "reform" it) or to pursue a real alternative. When were real alternatives ever implemented from above? So why does the Left not want an alternative?

---

28 Claudia v. Werlhof, 1985, *op. cit.,* Claudia v. Werlhof, 1986, *op.cit.*, Claudia v. Werlhof, 2001, *op.cit.*, Claudia v. Werlhof, "Das Patriarchat als Negation des Matriarchats. Zur Perspektive eines Wahns", in Heide Göttner-Abendroth (Ed.), *Gesellschaft in Balance. Dokumente vom 1. Weltkongress für Matriarchatsforshung* 2003 (Stuttgart: Kohlhammer, 2006); Claudia v. Werlhof, Annemarie Schweighofer, and Werner Ernst (Eds.), *Herren-Los. Herrschaft – Erkenntnis – Lebensform* (Frankfurt/Paris/New York: Peter Lang, 1996)

What Does Patriarchy Mean, and What Does It Have to Do with Capitalism?

The Left's analysis of capitalism is limited: one, because the Left exists, thinks, and feels *within* capitalist logic; and, two, because it is deeply entrenched in patriarchy. Only as the limits of capitalism come into sight can we look at the before and the after of capitalism. And once we do this, we encounter (non- or precapitalist) patriarchy and matriarchy. The analysis of these concepts as theoretical concepts (and not only as polemic ones) has characterized our work more and more since the 1990s.[29] Women have long spoken of patriarchy, especially since capitalism is so obviously hostile to women and exploits them in specifically scrupulous ways.[30] It always remained unclear, though, what patriarchy really meant. For most women, it has meant merely the rule of men or fathers – within the family, the work place, or the state. It is known that patriarchy is older than capitalism. But some on the Left thought that patriarchy was mainly a quasi-irrational historical remnant that would eventually be discarded by capitalism and "progress". However, in this respect, too, things are not always what they seem to be.

Thesis I: Patriarchy is the basic foundation, "Tiefenstruktur" or "deep structure" of capitalism.

If one goes beyond capitalism and explores historical depths, one finds patriarchy and with it many realities that characterize capitalism too: war as a means to plunder and conquer; systematic domination (the state system); the categorical submission of women; class divisions; systems of exploitation of humanity and nature; ideologies of male "productivity" and religions of male "creation"; alchemical practices that are supposed to "prove" them; and the dependence on the real productivity and creative forces of others – a thoroughly "parasitic civilization". Patriarchy has been known to reach back for at least 5-7000 years.

---

29 Heide Göttner-Abendroth, *Das Matriarchat I: Geschichte seiner Erforschung* (Stuttgart: Kohlhammer, 1988). Veronika Bennholdt-Thomsen, 1994, *op.cit.*, Claudia v. Werlhof, 1991, *op.cit.*, Claudia v. Werlhof 1991b, *op.cit.*, Claudia v. Werlhof, *MutterLos. Frauen im Patriarchat zwischen Angleichung und Dissidenz* (München: Frauenoffensive, 1996). Claudia v. Werlhof, „Frauen, Wissenschaft und Naturverhältnis. Oder: Was heißt heute Kritik am Patriarchat?", *Widerspruch*, Nr. 34, 17. Jg./ 1. Halbjahr 1997b, Zürich, pp.147-170. Claudia v. Werlhof, 2000, *op.cit.*, Claudia v. Werlhof, „Gewalt und Geschlecht", *Widerspruch*, Nr. 42, 22. Jg./1. Halbjahr 2002, Zürich, pp. 13-33; Claudia v. Werlhof, 2001, *op.cit.*, Claudia v. Werlhof, 2003, *op.cit.*, Claudia v. Werlhof, 2004, *op.cit.*, Claudia v. Werlhof, 2006, *op.cit.*

30 Maria Mies, 1986, *op.cit.*

During this time, Europe experienced several waves of patriarchalization.[31] These are variously described as "Kurgan" invasions, Romanization, Christianization, and the Feudalism that followed it.[32]

What are the differences between patriarchy and capitalism, and what do they have in common? Capitalism has old and far-reaching patriarchal roots; capitalism is, in fact, patriarchy's latest expression. In this sense, capitalism and patriarchy belong together. The differences lie in what is specific to capitalism: the extension of wage labor; the invention of unpaid house work (which is directly tied to the former); the generalization of commodity production (in various ways); the guiding role of capital as abstract wealth; the creation of a "world system" that replaces the former "empires" (Wallerstein); and the globalization of the entire capitalist enterprise to the point of its possible collapse due to reaching the limits of what the earth can take and what can technologically be transcended.[33] Yet all these specific developments still lie within the general patriarchal trajectory[34]

Thesis II: Capitalism attempts to realize the utopia of patriarchy: a world without nature or mothers ("full patriarchalization")

The one aspect that is entirely new to the patriarchy of modernity is the attempt to turn the ideologies of male "productivity" and male-divine "creation" into material reality. This transition from patriarchal idealism to patriarchal materialism – which first occurred in Western Europe – is what truly distinguishes capitalism from all other forms of patriarchy and all other modes of production. However, this transition is still not to be misunderstood as a rupture in patriarchal history. To the contrary, it brings it to its end and full realization by proving once and for all (in "reality") that it was indeed the *ruler, father, Man, god*, who has created the world and is the true creator of life.[35] Capitalism is the utopian

---

31 Marija Gimbutas, *The Goddesses and Gods of Old Europe - 6500-3500 Myths and Cult Images* (London: Thames & Hudson, 1984); Claudia v. Werlhof, 2002, *op cit.*
32 Maria Mies, Über die Notwendigkeit, Europa zu entkolonisieren, in Claudia v. Werlhof, Veronika Bennholdt-Thomsen and Nicholas Faraclas (eds.), *Subsistenz und Widerstand. Alternativen zur Globalisierung* (Wien: Promedia, 2003), pp.19-40
33 Immanuel Wallerstein, 1974, *op.cit.*, Ronald Wright, *Eine kleine Geschichte des Fortschritts* (Reinbek: Rowohlt, 2006)
34 André Gunder Frank and Barry Gills (eds.), *The World System. Five Hundred Years, or Five Thousand?* (London: Routledge, 1996)
35 Claudia v. Werlhof, "The Utopia of a Motherless World – Patriarchy as War-System", paper, *2nd World Congress of Matriarchal Studies: Societies of Peace*, Austin 2005 (publ. 2009 Toronto, Inanna, see chapter 8)

project of modern patriarchy. Its aim is to make an ideological justification of domination unnecessary. It is now the material achievements of capitalism themselves that are supposed to prove that the patriarchs are indeed "creators". The ultimate objective is to end the dependence on who will always be the only *true* creator and producer: *nature*, the *goddess*, the *mother*. The idea is to substitute her by something supposedly superior.

What is at least implicit in these efforts is the fact that there has never been any true patriarchal creation. In fact, until modernity the notion of patriarchal creation was a mere abstract claim. What distinguishes the modern or capitalist-patriarchal project from its predecessors is that it does not content itself anymore with trying to appropriate or imitate the creation of nature (an obviously futile attempt), but that it actively tries to substitute this creation by something entirely new. What we are facing today is a "real utopian" project directed against the order of life. This is what I call patriarchy as an "alchemical" or "war system".[36] The capitalist form of patriarchy is the apex of patriarchal development, of the "evolution" that patriarchy itself has invented. It tries to establish a "pure", "complete" and "eternal" patriarchy as a new paradise, bereft of all matriarchal and natural traces. The intention is to go beyond the world as we know it and to reach an allegedly superior one – by a process of metaphysical "birth giving".[37]

Thesis III: Patriarchy will not be overcome by progress; since it is progress itself in its capitalist form.

From its beginnings, modern science stood in relation to nature "as an army in enemy territory, knowing nothing about it".[38] In the form of modern technology, namely: in the form of the machine, modern science set out to virtually extinguish ("substitute") not only life, death, and the creation of life as we know it; but also humanity, women, and mothers; the earth, plants, and animals; and matter itself.

The new technologies – "nuclear alchemy", biochemistry, nanotechnology, reproduction technology, and genetic engineering – ("algeny", Rifkin) clearly reveal the intentions of this modernized form of patriarchal alchemy: to prove the alleged existence of male creation/production. But of course, this project is carried out not in cooperation with women and nature but in opposition to them.

---

36 Claudia v. Werlhof, 2000, *op.cit.*, Claudia v. Werlhof, 2001, *op.cit.*, Claudia v. Werlhof, 2006, *op.cit.*
37 Christel Neusüß, *Die Kopfgeburten der Arbeiterbewegung. Oder: Die Genossin Luxemburg bringt alles durcheinander* (Hamburg: Rasch & Röhrig, 1985)
38 Otto Ullrich, *Technik und Herrschaft. Vom Handwerk zur verdinglichten Blockstruktur industrieller Produktion* (Frankfurt: Suhrkamp, 1977)

The machine itself represented the first attempt to substitute humanity and nature (the machine of killing, work, sex, and reproduction). By now it is complemented by a "machinization" of nature itself. The machine as an "open system" does not substitute for nature by a mere apparatus. Rather it forces nature to do by itself what genetic modification and "information" induced by the molecular-machinist means demand.[39] This technology wants to do away with the "gestalt", the forms of life themselves.

For instance, the trick of the machine as an "open system" instead of a closed one, is to use technologies like GM or Nano to replace the information of cells by new information resulting from forced genetic combination or mini-pics. Once introduced into the living body, these are supposed to reproduce themselves therein. But natural cycles are partially put out of order as this other order is installed, a programmed one from outside.

So far, these attempts have fallen short of men's aspirations for control. In fact, for those of us with a non-capitalist/non-patriarchal understanding of nature and the body, it seems obvious that any attempt to produce an immortal, better, higher, superior, more perfect being or form of "life" is doomed to fail. All that the current capitalist attempt has done is un-leash forces of violence that are destroying ultimately all natural relations and cycles – both from outside and from within. Recent plans for "trans-human" or even "post-human" life illustrate the system's ludicrousness and danger: if human beings cannot be artificially created, they might as well be eliminated![40] Modern capitalist patriarchy obviously knows no moral restrictions and has already done a lot of irreversible harm to life on this planet.

Thesis IV: As long as capitalist patriarchy remains the utopia of the Left, the Left can provide no alternative.

Analyzing patriarchy makes it much easier to understand why the Left has such difficulties in finding alternatives to capitalism. Capitalism is capitalist patriarchy, and if the former vanished, so would the latter. Patriarchy would then only survive in a pre-capitalist form, one that does not imply the notion of "utopian materialism". However, it is highly unlikely that the Left would ever forsake technological progress – the heart of capitalist patriarchy. Hence, the "libera-

---

39 Jeremy Rifkin, 1983, *op.cit.,* Frank Schirrmacher, 2001, *op.cit.*,
40 Damien Broderick, *Die molekulare Manufaktur. Wie Nanotechnologie unsere Zukunft beeinflusst* (Reinbek: Rowohlt, 2004). Bernhard Irrgang, *Posthumanes Menschsein?* (Wiesbaden: Franz Steiner, 2005). Martin Kurthen, *Die dritte Natur. Über posthumane Faktizität* (Münster: LIT, 2004)

tion" of patriarchy from capitalism is not in sight. The reverse is of course utterly impossible: capitalism can never be liberated from patriarchy because without patriarchy no capitalism would ever exist. It is the utopia of patriarchy and the attempt at realization that has allowed capitalism to appear. There is no capitalist mode of production outside of patriarchy.

A true alternative to capitalist patriarchy would have to be an *alterna-depth*.[41] This is to say that scholars would not deal with 500 years of capitalism anymore – rather, we would take on 5000 years of patriarchy![42] We need to free ourselves from a religion that counts even atheists amongst its followers and that is characterized by a firm belief in the systems of violence that have defined patriarchy's history since its beginnings. Especially in the North, Leftist and academic men have long adhered to this belief, and these days increasing numbers of women do so as well.[43] We need to find entirely new ways of feeling, thinking, and acting. We have to follow the iceberg from its tip to the enormous depths that really define it. Only this will allow modern humanity, the Left and many feminists among them, to turn it upside down and reveal the hidden truths of our society.

Thus, the problem of the Left when searching for an alternative is even more fundamental than what we had already suspected. The Left is not interested in an alternative to real existing capitalism because capitalism intends to realize the patriarchal utopia and patriarchy is firmly inscribed into the Left's "collective subconsciousness".[44] What needs to be addressed is the *whole*, the *alterna-depth*, which shines through historical matriarchy (the "maternal order") as well as the relics of matriarchy that still exist even in the midst of patriarchy.[45] Until today the Left does not acknowledge the result of recent research that confirms that the world's matriarchal societies – contrary to capitalist modernity and all

---

41 Translator's note: The German term for "depth" is "Tiefe". The author's word play - "Alternative"/"Alterna-*Tiefe*" – cannot be reproduced in English.
42 Immanuel Wallerstein, "World System versus World Systems. A critique", in André Gunder Frank and Barry Gills (Eds.), 1999, *op.cit.,* pp. 292-296
43 Dirk Baecker (ed.), *Kapitalismus als Religion* (Berlin: Kadmos, 2003)
44 Mario Erdheim, *Die gesellschaftliche Produktion von Unbewusstheit* (Frankfurt: Suhrkamp, 1984)
45 Heide Göttner-Abendroth, 1988, *op.cit.,* Veronika Bennholdt-Thomsen, 1994, *op.cit.,* Renate Genth, „Matriarchat als zweite Kultur", in Claudia v. Werlhof, Annemarie Schweighofer and Werner Ernst (eds.), 1996, *op.cit.,* pp. 17-38. Veronika Bennholdt-Thomsen, Nicholas Faraclas and Claudia v. Werlhof (eds.), 2001, *op. cit.,* Claudia v. Werlhof, 2006, *op.cit.,* Claudia v. Werlhof, „Capitalist Patriarchy and the Struggle for a „Deep" Alternative", in Genevieve Vaughan (Ed.), *A Radically Different World View is Possible. The Gift-Economy Inside and Outside Patriarchal Capitalism* (Toronto : Innana, 2006a, appeared in 2007)

patriarchal societies – have never known a state, domination, classes, war, gender conflicts, or ecological catastrophes. We can draw no other conclusion than to let go of all hope that the Left can be of any support for us as we face future challenges. Hence we will not waste our energies any longer trying to explain our point of view. We will focus on the *alterna-depth* instead.

Bibliography

Anders, Günther 1989: Die Antiquiertheit des Menschen, 2 volumes, München: Beck
Arbeitsgruppe Bielefelder Entwicklungssoziologen (Ed.) 1979: Subsistenzproduktion und Akkumulation, Saarbrücken: Breitenbach
Baecker, Dirk (Ed.) 2003: Kapitalismus als Religion, Berlin: Kadmos
Bell, Diane / Klein, Renate (Eds.) 1996: Radically Speaking. Feminism Reclaimed, London: zedpress
Bennholdt-Thomsen, Veronika 1980: Marginalität in Lateinamerika. Eine Theoriekritik, in: Lateinamerika. Analysen und Berichte 3: Verelendungsprozesse und Widerstandsformen, Berlin: Olle & Wolter, pp. 45-85
Bennholdt-Thomsen, Veronika 1981: Subsistenzproduktion und erweiterte Reproduktion. Ein Beitrag zur Produktionsweisendiskussion, in: Gesellschaft. Beiträge zur Marxschen Theorie 14, Frankfurt: Suhrkamp, pp. 30-51
Bennholdt-Thomsen, Veronika 1982: Bauern in Mexiko zwischen Subsistenz- und Warenproduktion, Frankfurt/New York: Campus
Bennholdt-Thomsen, Veronika 1994: Juchitán – Stadt der Frauen. Vom Leben im Matriarchat, Reinbek: Rowohlt
Bennholdt-Thomsen, Veronika / Holzer, Brigitte / Müller, Christa (Eds.) 1999: Das Subsistenzhandbuch. Widerstandskulturen in Europa, Asien und Lateinamerika, Wien: Promedia
Bennholdt-Thomsen, Veronika / Mies, Maria 1995: Eine Kuh für Hillary. Die Subsistenzperspektive, München: Frauenoffensive (1999: The Subsistence Perspective. Beyond the Globalized Economy, London: zedpress)
Bennholdt-Thomsen / Faraclas, Nicholas / Werlhof v., Claudia (Eds.) 2001: There is an Alternative. Subsistence and Worldwide Resistance to Corporate Globalization, London: zedpress
Bloch, Ernst 1991: Naturrecht und menschliche Würde, Frankfurt: Suhrkamp
Broderick, Damien 2004: Die molekulare Manufaktur. Wie Nanotechnologie unsere Zukunft beeinflusst, Reinbek: Rowohlt

Erdheim, Mario 1984: Die gesellschaftliche Produktion von Unbewusstheit, Frankfurt: Suhrkamp

Frank, André Gunder 1977: On so-called Primitive Accumulation, in: Dialectical Anthropology, 2, pp. 87-106

Frank, André Gunder / Gills, Barry (Eds.) 1996: The World System. Five Hundred Years - or Five Thousand? London: Routledge

Genth, Renate 1996: Matriarchat als zweite Kultur, in: Werlhof v., Claudia / Schweighofer, Annemarie / Ernst, Werner (Eds.): Herren Los. Herrschaft – Erkenntnis – Lebensform, Frankfurt, Paris, New York: Peter Lang, pp. 17-38

Genth, Renate 2002: Über Maschinisierung und Mimesis. Erfindungsgeist und mimetische Begabung im Widerstreit und ihre Bedeutung für das Mensch-Maschine-Verhältnis, Frankfurt/Paris/New York: Peter Lang

Gimbutas, Marija 1984: The Goddesses and Gods of Old Europe. 6500-3500 Myths and Cult Images, London: Thames & Hudson

Göttner-Abendroth, Heide 1988: Das Matriarchat I: Geschichte seiner Erforschung, Stuttgart: Kohlhammer

Irrgang, Bernhard 2005: Posthumanes Menschsein? Künstliche Intelligenz, Cyberspace, Roboter, Cyborgs und Designer-Menschen – Anthropologie des künstlichen Menschen im 21. Jahrhundert, Wiesbaden: Franz Steiner

Klein, Renate 2001: Globalized Bodies in the Twenty-first Century: The Final Patriarchal Takeover? in: Bennholdt-Thomsen, Veronika / Faraclas, Nicholas / Werlhof, v. Claudia (Eds.): There is an Alternative. Subsistence and Worldwide Resistance to Corporate Globalization, London: zedpress, pp. 91-105

Kurthen, Martin 2004: Die dritte Natur. Über posthumane Faktizität, Münster: LIT

Luxemburg, Rosa 1967 (1913): The Accumulation of Capital, London: Routledge

Merchant, Carolyn 1982: The Death of Nature: Women, Ecology and the Scientific Revolution, San Francisco: Harper & Row

MEW (Marx-Engels-Werke) 1974, Bd. 23, Das Kapital 1, Berlin: Dietz

Mies, Maria 1978: Methodische Postulate zur Frauenforschung – dargestellt am Beispiel der Gewalt gegen Frauen, in: Beiträge zur feministischen Theorie und Praxis, Nr. 1: Erste Orientierungen, München, pp. 41-63

Mies, Maria 1986: Patriarchy and Accumulation on a World Scale. Women in the International Division of Labour, London: zedpress

Mies, Maria 1992: Wider die Industrialisierung des Lebens, Pfaffenweiler: Centaurus

Mies, Maria 2001: Globalisierung von unten, Hamburg: Rotbuch

Mies, Maria 2003: Über die Notwendigkeit, Europa zu entkolonisieren, in: Werlhof,v. Claudia / Bennholdt-Thomsen, Veronika / Faraclas, Nicholas

(Eds.): Subsistenz und Widerstand. Alternativen zur Globalisierung, Wien: Promedia, pp. 19-40

Mies, Maria 2004: Krieg ohne Grenzen. Die neue Kolonisierung der Welt, Köln: PapyRossa

Mies, Maria / Shiva, Vandana 1993: Ecofeminism, London: zedpress

Mies, Maria / Werlhof, v. Claudia (Eds.) 1998/2004: Lizenz zum Plündern. Das Multilaterale Abkommen über Investitionen, MAI – Globalisierung der Konzernherrschaft, und was wir dagegen tun können, Hamburg: Rotbuch

Neusüß, Christel 1985: Die Kopfgeburten der Arbeiterbewegung, oder: Die Genossin Luxemburg bringt alles durcheinander, Hamburg: Rasch & Röhrig

Raymond, Janice 1994: Women as Wombs. Reproductive Technologies and the Battle over Women's Freedom, San Francisco, Melbourne: Spinifex

Rifkin, Jeremy 1983: Algeny, New York: Viking

Salleh, Ariel 1997: Ecofeminism as Politics: Nature, Marx and the Postmodern, London, zedpress

Schirrmacher, Frank (Ed.) 2001: Die Darwin AG. Wie Nanotechnologie, Biotechnologie und Computer den neuen Menschen träumen, Köln: Kiepenheuer & Witsch

Ullrich, Otto 1977: Technik und Herrschaft. Vom Handwerk zur verdinglichten Blockstruktur industrieller Produktion, Frankfurt: Suhrkamp

Wallerstein, Immanuel 1979: Aufstieg und künftiger Niedergang des kapitalistischen Weltsystems, in: Senghaas, Dieter (Ed.): Kapitalistische Weltökonomie. Kontroversen über ihren Ursprung und ihre Entwicklungsdynamik, Frankfurt: Surhkamp, pp. 31-67

Wallerstein, Immanuel 1996: World System versus World Systems. A critique, in: Frank, André Gunder / Gills, Barry K. (Eds.): The World System. Five hundred years of five thousand? London: Routledge, pp. 292-296

Weizenbaum, Joseph 1976: Computer Power and Human Reason: From Judgement to Calculation, San Francisco: W.H. Freeman & Company

Werlhof v., Claudia 1978: Frauenarbeit: der blinde Fleck in der Kritik der Politischen Ökonomie, in: Beiträge zur feministischen Theorie und Praxis, Nr.1, Erste Orientierungen, München, pp. 18-32 (in English 1988: Women's Work: The Blind Spot in the Critique of Political Economy, in: Mies, Maria / Bennholdt-Thomsen, Veronika / Werlhof v., Claudia: Women, The Last Colony, London, zedpress)

Werlhof v., Claudia 1983: Lohn hat einen „Wert", Leben nicht? Auseinandersetzung mit einer „linken" Frau, in: Prokla, Nr.50: Marx und der Marxismus, Berlin, pp. 38-58

Werlhof v., Claudia 1985: Wenn die Bauern wiederkommen. Frauen, Arbeit und Agrobusiness in Venezuela, Bremen: periferia/CON

Werlhof v., Claudia 1986: Wir werden das Leben unserer Kinder nicht dem Fortschritt opfern, in: Gambaroff, Marina. et. al.: Tschernobyl hat unser Leben verändert. Vom Ausstieg der Frauen, Reinbek: Rowohlt, pp. 8-24

Werlhof v., Claudia 1991: Was haben die Hühner mit dem Dollar zu tun? Frauen und Ökonomie, München: Frauenoffensive

Werlhof, v. Claudia 1991b: Männliche Natur und künstliches Geschlecht. Texte zur Erkenntniskrise der Moderne, Wien: Frauenverlag

Werlhof v., Claudia 1996: Mutter-Los. Frauen im Patriarchat zwischen Angleichung und Dissidenz, München: Frauenoffensive

Werlhof v., Claudia 1997: Ökonomie, die praktische Seite der Religion. Wirtschaft als Gottesbeweis und die Methode der Alchemie. Zum Zusammenhang von Patriarchat. Kapitalismus und Christentum, in: Ernst, U. et.al. (Eds.): Ökonomie M(m)acht Angst, Zum Verhältnis von Ökonomie und Religion, Frankfurt/Paris/New York: Peter Lang, pp. 95-121

Werlhof v., Claudia 1997b: Frauen, Wissenschaft und Naturverhältnis. Vier Thesen wider den Emanzipationsansatz. Oder: Was heißt heute Kritik am Patriarchat? In: Widerspruch, Nr. 34, 17. Jg./1. Halbjahr, Zürich, pp. 147-170

Werlhof v., Claudia 2000: Patriarchat als „Alchemistisches System". Die (Z)ErSetzung des Lebendigen, in: Wolf, M. (Ed.): Optimierung und Zerstörung. Intertheoretische Analysen zum menschlich Lebendigen, Innsbruck: STUDIA, pp. 13-31

Werlhof v., Claudia 2001: Losing Faith in Progress: Capitalist Patriarchy as an "Alchemical System", in: Bennholdt-Thomsen, Veronika / Faraclas, Nicholas/Werlhof, v. Claudia (Eds.): There is an Alternative. Subsistence and Worldwide Resistance to Corporate Globalization, London: zedpress, pp. 15-40

Werlhof v., Claudia 2002: Gewalt und Geschlecht, in: Widerspruch, Nr. 42, 22. Jg./1. Halbjahr, Zürich, pp. 13-33

Werlhof v,. Claudia 2003: (Haus)Frauen, „Gender" und die Schein-Macht des Patriarchats, in: Widerspruch, Nr. 44, 23. Jg./1. Halbjahr, Zürich, pp. 173-189

Werlhof v., Claudia 2004: Natur, Maschine, Mimesis. Zur Kritik patriarchalischer Naturkonzepte, in: Widerspruch, Nr. 47, 24. Jg./2. Halbjahr, Zürich, pp. 155-171

Werlhof v., Claudia 2004b: Using, Producing and Replacing Life? Alchamy as Theory and Practice in Capitalism, in: Wallerstein, Immanuel (Ed.): The Modern World System in the *Long Durée*, Boulder: paradigm, pp. 65-78

Werlhof v., Claudia 2005: The Utopia of a Motherless World – Patriarchy as War-System, paper, "2nd World Congress of Matriarchal Studies: Societies of Peace", 29.9.-2.10, Austin, Texas (see chapter 8)

Werlhof v., Claudia 2006: Das Patriarchat als Negation des Matriarchats. Zur Perspektive eines Wahns, in: Göttner-Abendroth, Heide (Ed.): Gesellschaft in Balance. Dokumente vom 1. Weltkongress für Matriarchatsforschung 2003, Stuttgart: Kohlhammer, pp. 30-41

Werlhof v., Claudia 2006b: Capitalist Patriarchy and the Negation of Matriarchy. The Struggle for a „Deep" Alternative, in: Vaughan, Genevieve (Ed.): Women and the gift Economy. A Radically Different World View is Possible, Toronto: Innana, pp. 139-153

Werlhof v., Claudia/ Bennholdt-Thomsen, Veronika/ Mies. Maria 1983: Frauen, die letzte Kolonie, Reinbek: Rowohlt (in English 1988: Women, the Last Colony, London: zedpress)

Werlhof v., Claudia / Ernst, Werner / Schweighofer, Annemarie (eds.) 1996: Herren Los. Herrschaft – Erkenntnis – Lebensform, Frankfurt/Paris/New York: Peter Lang

Werlhof v., Claudia / Bennholdt-Thomsen, Veronika / Faraclas, Nicholas (eds.) 2003: Subsistenz und Widerstand. Alternativen zur Globalisierung, Wien: Promedia

Widerspruch 2005: Nr. 49, Prekäre Arbeitsgesellschaft, Zürich

Wright, Ronald 2006: Eine kleine Geschichte des Fortschritts, Reinbek: Rowohlt

6. Patriarchy as Negation of Matriarchy – Perspective of a Delusion[*]

- unpublished -

[in German: Das Patriarchat als Negation des Matriarchats. Zur Perspektive eines Wahns, in: Göttner-Abendroth, Heide (Hg.): Gesellschaft in Balance. Dokumentation des 1. Weltkongresses für Matriarchatsforschung in Luxemburg 2003, Stuttgart (Kohlhammer) 2006; S. 30-41; in Spanish: El Patriarcado como Negación del Matriarcado. Perspectiva de una Chímera, in: Claudia v. Werlhof/Mathias Behmann: Teoría Crítica del Patriarcado, Frankfurt a. M., Peter Lang 2010, pp. 121-138]

Preliminary remark

This is the English translation of my contribution to the "1. World Congress of Matriarchal Studies" in Luxemburg in 2003 which was held in German language.

So far, I have been studying patriarchy rather than matriarchy simply because I consider myself to be a matriarchal woman who does not really understand patriarchy. That is why I want to analyze it, which is just another way of saying that it is not matriarchy but patriarchy which is the problem. My analysis rests on the thesis that patriarchy is not an independent order of society but, squatting on matriarchy, exploits, changes, and destroys all formerly matriarchal ways of living and thinking. Binary and antagonistic in its form, this thesis may appear to neglect society's complexity, but it serves the purpose of working out as distinctly as possible the differences between matriarchy and patriarchy. Only on this basis can the complexity of society be adequately analyzed.

What is "Patriarchy"?

Thesis and Field of Research

According to my thesis and seen from a matriarchal viewpoint, patriarchy is neither in itself nor of its own an order of society, culture, or civilization. It is not independent of matriarchal forms of society but has developed out of the

---

[*] Translation from German by Dr. Ursula Marianne Ernst

negation of matriarchy. Seen as such, patriarchy has to be called a delusion. The fact that it cannot exist or cannot have its own reality in the sense of its own definition enhances its phantasmagoric character. Patriarchy literally means "the father is the beginning", "father origin" or "father uterus", because the Greek word arché, which is part of the words "patriarchy" and "matriarchy", originally means "beginning, origin, Uterus". Only much later, in times of patriarchy, "arché" acquires the meaning of "dominance" or "domination". Patriarchy as such remains a perspective, an idea, a Utopia, the project of a society that wants to be absolutely without a mother and independent of nature, cut off from its inter-connectedness with all other forms of being.

Efforts to make this Utopia concrete are, however, under way and will result in "patriarchy" or "the father's dominance" (that is "arché" in the second, the patriarchal sense of the word). The project of not only conceptualizing but also materializing patriarchy or of "technically" realizing it is a project of modern times. Patriarchy in the original sense of the word was and still is scarce, if it exists at all.

In the process of materializing the patriarchal project such an enormous destruction of life, especially of women and nature, has occurred that patriarchy appears to have reached its limits. It seems that the race of destruction and "production", that is the construction of patriarchy, is in its final stage and will probably be decided in the very near future.

Patriarchy, seen from this perspective, must be understood as a *process* which continually extends its borders and which, at the same time, goes deeper and deeper. This process obviously tends towards becoming a *system* but, as basically never ending, cannot come to its conclusion. Its present phase of capitalism as a global system ("globalization") appears to be its, so far, last and most violent period in which many patriarchal tendencies of history come to a peak or *accumulate.*

With this thesis I oppose and contradict those who understand patriarchy as "the father's dominance" without asking for the reasons of the will to dominate, as if domination were, per se, a male need. I also oppose and contradict those who – literally standing at the other end of my thesis – do not see the connections between patriarchy and modernity but consider it to be a pre-modern or old-fashioned, "traditional", and backward phenomenon, a phenomenon which – seen from the perspective of technical progress – seems anachronistic and in the process of disappearing – all by itself!

In general, I also oppose and contradict those who fight against any periodization of history that goes beyond modern times, the Middle Ages or antiquity and, therefore, refuse to look back upon "pre-historic" times or the predecessors of patriarchy. This approach allows them to deny both the existence of matriarchies and the origins of patriarchies and to consider the former as irrelevant. Against that view let me warn with Johann Wolfgang von Goethe:

Wer nicht von drei Tausend Jahren	*Who never looks beyond*
sich weiß Rechenschaft zu geben,	*more than three thousand years,*
bleibt im Dunkeln, unerfahren,	*will stay in darkness, fond*
mag von Tag zu Tage leben.	*of living day by day in tears.*
(West-Östlicher Divan, 1819)	(Transl. UE)

And finally, I certainly oppose and contradict those who simply think systemically and do not want to see patriarchy as a historical phenomenon. Instead, they consider it to be unhistorical, as if it had existed from times immemorial as an independent, "necessary", or even "the best possible" order of society, an order with the special capacity of "evolving" into "civilization", the only relevant order worth noticing.

From my viewpoint, patriarchy is not only a general and vague term of political combat, but primarily a basic theoretical concept for the global understanding of origin, development, and future of our present order of society (C. v. Werlhof 2003).

Attacks on Matriarchal Studies and on the Critique of Patriarchy

It is not insignificant that feminist *matriarchal studies* and *the critique of patriarchy* are presently *under attack* again in the way they had been attacked at the time of National Socialism (s. AutorInnengemeinschaft 2003). National Socialism was clearly interested in these topics and used them for its own purposes. Of course, its leaders did not pay attention to matriarchal studies or a feminist critique of patriarchy. On the contrary, such studies were forbidden by them, while they tried, with something like their own "critique" of patriarchy, to patriarchally utilize matriarchal studies with the purpose of both, defaming Jews and recruiting women for their national socialism. Of course, they carefully avoided to apply their critique of patriarchy to National Socialism itself.

At present, attacks on matriarchal studies and on the critique of patriarchy come rather from the left and from women's groups that do not want to have anything to do with feminism. Women's lobbies, neo-liberal politicians, and, especially, post-modern as well as post-feminist "gender" researchers (B. Röder et al. 1996) vehemently fight against the concepts of matriarchy and patriarchy, and they probably do so because they could otherwise no longer legitimate their politics of participating in the global project of patriarchy (for a critique s. D. Bell/R. Klein 1999).

Certain left groups locate matriarchal studies and the critique of patriarchy on the extreme right, though they have formulated a much more radical critique of capitalism than the Left itself (c.f. Mies 1986). The leftist critique, however, remains "within the system" by still considering "socialism" to be an alternative to "capitalism" and not as a component of one and the same "capitalist world system". Since these critics include neither the so called "second", supposedly "post-capitalist" nor the so called "third", supposedly "pre-capitalist" (not to speak of a matriarchal) world, they are not interested in issues such as:
1. Alternatives to the state/to systems of domination;
2. Alternatives to technical progress/to the machine;
3. Alternatives to modern relations to nature/the impact of the question of ecology;
4. Alternatives to patriarchy as the historical background or bearer of capitalism.

And they are, finally, not interested in:
5. A serious discussion of the so called women's question, although only from such a discussion the above mentioned problems could be seen within and as part of the *patriarchal syndrome*.

Accordingly, the fast points of this avoidance debate against matriarchal studies and the critique of patriarchy are:

Technical progress, especially technology as machine, hostile relations to nature, and (men's) domination must remain untouched, to the effect that eco-feminists, feminist critics of domination, subsistence theorists, and, even more so, subsistence practitioners, or so called "spiritual" women and matriarchal researchers, who plead for alternatives, are seen as "esoteric", "conservative", and have to be, more or less, located on the right. Never mind, how much critique of capitalism they may have formulated! (c. f. Bennholdt-Thomsen/ Faraclas/Werlhof 2001)

The bottom line of all this debate is: Capitalism must not really be criticized. All that matters is the seizure of power by another group inside capitalism, and the critique is valid only as long as no change of power has taken place.

As a consequence of this attitude, the concepts of capitalism and patriarchy as well as their connections are taboo and must not be analyzed to their full extent. With *capitalist patriarchy* moving toward its critical point, this taboo becomes even stricter and it seems that a discussion of alternatives to capitalism and to patriarchy must be avoided by all means (s. H. Göttner-Abendroth 2003).

Instead, I am pleading for understanding our social order as basically a global patriarchy which has evolved over a period of 5 to 7000 years, with global capitalism as its, so far, last and "highest" form of expression which marks the limits of its development.

Thus, once again after the times of National Socialism and, historically for the first time within a global context, the question of *alternative/s to patriarchy* – and not only to capitalism – is on the top of the agenda. Matriarchal studies are, more than others, summoned to answer the following questions: Would neo-matriarchal or generally non-patriarchal and no longer capitalist social relations present an alternative? What is already being done in this field? How could one conceptualize this alternative and in which form should it be materialized?

Matriarchy as a "2nd Culture" within Patriarchy

Accepting the reversal of the common view of things and considering the problems of social development(s) within patriarchy as inter-connected, that is by using a more powerful "telescope" to look upon pre- and non-patriarchal times in order to learn for the present, two phenomena appear very clearly: the phenomena of under- or overrating patriarchy.

1. Once we realize that patriarchy is not only a system of domination, especially of that of men over women, it will no longer be *underrated*. Patriarchy aims at much more than just the domination of men over women. It has an objective which goes far beyond that form of domination.
2. Patriarchy has a beginning and it will, therefore, eventually have an end. Seen from an evolutionary perspective, it is not "necessary" and it should, therefore, not be *overrated*. In other words: Societies organized according to "non-patriarchal" principles must, simply for logical reasons, have existed. Therefore, they can and possibly will, for the same logical reasons, develop again.
3. The fact that different matriarchies still exist today proves that patriarchies have neither at all times nor everywhere been the only form of society. At the same time, the existence of matriarchal societies in our time or their survival within patriarchies point toward the danger of continuous patriarchalization of still existing or newly formed matriarchal social relations.
4. There is, however, no easy answer to the question how and to what extent new no longer patriarchal societies resemble historical and still existing "older forms" of matriarchies. Living matriarchies can only give us clues for alternatives just like global alternative movements do.

When we look at the etymology or at archaeology – which archaeologist could explain what it means that the sphinx is about 14000 years old?! – or when we look at societies of old or new living matriarchies, and finally when we look at non-patriarchal social relations inside patriarchy, we must realize that for very long periods of human history there globally existed a many-faceted matriarchal world culture, and that patriarchy is, in its different forms of appearance, simply an evolutionary error of very recent origin, although an extremely dangerous and violent one.

Against this background the following questions have to be asked: Why do so many people still and in spite of patriarchy think in matriarchal forms and find it so very hard to understand the patriarchal rules of thinking, acting, feeling, and being – in spite of continuous social pressure? Is this due to the fact that they "remember" matriarchal social relations, or is it only because of their resistance to acute patriarchal oppression? But even though the latter may be the case one has to ask: Where does this resistance come from in a person who has had no experience with conditions other than patriarchal ones? This question harbors a genuine problem of epistemology. Is it possible that resistance to patriarchy or dissident thinking and behavior goes back to some form of matriarchal experience or memory? What would this question imply for the issue of "consciousness" in general? How and to what extent does a matriarchal consciousness still influence people's lives? To what extent can such influence be explained by indicating that human consciousness not only comprises a person's direct experience but also early stages of human existence as such? What is the role of still surviving matriarchal social relations or relations that point toward *matriarchy as a "2nd culture"* within patriarchy (R. Genth 1996)?

Only one thing is obvious: Matriarchal social relations and societies not only existed in forgotten pre-historic times which no longer have any impact upon our lives today and can, therefore, be neglected. On the contrary: The question, whether they have existed or not, is more important than ever. Today, matriarchal social relations or forms become more and more vital, they may even have always run like a red thread through our experience, our memories, and our states of consciousness; they may, as such, still influence our impressions, behavior, social relations, desires, feelings, ideas, and forms of thinking. From this perspective, it might be advisable, even wise, to study matriarchal social relations and phenomena right in the center of contemporary patriarchies. Such studies could help them surface and make us aware of them to such a degree that we could use them in our search of alternatives to patriarchy as immediate starting points.

Patriarchy as the Development of a War System

Matriarchal and Patriarchal Social Relations:
Patriarchy as a Process of Patriarchalization

According to the relevant literature, social relations probably lost their matriarchal character in a situation of need, danger, or emergency that might have occurred on account of climatic changes that were followed by "catastrophic" migrations in the course of which matriarchal social relations were injured and spoilt and finally destroyed (M. Gimbutas 1994; H. Göttner-Abendroth 1989; J. de Meo 1997).

Let me define as *matriarchal* those *social relations* which most suit the life of human groups and communities that are closely connected with nature and other non-human forms of being and which best guarantee the groups' or communities' survival wherever they may live. According to this definition, such relations will have evolved in different forms all over the world and in a long historical process. The common feature of potentially manifold matriarchal cultures is – to take the word "culture" literally – the care of life and there can hardly be any doubt that it was the long history of the mother-child-relationship which led to the "evolution" of matriarchy and toward matriarchy. One may assume that, if there has ever been anything like "evolution" in human history, it has to be searched for in the mother-child-relationship.

In this sense indigenous matriarchal cultures in North America know, for instance, two basic rules according to which they orient their lives: All life comes from women. Life must not be endangered.

Matriarchal societies all over the world and at all times would probably stick to these two basic rules.

Patriarchal social relations will, according to the above given definition of matriarchy, most probably not have developed out of a project that arose within matriarchy against matriarchy. Such a development would imply that there existed, within matriarchal societies, social contradictions of a form in which they systematically only develop in long periods of violence, domination, oppression or subordination, exploitation, robbery, class formation, and the like. Such conditions are, however, only known to exist in patriarchies. In fact, it is exactly such conditions which define patriarchy. Yet, there are some researchers who propose endogenous causes for the development of patriarchy out of matriarchal societies themselves (s. C. Meier-Seethaler 1992 (1988)).

It seems, however, much more likely that patriarchal social relations have first developed in reaction to the fact that matriarchal social relations could no longer be continued in the way they had existed before. This would also explain why some societies, such as the Celts, for instance, preserved a great number of matriarchal traditions long after they had changed to patriarchal social relations (J. Markale 1984).

There are, in any case, many instances that indicate that matriarchal societies could successfully prevent the endogenous development of domination and that they were not naïve in regard of the potential dangers of power, domination, and violence that otherwise could have developed within their own social order (s. P. Clastres 1976; Ch. Sigrist 1979 (1994)).

Apart from all these considerations, there is no doubt that the decision to raid others comes about in a situation of emergency or a situation which may be (even fraudulently) interpreted/defined as emergency. It is raid to hunt animals that had previously been taboo, and/or to invade another human community in order to get food supplies. Most probably, in many cases people will have, in the long run, arrived at some kind of agreement. In any case, according to Marija Gimbutas, the Kurgans needed hundreds of years of organized waves of conquest though not being able to erect a regular system of domination such as the state (Gimbutas 1994) To the contrary see for example, the history of the invasion of Sumer in Ancient Mesopotamia, modern Iraq, in the 4th millennium B.C.

"Oriental despotism" which arose in those areas largely determined the rise and development of patriarchies in antiquity (s. K. Wittfogel 1977) and thus also the rise and development of Western patriarchy which was later established by means of Roman colonization and of violent waves of Christianization starting from Rome (s. M. Mies 2003).

In any case, the tremendous use of violence which, right from the beginning, characterizes patriarchal systems of domination (s. D. Wolf 1994) can hardly be explained, if one assumes that patriarchy arose within matriarchal societies as endogenous formation.

It does, however, make sense to speak of endogenous waves of patriarchalization as the result of outside influences which continue inside and lead to more and stronger waves of patriachalization within a matriarchal society. Such an endogenous process within matriarchal societies, which I would like to call "*secondary patriarchalization*", may have been started as protection against violence, particularly against the threat of war: "Protective or defensive forces" not only take over the defense against outside enemies but they also produce a power system inside society. This has been "the logic of war" up to present times.

The question when to call a certain society no longer matriarchal or when to consider it to be primarily patriarchal is probably mostly a question of periodization. If matriarchy is the first social order and if the development of patriarchy comes after and out of the conquest of matriarchy, it must follow that some matriarchal social relations have outlived patriarchalization, have developed as new, oppressed, pauperized forms, or have been propagated only to veil domination or to legitimize it.

The "Logic" of (the Development) of Patriarchy

From our *thesis* that patriarchy is always based upon the destruction of matriarchy and as such "squats on" originally matriarchal social relations, it follows that there must be some basic principles which are at least "necessary" for the formation of patriarchies as long as they compete with and are opposed to matriarchies. To put it differently: If patriarchies do not "as such" exist on their own but develop only in opposition to matriarchal societies, then such basic principles should state what a patriarchal society or a society on its way to patriarchy "logically" and in any case requires in order to develop and to continue. As minimal principles they would form the basis of any patriarchy, no matter how different its social order in other respects may be, and, since they are basic and necessary for any patriarchal society, they would have to be defended by all means and at all costs. According to "patriarchal logic" any attack upon these principles would have to be seen as an attack upon the basis of society itself.

Since most of us have come to consider patriarchy as the normal form of society, the monstrosity of this logic and its fundamental opposition to everything that was and still is considered normal in matriarchal societies do not strike us as terrible. We become aware of its monstrosity only when we are directly confronted with it or when we really experience the moment when patriarchal logic bursts and suddenly turns its "structural" or latent violence into direct violence.

In the following passages I will present the "logic" of patriarchy as *a "necessary" negation of matriarchal social relations*. Once the scandal of patriarchy has again become evident and entered our consciousness, we will be able to clearly differentiate between patriarchal and matriarchal principles. Then we will also realize that patriarchy always includes the usurpation or robbery of matriarchal acquisitions and achievements which, in the end, are presented to be genuinely patriarchal ones.

My analysis of this patriarchal logic is based on only one prerequisite: Patriarchy wants to exist and wants to assure its existence against the matriarchal society upon which it squats. This, however, is beyond doubt.

Patriarchy as "War System"

As far as we know today, patriarchy always and everywhere begins with war (R. Eisler 1993; M. Mies 2003; C. v. Werlhof 2003 a). War develops out of armed men on horseback raiding unarmed villages and towns, looting them, destroying them, and conquering them (M .Gimbutas 1994). Only after conquering strangers, the people of one's own clan or group, and especially the women, can be conquered and enslaved (the words for slaves and women are the same in some cases). In this process, hostility of the sexes, different classes, private property as the result of robbed property (privare = rob), and the state are established.

"Violence" in patriarchy is not vague or some kind of incidental phenomenon which only appears at the moment when it is socialized or legalized and legitimized "from the top". In patriarchy, individual as well as collective violence, ordered from the top of society, is always the result of war and part of war. War is, in this process, not a temporary, sudden outbreak of "generative violence" (see R. Girard 1992), it is rather continuous generative violence. Patriarchy, according to our *thesis,* does, therefore, not only begin with war, but takes war as its model for the time after war and for all times, those of so called "peace" included.

1. *In patriarchy social relations orient themselves on war and imitate war as their model.* It is only the perspective on patriarchy as war which can explain its social relations and which allows to analyze the latter adequately. Violence in patriarchy must, according to this perspective, be characterized as "legitimate" violence in so called "just" wars. When we look at human history and at the world as it presents itself right now to the socio-political observer, it is obvious that patriarchal forms of violence are, as such, "invented" in war. War is the "father" (and, indeed, not the "mother") of patriarchy as a whole system of violence with thoroughly planned - or "cold" - violence as one of its main "inventions". Patriarchal violence, socially produced, organized, and institutionalized, could not develop without war but arose with and in it: Violence is always and foremost violence of war. For hundreds of centuries, war as capital invention of patriarchy has supplied and still supplies the "necessary" empirical knowledge for itself (see Sunzi 500 B. C., 1999). This also explains the establishment of violence as military and state monopoly, removing or suppressing other forms of coercion, such as quasi "autonomous", state independent violence.
2. If war not only marks the beginning of patriarchy but if patriarchy, as such, is war, that is war at all times, everywhere, in principle, and in all areas of life and society, then patriarchy is not only a system of violence but a *system of*

war (for this new concept see M. Mies 2004). War is the typical "order" of patriarchy, even in times of so called peace. The immediate and early phase of direct war will, in the course of time, have developed into patriarchy proper. Accordingly, processes of patriarchalization work to the effect that all social areas and relations are turned into "warlike" or militarized conditions which systematically refer to each other. In this way, war will, step by step and always more deeply, penetrate all of society (U. Bröckling 1997). Virilio would call such a state that of "pure war" (see Virilio/Lotringer 1984). It is a state in which social development solely turns around the "logistics" of the "war machine" (ibid., p. 121).

3. *War as the method of patriarchy must be re-defined.* War in patriarchy, even though it may begin as a raid, is not only an attack that passes away, not a momentary conquest or an "offensive war". Nor is it anything like a more or less "fair" race or competition among opponents of equal strength (s. C. Schmitt 1932). War, according to its own logic, never ends with conquering what it wants to conquer, it always remains as "method" for further conquest, and it will be continued after the conquest inside the conquered area to prevent the conquered from freeing themselves (colonialism). Furthermore, war is not only about killing the "enemy" but rather aims at subjecting the enemy to be used for the "victor's" purposes, such as cheap labor or "producers" of human beings. War is, therefore, not a kind of "continuation of politics by different means", it rather is the other way round: Politics, the economy, the technology, the relations to nature and the relationship between the sexes, and the strategies of their legitimization in science, ethics, and religion in patriarchy are the *continuation of war* by – only partially – different means. What follows after "hot" war is, in the best case, cold war or equally *"cold peace"*.

Since the return to peace would be a return to matriarchal social relations, there is no peace in patriarchy. We are not aware of this, because we have got used to considering as peace a state which is no more than the temporary absence of direct murderous violence. What we take for peace is simply the disappearance of obvious violence in our closer neighborhood. But when it seems to be taboo or invisible, violence is just hiding in the form of "cold" violence. From a patriarchal perspective, society is seen as something that has to be permanently conquered and subjected. Since the groups or communities that were first conquered (and still are being conquered) were women's cultures with close relations to nature, it is no incident that the population of a country or the people are still considered to be "feminine" or somehow "natural".

4. Patriarchy is a *Utopia* which systematically uses war to become real and concrete. This war system paradoxically legitimizes itself by claiming to be capable of bringing about a "nobler" and "higher" world, a new creation of the world – by means of war and destruction. This *"alchemical project"* (s. B. Easlea 1986; C. v. Werlhof 2003) aims at a "society" in which women and nature are no more than matter to be transformed, that is mother-material seen as dead matter or as matter to be killed. The outcome of this project would be something like a *"pure patriarchy"* that finally got rid of everything matriarchal and that would need neither women nor nature any more. Only then, patriarchy would have utterly emancipated itself from matriarchal society and would, standing on its own feet, have become an independent order of society. "Patriarchy" would then, in the fullest sense of the word, have realized itself. "Social formation" would have given way to "technological formation" or to the *"alchemical system"* (C. v. Werlhof 2003) that would finally exist ex nihilo.

This illusion might represent the last and final legitimization of patriarchy. It would consist in the idea that patriarchy, in its proper form, wants to create *a new "paradise"*, a place without scarcity and conflict. All forms of violence and war would be seen as passing, yet "necessary", phenomena on this way to progress which appears to be desired by god and nature, and even by the women.

Summarized Interpretation:

Patriarchal Forms of Negating Matriarchy

1. Patriarchy negates matriarchy by tautologically pre-supposing itself as its own origin. Social alternatives to patriarchy are ignored, ridiculed, or demonized. Society is being reduced to patriarchy.
2. Patriarchy negates matriarchy by trying to usurp, appropriate, and incorporate the acquisitions of matriarchal cultures which are then presented as its very own creations. Accordingly, the lord, god, father presents himself as the better mistress, goddess, creatrix, mother, and nature (natural power). The ancient "mother right" is turned into the "father right" over life and death.
3. Patriarchy negates matriarchy by turning its rules and principles upside down or by perverting them. Matriarchal society is literally turned over to stand on its head. To do so, matriarchal taboos concerning food, sexuality, domination, exploitation, and killing have to be broken. With war as "the father of all things" instead of life as "the mother of all things", creation and wealth

appear to come from willful destruction instead of from the cooperation of all things alive. War is considered to be beautiful, true, and good. Faith in the absurd stands against knowledge of the world. Sarcasm and cynicism toward life are considered as adequate and intelligent. Human intelligence is primarily used for destructive purposes.
4. Patriarchy negates matriarchy by destroying the latter. Murder of goddesses, mothers, and women become the rule. The sacrifice of women, nature, and culture are at the center of society with internal and external destruction as the result. The knowledge of subsistence, of life, and of peace, wisdom in dealing with conflicts, and empirical knowledge of nature, all these are, together with their witnesses, destroyed. Against all these, patriarchy sets up its nihilism.
5. Patriarchy negates matriarchy by trying to transform matriarchal societies into patriarchal ones. This leads to the "alchemical project" of constructing and producing patriarchal "creations" on the basis of a violent "divide and rule!" in all areas of life. Modern times and capitalism are, more than other historical periods, characterized by this project of direct material patriarchalization, particularly in the form of the production of commodities, of money bearing interest, and of machine technology ("the military industrial complex").
6. Patriarchy finally negates matriarchy by trying to replace matriarchal society by patriarchal order. To do so, it has to totally abstract from matriarchal social relations or to absolutely set itself off from them. This is possible only when the constructs and products of patriarchy lead to an independent *second "creation"* which, in fact, replaces the former creation to such an extent that one can do utterly without it. Only with the establishment of such a "pure patriarchy" the annihilation of women and nature are – in retrospect – "legitimized". Such hubris, that is the willingness to stake the entire life on earth, is the true "*secret*" of patriarchy.

Toward a Neo-Matriarchal View of Inter-Connectedness

Alternative projects, even if they do not explicitly mention matriarchy, globally start with equality, subsistence, mutuality, the affirmation of life, and cooperation. The simple self-evident truth of life without dominance is again right at the center of thinking, acting, and feeling. The relation to internal and external nature is understood to be based on the idea of all things alive and all phenomena being inter-connected. A matriarchal view of the world realizes its inter-connectedness and does not transcend it nor create another world beyond it. It rather goes right through it (transcendere) without disconnecting the individual beings. On the contrary, it realizes the transcendence of their limits and sees every being connected with every other being. Thus, the thoughts pick up the threads of ancient wisdom woven by matriarchal cultures (s. Bennholdt-Thomsen/Faraclas/v. Werlhof 2001).

The delusion of patriarchy will, like a phantom, disappear from the surface of the Earth...

If we then turn back upon the times of patriarchy and look at it from an "archaeological perspective", we shall soon wonder how it could ever have existed.

Bibliography

AutorInnengemeinschaft (Eds): Die Diskriminierung der Matriarchatsforschung. Eine moderne Hexenjagd, Bern (Amalia) 2003
Bell, Diane and Klein, Renate (eds.): Radically Speaking: Feminism Reclaimed, London (Zedpress) 1996
Bennholdt-Thomsen, Veronika/Faraclas, Nicholas /Werlhof, Claudia v. (Eds.): There is an Alternative. Subsistence and Worldwide Resistance to Corporate Globlization, London (Zedpress) 2001
Bröckling, Ulrich: Disziplin. Soziolgie und Geschichte militärischer Gehorsamsproduktion, München (Wilhelm Fink) 1997
Clastres, Pierre: Staatsfeinde. Studien zur politischen Anthropologie, Frankfurt (Suhrkamp) 1976
De Meo, James: Entstehung und Ausbreitung des Patriarchats – die Saharasia-These, in: De Meo et. al. (Eds): Nach Reich. Sexualökonomie, Frankfurt/Main (2001) 1997, pp. 377-410
Easlea, Brian: Väter der Vernichtung. Männlichkeit, Naturwissenschaftler und der nukleare Rüstungswettlauf, Reinbek (Rowohlt) 1986
Eisler, Riane: Kelch und Schwert. Weibliches und männliches Prinzip in der Geschichte, München (Goldmann) 1993 (The Chalice and the Blade)
Genth, Renate: Matriarchat als 2. Kultur, in: Werlhof/Schweighofer/Ernst (Eds): Herren-Los. Herrschaft – Erkenntnis – Lebensform, Frankfurt/Main (Peter Lang) 1996, pp. 17-38
Gimbutas, Marija: Das Ende Alteuropas. Der Einfall von Steppennomaden aus Südrussland und die Indogermanisierung Mitteleuropas, Innsbruck (Innsbrucker Beiträge zur Kulturwissenschaft, Sonderheft 90) 1994
Girard, René: Das Heilige und die Gewalt, Frankfurt (Fischer) 1992
Goethe, Johann Wolfgang von: West-Östlicher Diwan, 1819
Göttner-Abendrohth, Heide: Das Matriarchat I, Geschichte seiner Erforschung, Stuttgart (Kohlhammer)1989
Göttner-Abendroth, Heide: „Verhindert sie mit allen Mitteln!" Die Diskriminierung der Matriarchatsforschung und die praktischen Folgen, in: AutorInnengemeinschaft (Eds): Die Diskriminierung der Matriarchats-forschung. Eine moderne Hexenjagd, Bern (Amalia) 2003, pp. 63-87
Markale, Jean: Die Keltische Frau, München (Goldmann) 1984
Meier-Seethaler, Carola: Ursprünge und Befreiungen. Die sexistischen Wurzeln der Kultur, Frankfurt/Main (Fischer) 1992
Mies, Maria: Über die Notwendigkeit, Europa zu entkolonisieren, in: v. Werlhof/Bennholdt-Thomsen/Faraclas (Eds): Subsistenz und Widerstand. Alternativen zur Globalisierung, Wien (Promedia) 2003, pp. 19-40

Mies, Maria: Patriarchy and Accumulation on a World Scale. Women in the International Division of Labour, London (Zedpress) 1986

Mies, Maria: Krieg ohne Grenzen, Köln (PapyRossa) 2004

Schmitt, Carl: Der Begriff des Politischen (1932), Berlin (Duncker & Humblodt) 2002

Sigrist, Christian: Regulierte Anarchie. Untersuchungen zum Fehlen und zur Entstehung politischer Herrschaft in segmentären Gesellschaften Afrikas, Hamburg (EVA) 1994 (1979)

Sombart, Nicolaus: Die deutschen Männer und ihre Feinde. Carl Schmitt. Ein deutsches Schicksal zwischen Männerbund und Matriarchhatsmythos, München/Wien (Carl Hanser) 1991

Sunzi: Die Kunst des Krieges, ed. by James Clavell, München (Droemer) 1999

Virilio, Paul and Lotringer, Sylvère: Der reine Krieg, Berlin (Merve) 1984

Werlhof, Claudia von: Der Verlust des Fortschrittsglaubens. Das kapitalistische Patriarchat als „Alchemistisches System", in: Werlhof et. al. (Eds.): Subsistenz und Widerstand, Alternativen zur Globalisierung, Wien (Promedia) 2003, pp. 41-68

Werlhof, Claudia von: Gewalt und Geschlecht, in: AutorInnengemeinschaft (Eds): Die Diskriminierung der Matriarchatsforschung. Eine moderne Hexenjagd, Bern (Amalia) 2003 a, pp. 13-33

Wittfogel, Karl A.: Die orientalische Despotie. Eine vergleichende Untersuchung totaler Macht, Frankfurt (Ullstein) 1977

Wolf, Doris: Was war vor den Pharaonen? Zürich (Kreuz) 1994

7. Loosing Faith in Progress?
Capitalist Patriarchy as an "Alchemical System"[*]

in Veronika Bennhold6t-Thomsen, Nicholas Faraclas and Claudia von Werlhof (Eds.): There is an Alternative. Subsistence and Worldwide Resistance to Corporate Globalization, London 2001, Zedpress, pp. 15-40

- new revised version -

Preliminary remark 2010

"Critical Theory of Patriarchy", as a new trans-disciplinary paradigm, is advancing by the concept of capitalist patriarchy which is a result of the work of the "Bielefeld School". Since patriarchy is much older than capitalism, necessarily research has to be done about the relationship between modern patriarchy and historical forms of patriarchy.

In the next chapter we are dealing with such a "periodization" of historical patriarchies and how they merged with the modern patriarchy – especially the western form of patriarchy.

The central concept which makes such a periodization possible is found in the idea and practice of Alchemy, which is defined as being the first general patriarchal natural science, technology, philosophy, religion, and psychology.

How did Alchemy find its way from antiquity and the Latin Middle Ages into European, Western modernity? How was it even able to grow so much that it is nowadays the determining characteristic regarding all dimensions of modern civilization? And how was it able to become a generalized phenomenon – as a patriarchal utopian project of a supposed better world and future?

This unique hypothesis contradicts most of the research done on Alchemy until today. In this paper, it can only be treated in its general aspects. A detailed historical analysis is still in the making (von Werlhof, man.). The analysis of Alchemy is and will be the core of the "Critical Theory of Patriarchy", as it can be applied to each discipline of modern natural and social sciences, as it is and will be able to answer many of still unresolved questions, even of those that

---

[*] Translation from German by Danny Lewis (based on C. v. Werlhof 1997), lectured by Nicholas Faraclas and revised by the author in 2009

have not been asked yet, and as it is and will especially be able to explain the inevitable failure of modern civilization. Interestingly the popular and even academic belief that alchemical thinking, acting and believing was eradicated centuries ago still exists.

Introduction

Why is it that we in the West have such a hard time conceptualizing alternatives to corporate globalization, particularly Maria Mies' "Subsistence Is The Alternative" – SITA? I contend that the difficulties that we have in imagining alternatives stem directly from the fact that especially women, nature, and the colonies have been subjected to domination, exploitation and also a fundamental *transformation*. The concept we normally use to refer to this exploitative, violent, and sexist history is "patriarchy" (along with its flipside "matriarchy"). In my opinion, patriarchy has not yet been fully analyzed, and I will therefore attempt to deepen this analysis in order to redefine the very concept of patriarchy.

Patriarchy has neither been *systematically* related to other significant phenomena of our society nor has it been interpreted as a system of changing and multifunctional concrete politics in every day life as well as on a general social level. In one word, it has been *underestimated* as an interdisciplinary historical category and reality. Patriarchy has not vanished with progress. On the contrary, it is developing with progress: It is progress itself! Capitalism is only the latest stage of patriarchy and not its contradiction, as many people (especially women) seem to believe today. So we live in a society that should be defined as "capitalist patriarchy".

My contribution to this theoretical debate consists in the use of the seemingly obsolete historical concept of *"alchemy"*. In relating alchemy to patriarchy, however, I found the "key" (the key is the main symbol of alchemy) not only to understand the history and concrete versions of patriarchy, but also the forms of patriarchal behaviour, of concrete patriarchal politics towards people, women, nature, society, and the world in general. In one word: I found out that alchemy is the "method" of patriarchy. Using this method, politicians, technocrats, scientists and experimenters try to transform the world not just into a modern one, but also into a patriarchal one. This way patriarchy has become what I call an "Alchemical System".

I will first consider religion, namely Christianity, and how it is related to alchemy and to the violence of capitalist patriarchy. In reality, we in the West believe in violence. The "Alchemical System" as the form, capitalist patriarchy has developed, can only survive because people put all their faith in it. Therefore the question is how to rid ourselves of this misguided and self-destructive belief. Only then can our eyes be opened to real alternatives to the limited choices that global capital is forcing us to accept. I am sure that my friend Maria Mies will like this approach as an extension of her own analysis of "Patriarchy and Accumulation on a World Scale" (Mies 1986).

The thesis

Is it possible to say that our economics and technology, capitalism, is the practical side of our religion, Christianity? Is it possible to say that with capitalism society has assumed the Christian goal and task of proving the existence of God? If so, what would "God" then be?

From this point of view our economics and technology would actually be a form of religious practice, while our religion would, in truth, be an economic and technological theory. However, whereas this is not necessarily true for all systems of economics and for all religions, it could nonetheless be true for us in the west (see Weber 1993).

If our hypothesis about such a narrow relationship between capitalism and Christianity is true, then we would need to abandon this faith in order to be able to change the economic and technological order. In the search for real alternatives we therefore are required to liberate ourselves from a set of beliefs. But what is wrong with our beliefs?

If we begin with the results, then we are certainly forced to admit that our modern economic and technological system, capitalism (including socialism) as "modernity", is in fact systematically destroying the earth: the final outcome having much less to do with "God", than with the question of ecology (Brown/Ayres 1998).

On the other hand, if we focus on religion, we see, surprisingly, that at least our religious institutions, paramount among them the Church, are apparently not at all opposed to this destruction. In any case, the Church seen as the centre of a world power has until now said or done very little about the ecological problem (as exception see Drewermann 1991). Of course, this is not true for many Christian grass-root movements around the world or for feminist theology. But these groups did not succeed in changing the attitude of the "top ten" of the church. At first glance this might seem very surprising, because it is "God's creation" which is being destroyed, and we would expect the Church as such stand up and say, "Stop! We can't do this". Yet this seldom happens, let alone is it followed by concrete political acts. In my opinion this is tantamount to saying that the Church, along with most other institutions – like the majority of the governments, political parties, trade unions, entrepreneurs and social movements

– is in agreement with the destruction that is happening. The real question is: "Why?" We must take the lack of the Church's response very seriously, and we cannot make excuses by saying that the Church has only forgotten to respond or does not properly understand that the earth is gradually being destroyed, or that a distinction must be made between the Church and Christianity, or between the Church and its members. Thus I have to conclude that the Church – in theory and in practice – is in agreement with the destruction of the earth by the modern economic and technological system (see Hunke 1987). So, having faith either in our religion or in capitalist progress is to have faith in the destruction that corporate globalization is visiting on the earth.

The patriarchal project

From this perspective, the Church and Christianity on the one hand and the capitalist system on the other hand appear in reality as one and the same project. I call it "The patriarchal project". But, what is it that both are attempting to achieve, and by which practical method? How can this explain the negative results for most of us and our planet?

I will hereafter refer to this common denominator of Christian religion and capitalist system as "Patriarchy". Thus, for me the first and most central question is: what is patriarchy really? As of yet there has been no proper definition of patriarchy which can offer an explanation for the observable relationship between Christianity and capitalism.

"Pater" and "arché"

If one examines the word patriarchy from a literal viewpoint – and this is always a good starting-point, because the names of things are no accident – we see that it is a combination of the words *pater* and *arché*. Pater means "father", and arché basically means "origin", "beginning", or also, in a concrete sense, "uterus". Over the centuries the meaning of "arché" shifted to include "power, rule, domination", which of course is something rather different. We generally only think of this second meaning when we see the word "arché", thus patriarchy and matriarchy translate to mean "rule of fathers" or "rule of mothers", and accordingly we wrongly think of matriarchy as society ruled by mothers/women. This, however, is a condition which has never existed: in any case there is no evidence of it in pre-patriarchal societies anywhere on our earth (see Weiler 1993, Lerner 1991; Göttner-Abendroth 1988; Meier-Seethaler 1992; Eisler 1993). Correspondingly, many people wrongly explain and justify patriarchy as the logical reverse of "mothers'"/or "women's rule".

Much of this confusion can be eliminated if we return to the older meaning of arché. With the older meaning in mind, matriarchy translates simply as "in the beginning the mother" (see Göttner-Abendroth ibid). All life originates from and is born of mothers, *in the last instance of Mother Earth*. This is and always has been simply the state of things here on earth, a fact which banal may seem at first glance, but which has potentially paradigm-shattering implications. With that in mind, the concept of patriarchy, translating as "in the beginning the father", seems like a strange notion. This would be like saying that fathers are the originators of life, i.e., fathers are men with uteruses. Suddenly patriarchy, pater arché, seems like a seriously more complicated and difficult concept than that of mater arché, or matriarchy, because it is not referring to any concrete event, fact, or state of things. Therefore pater arché cannot be the reverse of mater arché, simply because it does not exist.

The second problem arises from the transformation of the meaning of arché from "origin" to meaning "rule, domination". First, a "right to rule" is deduced from the fact of origin. This could mean either the power of the body of the mother, of the female (e.g. Mühlmann 1984), or mother-power (Canetti 1986), or "mother-right" as well (Bachofen 1978). But in this case there is no "rule". Or possibly what is meant is that the maternal power, which by nature is necessary for nurturing, protecting, and accompanying new life until it is able to take care of itself, is replaced by a father's "right to rule". Either the father "rules" and assumes the power of the mother while she is giving birth, or the "father" makes his claim to the power because he himself is the one giving birth. This would mean a kind of "father's power". However, since fathers are not (yet) able to give birth and thus are not by nature "powerful" in this sense, we still have the problem of explaining which non-maternal birth and non-maternal ruling power we are talking about here.

Things are just as difficult when we look at the word "pater". In the discussion on patriarchy it is often not taken into account that – as far as we know – the word father did not even exist in pre-patriarchal society, and when it finally appears with patriarchy, it does not mean any of the things we usually associate with it. When the concept of father appeared in history, it did not mean the physical father who takes care of his children. The concept of father was from the beginning an abstract institutional one *instead*, a concept of hierarchy, rule and domination (e.g. von Braun 1990). The father appears from the beginning in connection with the concept of domination, the lawful ruler, God, something superhuman (see Freud 1974). The father concept thus did not necessarily mean physical fatherhood, and it did not originate in the sensual culture of matriarchies (here and elsewhere in the text I will use the term "matriarchy" with the concrete pre-patriarchal meaning "in the beginning the mother" rather than the mythical "rule of the mothers"). Only with this in mind can we understand that the concept of father is a purely *utopian* concept, in the sense that the "rule" of the "father" is: a) possible; b) desirable; c) so all-comprehensive that it could even include the maternal, real origin, the birth event; and/or d) no longer needs the maternal, because it has completely "replaced" it.

Patriarchy as Utopia

This way patriarchy is basically the expression of a *social utopia* which states that it is the father and not the mother, in the abstract institutional form of "fatherhood", i.e., as a supposed God or his "law", or even a "natural law", who creates life, or who ideally one day will be able to do so.

So patriarchy is in the end an unimaginable, incomprehensible, almost inexpressible claim totally unattached to and abstracted from the concrete conditions of earthly existence, going far beyond anything as banal as some sort of "birth envy". Its goal is nothing less than the transformation of the birth-giving female body into an all-producing and universally re-producible thing, to replace the birth-giving body with non-bodily, non-female machinery and claim this machinery to be the goal and end of human history. The same is true for Mother Nature and the earth herself. Patriarchy thus means "motherless society" and ends in the policy of attempting to replace the concrete mother/nature with the abstract father/"second" nature (Bruiger 2006). Only when we realize this can we really understand why patriarchy begins with matricide and the conscious killing of animals (see Weiler 1991; Tazi-Preve 1992; Wolf 1994), with the subjugation of maternal culture co-operative with nature, and ends by trying to replace it with an artificial social "design", which means to have finally replaced society and nature by a "system", the "machine" (Merchant 1987, Genth 2002).

This attempt at substitution is a true obsession which continues to haunt us and whose menace is as immediate and threatening as ever. Accordingly, as long as there are real, concrete mothers and independent natural processes in this world, patriarchy is not complete and does not really even exist. And so there is a continuous, repeated need to prove over and over again that the Father, as the "Also-Mother", lording over the world, i.e., God, as presented in all monotheistic religions (not just Christianity), really exists. Thus, from a religious point of view, the real "sin" of women and nature is simply the fact that they still are needed as mother/s because of the fact that life comes into the world only through their bodies. In Christian (or monotheistic) religion, all women are by nature sinners, unless, like Mary, they are mothers without sensual bodies or nine-month pregnancies. This is because in patriarchy a "spirit" does what is normally done by (fe)male bodies, a spirit which does not inhabit the supposedly "spirit-less" body and which enters it from outside in the form of a masculine-godly act, an act which also calls the latest reproduction technologies to mind, not to mention the many sperm-theories in the history of breeding (Aristotle et. al. in Treusch-Dieter 1990). In any case this vision presupposes a paradoxical separation of body and mind, matter and spirit, "mater"/mother and life. Just as Mary was the ideal image of a patriarchal Yet-Mother, we are also in possession of an even older image of the father as Also-Mother, namely the Egyptian pharaoh Echnaton, who, as the founder of the first monotheistic religion, the Egyptian religion "Aton", is said to be also the founder of Judaism (see Freud 1974). The god Echn-Aton appears as a pregnant man (see Wolf 1994). Thus from the very beginning of monotheistic religion we witness the claim of the Father uniting all into one, God as the "One and All". The "one and all" is no longer the cosmic all-mother, the goddess Nut, who interestingly enough had her name stolen and used – written backwards – as the name of the new reversed father religion. The so-called Father was established in her stead, a completely unnatural, contradictory and paradoxical artificial being placed in (and above) the world as a political theory about the goal and end of history. So, long before our present economical and technological system developed, the political theory of monotheism was accompanied by the politics of despotism, which from then on defined and determined the practical, daily methods for the realization of the patriarchal obsession of replacing the mother and Mother Nature. The ideological part of this system is that which we refer to as monotheistic religion (see Assmann 1998, Girard 1992).

Patriarchy is the concept of a utopian system which goes hand in hand with monotheistic religion. Patriarchy wants to construct a form of society which not only makes a claim, but also in the course of time attempts to prove it. This claim is non other than the assertion that the better, more divine world is the one inhabited by the pater arché, the "birth-giving" and thus legitimately ruling Father-God, or his "Father-Law", instead of the "natural right" of the mother and of the laws of nature (see von Werlhof 1996, Lauderdale 1996). But since the political theory of patriarchy, the rule of the birth-giving-origin-father, is purely a claim, it needs a whole system of proofs while at the same time calling for the actual realization of its utopia. This is necessary, because in the long run a whole civilization cannot be based on something which does not exist and which contradicts everything that our daily experience teaches us.

Patriarchy as violence

Thus it becomes typical and necessary for patriarchy to attempt to construct its own reality and that it speculates upon rather than explaining existing reality. This speculation goes along with a sort of "violent thinking" (Ernst 1986) which is formative for the reality it constructs. From that point on "violent thinking" is permanently connected to a politics of brutal force which will ruthlessly remake anything in its way which does not fit its theory. This practice of force and violence also turns up in science and technology, as well as, last but not least, in economics. From then on there is a constant effort to turn the world completely upside down, to transform nature, which is no longer regarded female-maternal, into something male-paternal (see Boehme 1988; Merchant 1987).

In recent history modern technology gives us a very clear picture of this. In particular, modern reproductive technology "reproduces" not so much actual life itself as the ideal process of life "production": the pregnancy machinery, or birth machine, in the true sense of the word, which in the end would function without the female body, or at least without parts of it (see Rifkin/Perlas 1983). This goes even so far as to include the fiction of the pregnant man (no matter how simple, stupid, and ugly this fiction might be), into whom birth-giving organs can be implanted. The perverse idea of an artificially pregnant man goes all the way back to the pharaoh Echnaton.

The same is true for all the intents to produce an "artificial life" outside of the human sphere in animal and plant-life and even within the machinery itself (Weizenbaum 1978, Rifkin/Perlas 1983).

Still today not all thinking takes place upon purely patriarchal lines, neither consciously nor unconsciously. But those who are busy shaping our destinies certainly do think in this way, as evident by their constant, unmitigated thirst for power and money, a fact for which we would otherwise have no explanation (see von Werlhof/ Schweighofer/ Ernst 1996).

We thus can say that the patriarchal project is both an ideological (religious, philosophical) and a practical (technological, political, economic, cultural) attempt to convert the entire world into its opposite, a world which would then be "better", more "divine", and more in line with what is assumed to be its own, real "evolutionary" tendencies. For this reason, from a religious as well as from a technological and economical perspective, the world appears as a place in need of improvement, an imperfect, "evil", "unclean", worthless, low, or somehow insignificant place. Thus there is always a basic need for redemption or salvation – not only *of* the world, but also *from* the world (see Kippenberg 1991). In patriarchal religions (beginning with the Gnosis: see Sloterdijk/Macho 1991; and also Buddhism) the world, all earthly existence, is seen as a form of suffering, and must be overcome, the most important difference among them being the way salvation is to be attained.

From a pre-Socratic viewpoint (see Ernst 1997), the world was originally a Garden of Eden, which is then lost: for we have been driven from Paradise. It is also believed that, although we might be able to construct a new paradise, we can never go back to the old one. And this is the point where the new concept of economics and technology comes into play: the construction of that new world, that new paradise. We can never be satisfied with the way the world (supposedly) is, with nature as it (supposedly) is, we can never be satisfied that nature is something "maternal", that life comes from the female. No, for us this seems to be something almost outrageous, even diabolical. This is why from the religious point of view all women and nature itself are seen as automatically "low" and "bad". This "fundamentalist" damnation of all that is female and/or natural (see Girard 1992) stems from the belief that women/nature should not bring forth life, but only God, the Father. In reality, nevertheless, heterosexual intercourse and sexual desire are necessary to the life-process, as well as to the entire scope of bodily, spiritual, intellectual, and sensual experience, all the things which are capable of uniting men, women, and children in a completely non-patriarchal way, in a this-worldly, erotic and creative community (see Schubart 1989). Patriarchy's task is thus to break the power of the senses, the power of sense, and to get rid of the entire bodily sphere, along with all life-celebrating emotions and sensibilities. What is meant is the dulling of the senses and the replacement of the sensual world, of sense itself, with an un-sensual, sense(s)less world in which all sensibility has been lost, a world which makes no sense (see Kutschmann 1986), and a world that has nothing to do with original nature any more.

And thus we can explain why the patriarchal project, beginning with its very basic concept of "pater arché", is such a thoroughly violent one, making use of the most systematic, all-inclusive, and thoroughgoing violence in all of known history; why it has grown to such insane proportions and spread itself so globally: and why it is a thoroughly irrational project in which all of rationality itself is used as a tool to achieve its irrational and illusionary ends of turning the entire globe upside down along with all previous culture, and of changing nature into something which it exactly is not: an *anti-nature*. And this is what women-kind, or people in general, still do not grasp: the perpetuators of this system are dead serious, *they really mean it.*

What we are dealing with here is not the denial of the testing or of the development of something new, as many voices perhaps would say. What needs to be recognized is that this something new which patriarchy is seeking is really something thoroughly *opposed* to the world, something inimical, perverted, and destructive for it. We cannot seriously desire that everything non-patriarchal be destroyed and eventually be prevented from existing at all (Deschner 1994; Ullrich 1980; von Paczensky 1970; Illich 1982, 1983).

In the meantime we quietly assume that the new is better than the old, no matter how, why, or at what cost this "new" is constructed. Where living beings are constantly suffering injury, we ought to be hearing alarm bells ringing everywhere, but this alarm is not heard: Destruction supposedly has a creative aspect, or will be followed by "creation". See for example the concept of the world-renowned Austrian economist Joseph Schumpeter who literally speaks of "creative destruction" (Schumpeter 1962). All that religious guilt, so present otherwise, is gone here, because Christianity is not concerned at all with any of these questions. Instead, the crimes against nature, against women, matricide, the murder of "sweet and wise body", the murder of women's culture and of Eros – these are the very goals of the patriarchal project and the prerequisites for its achievement. Thus the persecution of witches has never really stopped – it just changed shape (Kimmerle 1980) – yet no one seems to feel very guilty about it, there is no evidence of any strong present or future feeling of responsibility, neither in the Church nor among men in general. So, the murder of women appears as a somehow normal and understandable event in criminal history, too (see Trube-Becker 1987). From the logic of this point of view it is – to the contrary – sinful to love women and not to punish them, and to love nature instead of trying to dominate it.

Patriarchy and "improvement" ("evolution", machinery)

The patriarchal utopia could therefore not be realized as long as (unless) women/nature still did (not) exist, except in some "improved", i.e., perverted, form, twisted through some unspeakable method, some new form which has nothing at all to do with the reality of nature or of women. When everything is seen as evil – the human being, especially women and nature - then this legitimizes the right to "improve" them, make them "ripe" for civilization, or to "cleanse" the world of them. This principle of human "evolution" is very obvious if we look at all sexist, racist, and especially educational practices (Dressen 1982; Hammer 1997).

To this end the human being, the world, nature and women, must – firstly – all be *transformed* into something really evil, a dirty, low or bad matter, not only ideologically but also empirically, in reality. This is the initial task of religion, technology, politics, and economy. Without first undergoing degradation, there would have been no need for "improvement". However, the original act of degradation, of "making out" something to be bad, i.e., making it bad, leaves some pretty irreversible results. That is how it is supposed to be, so that afterwards almost anything would seem to be an improvement. We see the same thing happening in the destruction of the jungle, in land erosion and desertification due to modern farming and mining-techniques, or in the "breeding" of "ennobled" species and "races" (Chargaff 1988).

After having degraded the world and its beings one has a justification for their improvement or even replacement. Investment in "human capital" seems to liberate us from the "risks" living beings mean for the system. It seems to be able to produce a purified, healthy, happy and perfect life "free" from suffering (Bergmann 1992): a life which has been transformed into machinery. In this way we have become accustomed to accepting a new primitiveness, brutality and irrationality, combined with a planned ignorance – the totalitarian outcome of "violent thinking".

Thus economics – in conjunction with technology – appears to be the secular arm of the patriarchal project, as originally formulated theologically in religion and politically-philosophically in politics. Despite its claims of having left all its irrational and religious aspects behind it, it seems that capitalism today, in exact continuity with religious patriarchal thought, is attempting to take that very same religious patriarchal utopia and turn it into reality: to prove the existence of One (male) God and to create a "divine" world as the realization of Utopia, the "good", the "beautiful", and the "true" world, a new "Paradise" on earth (compare with Plato 1962).

Patriarchy as scarcity

It thus becomes apparent why our modern system defines itself in terms of the task of overcoming scarcity (Illich 1982; Gronemeyer 1988; Sachs 1993). There are, however, two interesting aspects to this scarcity. One of these, which as far as I can discover has never been examined, is the "*scarcity of patriarchy*". For, there simply are no "birth-giving" fathers, nor are there any real substitutes for nature, nor any nature-less, motherless worlds. One can thus say that patriarchy itself is in fact scarce, extremely scarce. What is utopian about patriarchy is that it is presented as normality, as anything but scarce. In order to prove this one tries to make it plentiful. Not only much money and giant masses of commodities in a literal "production-battle" are the outcome, but also "great" men (Godelier 1987) and many small "lords", as well as conception and fertilization theories which claim – the same way as in antiquity already – that it is only the male sperm which carries life, and that women are merely "black boxes" for its transformation and growth (see Treusch-Dieter 1990). It constructs a "second nature", no longer born as "natura naturata" from "natura naturans" any more, not self-creating nature, but rather a "nature" put upon or forced into nature, an artificial un- or anti-nature. Like Ernst Bloch one could say, patriarchal civilization moves in the world like "an army in the enemy's territory" (1967). In the meantime even women see their bodies and their ability to give birth as something unimportant, ugly or old-fashioned; to the point that they themselves campaign its abolishment and replacement through industry (see the "gender" approach of Firestone 1975 to Haraway 1995).

There is also a second aspect to the overcoming of scarcity through capitalism, one which has been well-documented. I am referring to the fact that scarcity, i.e., need, which the economic system is supposed to free us from, is actually caused by it, i.e., created through policies of monopolization, accumulation, and destruction (see Bergfleth 1992; Mies/von Werlhof 1999). On the one hand we possess an entire artificial wealth of means and products, and on the other hand we see an unbearable, artificially-produced scarcity of these very means and products, as well as the supposed lack of any alternatives to them. This becomes especially obvious when we look at the means and products which are basic and essential for life (see von Werlhof 1983; Krieg 1980; Mies/Shiva 1993). Economics presents itself as the saviour, but it actually creates the problem it is supposed to save us from (see George 1980; Imfeld 1985). This is essential to the general acceptance of the economic program. Only then, when misery, disaster, infertility, and destruction, i.e., a scarcity of paradise, really do exist, is there also the necessity for constructing a "better world" with less scarcity, a new paradise: but this time a paradise that is assumed to never disappear – like "evolution".

The belief in progress is going to run into the last form of scarcity which emerges when non-renewable resources are unlimitedly looted, always more species go extinct and soils and waters have irreversibly died.

So, in reality, things go the opposite way than pre-supposed. Instead of heaven we are inventing hell on earth.

Patriarchy as metaphysics

This cynicism of producing scarcity through accumulation and destruction leads to a *delusion*: that it would be possible and recommendable to construct a new world which, in the final analysis, would certainly be a metaphysical one, beyond physics, beyond the body, matter, the mother (physein in Greek also means to give birth), i.e., beyond all of nature (Shiva 1989). The incredible strength of our faith in this patriarchal religion is revealed in our acceptance of the nihilistic notion that the existing world must first be destroyed in order to get a better one: for, what happens if this self-generated natural catastrophe, this apocalypse, only ends in a big "self-made" Nothing – instead of God, instead of the world as a "functioning machinery"? And much seems to speak for this eventuality (see Schütz-Buenaventura 2000). It is an incontestable fact that there is not even a shred of evidence for any credible replacement for this Nothing on the horizon. The project of the supposed conquest of nature, originally expressed in religious terms as God's instruction to Adam to "rule over the earth", has ended in her accelerating retreat (see Colburn et. al 1996).

But, our behaviour towards nature and women remains the same, and the legitimization of this behaviour remains the same, although everyone knows what a lie it is. The "valuation" of nature means the destruction of its real value, its transformation into waste. Patriarchal thinking has "penetrated" our consciousness so deeply that it is nearly impossible for us to imagine anything other than the destruction and subsequent "improvement" of the world, even when we see that this is not possible. For example, the mention of the "curse" of technology is always countered with mention of its apparent "blessings", which are nothing but short-lived illusions of "improvement" that can only be sustained if we manage to ignore the violence and degradation that was necessary to produce them and/or is their consequence. Yet there is only one real alternative to this dire situation: the acceptance of nature as it is, and a relationship with it based on this acceptance (see Mességué 1989). This acceptance is prerequisite to any co-operation with her. But this sort of reasoning has not been possible in our "reasonable" age and civilization. We are no longer (even) capable of recognizing what nature is, and (even less capable) of knowing who women are.

The method of patriarchy: Alchemy

In a second step I deal with the methods used to set up the patriarchal utopian dream as a "concrete" utopian world and to prove this "new world" through religion and belief-systems and, particularly, through economics and technology. That there must be such a method clearly follows from the fact that patriarchy, as a utopian theory, initially does not exist; it is a *"wannabe"*. Patriarchy as a social system must remain unproven as long as reality does not conform to the theory or to the utopia. Patriarchy is always in need of a proof, especially over the longer term, for we have often seen that mere terror and lies will not work forever in keeping people in bounds, and intimidation and deception alone will never turn them into true believers in patriarchy. All over the world we can still hear women laughing – those that still are able to laugh – at the male patriarchal version of how life is created and of what a tremendous role they play in it (see Diotima in Plato 1985). Moving beyond the religious or ideological expressions of patriarchy one has always felt the need to put its theory into practice through politics, technology, science, and economics, in order to prove the correctness of its hallucinations. And in fact, from the beginning in all of patriarchy's theories, even in philosophy and in other supposedly nonreligious disciplines, we have seen the attempt to formulate patriarchy's perverted train of thought in such a way as to expand the *faith* in the correctness of its claims, although – or perhaps because – there can be no real *knowledge* of these claims (see Hunke 1987). And so we have here a system of belief which is considered as particularly divine and which must be maintained over and against everything we know. This faith begins where there is no knowledge, and where knowledge cannot exist. The absurd can only be believed, it cannot be known: "credo quia absurdum" (Galtung 1995). In the long term, however, the problem of the practical realization of the theory plays an increasingly important role. How can a patriarchal world really be brought about, so that faith in it, permanently precarious, can be replaced by "concrete" knowledge of it?

After examining various natural sciences and the history of technology, I have gradually come to the conclusion that the method for realization of patriarchy was and still is *alchemy*. Alchemy, as a kind of all-comprehensive theology, philosophy, psychology and technology is the key to the question of *how* patriarchy puts its theory into practice, in all areas and at all levels of society.

The word alchemy goes back to the Arab word "keme", the meaning of which includes "the black mud of the Nile". The annual flooding of the Nile left behind thick layers of this black mud on its banks, making them fertile. Through nature's chemistry of mixing water and earth new life was created. Alchemy must originally have been the attempt to observe this natural phenomenon, to understand it, to help it along, and to imitate it. This is most likely the phase of the pre-patriarchal alchemy of gardeners and peasants, of men and women who wished to help this process along and co-operate with this natural process, without changing the principles behind it (e.g., the early notion of the Garden Eden or the famous "Hanging Gardens" of Queen Semiramis).

Alchemy is known to us through the history of religion, philosophy, psychology and technology. It has existed throughout the world in many forms. Most certainly alchemy had its origins in ancient matriarchal cultures and over time became more and more patriarchalized and perverted – turned into its opposite. There is much evidence of alchemical practices and theories in China, India, Africa, Middle East, and throughout Europe, especially in Eastern and South-Eastern Europe (see Eliade 1980; Jung 1985; Binswanger 1985; Bologne 1995; Gebelein 1996; Biedermann 1991; Schütt 2000). But as far as I can discover, there have been no attempts until now to examine alchemy from the perspective that I have suggested here. Thus I am crossing into new territory, at least subjectively. However the time appears ripe to attempt an initial thesis on the role of alchemy in patriarchy and vice versa, and later to substantiate these beginnings with further research (von Werlhof 2000a).

Whereas our economy, the "capitalist world system" (Wallerstein 1974, 1986, 1989), appears to be the practical side of our religion with the goal of achieving patriarchy by adding "In the beginning was the father" to the idea of "paradise", then alchemy, according to the thesis, is the concrete method for achieving this goal.

Let us examine what the method of alchemy is. The central concept in Egyptian alchemy, going back much more than 5000 years is the key (Binswanger 1985). Egyptian alchemy actually saw itself as the key to deciphering the world. I will similarly use alchemy as the key to the interpretation of the method for constructing patriarchy.

Patriarchal alchemy

The principles of nurturing and co-operation of early alchemy are entirely different from those of patriarchal alchemy, such as the production of the so called "materia prima", (or) "massa confusa" or "nigredo" on the one hand, and of "dissolve and combine", in Latin "solve et coagula" on the other hand. The "materia prima" is the outcome of a process in which the alchemist wants to go back to the supposed origins of matter. For this purpose he has to "blacken" and to dissolve all matter mostly by using fire, producing the so called "nigredo" which is supposed to be the all including original substance of matter. In other words, the alchemist starts with bringing death to matter. This process is called "mortification", from latin "mors" = death (Bologne 1995). It is no coincidence that blacksmiths and all forms of pyro-techniques played a special role in alchemy, (Eliade 1980), and that women, seen as witches, were burned.

After that, according to the principle of "dissolve and combine", "elements" like mercury in a first and sulphur in a second step, in the case of metals, are recombined with the materia prima – here mostly lead – which through this procedure is supposed to gain the "higher" level as silver or the highest as gold.

It is the same process which in the social sciences we refer to as "divide and rule". This is also the principle of patriarchal technology. The "raw" material first undergoes the process of abstraction, dissolution and "death" (filtering, isolation). The "mortificated" substances are then combined with other substances that have been "abstracted" from their natural surroundings (see Ernst 1993). This method anticipates machine technology (Mumford 1977), which, although appearing much later, does the same thing (see Bammé et al.

1983). Machine technology shares with alchemy this principle of separation and "purification" of "elements" (see the experiment in sciences), as well as the principle of producing "raw materials" primarily as "resources" first of all. Here we have a context, a common ground, reaching through various epochs and expressing itself in the development of various periods of patriarchal thought, intention, and practice. Thus alchemy shows up right within the capitalist system, despite the fact that our modern world claims to have left the superstitious and ignorant or naive method which alchemy is labelled to be, far behind it. The reason is that alchemy failed to succeed in producing the "highest", "godly" matters: *gold and life*. Nobody would therefore want to relate to it any more.

But if we compare alchemy with the modern experiment it is obvious that there are many similarities.

The central principles of "blackening" and of "dissolve and combine" are those of force and violence. They require sacrifice, that of matter e.g. nature, and that of people, especially women (Eliade 1980). The isolation of so-called "elements" as "pure" substances (characteristic of modern chemistry as well), comprises the "construction" *on the basis of* the destruction of the "materia prima", reducing it to essences which do not occur in nature. Alchemy goes about its work of producing new, "improved" substances and materials by combining these "pure" substances with the raw material of the materia prima and with one another.

The alchemist completes his *"great work"* through the so-called "chemical" or "holy marriage" of matter. "Holy marriage" is a metaphor taken from matriarchal culture. Whereas "holy marriage" originally was the coming together of the goddess and her hero in a great celebration of Eros from which all life springs and is confirmed (see Weiler 1993), in alchemy it appears as a connection between, and forced upon, artificially abstracted substances characterized as either "male" or "female" (e.g., gender as a truly "social construction"; see Jung 1985). For example, the blacksmith often was responsible for circumcision, thus producing "pure" sexes (see Wolf 1994). The ceremony is no longer one of the mixing of the natural manifoldness and polarity of matter (materials) as a "great work" of nature, it is the forced putting together of artificial opposites (see Ernst 1993; 1996), from which the "great work" of the alchemists springs. The alchemist sees himself (here) as the true creator, as the procreator of a completely new kind of "higher" matter or life. He sees himself as a sort of new "great mother", or rather, God. Apparently in the name of the latter, like the priest at a wedding, he completes the holy ritual in the "sacrament" of bringing the couple together. Only from this established act of bringing together – and, correspondingly, the first sexual act is only permitted following this ceremony – springs something (entirely) new, so it is supposed, in particular new life (see "heterosexual reproduction"). This life is even defined as a "higher" one than "normal life" as it is based on the sacrifice of the woman's life, because she is denied in her self-creative power and by ritual "mortification" reduced to the "raw material" for the "creation" of the alchemist.

However, the whole principle of the combination of pure substances or "elements" with the materia prima as raw material seems all the more puzzling in that "pure" substances as well as the mortificated material prima are essentially dead ones, from which no life is very likely to grow. And so patriarchy is in principle *barren* (see Colburn et al. 1996). This fact is gradually being noticed by modern chemistry which has begun mixing its pure substances with "impure", living ones (Rifkin/Perlas 1983).

But the supposedly higher life is meant to come into being in a way that makes the alchemist, rather than nature or women, appear as the "divine creator" (c.f. patents on life forms). And above all, the alchemist's goal is to construct not just any (old) new life, but rather a very special new form of life which is not only supposed to be better, but which also leads to the discovery of the so-called "philosophers stone" – the "tincture", the "elixir", the "powder" – all terms for the "quintessence", the "fifth" element or final "essence", with which all matter can be transformed into the most valuable of all matter: gold, meaning: "life". Finding life in its "pure" form is the ultimate goal of all alchemical filtering.

The purpose of alchemists, however, is not to promote and protect life and fertility. It needs the philosopher's stone in order to get hold of the "essence of life" which is thought to be lurking somewhere inside all matter. Here, the pre-patriarchal experience in the unity of matter and mind is still maintained. But the (eventual) rejection of this unity is foreshadowed by the attempt made by the alchemist to *produce and to get hold of a combination of the highest matter with the highest spirit*. This is the *philosopher's stone*. It seems to be the pure power of life in a material form, with which one believes to be able to produce living beings even beyond nature and women: the so-called "homunculus", the small human often depicted as sitting in a test tube. Homunculus would be, so to speak, the first successful test tube baby, a creation of the alchemist experimenter – something that has never really (happened or) existed. For example, Paracelsus, the famous alchemist and physician of the 16th century, still tried to produce new life by combining male sperm with human (female?) blood (see Paracelsus 1990). Similar experiments using alchemical methods have taken place through the centuries up until the present day (von Worms 1988).

Unlike earlier, pre-patriarchal "alchemy" with its principle of co-operation with nature, what we see here is an attempt at the *usurpation* of the female pregnancy and birth process, not only in theory, but also in *reality*, an attempt to "improve" them and "replace" them with something else. This is what we have previously referred to as the attempt to prove the existence of God: the proof that a male, omnipotent creator *above* matter really does exist. For previously there were only female gods and female creators *within* matter.

Until today the patriarchal belief has been maintained. Modern scientists are using alchemical principles today as well and are still attempting the same thing. Since earlier times, nevertheless, they have not succeeded in proving the existence of a metaphysical God and have not brought about a "male" creation of (new) life as it springs from nature and from women. In this sense alchemy has been a failure, but it has in its current form – in "chemistry", physics and the scientific experiment in general – produced something else, namely artificial forms of a so called *"life", partly "created" beyond the cycles of nature – like clones and "in vitro"-fertilized embryos* – effectively retaining all of the former goals and methods of alchemy. The main question, however, remains: Can these anti-natural "life" forms *"replace"* life and nature *on the basis of the destruction* of which they have been and are "created"? Only when this question can be answered with Yes, this would be a proof for the existence of "God", be he beyond the world or within it – namely in the form of the modern alchemist as a "demiurg" himself. But as far as we can see, the logical answer is No. *"Creation out of destruction"* can, of course, not replace creation as such (Chargaff 1988).

Alchemy, capitalism (speculation) and individual identity

Let us now turn to alchemy as the patriarchal method in the field of economics (itself). The Swiss economist Hans Christoph Binswanger, in his book "Geld und Magie" (money and magic), discusses the connection between modern economics and alchemy – without, however, any reference to patriarchy (1985). For Binswanger, Goethe's "Faust" symbolizes modern capitalist economics as an alchemical process. The goal is a new creation out of nothing, which in the end is supposed to be possible as a pure abstraction. Whereas previous alchemists attempted to reduce matter to its supposed "basic essence", last but not least gold, i.e., to suggest that gold, the "pure metal", respectively "life as such", is the ultimate essence of matter – this would be a good place to apply the term "essentialism" –, modern economy for its part starts with the belief that gold is the ultimate value and most convincing symbol of wealth and power. After the invention of paper-money this belief changes from having gold = having power over life, to having money = having power over life (see Binswanger 1985 and Beiträge zur feministischen Theorie und Praxis, 1985). This way the belief is changing into speculation: the belief in a piece of paper. This means to attempt to change even paper, or just "information", as today, back into money or gold, and last but not least into life/power over life, be it now or in the future. Whereas in alchemy real materials served as the basis, today the belief in the potential of paper – currency notes – or information must suffice to serve as the claim to the treasure, namely gold and life. And thus, in our economic system, money as a form of "capital", even more so than gold or life as such, by the time is raised up as the "better matter", if not the philosopher's stone, and its existence then, logically, represents the proof of the supposed existence of God.

In the real world, money, as the new philosopher's stone (itself), appears to be the means for turning everything else into money as well. Money appears to be life itself, or the cosmic life power, which can incite or force the continual production of something new, even something previously unknown. Money "is born" through the "alchemical" mixing of land and labor, later increasing (even) more by being mixed again with capital, itself the "product" of labour and land. Capital, soil and labour are filtered out of the world and of human existence as more or less "pure substances". As such they exist in the form of the "labourer", the cultivated field, *"Blut und Boden"* as parts of the alchemical machinery. They amalgamate to form new "life", the commodity as *fetish* (see Marx 1974). The commodity, rather than any other "antiquated" form of life, seems to guarantee, even to be, a new and "better" form of life. (Later) The same increasingly applies to machines, which today are referred to as "beings" – this is the "essentialism" of the "post modern" discourse –, while human beings are conversely regarded as post-human "systems" (see Weizenbaum 1978). This way the machine is qualified as a sort of a new and "better" or "higher" life, whereas life is regarded as a lower form of organized matter.

Money really does begin to seem like a kind of philosopher's stone, because it keeps this process in motion, in particular by mobilizing people as "labour" and placing them at the service of the alchemical process of turning – their – life into money/capital while at the same time succeeding at keeping them faithful to the beliefs that underpin the system, namely that they contribute to "improve" not only their own lives, but also the life of the whole society. The separation (abstraction) of humans from their surroundings by so-called "original accumulation", i.e., their separation from land and other means of production – from the alchemical point of view their "mortification" – forces them to concentrate all their productive capabilities onto the production of pure "human material", the "labour power", and to reduce all their hopes and desires to the goal of making money like a modern alchemist, or of placing themselves at his disposal as "pure substances". And the women have to play the part of the general "materia prima" without developing into "pure substances", having been transformed from witches into "housewives". So, the women were forced into sacrifice and then had to continue to sacrifice themselves in the process of patriarchal "life-production": Going all the way from mothers to "mother-machines" (Corea 1980), they are even told to have become a more essential part in the male creation of life-process, a sort of a new pure substance, whereas in reality they contribute to the alchemical aim of being in the end totally replaced by machines. This indeed would be the ultimate sacrifice of women: the general murder of the mother *as such*.

"Homo oeconomicus" and "femina domestica" (Illich 1982) are the product of a total mobilization in service of the artificial "uterus". This way they seem to regard themselves as a kind of philosopher's stone, which each individual in the economic "melting pot" of human raw materials has created in, "for", and "of himself": "self-realization" is a word for "self-alchemization". Nowadays everybody has become his/her own alchemist – see the truly alchemical notion of "gender". Individualization seems to mean to become ones own alchemist ("*alchemization*"). This is the *generalization* of alchemy instead of its retreat from the world which supposedly happened when modernity began (Schütt 2000).

Today, the stated goal of people is to do anything for money, to be eternally "prepared" for money, in order to have a God-related, "self-determined" modern "piece of life" (Duden 1991). And the necessity of this goal, including the faith in it, is what defines the person as a "homo christianus": a "good Christian", someone to be found especially among the prosperous, who are considered to be God's chosen ones. According to Calvin, to have money is proof of the proper faith in God's existence, for He has provided those riches, and He does not do the same for everyone. *Faith in God and faith in money* has become one and the same thing. It becomes a (matter of, a) proof of faith when the individual spends all his time and thought on nothing other than making money. Otherwise one is regarded as heretic, immoral or vagabond (see the debates in Weber 1993; Foucault 1977; Dreßen 1982; Schütz-Buenaventura 1996). Faith itself, Christianity, through its connection with modern economics, becomes a kind of philosopher's stone. For, where there is a (permanent) lack of money, this lack is replaced by faith, which assumes the task of calming the poor and the losers, while at the same time motivating them to continue doing exactly that which caused their misery in the first place.

The fact that everyone is busy doing the same thing, is searching for the same "main thread", is characterized later by Adam Smith as being God's secular will set in motion and directed by the great "invisible hand" (see Smith 1823). It is as if the new cooperation between economics and religion were a holy act, although it should more appropriately be regarded as a "black mass" or "conjuring the devil". And thus the murderous egoism of each individual, which is thus systematically brought to the fore, appear afterwards to be beneficial for society, socially good and (socially) valuable, part of a good or godly society, in any case as a part of the best of all possible worlds. What other social system and religion has ever managed to view humankind as bad, to literally make them bad, and to push this fact off as an *improvement* or as "evolution" of humankind, as the triumph of humankind over nature? (e.g. Hobbes 1984, Locke 1970). How is it possible that the "mind who wants the evil" – violent thinking = alchemical thinking – nevertheless "creates the good"? (c. f. Ernst 1986) – the answer is: It has not been possible!

With the *great alchemist reversal*, we finally have the explanation for modern Europe's success at and through its colonization of most parts of the world. Who else among the world's peoples were individually and collectively as mobile, laborious, arrogant, active, unscrupulous, merciless, violent, convinced of their mission to bring real i.e., patriarchal civilization to the entire world: united, like an army, oriented towards a single goal, everywhere, permanently, and without needing even a command from above? (cf. Todorov 1980). The *alchemy of patriarchy*, especially in the *mixture of Christianity and capitalism*, has transformed the entire world, has turned it upside down. After all, it possessed "pure" Christian faith and "pure" cold economic calculation – God and Money – as "pure", abstract "substances", both originally separate things (and they still are made to appear as such today). And then they were put together in an unholy marriage built upon the decline of nature and women's culture: transformed into "capital" – money, command, machinery – as the proof of the existence of God.

The other result of this mixture is, however, not the noble Civilized Man and Paradise on Earth: on the contrary, the result rather resembles something like hell on an earth serving as a home for Dr. Jekyll and Mr. Hyde. Evil, the devil, sin, "scarcity", all those things from which religion claims to free us, and which economics claim to improve, are really produced by them, and then systematically spread throughout the world. Alchemy has not generated any jolly homunculus, or any gold; it has generated a menagerie of freaks and monsters, e.g., the god-fearing exploiter, the honourable mass murderer, the gentleman conqueror, the salvation-bringing missionary, the torturer in service of the good cause, the innocent rapist, and the creative maker of the atom bomb; it has invented such marvels as "creative destruction", war as the "father of all things", the "ethics" of degradation, the "morale" of repression, education to self-destruction, "modesty" as toleration of domination, violence in sexuality, cynicism as the "normal" intellectual posture, and war as a "humanitarian" act (Chossudovsky 1996; Klöss 1985; Daly 1970; Theweleit 1977; Easlea 1986; Sloterdijk 1983).

And yet, in patriarchy all of this is considered as neither evil, sinful nor diabolical, because, in contradiction to what really has taken place, patriarchy sees itself as the one and only instrument, the "weapon", against evil, sin, and the devil which it sees lurking everywhere in nature, in life, in everything feminine, sensual and erotic, and ultimately in the very world itself. This is *the real distortion* of things.

The alchemical system, with its goal of patriarchy, has in the meantime become so internalized and is so strongly present in the back of the mind that for humankind, driven from its "paradise", there generally is no need of any external force for one to be squeezed into the alchemical mortification and purification process. The modern person continually "alchemizes" himself by transforming his "passions" into "interests" (see Hirschman 1987). And although his empirical experience tells him that his life does not seem to be improving and is neither becoming "precious", nor attaining a special "identity" or "individuality", but is in the end wasted, that his life is being hardened into something dead – Marx' s concept of capital as "past", "dead" labour –, he still hangs on to his *alchemical superstition* without knowing that the whole process is, as it always has been, nothing but a swindle (see von Werlhof 1983/92).

Even women, who ought to know better because it is still they through whom self-creating life enters the world without the assistance of any alchemy, have begun to believe this dangerous patriarchal non-sense. They, too, now wish to be "equal" with patriarchal men, as labourers, individuals, as possessors of commodities, sexuality, power and money. They want to catch up with men's supposedly more advanced development to make this development generally accessible, copy it, rather than to see to it that the insane notion of a "better" life be exposed as the *deadly illusion* it is. Many of them even accept the new reproductive technologies dealing with pregnancy, birth, and maternity, not realizing that the goal of these technologies is the final, last possible – or impossible – step towards their total removal from the "power to be", as well as the replacement and destruction of the last remaining form of life and subsistence which have not yet been split asunder. Many women today act as if they did not know what this means, as if the patriarchal attempts to construct a *motherless world* were possible, even desirable (Butler 1991)!

In the final analysis, of course, there is no such thing as the philosopher's stone. Money, God, the male "creator" and the faith in these things are all illusions. The belief in the philosopher's stone is the superstition that blinds us all to the strength and power with which we are naturally endowed from birth, the erroneous belief that drives us to seek strength and power instead in God, in money, in dead objects – capital – or in political and military "power". Indeed we cannot imagine finding strength and power within ourselves, unless and until our lives have somehow been "cleansed" of everything living. Thus we seem not to object in the slightest to sacrificing either ourselves or others, because we believe that it is all for the cause of the improvement of humankind and of the world. This explains the paradox of "progress" demanding sacrifices (Gambaroff et al. 1986). And from a theological point of view it seems that the sacrifice and further "higher existence" of Christ is seen as the "model" for our own alchemical transformation. Christ himself appears as *"Christus lapis"* (Jung 1985), as the "philosopher's stone" for the redemption of humanity.

In the modern world we only maintain the illusion of the effectiveness of the so-called philosopher's stone, because pure substances have been mixed not only with the "nigredo" of all sorts of raw materials as well as with other pure substances – as already invented in pre-modern patriarchal alchemy – but have also been combined with living ones, with life itself. Just as in chemistry: as long as the artificial fertilizer is not put into the fields, it will never have any effect; as long as no one uses those machines, they are only heaps of junk; and the artificially fertilized egg still needs a uterus for the embryo to develop. Without *impure life* there is still no outcome at all. This is of course why so much money is being spent on research in such areas as plant growth without earth, self-producing and self-maintaining systems – so-called artificial intelligence – as well as artificial birth machines. But in the meantime it has become obvious that patriarchal "new life" – beyond a simple cell-combination! – is not the better or even "higher" form of life at all, but it is a weak, susceptible, monotonous, dependent, primitive, reduced form of life, life without spirit/mind, machine-"life", a pseudo-life beyond the cycles of nature and therefore without a past and a future – not to mention the ecological destruction which generally seems to go hand in hand with it (see Chargaff 1988; Dahl 1989; Shiva 1992).

Paradoxically, this is becoming even more apparent in the most recent phase of alchemy, the combination of different, but living substances in genetic engineering and all sorts of biotechnology (called "algeny" by Rifkin 1983). This is essentially because artificial life can in a way "be made", but it would never be able to "replace" born life - and, may be, it even does not want it!

Alchemy without matter?

The power of money to force all of life into prostitution and to present this perversion as a quasi-religious act characterizes our system to be a kind of Christian pimping, or, in other words, shows up procuring (souteneuring) to be the real kernel of the patriarchal economic system, especially of capitalism. This means that western, Christian capitalism is a form of exploitation of peoples' life-powers and their alchemical transformation into the life power or -energy of others. In reality it is general *cannibalism*.

Where money is concerned, the alchemical procedure still appears to be a success – even after the breakdown of the financial markets. It is no accident that the word for a return on money is "interest". The money which comes to exist in the alchemical process of the modern economic system, capitalist money, appears to "give birth" to more money. Money has children and grandchildren, i.e., simple interest and compound interest. It really does seem to appear – to be "created" – almost out of nowhere, from pure abstraction. In the earlier stages of alchemy, as long as someone had to work in order to produce simple and compound interest, this was not the case. However, we can observe how interest is meanwhile being paid out on future, not yet accomplished, supposedly potential, production and services whose eventual realization we are required to simply believe in. Interest thus is actually coming out of a temporary nothing, a not-yet, it is a mortgage on the future which will soon be due for payment. Today, in the sphere of floating speculation – i.e., faith – capital is no longer directly connected to actual production processes (see Kennedy 1990). The material alchemical transformation process of economics seems to be no longer applicable, and is being temporarily replaced with an invisible, "non-material alchemy", alchemy without matter (see von Werlhof 1997). But it is alchemy nonetheless, although on a level of the "pure" mind – without matter – and "pure" theology – without nature (though matter and nature will play their role later, so to say, temporarily divided and postponed from the "production" process!). For, certainly the images of the goose who laid the golden egg, or of water transformed into wine, without anyone lifting a finger, amazingly still do not appear to incite people's doubts. On the contrary, alchemy appears to have finally reached its goal of creating a world in which milk and honey flow – for no reason: As if the self-creating original nature has finally really been replaced:

- by philospher's stones everywhere – a machinery out of which automatically flows all we want;
- by "pure" money that is not the result of work and the transformation of nature any more;
- by the "pure" mind, a sort of life -"energy" divided from matter;
- by the One-and-All God beyond the world, appearing in this world.

It even seems as if the "post-modern" economic system has only need of imaginary services in order to reach a stage, in which the philosopher's stone in the end apparently is made of only "pure thought" or "pure life" without matter. What progress for alchemy! Thought as a sort of "life power" or "energy" alone is now all that is needed. This is then seen as "intellectual development" and spiritual "energy supply". Would non-material alchemy not be the best proof that

God, the "Creator", patriarchy, really exist? And would alchemy without matter not be the best proof, that producing the Nothing via the destruction of the world is no problem at all, but to the contrary, that the Nothing is even God himself? In this case patriarchy would really have come through!

One simply assumes that it will all work out in the end, for everyone, and forever. What a rude awakening is in store for the "true believers"!

The necessary failure of the "Alchemical System"

One can say that in contrast to former times, alchemy as a method of thinking, feeling and acting has been expanded to all spheres of society, all sorts of production processes and all people living under modern conditions. Therefore it is justified to speak of the existence of an "alchemical system" today. Alchemy has progressed by means of generalization and "globalization" (see von Werlhof 2000b). Its methods of usurpation/negation, mortification/degradation, abstraction/isolation, perversion/"improvement", construction/production and speculation/nihilism seem to leave us without any alternative. After 5000 years of the alchemical implementation of the patriarchal project, we feel incapable of imagining that the world could function in another way.

But, meanwhile it is finally becoming obvious that the utopian project of constructing patriarchy, of creating the pater arché, is a true catastrophe. Our belief in alchemy is being shaken as we come to realize that countless human and nonhuman beings are being pushed towards their destruction and driven to extinction. Alchemy has never produced a better or even higher form of life without producing its opposite at the same time, nor has it come up with anything with which to replace the original form. The construction of patriarchy as an empirical fact rather than as a utopia has still not succeeded and is further from success than ever. (And) It cannot succeed, because the world is being ruined in the process. There is nothing after the devastation. From nothing comes nothing. The "scarcity", the waste, the loss of faith, they are all pointing to this fact. It makes room for a different, "dissident" world view, the scope of which is no longer anthropocentric and "andro"-centric. The "Goddess comes back" – the women say – though only to a world in which not only "holy water" is holy, but all water.

The first decisive step beyond the nihilistic-tautological forms of patriarchal thinking, feeling and doing would therefore be to finally stop believing that the destruction of the earth is not such a terrible thing after all, or will even lead to our redemption from nature: Yet it is believed that the world will be followed by something better, a "post-natural", "post-worldly", "post-human" paradise.

Seen worldwide, I think that we are already approaching the "critical mass" needed to rid ourselves of the alchemical belief in deadly miracles. Let us restore our view of the world by putting our feet back on the earth and turning our reality right-side-up again. Let us begin to celebrate the liberation of our earth, our bodies, our minds and our souls from the destructive faith in patriarchy, alchemy, and corporate globalization!

Bibliography

Assmann, Jan (1998) *Moses der Ägypter. Entzifferung einer Gedächtnisspur*, München: Carl Hanser
Bachofen, J. J. (1978) *Das Mutterrecht*, Frankfurt: Suhrkamp
Bammé, A. et al. (Eds) (1983) *Maschinen-Menschen, Mensch-Maschinen, Grundrisse einer sozialen Beziehung*, Reinbek: Rowohlt
Beiträge zur feministischen Theorie und Praxis (1985), Geld oder Leben?, No. 15/16
Bergfleth, G. (1992) Perspektiven der Antiökonomie, *Niemandsland. Zeitschrift zwischen den Kulturen*, Jahrg. 4, Heft 10/11: Tugendterror, pp. 251-259
Bergmann, A. L. (1992) *Die verhütete Sexualität, Die Anfänge der modernen Geburtenkontrolle*, Hamburg: Aufbau
Biedermann, H. (1991) *Lexikon der Magischen Künste. Die Welt der Magie seit der Spätantike,* München: Heyne
Binswanger, H. Ch. (1985) *Geld und Magie*, Stuttgart: Weitbrecht
Bloch, E (1967) *Das Prinzip Hoffnung*, Frankfurt a. M.: Suhrkamp
Böhme, H. (1988) *Natur und Subjekt*, Frankfurt a. M.: Suhrkamp
Bologne, J.-C. (1995) *Von der Fackel zum Scheiterhaufen. Magie und Aberglauben im Mittelalter*, Solothurn/Düsseldorf: Walter
Braun, C. von (1990) *NichtIch, Logos-Lüge-Libido*, Frankfurt: Neue Kritik
Brown, L. and E. Ayres (1998) *World Watch Reader on Global Environmental Issues,* New York/London: W.W. Norton & Co
Bruiger, Dan (2006): *Second Nature. The Man Made World of Idealism, Technology and Power*, Victoria, BC: leftfieldpress
Butler, J. (1991) *Das Unbehagen der Geschlechter*, Frankfurt: Suhrkamp
Canetti, E. (1986) *Masse und Macht*, Frankfurt: Fischer
Chargaff, E. (1988) *Unbegreifliches Geheimnis, Wissenschaft als Kampf für und gegen die Natur*, Stuttgart: Klett-Cotta
Chossudovsky, M. (1996) *The Globalization of Poverty*, London: Zed
Colburn, Th. et al. (1996) *Our Stolen Future,* London: Abacus
Daly, M. (1970) *Gyn/Ökologie*, München: Frauenoffensive
Dahl, J. (1989) *Die Verwegenheit der Ahnungslosen. Über Gentechnik und andere schwarze Löcher des Fortschritts*, Stuttgart: Klett-Cotta
Deschner, K.-H. (1994) *Kriminalgeschichte des Christentums,* Band 1-4, Reinbek: Rowohlt
Deschner, K.-H. (1992) *Das Kreuz mit der Kirche: Eine Sexualgeschichte des Christentums*, München: Heyne
Drewermann, E. (1991) *Der tödliche Fortschritt. Von der Zerstörung der Erde und des Menschen im Erbe des Christentums,* Freiburg: Herder

Duden, B. (1991) *Der Frauenleib als öffentlicher Ort. Vom Mißbrauch des Begriffs Leben*, Hamburg/Zürich: Luchterhand

Easlea, B. (1986) *Die Väter der Vernichtung. Männlichkeit, Naturwissenschaftler und der nukleare Ruestungswettlauf*, Reinbek: Rowohlt

Eisler, R. (1993) *Kelch und Schwert. Von der Herrschaft zur Partnerschaft. Männliches und weibliches Prinzip in der Geschichte*, München: Frauenoffensive

Eliade, M. (1980) *Schmiede und Alchemisten*, Stuttgart: Klett-Cotta

Ernst, U. M. (1997) *Die Schrift der Göttin*, in: Ernst, U. M. et al. (Eds.) *Ökonomie (M)macht Angst*, pp 147-174, Frankfurt/New York/Paris: Peter Lang

Ernst, W. W. (1986) *Legitimationswandel und Revolution, Studien zur neuzeitlichen Entwicklung und Rechtfertigung politischer Gewalt*, (insbes. Einleitung), Berlin: Duncker & Humblodt

Firestone, S. (1975) *Frauenbefreiung und sexuelle Revolution*, Frankfurt: Fischer

Freud, S. (1939) *Der Mann Moses und die monotheistische Religion: 3 Abhandlungen*, in: Freud, S. (1974) *Fragen der Gesellschaft - Ursprünge der Religion*, pp 455-581, Frankfurt: Fischer

Foucault, M. (1977) *Überwachen und Strafen, Die Geburt des Gefängnisses*, Frankfurt: Suhrkamp

Galtung, Johan (1995) Credo quia absurdum: Über die Grenzen der Konsequenz Ethik, in: Rudolf Bahro (Ed.): *Apokalypse oder Geist einer neuen Zeit*, Berlin: edition ost, pp. 56-74

Gambaroff, M. u.a. (1986) *Tschernobyl hat unser Leben verändert. Vom Ausstieg der Frauen*, Reinbek: Rowohlt

Gebelein, H. (1996) *Alchemie. Die Magie des Stofflichen,* Müenchen: Diederichs

Genth, Renate (2002): *Über Maschinisierung und Mimesis*, Frankfurt a. M.: Peter Lang

George, S. (1980) *Wie die anderen sterben. Die wahren Ursachen des Welthungers*, Berlin: Rotbuch

Girard, R. (1992) *Das Heilige und die Gewalt*, Frankfurt: Fischer

Godelier, M. (1987) *Die Produktion der Großen Männer*, Frankfurt: Campus

Göttner-Abendroth, H. (1988) *Das Matriarchat I: Geschichte seiner Erforschung*, Stuttgart/Berlin/Köln: Klett-Cotta

Gronemeyer, M. (1988) *Die Macht der Bedürfnisse*, Reinbek: Rowohlt

Hammer, S. (1997) *Humankapital. Bildung zwischen Herrschaftswahn und Schöpfungsillusion*, Frankfurt/Paris/New York: Peter Lang

Haraway, D. (1995) *Die Neuerfindung der Natur. Primaten, Cyborgs und Frauen*, Frankfurt/New York: Campus

Hirschman, A. O. (1987) *Leidenschaften und Interessen, Politische Begründungen des Kapitalismus vor seinem Sieg*, Frankfurt: Suhrkamp

Hobbes, Th. (1984) *Leviathan oder Stoff, Form und Gewalt eines kirchlichen und bürgerlichen Staats*, ed. Iring Fetscher, Frankfurt: Suhrkamp

Horkheimer M., Th. W. Adorno (1988) *Dialektik der Aufklärung, Philosophische Fragmente*, Frankfurt: Fischer

Hunke, S. (1987) *Glauben und Wissen. Die Einheit europaeischer Religion und Naturwissenschaft*, Hildesheim: Olms

Illich, I. (1982) *Vom Recht auf Gemeinheit*, Reinbek: Rowohlt

Illich, I. (1982) *Gender*, New York: Pantheon

Imfeld, A. (1985) *Hunger und Hilfe*, Zürich: Rotpunkt

Jung, C. G. (1985) *Erlösungsvorstellungen in der Alchemie*, Solothurn/ Düsseldorf: Walter

Kennedy, M. (1990) *Geld ohne Zinsen und Inflation*, Steyerberg: Permakultur

Kimmerle, G. (1980) *Hexendämmerung. Zur kopernikanischen Wende der Hexendeutung*, Tübingen: Konkursbuch

Kippenberg, H. G. (1991) *Die vorderasiatischen Erlösungsreligionen in ihrem Zusammenhang mit der antiken Stadtherrschaft*, Frankfurt: Suhrkamp

Klöss, E. (1985) *Die Herren der Welt. Die Entstehung des Kolonialismus in Europa*, Köln: Kiepenheuer & Witsch

Krieg, P. (1980) Manuskript zum Film „*Septemberweizen*", Freiburg

Kutschmann, W. (1986) *Der Naturwissenschaftler und sein Körper*, Frankfurt: Suhrkamp

Lauderdale, Pat (1996): Indigene nordamerikanische Alternativen zur Vorstellung von Recht und Strafe in der Moderne: Was die natur uns lehrt, in: C. v. Werlhof/A. Schweighofer/W.Ernst (Eds.): *HerrenLos. Herrschaft – Erkenntnis – Lebensform*, Frankfurt a. M.: Peter Lang, pp. 133 -156

Lerner, G. (1991) *Die Entstehung des Patriarchats*, Frankfurt/New York: Campus

Locke, J. (1970) *Gedanken über Erziehung*, Stuttgart: Reclam

Marx, K. (1974) Der Fetischcharakter der Ware und sein Geheimnis, in: Marx, K. (1974) *Der Produktionsprozeß des Kapitals (Das Kapital Band I)*, in: Marx/Engels-Werke Band 23, pp 85-98, Berlin: Dietz

Meier-Seethaler, C. (1992) *Ursprünge und Befreiungen, Die sexistischen Wurzeln der Kultur*, Frankfurt: Fischer

Mességué, M. (1989) *Das Gesetz der Natur*, Frankfurt a. M./Berlin

Merchant, C. (1987) *Der Tod der Natur, Ökologie, Frauen und neuzeitliche Naturwissenschaft*, München: Beck

Mies, M. (1988) *Patriarchy and Accumulation on a World Scale. Women in the International Division of Labour*, London: Zed books

Mies, M., Bennholdt-Thomsen, V. and C. von Werlhof (1988) *Women, the Last Colony*, London: Zed books

Mies, M. and V. Shiva (1993) *Ecofeminism*, London: Zed books

Mies, M., C. von Werlhof (Eds.) (1999) *Lizenz zum Plündern - Das Multilaterale Abkommen über Investitionen – MAI – Globalisierung der Konzernherrschaft – und was wir dagegen tun können*, Hamburg: Rotbuch EVA

Mühlmann, W. E. (1984) *Die Metamorphose der Frau, Weiblicher Schamanismus und Dichtung*, Berlin: Dietrich Reimer

Mumford, L. (1977) *Mythos der Maschine*, Frankfurt: Fischer

Paczensky, G. von (1970) *Die Weißen kommen. Die wahre Geschichte des Kolonialismus*, Hamburg: Hoffman & Campe

Paracelsus (1990) *Die Geheimnisse, Ein Lesebuch aus seinen Schriften*, hgg. von Peuckert, W.-E., München: Knaur

Plato (1985) *Das Trinkgelage. Über den Eros*, Frankfurt: Suhrkamp

Plato (1962) *Politeia*, in: Werke, Band III, Reinbek: Rowohlt

Rifkin; J., Perlas, N. (1983) *Algeny*, New York: The Viking Press

Sachs, W. (ed.) (1993) *Wie im Westen so auf Erden*, Reinbek: Rowohlt

Sloterdijk, P. (1983) *Kritik der zynischen Vernunft*, Frankfurt: Suhrkamp

Schütt, Hans-Werner (2000) *Auf der Suche nach dem Stein der Weisen. Die Geschichte der Alchemie*, München: C.H. Beck

Schütz-Buenaventura, I. (1996) *Die Vergesellschaftung des destruktiven Konstruktivismus*, in: v. Werlhof/Schweighofer/Ernst (Eds.): *Herren-Los*, pp 270-301, Frankfurt/ Paris/New York: Peter Lang

Schütz-Buenaventura, I. (2000) *Globalismus contra Existentia. Das Recht des ursprünglich Realen vor dem Machtanspruch der Bewußtseinsphilosophie*, Wien: Passagen

Schubart, W. (1989) *Religion und Eros*, München: C.H. Beck

Schumpeter, J. A. (1962) *Capitalism, Socialism, and Democracy*, New York: Harper Torchbooks

Shiva, V. (1989) *Das Geschlecht des Lebens. Frauen, Ökologie und Dritte Welt*, Berlin:

Shiva, V. (1992) *Monocultures of the Mind*, London: Zed books

Smith, A. (1776) *Eine Untersuchung über Natur und Wesen des Volkswohlstandes („Wealth of Nations")*, Jena 1823 (An Inquiry into the Nature and Causes of the Wealth of Nations, London

Tazi-Preve, I. (1992) *Der Mord an der Mutter*, Diplomarbeit, Innsbruck

Todorov, T. (1980) *Das Problem des Anderen*, Frankfurt: Suhrkamp

Treusch-Dieter, G. (1990) *Von der sexuellen Rebellion zur Gen- und Reproduktionstechnologie*, Tübingen: Konkursbuch

Trube-Becker, E. (1987) ‚Sexuelle Misshandlung von Kindern', in: Faessler, H. (Ed.) *Das Tabu der Gewalt*, Innsbruck: Eigenverlag, pp 186-194
Ullrich, O. (1980) *Weltniveau*, Berlin: Rotbuch
Wallerstein, I. (1974) *The Modern World System I: Capitalist Agriculture and the Origins of the European World-Economy in the Sixteenth Century*, New York: Academic Press
Wallerstein, I. (1980) The Modern *World-System II: Mercantilism and the Consolidation of the European World-Economy, 1600-1750*, New York: Academic Press
Wallerstein, I. (1989) *The Modern World-System III: The Second Era of Great Expansion of the Capitalist World-Economy, 1730-1840s*, New York: Academic Press
Weber, M. (1993) *Die protestantische Ethik und der „Geist" des Kapitalismus*, Bodenheim: Athenäum-Hain-Haustein
Weiler, G. (1991) *Der enteignete Mythos, Eine feministische Revision der Archetypenlehre C. G. Jungs und Erich Neumanns*, Frankfurt: Campus
Weiler, G. (1993) *Eros ist stärker als Gewalt. Eine feministische Anthropologie I*, Frankfurt: Campus
Weizenbaum, J. (1978) *Die Macht der Computer und die Ohnmacht der Vernunft*, Frankfurt: Suhrkamp
Werlhof, C. von (1988) On the Concept of Nature and Society in Capitalism, in: Mies, M. et al. (Eds.) *Women, the Last Colony*, pp 96-112, London: Zed Books
Werlhof, C. von (1996) Das Rechtssystem und der Muttermord, in: Werlhof, C. von (1996) *Mutter-Los*, pp 27-60, München: Frauenoffensive
Werlhof, C. von (1997) Ökonomie, die praktische Seite der Religion. Wirtschaft als Gottesbeweis und die Methode der Alchemie, in: Ernst, U. M. et al. (Eds.) (1997) *Ökonomie (M)macht Angst*, pp 95-121, Frankfurt/Paris/New York: Peter Lang 1997
Werlhof, C. von/A. Schweighofer/W. Ernst (Eds.) (1996) *Herren-Los, Herrschaft-Erkenntnis-Lebensform*, Frankfurt/Paris/New York: Peter Lang
Werlhof, C. von (2000a) ‚Patriarchat als „Alchemistisches System". Die (Z)ErSetzung des Lebendigen', in: Wolf, M. (Ed.) *Optimierung und Zerstörung. Intertheoretische Analysen zum menschlich-Lebendigen*, pp 13-31, Innsbruck: STUDIA Universitätsverlag
Werlhof, C. von (2000b) "Globalization" and the "Permanent" Process of „Primitive Accumulation": The Example of the MAI, the Multilateral Agreement on Investment, in: Arrighi, G. and W.L. Goldfrank (Eds.) *Festschrift for Immanuel Wallerstein, Part II, Journal of World-Systems Research*, Vol VI, No 3, Fall/Winter, pp 728-747

Wolf, D. (1994) *Was war vor den Pharaonen? Die Entdeckung der Urmütter Ägyptens,* Zürich: Kreuz

Worms, A. von (1988) *Das Buch der wahren Praktiken in der göttlichen Magie* (ed. Jürg von Ins), München: Diederichs

8. The Utopia of a Motherless World – Patriarchy as "War-System"

in Göttner-Abendroth, Heide (Ed.): Societies of Peace - matriarchies past, present and future, Toronto (Inanna) 2009, S. 29-44

- revised version -

Preliminary remark 2010

Matriarchal studies have become widespread internationally. This is also due to the fact that two World Congresses on Matriarchal Studies took place, the first one in Luxemburg in 2003 (my contribution see Chapter 5) and the second one in Texas 2005 (my contribution see this Chapter). Personally, I have not been researching so much about matriarchies, but concentrated my efforts on patriarchies. I am therefore on the one hand investigating the question of matriarchy from an outside perspective and on the other hand from the point of view of the world as it looks like nowadays. From a global perspective, our problem is the "modern", capitalist (and "socialist", see Chapter 4) patriarchy, not matriarchy. It is an illusion to think that those who are – still or again – living in more or less matriarchal social relations/matriarchal societies have successfully escaped patriarchy for ever and do not need to bother about it any more. The reason is that the global capitalist patriarchy is a terrible threat to matriarchies as the violent war-based-system of patriarchy does not tolerate any alternative(s). Nowadays, patriarchy is an even greater threat as the Military in East and West has started to use – and has since then been using – "environmental weapons" and the planet as a weapon itself (see Introduction, and part D.). It is now able to destroy the basic conditions for the existence of life everywhere on Earth, if not Mother Earth herself. This reality teaches us that we have to fight on two fronts: on the first one we have to fight for matriarchy and on the second front we have to fight against patriarchy. It is not sufficient to re-build matriarchal social relations and even "whole" matriarchies, but we have to defend them against the threats of modern patriarchy. Patriarchy is able to commit atrocities everywhere nowadays, although its logical and "spiritual" foundations are probably weak already and although it seems to have reached its own material limits ("peak oil" – and probably "peak of everything").

With my speech I intended to explain the overall historical framework necessary for the development of patriarchy and its actions against matriarchy as well as the global tendencies of today which are counter-productive for "matriarchal politics".

Introduction:

I am sorry, but we still live in patriarchy! It is, therefore, my task to make clear what that really means. Because, patriarchy is not only a threat to matriarchal societies still alive on earth and of matriarchy as a sort of "second culture" within patriarchy, but it is also a still growing threat to humankind as a whole, including the patriarchs themselves.

Hypothesis: Patriarchy, a "Dark" Utopia

A "deep" analysis of patriarchy shows:
1. Patriarchy tries to build a supposed "new paradise" on earth.
2. The way to this paradise is war.
3. The new paradise is supposed to be a motherless world.

Patriarchy, therefore, is a "dark" utopia. As a utopia against the world and against women it has to be forced upon the world and women, if it is going to be realized.

Patriarchy is a "Civilization" Dependent on Matriarchy

Patriarchies never existed based on their own capacities and never had their own independent civilizations, but developed only after the conquest of matriarchal societies. Seen from this perspective, patriarchy is a social process still evolving. What is called civilization today is a dependent (patriarchal) civilization that has been built upon matriarchy, or what is left of it, up to the present day and everywhere on the globe. In reality, patriarchy is a mixed society, which still depends on matriarchy for its life.

The utopia of patriarchy consists in becoming totally independent from matriarchy. The question is, nevertheless, can patriarchy develop into an independent civilization, and if so, what will happen when the last vestiges of matriarchy have been destroyed?

Patriarchy, "Militarization" Instead of "Civilization": A Developing "War-System"

What is the real meaning of war?

Matriarchal societies are societies of peace. But patriarchy came into the world by conquest, by war. War is not just violence, but organized mass violence, based on calculated planning.

After the conquest the war continues. It becomes institutionalized. The war takes the form of the State. The new order is more militarized than civilized, because it has to be protected from being dissolved by the people, and by life. Thus, war is not the exception, as is normally assumed, but the rule in patriarchy.

We can say that the new society becomes a system because, in contrast to matriarchal society, it is based on systematic contradictions within society and between society and nature. The belief in violence becomes the general religion of patriarchy. Violence is looked upon as the main truth in life (Girard 1972).

A complete, "pure," closed war-system that is embracing all spheres of society and nature is the utopia of patriarchy.

What is the real meaning of the patriarch, the "father"?

Let us explore what "patriarch" or "father" means. The analysis of the etymology shows: Fathers are allegedly legitimate rulers over conquered paradises that have been transformed into kingdoms/empires of the sky and on earth; fathers are supposed to be the real creators of life and wealth, being somehow mothers, too; fathers seem to have the knowledge about the secrets and miracles of creation from the beginning of time, so that there is neither an independent mother, nor a Goddess anymore; and the mother has been defined away or reduced to an attribute of the almighty cosmic-and-earthly ruling Father-God, who has stolen her power and wisdom (Budge 1969, 1978; Frankenberg 1985; Walker 1988; The American Heritage Dictionary 2001). Thus, the Father-God is a fiction in contrast to the Mother-Goddess as a reality.

The earthly fathers and patriarchs, therefore, get into a difficult situation. They have to prove in reality that they are able to create, that this creation is the highest and best, and that they can even replace the supposed lower forms of existing creation. This is their utopia. The question now becomes: What is it that fathers create? And how are they doing it?

What are patriarchal meanings of death and life? How are death and life related to patriarchal creation?

The first patriarchal creation is "creation" out of destruction. The looting that takes place during war provides wealth and life to warriors and their society (Mies 1986). Hence, the cult of the artificially produced second, supposedly good death, the death under control, the non-natural death that occurs through war, murder, torture, rape, and other forms and techniques of violence.

The second main creation of patriarchy is a so called creation out of nothing. It is based on the invention of a fictitious life and world beyond the existing one, a metaphysical, supposedly existing second, higher and better life and world (Plato 1994).

We can be certain that the world had never before been perceived as divided in that way. We can further assume that foreign invaders invented a world beyond the existing one because they had to explain where they came from in order to legitimize their rule. In sum, patriarchal acting and thinking follow the same principles:

1. Negate what existed before conquest by destroying it, usurping it, perverting it, transforming it, trying to do without it, trying to replace it, and, as long as it still exists, looking down on it as bad, low, wrong, and sinful.
2. Make propaganda for utopia, a supposedly better world than the one that exists after the conquest and/or the one that is still remembered as having existed before the conquest.
3. Invent a division between supposedly good and supposedly evil worlds, justifying the principle of "divide and conquer."
4. Feel legitimized to start to realize the utopia of a "better" world by a "creation" that consists of the plunder of the existing supposedly evil world, and by the "creations" of the supposed "good," metaphysical world, the world of the (future) "higher" and "holy" creation.

The metaphysical world is the model of a utopia that will have to be materialized on earth (Sloterdijk and Macho 1991). However, in reality, the patriarchs as the "fathers" of this world still depend on women and nature. This is why they are desperately trying to accelerate "progress".

How the alchemist tried and still tries to become the first concrete utopian father

Why is the new "creation" destructive even after war, in so-called "peaceful" times? The analysis of patriarchal creation beyond immediate war can be undertaken by using a new concept of "alchemy" and of the alchemist who is helping to expand the war-system to non-military, if not all spheres, of life. "War is the father of all things!" as Heraclitus put it. If we look at the methods and principles of about 5000 years of alchemical processes and manipulations, we see that they have become typically patriarchal: "Divide – transform – and rule!" "*Solve et Coagula!*" (Werlhof 1997, 2000, 2001, 2004).

The first step in the alchemical process of "creation" is called "mortification," from the Latin word *mors*, or death. *Mortificatio* means bringing death to living matter. This occurs in order to take control over matter and is mostly done by using fire (see Eliade 1980). This is most probably due to the war-tradition. The process finishes with a sort of black matter, the "Nigredo", which is considered to be the primordial matter, *materia prima* or *massa confusa*, out of which – so the alchemist supposes – life as such came into being. At that point, the alchemist thinks to start at point zero of creation like God himself, but on earth.

In case of working with metals as matter the alchemist continues his work based on the "black matter" as his materia prima which he has produced in the first step.

In a second step, the alchemist tries to produce a sort of silver, which he calls the "white matter", "Albedo", by giving mercury as "semen" into the materia prima, mostly lead, the lowest in the supposed hierarchy of metals.

In a third step, the alchemist continues with trying to produce alchemical "gold", which he calls the "yellow matter", "Gold", by giving sulphur as "semen" into the silver. Gold is supposed to be the highest of all matter.

The substances, which the alchemist is putting together, are supposedly male and female. The lower matter is thought of as the female, the higher one and the "semen" as the male one.

Using pyrotechnics (for example, a melting process in his oven that looks like an artificial uterus) the so called "chemical marriage", a perversion of the concept of the "holy marriage" in matriarchy, takes place. It is said (see Eliade 1980) that if the melting process at one of its stages is not successful, a woman has to be sacrificed, usually the female assistant of the alchemist, who then has to jump into the oven. That seems to have worked.

In a fourth step, the so called "red matter", "Rubedo", a form of red gold or a red powder can eventually result from putting "coral semen" into the gold (cf. Schütt 2000). This substance is already next to what is called the "philosopher's stone", a sort of matter that contains all live creating forces which would finally allow the alchemist to become a godlike creator.

The alchemical process can also be undertaken on the basis of plants or animal, organic or inorganic substances. It depends on the type of "creation" the alchemist is interested in.

If human life is concerned the alchemical process occurs on the basis of human blood and sperm with which the alchemist tries to produce the so called *homunculus,* or little man, in a test-tube. For this creation, no mother is needed aside from female blood as "substance," and no biological father is needed aside from sperm as "substance". The "marriage" occurs in a sort of test-tube, which again looks like an artificial uterus. On top there is the alchemist as the "priest" or "father" who is inventing, leading, and controlling the procedure.

The alchemist intends to create a utopian life, a life u-topos, which means that it is a life or a matter without a genuine place on earth, without origin, without a navel, and without the participation of real persons – except the alchemist himself – without a concrete locality, without love, and *without a mother*, especially without Mother Earth. This idea is central to all his creations, not only when human life itself is concerned. Gold, for instance, is seen as a mature child of Mother Earth. When taking the different metals out of her womb, the alchemist considers them to be the immature children of Mother Earth that he is receiving by forcing her to abort them. By transforming the immature metals/children into mature ones, namely "from lead to gold", he thinks to help Mother Earth to be faster and even more perfect in her birth giving process, so that finally the alchemist himself is becoming the real creator – God!

The alchemist finally wants to become an independent creator who is able to force life into existence. Hence, the *"philosopher's stone"*, the paradoxical combination of an artificially created higher matter with something perceived as the essence of life with which the alchemist would be able to create life not only independently from mothers, but also independently from women and nature as such. Only then a sort of *creation even out of the Nothing* would be possible.

But the problem of the general alchemical procedure is that there is dead matter – after its "mortification" – brought together with other more or less dead matter that has been abstracted and isolated from its original surroundings. This way the creation of real new life is in fact impossible. The alchemist seems to have had a somehow mechanical view of nature and life already in antiquity, but in reality life is not being created mechanically.

In modern times the mechanical view even has become the foundation of progress as such, and as modern alchemy therefore was confronted with its constant failure, too, it started to overcome this problem by combining dead matter with living matter. This is the principle behind the invention of the so called *cyborg* today which is conceived of as a mixture of a living being and a machine (see Haraway 1983).

Generally, ways to combine dead matter with living matter was the result of industrialization which brought about a new technology, the machine, and a definition of living human labor linked to and combined with the machine(ry).

During the labor day the laborer himself was – so to say the first cyborg – being transformed into a combination with something dead, the machine(ry). From this definition of the laborer stems the definition of his labor power as something he can dispose of as a commodity to be sold to the owner of the machine(ry). From this point of view the laborer was considered to be himself a combination of separable parts, namely his labor power, which belonged to the machine, and himself as a living being. This way the laborer as such, even without the machine, was seen as a sort of combination of a living being and something that did not really belong to him, an abstract labor potential that he could give away by selling it to the machine owner (on the problems with the definition of the labor power under capitalism see Marx 1974, pp.192-330, 391-460). The laborer from then on was – like a cyborg – considered to be neither really alive nor really dead, but rather a living machine or commodity, living a life that is half dead because it has to be given away in the labor process.

This modern, capitalistic perspective on the laborer and the experiences he is making in the labor process show how much alchemical thinking and organizing has been implemented since the beginning of modern economy and technology, having gone unnoticed since then. This is because modernity is seen as a full success and therefore it never wanted to be seen in relation to pre-modern alchemy that – in reality – had failed in trying to produce "gold" and "life".

Another way to avoid a further failure of alchemy today is the *hybrid*, the combination of living matter with other living matter as it can be observed in all life-industries: bio-chemical, reproductive, and genetic engineering (see Rifkin 1998).

In any case, modern alchemy cannot renounce life as such. But it is always influencing more deeply life cycles and life processes as such, changing them from within. Jeremy Rifkin (1983) calls it "algeny", a mixture out of alchemy and genetics. The latest attempts are those of "nano-technology" which operates at levels of matter tinier than the atom (Schirrmacher 2001; Mooney 2010).

Though the pre-industrial alchemist already thinks according to machine-principles of destruction through division and re-combination, the machine as such was not yet invented. But the modern sciences – though they are denying it because alchemy was not able to produce gold and life – took over the methodological principles of alchemy as well as its aims. This endeavor is from now on called modern production and technological progress. I, therefore, consider alchemy to belong not only to patriarchy as a whole, but to have been adapted to modernity, too. In reality, *the machine has saved patriarchal alchemy from disappearing from the world.* The machine is the most important invention of alchemy during modernity. And saying this implies its present and future failure as well, as its method of *"creation by destruction"* is maintained, if not generalized by machine technology. Counteracting against its mortal effects by integrating living creatures as such into the alchemical process will not help in the long run. On the contrary, this integration will only widen the range of beings that are going to experience a loss of life and its damage to death: modern alchemy has become *cannibalistic*.

It is clear that nearly nobody wants to hear this today, of course!

In the meantime the methods of alchemy have spread to all spheres of society, so that we can speak of the development of what I call an *"alchemical system"* today as a sort of system of seemingly "peaceful" destruction, a paradox typical of patriarchy.

The *alchemist*, like the modern scientist, too, has a patriarchal view of the world. He does not want to create the same as women and nature do. He sees himself as helping nature to become the supposedly better, higher life, and to get there faster than it would have been possible by eventual natural evolution. He believes that nature and matter *want* to be improved the way he is acting upon them and *agree with being sacrificed* for patriarchal development. He does not see himself as being needlessly destructive, because for him violence is needed for creation, as his creation is a higher creation that seems to legitimize everything. He never looks from "below," from the point of view of matter/life itself, because he sees himself as being part of the "holy rule" of the fathers and as being "above" matter and natural life. He always looks down from his metaphysical, "spiritual," "higher," and supposedly more "noble" point of view. The *sacrifice* he is demanding from matter, women, and nature is self-evident to him. Progress needs sacrifices – from others.

Patriarchal alchemy helped change the view of nature and women completely, already before modernity. The alchemist is not looking with enchantment into the world; he does not respect the forms that nature brings into existence; he does not wonder about the beauty and grace of Her beings. On the contrary, his mind is gloomy. He works with tricks, fraud, and violence against nature; he is competing with her as his ovens and test-tubes show, and he has no emotional problem with being Her murderer. For him, sex and death belong to each other in more than one way. He is already on the way to *modern rationality* (Kutschmann 1986).

The alchemist is somebody who tries to find a new male identity within patriarchy, a form of patriarchal maleness or "masculation" (Vaughan 1997) that is not exactly like the warrior, the ruler or the priest, but a combination of the three, and of – in modern terms – a patriarchal scientist and engineer: the *concrete utopian "father"*. Until modern times, the alchemists were exceptions. Few men were dedicating their lives to alchemy. This is changing with modernity. Not contemplation, but action is wanted. The time for the alchemist is now or never.

The War-System is Expanding by Becoming an "Alchemical System"

The alchemists wanted to achieve too much too early. The project of realizing patriarchy needed a broader foundation. There was no direct path to utopia. Today, nevertheless, we can identify what have become the results of modern alchemy.

What is a commodity?

Alchemy had to go through capitalism, the so-called "Great Transformation" (Polanyi 1978) that transformed women into the first "black matter" of modernity, its first basic raw material (Federici 2004). In this way, women became the (subjected) "nature" of modern society and its first living machine and/or commodity, equipped with a form of *labor power without value*, price, or wage – in contrast to men. "Black matter" and women in modern society are considered a natural resource that can freely be appropriated. After the witch hunt women became "housewives" and "housewifized" (Mies, Bennholdt-Thomsen and von Werlhof 1988), a sort of natural commodity or commodified nature that had previously gone through the witch hunt as a process of concrete alchemical "mortification".

In general, capitalism has been defined as a society in which all things, including people and nature, are sought to be transformed into commodities in order to make money out of them (Wallerstein 1974), respectively into "capital" which takes the form of machinery, "command over labor" or the money that bears interest (Marx 1974, pp.168, 381, 391, 400, 424, 447). Capitalist technology, the machine(ry), is the method for how this transformation is occurring. I call it modern alchemy.

Capitalist economy, then, is the way to finally transform the commodity into money and profit by building up a new market, the capitalist world-market for commodities. This way *modern economy is alchemy* as well. It does not produce gold as the highest form of wealth, but money (in German "Geld") as the highest form of wealth. Gold is replaced by money (and in fact the gold-standard of money has been given up). And gold is generally replaced by capital (see Binswanger 1985).

So what does the transformation of nature and life into commodities, machinery, hierarchies, and money really mean? And is it not true that we consider this process to be the foundation of western society as, allegedly, the highest civilization ever, one that is creating a new paradise on earth?

As we have seen already, alchemy, including its modern version, is not creating or producing life or gold as such, but something else. In the phase of mortification it produces raw materials by killing nature and women in the meaning of a female "culture." When dead things are forced together in the factory they come out as "commodities," as *double-dead* things. They are dead because of their mortification into "raw materials" and because of using up, "killing", labor power during their production process. The past life of nature and the past life of the laborer are composing the commodity. Commodities, therefore, are not just dead, but *dead forever*.

This is a completely new situation on earth, because natural death is normally followed by new life. The systematic artificial death we are confronted with in modernity, on the contrary, is not followed by life any more, because this possibility is systematically excluded by "alchemically" destroying the natural life-death cycle. With this type of death, life does not go on any more.

Furthermore the new form of death is paradoxical. It is not just passive, but actively threatening and even destroying its environment, too, as if we existed in a world of zombies. This death is dangerous. It is like a post-death-"life" that is as aggressive, mortal, and warlike as its own production and destruction have been. Even after death this war continues.

Patriarchal "creation", therefore, does not lead to an artificial new paradise but to an *artificial hell on Earth*.

The more de-naturalization has taken place in the production process of the commodity, the more probable that it ends as special waste. This waste is a threat to life and to the earth as such, like nuclear, electronic, chemical, genetic and plastic waste. Always more waste, even organic waste, cannot be recycled within the natural environment any more, because it has turned into poison.

This is due to the fact that the commodity came out of a process of systematic and large-scale life-destruction. *The way of the commodity is paved with violent death from the beginning to the end.* Like a vampire that is neither dead, nor alive, the commodity has absorbed life, turning it into capital. Already Karl Marx defined capital as "past, dead labor", "labor that once was", but without drawing out the necessary consequences (Marx 1974, pp. 247, 209, 271, 446).

Another example of a mortal life-death combination is the genetically modified organism (GMO), be it plants, bacteria or animals. These organisms are dangerous and even lethal to other plants and animals. They root them out. They are aggressive. On the other hand, their life is weak. Most of them are purposely infertile, like "terminator" seeds. With some GMOs, mostly animals and bacteria, we do not know what the consequences of their existence will/might be. In the end, new "life forms" will have killed older life forms, whilst dying out themselves (Verhaag 2004). Only death forever will be left over – "gray goo" (Joy 2000).

Genetic engineering, which means "birth-giving war arts," started to create its own "life forms" by forcing different genes of different species together, producing the GMO. The GMO is a living commodity, a machine made out of nature-parts, consisting of a combination of at least two different living genes. It has no genealogy, no natural history, no mother, no morphological field and no species to which it belongs. It knows no stability, no meaning in itself and *no place in the cycle of death and life.* It is not embedded within nature and not related to bio-diversity. It is *utopian.* It is irreversible. And it is like a contagious, lethal, *epidemic disease.*

From this point of view, it is explicable that instead of getting life and death under control, patriarchal creation is causing a new kind of life and death that are getting completely *out* of control.

Only in its appearance the commodity seems to be related to nature and life in a positive way, and this is why people become confused with the perversion of *"fetishism"* (Marx 1974, pp. 85-98) which means that they believe in this appearance of the commodity, as if it would be even more alive than nature, so to say a better nature, and would therefore be able to fulfill the real needs for a happy life. In the meantime, people even believe that commodities stand for life and that nature is dead, turning everything upside down. This is of help for modern alchemists as their propaganda claims for the production of a better and higher matter and for the necessity of a "creative destruction" of the world.

After having created the reality of a bad world, the new alchemists told us to help create a good one. This new creation would now seem to be the only answer facing the catastrophes of the former. Patriarchy is *tautology*: The problems that have to be fought against first had to be created. Without problems there would be no need for patriarchy. In this way, it is not utopia that materializes, but *dystopia* – the opposite of utopia. It is utopia as a self made catastrophe.

What is money today?

Capitalist money contains all the former steps of the process, all former life, violence and death. Fetishists paradoxically perceive it as even more alive than anything else. They are assured by the fact that modern money as a system is organized as if it is "fertile". Via the interest it is growing as if it is "getting children and grandchildren" (Binswanger 1985), so that people forget about real fertility as an ability of nature alone, and do not find it scandalous when nature systematically is made infertile and destroyed. From this point of view money appears as if it was a sort of *"philosopher's stone"*, a concentration of life energy with which you can create more life wherever and whenever you want.

But, money is neither alive, nor fertile, nor does it create life. It is a violent fiction, like everything in patriarchy. It is the emptiness, the No-thing that is left over after the Great Transformation took place that started to liquidate matter, nature, and people, leaving them behind as and for the "liquidity" of the money system. There is no creation out of nothing. There has only been a "creation" *of* nothing.

What is the response of nature?

The time in which these facts could be hidden is disappearing rapidly. This is seen in ecology. The question is: How is nature responding? Her reactions are a mirror for us. Today She is showing everybody that She does not agree with being taken as the matter for a supposedly higher creation. Nature does not want to be developed into an alchemical paradise at all. She still is beyond human control instead of being dominated by modern man. Now She is going to show that She is not at all dead matter, but a living being that reacts actively and powerfully against the violence with which She is treated. Having a look on man made – *industrially made and militarily made* – global warming – *global warning* – and climate changes as well as "natural" catastrophes everywhere, this will be seen soon (Bertell 2000).

When the Catholic missionary Bonifacius, some 1300 years ago, cut the holy oak tree of the pagans in Saxony, this act mocked the pagan's belief system, as they believed that the sky would fall down now that the oak tree was no longer holding it up any more. Apparently, then the sky did not fall down. In reality, however, it did, seen from a spiritual point of view, but we only recognize it just now, as the consequences of this sort of behavior against nature everywhere cannot be denied any more.

Nevertheless, there is no way back from abstraction into interconnectedness. You cannot transform money, the commodity, the machine, capital, or a GMO back into living nature again. What has been killed this way cannot be brought to life again. Alchemy is a one-way undertaking only.

And, look at "nuclear alchemy" (Easlea 1986), which is trying to divide and rule even over the atoms, the tiniest spirit-matter of life, what holds together life as such, so that you need the most terrible violence to get it divided. Believe it or not, nuclear alchemists think the same way all alchemists do: that even the use of nuclear violence is creating new life on earth (Caldicott 2002). Of course, they neither consider the dead of today, nor those of the future who are sacrificed before they have been born (Anders 1994). Progress always seems to need more sacrifice, even in face of the fact that nuclear poisoning can never again be reversed. For nuclear alchemists, nevertheless, the curse can never be greater than the blessings that they think they are bringing to the world.

Most people do not look at the transformation processes of nature that are accompanying commodity production, because they believe in the creative character of modern economy and technology. Those who do look at the destruction that occurs consider this economy a "creative" destruction (Schumpeter 1962). This is an – unconscious – alchemical way of looking at capitalist patriarchy which means that in view of a possible creation the destruction that is occurring at the same time is not taken seriously.

The destruction that is necessary for the maintenance and expansion of capitalist transformation has become global and always more rapid, penetrating all spheres of life at the macro and micro levels. Global treaties like the General Agreement on Trade in Services, the GATS of the World Trade Organization, are organizing the final transformation into commodities of everything that has escaped this process so far (Mies and Werlhof 2003). They call it "privatization". It is the only way to maintain capitalist growth – the growth of *profits made out of life*. They are all alchemists. They literally want to liquidate everything forever. Furthermore, they even organize the *liquidation of the future* in order to appropriate its potentials now.

Most people do not understand the alchemical character of capitalist (including so-called "socialist") economy and technology. Like the Left, they consider the transformation of life and nature in general into commodities to be productive instead of destructive. They do not care about ecology, life and Mother Earth. They do not care about women, children, and about themselves. Generally, there is an "optimistic" perspective towards the future. Otherwise, they would have found out how the transformation into commodities, machinery, money, capital, and the overall "command over labor" did not only affect inorganic, but also organic matter, including their own lives. They do not see that the perpetrators are and will be affected as well.

What is the response of people?

It started with the transformation of women as so-called "witches" into housewives. Regarding this change, what are the problems of human ecology that we are facing today?

While people were told to become intelligent, healthy, wealthy, democratic, free, sensitive, civilized, equal, strong, and beautiful, the opposite is true. Something within us, something of our lives, our work, our behavior, our thoughts, our feelings, our future, has become commodified. We have, at least partly, become capital. We have become living machines. We are obeying nearly every order we are given. We seek a mimesis with money as if it were the "transcendental subject" of mankind (Sohn-Rethel 1970). We are still alive, but only partly. We are told that it is only our labor-power and not ourselves that is used as a commodity. So we think we are free people with a free life.

In reality, nevertheless, there is no separation. It is us, our life-energy, Eros, brain, fantasy, creativity, imagination, dreams, sex, soul, and spirit that are being transformed and "put together" with machinery, money, command, "capital". The separation between us and our labor-power is a fiction. If we are treated like commodities, we are forced to transform our life energy accordingly. We are called upon to kill parts of ourselves, divide and conquer ourselves, purify ourselves, take special abilities out of ourselves, force them together again and try to re-configure ourselves, *believing* that all this would be the best life we can possibly have. Emotionally we have to identify with this "self-alchemization", and enter into a *mimetic relationship with ourselves as commodities*, not as living beings. *How much of me is capital already?* How far [long?] can I make money out of my life, energy, body, brain, organs, labor, myself? How far [long?] can I function like a machine? How far [long?] can I do whatever I am ordered to do? Until I become a killer-solider, or an Eichmann? (Genth 2002)

Karl Marx (Marx 1974, P. 765) called the violence that we are committing against ourselves "economical violence" in contrast to the direct, "political" violence that comes from outside. The slave, he said, had to be forced to go to work (Marx, 1974, ibid and pp. 447; 624). We force ourselves to go. This is one of the differences between today and former periods in history. We have learned to internalize the system, the commodity, the machine, the command, capital. We were made to identify with those processes that rob and loot our lives and those of others worldwide. We gain our identity from becoming "like them", the capitalists, the modern alchemists and the system itself. We apparently had no choice: we perverted our mimesis, fantasy, intelligence, energy, and feelings to become more and more like the system, the machine(ery) itself. We submitted to the system and let it define who we are. Finally, we ourselves are responsible for the system. Without us it would be dead. But we gave life to it and transformed it into a "living machine." Without our consent it would immediately break down (Holloway 2006). We, in reality, produced the paradox of a "living system," because we fed it constantly. By feeding the "creation out of destruction" we behave like perverted patriarchal "mothers" within an alchemical system of "fathers".

We are called to justify this partial suicide of ourselves and the partial murder of others as progress and development. In reality it is a deadly alienation and separation from inter-connectedness with life that we are forcing upon us and our children. As a result, we get further away from the power of life, and become more and more helpless. In turn, our children get more and more frustrated and angry.

Once our labor-power is not only used as if it was a commodity, but has really become a commodity, the commodification-process does not stop. We may experience being treated like a *materia prima*, like raw material, like a "dividual" instead of the in-dividual. Or, we are chosen as a "substance," as an expert, for example. We are forced together with other "experts," forming a unit that has to function for projects defined by others. Such a project is a marriage, too: the female and the male "element" are bound together for the sake of the state as the alchemical father. The sacrifice is up to the woman and/as the mother (for a historical comparison see Treusch-Dieter 2001).

Nobody is left out. We are all facing the fact that parts of our lives have been damaged, stolen, destroyed, and transformed into their opposite. Therefore, we feel weak and half-dead and burnt-out. We do not love life any more; joy and laughter have disappeared. We have stopped playing and cannot feel anything anymore. When we do allow ourselves to feel, we feel something negative, because we are frightened, frustrated, greedy, depressed, and aggressive. And we don't know why.

Obviously we do not understand what the procedure of alchemical "creation" comprises. Neither the sciences, nor the Left, not to speak of "Gender-Studies" à la Butler is helping us in this respect (Butler 1991). On the contrary, they are leading us even deeper into the alchemical darkness of the realization of patriarchal utopia, called modernity. We therefore have to change the way we think and feel about it.

Finally, we have to stop to make the wrong choices in order to justify what we have done to ourselves and others in order to make us believe that we have reached the stage of a "better" and "higher" life. We are drawing false consequences out of our dilemma. We run into addiction, because the life perspective has been taken away from us. We go deeper and deeper into delusion, becoming more and more like machines, abstract like capital, fictitious and empty like money, or believers in the supposed holiness of command.

Our faith in the alchemical wonder of a metaphysical world on Earth makes us blind to reality. We believe in a "life after nature" or in the "post-natural human" and in a "post human nature" (see Bruiger 2006).

Patriarchy is the Dys-topia of a Motherless World, but We Can Do Something about It

Together with the war-system and its contraction into the alchemical system of capitalist patriarchy, western civilization and western peoples first have become murderers and now they are on route to suicide. They did not need more than a few hundred years. The accumulation of capital turns out to be the accumulation of eternal death. There is no infinite production – if it is destruction – on a finite globe. There are no "renewable resources". There is nothing that is able to replace what has been destroyed: soil, food, water, forests, cultures, peoples, subsistence, the gift, love, and even parts of the interconnectedness of life.

I call it *West End*.

The dark secret of patriarchy, the violence that is trying to literally annihilate life and death on earth, is coming to light in ourselves. For a long period of time, peoples, and especially women, have tried to remain "good people", even when they had to go through war, misery, and despair. Today, it seems that this form of resistance is disappearing rapidly, especially in the North of the World System, women included. The rationality that we have developed turns into its opposite, that is, irrationality and fundamentalism.

The spirit in which "production" takes place and the character of the alchemical methods used for it are falling back on us like a *boomerang*.

We are prisoners, in jail, behaving like inmates. This is because that is what we have become.

We have to, therefore, break out. We are confronted with the urgent need for an alternative, if we want to survive this war.

We know that a commodity, that money, capital, a machine, cannot be transformed back into living nature. Our only hope is that we are *not totally* commodified, machinized, monetarized, alchemized, housewifized, patriarchalized and enslaved.

We can remember what of our life's potential has not been totally absorbed by self-alchemization and strengthen ourselves again.

We can remember what is left of matriarchy as a "second culture" within and outside of us.

We can join with people and communities that are struggling for the same.

We can defend what is alive within us and others and strengthen it against the destruction within us, them and around us.

We can learn to struggle in favor of life on the globe, and struggle to get patriarchy out of our bodies, minds, behavior, emotions, and fantasies.

We can learn to use our mimetic capacities in order to get closer to Mother Earth again.

We can make experiments with gift-giving.

We can start to lose faith in violence and trust in life on Earth.

We can defend ourselves against those who are looking at life from the perspective of the death they produce.

We have to start to recognize what life, Earth, nature, natural death, and the Goddess, really mean, because never in history was there a society that knew less about them.

We, therefore, have to start to *revert what has been perverted*: Life into death and death into life, eternal death into a so-called paradise. We have to put back on its feet what has been turned upside down. We have to get rid of the confusion of our minds.

We have to become strong and we have to strengthen ourselves mutually, because patriarchs do not joke at all. When the patriarchs begin to understand that their whole system is failing, when the truth about the last five or seven thousand years of patriarchy is recognized, the patriarchs will not simply give up. Their last philosopher's stone is the bomb, followed by natural disaster-technologies today (Bertell 2000).

Therefore, *"take the toys out of the hands of the boys"*.

Because, without nearly any matriarchal vestiges and without nearly any life on the globe, when nearly everything is on the tilt toward death forever, when the Earth has nearly everywhere turned into hell, we then will not be able to invent a new matriarchal or post-patriarchal civilization any more.

So, let us do something now. Let us find out how to get rid of utopia and dystopia, the patriarchal hell, and how to get to the roots of "topia", the here and now of a post-patriarchal civilization.

The u-topos as the non-local, the non-vernacular, the opposite of concrete life, of the concrete mother and living matter, the abstract, the fiction, the nowhere, the No-thing, he motherless world will then disappear; maybe slowly, but it will.

Bibliography

Anders, Günther. 1994. *Die Antiquiertheit des Menschen*. München: Verlag Beck.
Bertell, Rosalie. 2000. *Planet Earth. The Latest Weapon of War*. London: The Womens Press
Binswanger, Christoph. 1985. *Geld und Magie*. Stuttgart: Verlag Weitbrecht.
Bruiger, Dan. *Second Nature - The Man-made world of Idealism, Technology and Power*. Victoria/Can.: Leftfieldpress
Budge, E.A. Wallis. 1969. *The Gods of the Egyptians*. Vol. 2, New York: Dover.
Budge, E.A. Wallis. 1978. *An Egyptian Hieroglyphic Dictionary*. Vol. 2, New York: Dover.
Butler, Judith. 1991. *Das Unbehagen der Geschlechter*. Frankfurt a. M.: Suhrkamp
Caldicott, Helen. 2002. *The New Nuclear Danger: George W. Bush's Military-Industrial Complex*. New York: New Press.
Easlea, Brian. 1986. *Die Väter der Vernichtung. Männlichkeit, Naturwissenschaftler und der nukleare Rüstungswettlauf*. Reinbek: Verlag Rowohlt.
Eliade, Mircea. 1980. *Schmiede und Alchemisten*. Stuttgart: Verlag Klett-Cotta.
Federici, Silvia. 2004. *Caliban and the Witch. Women, the Body and Primitive Accumulation*, New York: Autonomedia
Frankenberg, Gisela von. 1985. *Kulturvergleichendes Lexikon*. Bonn: Verlag Gisela Meussling.
Genth, Renate. 2002. *Über Maschinisierung und Mimesis. Erfindungsgeist und mimetische Begabung im Widerstreit und ihre Bedeutung für das Mensch-Maschine-Verhältnis*. Frankfurt and New York: Verlag Peter Lang.
Girard, René. 1972. *La violence et le sacré*. Paris: Éditions Bernard Grasset.
Haraway, Donna. 1983. *A Manifesto for Cyborgs: Science, Technology and Socialist Feminism in the 1980's*, in: *Socialist Revolution* 80. 65-107.
Holloway, John. 2006. *Die Welt verändern ohne die Macht zu übernehmen*. Münster: Westfälisches Dampfboot.
Joy, Bill. (2000). Warum die Zukunft uns nicht braucht, in: *FAZ, Frankfurter Allgemeine Zeitung*, 6. Juni
Kutschmann, Werner. 1986. *Der Naturwissenschaftler und sein Körper*. Frankfurt: Verlag Suhrkamp.
Marx, Karl. 1974. in MEW (Marx-Engels-Werke), Vol. 23: *Das Kapital 1*. Berlin: Verlag Dietz.
Marx, KARL. 1974. *Der Fetischcharakter der Ware und sein Geheimnis*, in: Marx, Karl und Engels, Friedrich, Werke, MEW, Vol. 23: *Das Kapital 1*. Berlin: Verlag Dietz. 85-98.

Mies, Maria. 1986. *Patriarchy and Accumulation on a World Scale: Women in the International Division of Labour* (esp. chapter on "Social Origins of the Sexual Division of Labour"). London: Zed Books.

Mies, Maria. 2005. *Krieg ohne Grenzen. Die neue Kolonisierung der Welt.* Köln: PapyRossa.

Mies, Maria, and Claudia von Werlhof (Eds.) 2003. *Lizenz zum Plündern. Das Multilaterale Abkommen über Investitionen – MAI. Globalisierung der Konzernherrschaft, und was wir dagegen tun können.* Hamburg: EVA.

Mies, Maria, Veronika Bennholdt-Thomsen, Claudia von Werlhof. 1988. *Women: the Last Colony.* London: Zed Books.

Mooney, Pat. 2010. *Next BANG! Wie das riskante Spiel mit Megatechnologien unsere Existenz bedroht*, München: oekom.

Plato. 1994. *Sämtliche Werke.* Vol. 2. Reinbek: Rowohlt.

Polanyi, Karl. 1978. *The Great Transformation: Politische und ökonomische Ursprünge von Gesellschaften und Wirtschaftssystemen.* Frankfurt: Suhrkamp.

Rifkin, Jeremy. 1983. *Algeny.* New York: The Viking Press.

Rifkin, Jeremy. 1998. *The Biotech Century.* New York: Tarcher/Putnam

Schirrmacher, Frank (Ed.). 2001. *Die Darwin AG. Wie Nanotechnologie, Biotechnologie und Computer den neuen Menschen träumen*, Köln: Kiepenheuer & Witsch.

Schütt, Hans Werner: *Auf der Suche nach dem Stein der Weisen. Die Geschichte der Alchemie*. München: Beck

Schumpeter, Josef. 1962. *Capitalism, Socialism, and Democracy.* New York: Harper Torchbooks.

Sloterdijk, Peter / Macho, Thomas (Eds.). 1991. *Weltrevolution der Seele: Ein Lese- und Arbeitsbuch der Gnosis.* Vol 2. Gütersloh: Artemis and Winkler.

Sohn-Rethel, Alfred. 1970. *Geistige und körperliche Arbeit: Zur Theorie der gesellschaftlichen Synthesis*, Frankfurt: Suhrkamp.

The American Heritage Dictionary. 2001. New York: Dell-Random.

Treusch-Dieter, Gerburg. 2001. *Die Heilige Hochzeit. Studien zur Totenbraut.* Herbolzheim: Centaurus.

Vaughan, Genevieve. 1997. *For-Giving: A Feminist Criticism of Exchange.* Austin: Plain View Press.

Verhaag, Bertram. 2004. *Leben außer Kontrolle.* München: Denkmalfilm.

Walker, Barbara. 1988. *The Woman's Dictionary of Symbols and Sacred Objects.* New York: Harper & Row.

Wallerstein, Immanuel. 1974. "The Rise and Future Demise of the World Capitalist System: Concepts for Comparative Analysis." *Comparative Studies in Society and History* 16 (4): 387-415.

Werlhof, Claudia von. 1997. "Ökonomie, die praktische Seite der Religion. Wirtschaft als Gottesbeweis und die Methode der Alchemie." Eds. Ulla Ernst, et al. *Ökonomie (M)macht Angst.* Frankfurt and New York: Peter Lang. 95-121.

Werlhof, Claudia von. 2000. "Patriarchat als Alchemistisches System. Die (Z)ErSetzung des Lebendigen." Ed. Maria Wolf. *Optimierung und Zerstörung. Intertheoretische Analysen zum Menschlich-Lebendigen.* Innsbruck: Studia. 13-31.

Werlhof, Claudia von. 2001. "Losing Faith in Progress. Capitalist Patriarchy as an 'Alchemical System' ". Eds. Veronika Bennholdt-Thomsen, Nicholas Faraclas, Claudia von Werlhof. *There is an Alternative: Subsistence and Worldwide Resistance to Corporate Globalization.* London: Zed Books. 15-40.

Werlhof, Claudia von. 2004. "Using, Producing, and Replacing Life? Alchemy as Theory and Practice in Capitalism". Ed. Immanuel Wallerstein. *The Modern World-System in the Longue Durée.* Boulder and London: Paradigm Press. 65-78.

Werlhof, Claudia von. 2006. "Patriarchy as Negation of Matriarchy – the Perspective of a Delusion." Ed. Heide Goettner-Abendroth. *Gesellschaft in Balance. Dokumentation des 1. Weltkongresses für Matriarchatsforschung.* Stuttgart: Edition HAGIA und Verlag Kohlhammer.

Werlhof, Claudia von. 2007. "Capitalist Patriarchy and the Struggle for a 'Deep' Alternative." *Women and the Gift Economy: A Radically Different Worldview is Possible.* Ed. Genevieve Vaughan. Toronto: Inanna Publications. 139-153.

C

The Globalization of Capitalist Patriarchy and the Alternatives

9. Globalization, Patriarchy, and Women's Movements[*]

Neoliberalism, Patriarchy, and Women's Movements, in: From Thoughts to Action, Journal of the ESF (European Social Forum) Action Network, Malmö/Sweden, 2008, short version, 2 p.

- revised and complete version -

Preliminary remark 2010

"Modernizing" the life conditions of women does not help them to escape patriarchy, as we can clearly see today. This is due to the fact that patriarchy is totally different in its character than even feminist women have thought it to be. This difference has to be analyzed and interpreted via the Critical Theory of Patriarchy. Its aim is to offer a better view on the alternatives to patriarchy, especially on the alternative(s) to capitalist patriarchy, in order to prevent women from participating in the further completion of patriarchy and from getting deeper into the maelstrom of "West-End" as is the case already.

Introduction

On the occasion of the International Women's Day, I want to present my views on the socio-cultural circumstances in which women find themselves in today and which define their possibilities of action. I will share my understanding of globalization, of globalization's consequences for women, and of patriarchy. My views on patriarchy and globalization are closely linked because globalization takes patriarchy to its conclusion. The main questions will be how this affects women and women's movements, and which possibilities for action remain. I will address both the examples we have seen in this respect and the difficulties we are facing.

1. Processes of Globalization

So-called globalization is an expression of the crisis of the "capitalist world system" (1). Since the 1970s, in particular since the US-administered coup in Chile in 1973, we are confronted with a new economic politics, so-called neo-

---

[*] Translation from German by Dr. Gabriel Kuhn

liberalism. In Chile, this economic politics was first introduced under a military dictatorship. Neo-liberalism undermines the welfare state and its role as a provider and caretaker for the people. The public sphere is destroyed and any extra-economic influence on economy, politics, and social life rendered impossible.

Through its redistribution of wealth from the bottom to the top, neo-liberalism maintains, even increases, the profits of big corporations. This reveals the crisis of the system as a whole. Neo-liberalism becomes necessary because the corporations' profits are threatened by global competition, the formation of oligopolies and monopolies, and the various crises of "development" and financial markets.

Neo-liberalism only serves the interests of corporations that act internationally and globally. Neo-liberalism means corporate politics (2).

Since the 1980s, many countries in the South have experienced the consequences of this politics. In the US and the UK it was introduced under Ronald Reagan and Margaret Thatcher respectively. Austria adapted to neoliberal politics by joining the European Union in 1995. The EU is a neoliberal project. This can be clearly detected from the treaties of Amsterdam and Maastricht all the way through to the drafts for an EU constitution (3).

The global trends of neo-liberalism become most obvious in the activities of the World Bank and the International Monetary Fund (IMF), as well as in the treaties of the World Trade Organization (WTO), particularly the General Agreement on Trade in Service (GATS). The GATS intends no less than "commodifying" all our actions, thoughts and feelings, and all natural elements – not only land, but also water, warmth/energy and even air. This will allow private corporations to gain profits from all of life's dimensions (4).

If modern economy is understood as the attempt to globally turn land and labor into commodities (5), then this process has so far always faced limitations. For a long time, certain wilderness areas remained inaccessible and certain political regimes would not yield to neoliberal force (for example pre-war Yugoslavia or pre-war Iraq). Also, the public and the domestic sectors were defined as "non-profit" sectors and were hence exempted from commercialization.

Neoliberal politics have changed this. The WTO's notion of Non-Agricultural Market Access (NAMA) provides for commercial exploitation of the last remaining wilderness areas. Wars are being waged to change governments, who are obstacles to Western interests, and to "open" new markets and allow the respective countries' resources to be plundered (6). Finally, the GATS-Agreement is facilitating the transformation of the public and domestic sectors into commercialized "services" (7).

What all this makes clear is that modern economy does not content itself with transforming local and regional subsistence economies (including "simple" commodity production following concrete needs) into capitalist commodity production that serves national and global markets (8). Neo-liberalism rather demands that this "Great Transformation" affects (the production of) reproduction as well, and hence all areas that have so far remained beyond its control. What the beginnings of industrialization revealed was that there was no production without reproduction. In other words, where life and living beings cannot be reproduced independently of market interests and immediate exploitation, no exploitation will, in the long run, be possible at all. This is why the modern nuclear family, the housewife and the housewife's unpaid labor have been established. This is what guarantees the (re)production of the workforce across generations without extra cost.

Today, cutting costs is still mandatory. Everything else, however, is about to change. Health, education, transport, communication, culture, and even the most basic needs like water, are turned into means for profit (9).

Neoliberal politics is usually justified by claiming that more development and more jobs are needed. This, in turn, will supposedly increase the common good. According to the neoliberal argument, this process can be administered much more professionally and efficiently by private companies than by the public or domestic sector.

Today we know that these claims are false. The products and services of private companies are increasingly more expensive while their quality is increasingly worse. To save costs, infrastructure is neglected and eventually one needs a lot of money to provide and receive goods and services. In the end, it is only the corporations that become more affluent, find new, profitable fields of activity, and reap the benefits of the restructuring and privatization of the public sector.

Of great importance to the "GLP politics" (Globalization, Liberalization, Privatization) are the SAPs, the Structural Adjustment Programs, of the World Bank and the IMF. These are levied against the countries of the South. The North calls them "austerity packages". They are part of what we might call a "global raid" intending to pull everything into the world market that still remains outside. Since it is international corporations that conduct this raid – often hailed as "development" – many small, medium and even some bigger corporations can only partake temporarily. The real global players are others.

The ways in which power structures increasingly turn into oligopolies and monopolies indicate that markets are characterized by unequal exchange much rather than "fair" or "just" exchange. They also indicate that it is crude exploitation, violent robbery and often irreversible destruction of life, living space and culture, which lies at the bottom of commodification. All human cultures are subjugated to a continued process of "original accumulation" and lose what they need for survival. The accumulation of capital increasingly takes on the form of simple expropriation. There are numerous examples of this, and the process has been analyzed by many (10).

The neoliberal treaties refuse to halt this process or adopt measures that would add a social or ecological dimension to economic interest. In fact, corporations perceive such measures as "indirect expropriation". In light of what is actually happening this allegation is ludicrous. Corporations assume that all resources, markets and investment areas are theirs alone (11).

This is why the neoliberal treaties contain special clauses that attempt to make international, national or communal resistance to their policies impossible. Such resistance can even be met by civil law suits according to WTO regulations. This is already happening.

The WTO treaties are negotiated by government representatives and corporations – always in secrecy. The public, whose opinion does not count in any case, has always remained excluded. The media usually does not report on the treaties at all. When they do, the reports are affirmative and trivial.

Not to make the politics transparent is intentional. The goal is to put it into effect without meeting resistance. "Speed kills" is the cynical slogan often used. Once a treaty has been ratified, it becomes international law. At that point, all resistance is futile. The GATS for example – like all WTO treaties – works effectively as if it was part of a global constitution. The goal is irreversible corporate privatization.

The enormous process to turn the whole world into a factory and marketplace hence receives absolute priority and becomes cemented in law. This also means that, if need be, it can be implemented by force (12).

In a sense, modernity reaches its "second phase". The transformation of the world into commodity, i.e. money, capital, machinery and command over labor (13) now reaches the most remote corners of the planet, the deepest levels of society and even our bodies. We can call this a sort of "revolution from above". In the process, democratic rules are – not only in Chile – ever more blatantly dismissed.

2. Globalization and Women

The dismantling of public services, the sale and privatization of socialized industries and the deterioration of the welfare state affect women in particular. Many of the most decent job opportunities for women disappear – without substitute. The new opportunities are all insecure, "precarious". Women increasingly find themselves in situations where the gap between labor and salary becomes enormous. While being forced to find wage labor, the only jobs available are poorly paid and often temporary. At the same time, living expenses are rising and education as well as health services are being privatized. Many women cannot afford such services any longer – many more will not be able to in the near future. This means even more and especially unpaid work for women because it is women who are expected to take care of the sick, the elderly and the young.

We can call this the second phase of "housewifization", i.e. the process of demanding women to do unpaid work both within the household and outside. Its second phase is characterized by the imminent collapse of traditional workforce reproduction, both in quantity and quality. This becomes obvious in the "Gebärstreik" (the refusal to give birth – women's own "labor strike"), as well as in the increasing number of divorces, poverty-stricken families, destitute elderly and neglected children.

The commodification of everything will reach its limits. However the system cannot allow to establish regular wage labor conditions – in particular with regard to unpaid housework. This poses a remarkable contradiction to the usual claims of those, advocating commodity production and its expansion.

Women have long demanded "wages for housework" (14). Today, housework has become partially commercialized and is loosing its subsistence character, i.e. it is no longer "real" non-commodity or subsistence production. Housework remains organized like subsistence work, but it generates a particular commodity (at least potentially): human labor. Housework becomes the most important mediator between life/subsistence and market/commodity. Its transformation into "obvious" commodity production and wage labor, however, is not accompanied by legal provisions that would guarantee real compensation or salaries. This means that despite of housework being "socialized", there is no "just" salary – or no salary at all. What we are witnessing is an increasing "housewifization" (instead of a "proletarianization") of women's labor in general. Today, the same applies to men. Labor conditions are "informalized" and "precarized" everywhere (15). I call the result "housewifized commodity production" ("wage-less commodity production") (16). This can take on the form of "commercialized" housework ("new maid question"), precarious employment, outsourced contracting, and even indentured labor or outright slavery of women as well as of men (17).

In this sense, neo-liberalism not only fails to overcome the modern principle of not remunerating the reproduction of the workforce (so vital for capitalism's profitability) (18); neo-liberalism extends, even generalizes this principle. The "cheap gender" becomes the model for cheapening labor in general. Most of today's profits are based on this development of "stealing" labor. The development is strongest in the global South and East. Not only does the unpaid housewife remain characteristic in these regions, but there are also masses of small commodity producers who earn practically nothing: small farmers, marginalized producers/laborers, and the new slaves and "housewifized" wage laborers of the outsourced industries in the "free production zones" or "world market factories" where contractors produce everything for corporations from sneakers to computer chips (19).

Today, the labor conditions of the North increasingly resemble those of the South, while those of men increasingly resemble those of women (20). Underdevelopment reaches everywhere. Instead of the Third World becoming like the First, the First increasingly becomes like the Third. It is simply more profitable not to pay wages – or only low ones. It has always been the "housewife" and not the "proletarian" who represented capitalism's ideal workforce (21). Today, this ideal is implemented globally, for men too.

Most have remained oblivious to the logic of this process since they were made to believe that housework is indeed not labor but a part of "woman's nature". In consequence, housework's role as the basis for a profitable capitalist economy has been notoriously denied.

The socialist claim that the liberation of women is possible through socializing/industrializing housework and through women entering the wage labor market has been proven wrong. There is no viable perspective for women. Neither will they survive based on housework and a providing "bread winner" alone, nor will they earn a decent living as wage laborers. Reality contradicts all ideologies claiming to improve the conditions of women. The workforce increasingly counts as nothing more but a "natural resource" that needs no (or hardly any) remuneration. Accordingly, a highly qualitative reproduction of the workforce seems no longer necessary.

Free wage labor and "normal wage labor conditions" have reached their end. Capitalism, however, has not, to the contrary. This contradiction is today's main contradiction of labor (22). But the trade unions do not respond to it.

It becomes ever more obvious that commodity production is destructive rather than creative. Commodity production means the destruction of resources. The whole world is used and exploited, including its people (as "forces of labor"). Capitalism is literally cannibalism. So far, there have only been few who have acknowledged this. The Austrian Joseph Schumpeter has called this process "creative destruction", suggesting creation to be its dominant feature, not destruction. In light of today's scarcity of resources, climatic changes, the production of seemingly "natural" catastrophes and the increasing problems of "human ecology", it seems impossible to sustain this illusion.

3. Patriarchy: "Replacing" Women and Nature?

Also technologically our economic system offers no solution. Modern economy and technology much rather wage a war against nature, women and life. All that counts is domination of nature and the transformation of everything natural into commodities, money and other alleged human "creations". No one is interested in satisfying the true needs of human beings, let alone in cooperating with nature.

This leads us to patriarchy which – contrary to capitalism which is only 500 years old – has been in existence for about 5000 years (23). By patriarchy I understand the presumption that it is the male gender that is creative and not the female. In patriarchy, one permanently tries to prove that creation comes from men, their institutions, their power and their technology – not from women, women's culture, and nature. Within this logic, life becomes a male invention and a male god becomes life's "creator".

The politics of destruction that goes along with this is justified by claiming that nature, even planet Earth and women have to be dominated and controlled. Eventually, they even ought to be replaced by artificial products: more male "creations".

This development is defined as "technological progress". Within its logic, life comes from men or machines. Reproductive technologies, genetic engineering or nanotechnology are all blatant examples of how modernity tries to render women unnecessary as mothers and to replace as many natural processes as possible by technological monster projects (24), not to speak of "geo-engineering" as a supposed means to "cool" the planet and to take control over it as a whole (25).

This is why modernity's commodity production is, unnoticed by the left, a project of destruction: production shows itself as devastation. One attempts to replace nature, motherhood and subsistence production, and even the planet by their exact opposites.

Modernity is an era in which patriarchal society wants to prove materially that men can count as creators of the world, today even of our planet, and are not dependent on women or nature as a whole anymore. Since there is a lot of "capital" to be generated, control to be gained and money to be made, this process has established its dominance in the name of "capitalism" and/as "globalization" on all levels.

The attempt to turn the world on its head and to replace reality with something else is based on an illusion. It is doomed to fail. However, only by recognizing its failure, the essence of the project becomes clear. Many still believe that the destruction we are facing is not that troubling – either because they themselves are not affected by it yet, or because they continue to believe that something different, a new and better world, a "higher" civilization will follow.

4. Women's Response and Women's Movements

The process of globalization seems to leave two options for women. Either they partake as much as they can (because they feel like there is no other way or because they too have come to believe in "progress") or they step out of line and start looking for alternatives.

Several problems keep many women from doing the latter: notions of patriarchy that are way too superficial; a general lack of understanding about the connections between patriarchy, capitalism and globalization; and the fact that an ever increasing number of women has bought into the notion of progress (26).

There exist divides between women – mainly along the lines of North/South and East/West – and much confusion. Western women, for example, have for the most part accepted a capitalist and patriarchal logic and, accordingly, display hostility towards body and nature. This phenomenon is part of the patriarchal venture itself and not restricted to Christianity. Many women give up on being creators of life. They have accepted the patriarchal notion that they can only overcome repression, exclusion and inferior social status by denying both their body and womanhood.

As a consequence, women are being transformed, and actively transform themselves, from a "truly bodily" (*leibhaftig*) witch to an "objectified" housewife, and from there via technology to a "gender" machine, work machine, sex machine and/or birth machine. The transformation of women veers ever more towards their abolishment/replacement – a process that many women themselves support today (27). Women's politics have become the politics of technology. For many the question has become how to best overcome their body and womanhood. Many try to escape a patriarchal female identity by patriarchal means. This is only logical, of course. It is a logical response to the desolate conditions that women have been facing for a long time and that are inherent in the patriarchal capitalist system. However, detaching oneself from one's own body is ultimately impossible and undesirable. No objectification without body? Maybe, but no life either.

The postmodern attempt to embrace new "identities" or to distance ourselves from those which define us now is usually a Pyrrhic victory for women. It also leads to abandoning solidarity because women – fulfilling patriarchy's needs – anticipate their own technological replacement and try to transform and replace themselves. The patriarchal hostility towards the body and womanhood can nowadays be found within women themselves. Some women have their breasts amputated and many become anorexic in order to escape their bodily womanhood through a kind of self-mutilation.

The women's movement is the attempt to escape conditions which provide no future. For a long time, this has meant to escape the household since women cannot survive as housewives and mothers alone. However, the prospect of finding liberation in wage labor is today more daunting than ever.

What then, is our future? Do we even have one? What we have is not working anymore, but the apparent alternative is not working either. "Independence" proves not to be the answer, as it mostly seems to be another, just more public form of housewifeization. While we cannot afford to be mothers alone, we can not be proletarians or capitalists either.

People fall into the trap of enlightenment when they start looking for equality where there is difference – for example between men and women. In the most extreme cases, one tries to eradicate difference technologically, for example women's ability to give birth. Ultimately, this means an attempt at abolishing women altogether – at least as mothers (28). Of course the attempt will be unsuccessful, but it will do huge damage to life.

Buying into patriarchal thought and the patriarchal project is what I consider the main problem of women and women's movements today, especially in the global North. Women have begun to accept the patriarchal allegations that, as "women", they are inferior, non-productive and worthless. This should not surprise us too much. They have been forced to believe in this as "truth" long enough (29).

I think we can see this as a prisoner phenomenon. Living within the system means for many that there is no escape, no outside – just as if we were in prison. It appears as if the system has incorporated everything. It appears as if there is indeed no more nature – or that it only exists as a source of exploitation. It also appears as if womanhood outside the system's definitions is not (or no longer) possible. The only option that apparently remains is to take "power" within the system (30) – but unfortunately, this translates into complicity. The challenge is to distance oneself from the system altogether.

The liberation of women does neither come from adapting to patriarchy nor from abolishing womanhood. It comes from the inner, spiritual detachment from capitalist and patriarchal assumptions and from another way of acting that is resulting from it. The intellectual capacity of women should not be used to affirm the system or to turn it into a "fetish" (31). It should be used to become dissident and subversive. The conditions we are facing today must not be accepted as an unchangeable reality.

The liberation of women happens neither through housework nor wage labor. It happens through liberation from patriarchy and its latest form, capitalism (including socialism).

The wrong turn that has led women into patriarchy has to be rectified. Women have to find their way out of the patriarchal system. There must be a future for women, in which they are not forced to deny their body and motherhood or to partake in their own depreciation. There must be a future for women in which they will not have to defend patriarchal interests as their own.

What is at stake is that women, in a radical and fundamental way, bid farewell to self-hatred and the patriarchal criteria that judge them. Women must remember their own culture which has existed everywhere on this planet – and which still exists, right among us, often as so-called "second culture" (32). It is revived in many alternative movements. It is no surprise then that most truly alternative movements are women's movements.

Women can regain their joy for life. Women can reject the nihilism of global patriarchy and the systematic destruction it implies. Women can recapture the richness of life. In fact, this is their only option.

References

1) Immanuel Wallerstein: The rise and Future Demise of the World Capitalist System: Concepts for Comparative Analysis, in: Comparative Studies in society and History, Vol. 16, No.4, 1974, pp. 387-415
2) Noam Chomsky: Profit over People. Neoliberalism and Global Order, New York: Seven Stories Press 1999; Michel Chossudovsky: The Globalisation of Poverty. Impacts of IMF and World Bank Reforms, Penang: Third World Network 1997; Maria Mies/Claudia von Werlhof (Eds.): Lizenz zum Plündern. Das Multilaterale Abkommen über Investitionen – MAI. Globalisierung der Konzernherrschaft- und was wir dagegen tun können, Hamburg: Rotbuch 2003; Claudia von Werlhof: Alternativen zur neoliberalen Globalisierung oder Die Globalisierung des Neoliberalismus und seine Folgen, Wien: picus 2007 (The Globalization of Neoliberalism, its Consequences, and Some of ist Basic Alternatives, in: CNS, Vol. 19, Issue 3, September 2008, London/New York: Routledge, pp. 94-117
3) Gerald Oberansmayr: Auf dem Weg zur Supermacht, Die Militarisierung der Europäischen Union, Wien: Promedia 2004
4) Mies/ Werlhof: Lizenz, pp. 7-23: Werlhof: Alternativen, pp. 46-51
5) Wallerstein: The rise....
6) Maria Mies: Krieg ohne Grenzen. Die neue Kolonisierung der Welt, Köln: PapyRossa 2004
7) Mies/ Werlhof: Lizenz, pp. 7ff
8) Karl Polanyi: The Great Transformation. Politische und ökonomische Ursprünge von Gesellschaften und Wirtschaftssystemen, Frankfurt: Suhrkamp 1978
9) Maude Barlow/Tony Clarke: Blue Gold. The Battle against Corporate Theft of the World's Water, Toronto: Stoddart Publishing, 2002
10) Claudia von Werlhof/ Veronika Bennholdt-Thomsen/ Nicholas Faraclas (Eds.): There is an Alternative. Subsistence and worldwide Resistance to Corporate Globalization, London: zedpress 2001
11) Maria Mies: Globalisierung von unten. Der Kampf gegen die Herrschaft der Konzerne, Hamburg: Rotbuch/EVA 2002, p. 7
12) Mies: Krieg...
13) Karl Marx: Capital, Vol. 1, Moscow: Progress Publ. 1887
14) Power of Women Collective/Lotta Femminista/Brigitte Galtier: Frauen in der Offensive. Lohn für Hausarbeit oder: Auch Berufstätigkeit macht nicht frei, München: Frauenoffensive 1974 (orig. in Italien language)
15) Widerspruch, Nr. 49: Prekäre Arbeitsgesellschaft, Zürich 2005
16) Claudia von Werlhof: The Proletarian is dead. Long live the Housewife?

The Economic Crisis and War Danger as Problems of a Restructuring of the International and Sexual Division of Labour, in: Maria, Mies/Veronika Bennholdt-Thomsen/Claudia von Werlhof: Women, the Last Colony, London: zedpress 1988, pp. 168-181
17) Kevin Bales: Disposable People: New Slavery and the Global Economy, Berkeley: Univ. of. California. Press 1999
18) Mascha Madörin: Zur Verknüpfung von Kapitalismus und Männerherrschaft, in: Elmar Altvater u.a.: Die Gewalt des Zusammenhangs. Neoliberalismus – Militarismus – Rechtsextremismus, Wien: Promedia 2001, pp. 125-142
19) Christa Wichterich: Die globalisierte Frau. Berichte aus der Zukunft der Ungleichheit, Reinbek: Rowohlt 1999
20) Veronika Bennholdt-Thomsen/Maria Mies/Claudia von Werlhof: Women, the Last Colony, London: zedpress 1988
21) C. v. Werlhof: The Proletarian... , Claudia von Werlhof: (Haus)Frauen, „Gender" und die Schein-Macht des Patriarchats, in: Widerspruch, Nr. 44: Feminismus, Gender, Geschlecht, Zürich 2003, pp. 173-189
22) Claudia von Werlhof: No Critique of Capitalism without a Critique of Patriarchy! Why the Left is No Alternative, in: CNS - Capitalism Nature Socialism, Vol.18, Number 1, March 2007, pp. 13-27
23) Claudia von Werlhof: Patriarchy as Negation of Matriarchy – On the Perspective of a Delusion, in: Heide Göttner-Abendroth (Ed.): Societies of Peace, Documents of the World Congresses on Matriarchal Studies in 2003 in Luxemburg and 2005 in Texas, Toronto: Inanna 2008, forthcoming
24) Claudia von Werlhof: Patriarchat als „Alchemistisches System". Die (Z)ErSetzung des Lebendigen, in: Maria Wolf (Ed.): Optimierung und Zerstörung. Intertheoretische Analysen zum menschlich Lebendigen, Innsbruck: Studia 2000, pp. 13-31
25) Claudia von Werlhof: What is Man Doing – What Mother Earth? The Planet in Growing Distress...www.pbme-online.org, 2010; generally see Bertell, Rosalie: Planet Earth. The Latest Weapon of War, London: The Womens Press 200
26) Werlhof: (Haus)Frauen...
27) Tina Thürmer-Rohr u.a. (Eds..): Mittäterschaft und Entdeckungslust, Berlin: Subrosa 1989
28) Hilde Schmölzer: Die abgeschaffte Mutter. Der männliche Gebärneid und seine Folgen, Wien: Promedia 2005
29) Silvia Federici: Caliban and the Witch. Women, the Body and Primitive accumulation, New York: Autonomedia 2004

30) Michel Foucault: Discipline and Punish: The Birth of the Prison, New York: Vintage 1977
31) John Holloway: Die Welt verändern ohne die Macht zu übernehmen, Münster: Westfälisches Dampfboot 2006 (orig. in Spanish language)
32) Renate Genth: Matriarchat als „zweite Kultur". in: Claudia von Werlhof/ Annemarie Schweighofer/Werner Ernst (Eds.): HerrenLos. Herrschaft – Erkenntnis – Lebensform, Frankfurt 1996, pp. 17-38

10. Capitalist Patriarchy, the Re-Emergence of Matriarchy and the Struggle for a 'Deep' Alternative

Parts of "Capitalist Patriarchy and the Negation of Matriarchy" in Vaughan, Genevieve (Ed.): Women and the Gift Economy. A Radically Different World View is Possible, Toronto 2007 (Inanna), pp. 139-153

Introduction

In her important book, *For-Giving: A Feminist Criticism of Exchange*, Genevieve Vaughan states: "In order to reject patriarchal thinking we must be able to distinguish between it and something else: an alternative" (Vaughan 1977: 23). I identify with this statement as I, too, have tried "to think outside patriarchy" although being inside it most of the time. At the "First World Congress of Matriarchal Studies," held in Luxemburg in 2003, where Vaughan and I first met, she stated, "If we don't understand society in which we live we cannot change it; we do not know where the exit is!" Therefore, "we have to dismantle patriarchy." In this article, I would like to add to Vaughan's analysis of capitalist patriarchy and tackle the task of dismantling patriarchy.

"A Different World is Possible!"

This has been the main slogan of the worldwide civilian movement against globalization for years. I have to add: "A *radically* different world is possible!" – it is not only possible but also urgently needed. But without a *vision* of this radically different world we will not be able to move in this direction. Therefore we need to discuss, first of all, a radically different worldview. For this purpose we have to analyze what is happening today and why. Only then will we be able to define a really *different* world, worldview and vision.

"Globalization"

A radically different worldview is necessary because today we are observing global social, economic, ecological, and political developments that are completely different from what they should be. "Globalization" is obviously not a movement toward more democracy, peace, general welfare, wealth, and ecological sustainability, as its propagators are pretending everywhere. On the contrary, the opposite is true. Never in history are so many people dying from hunger and thirst, environmental destruction, and war, most of them women and children. Never in history have so many people been confined to poverty, income reduction, expulsion, expropriation, and extreme exploitation, again, most of them women and children. Never in history has technological progress led to such intense and threatening destruction of the environment globally. Never in history has the nuclear threat been so acute. Never in history have the political systems been changing so clearly in the direction of authoritarian, if not despotic rule in many parts of the world. And never in history has such a tiny minority on the globe been so incredibly rich and powerful. For transnational corporations and their "global players" today, we, and the planet, are nothing but their "play material."

This situation can be called the "development of underdevelopment" (Frank 1978). But this time underdevelopment is not only taking place in the South, but also in the North. It is the result of a "new colonization of the world" (Mies 2004) that did and does not happen inexplicably, but is actively and aggressively promoted by governments as their general and apparently "normal" policy, beginning in the 1980s of the twentieth century. This policy consists in a "continuing process of primitive accumulation" (Werlhof 1988 and 2000) that leads to a forced economic growth through the direct expropriation of the peoples of the globe and the globe itself. The name of this policy is "neo-liberalism." This new liberalism serves exclusively the interests of the corporations. For the rest of humanity it means just the opposite, totalitarianism.

Is this "New World Order" (Chomsky 1999; Chossudovsky 1996) the "best of all possible worlds" that western civilization pretends to develop? Or is the current development of western civilization better defined as the peak and turning point towards its final decline (Wallerstein 1974)?

Capitalist Patriarchy: A Historical Concept

Many people have provided descriptions of globalization as global crisis and its dynamics (Chossudovsky 1996; Hardt and Negri 2000; Wallerstein 2004; Ziegler 2002). There seems to be "no future" – astonishingly enough even for the global players themselves. I call this situation *west end* (Werlhof 2002). Western civilization is in its final decline globally. With the self-given "licence to loot" (Mies and Werlhof 2003; Werlhof 2000), the resources of the earth will come to an end. The decline of resources is already underway. With the resulting "resource wars" (Klare 2001) – the new global wars for oil and water – we are witnessing the beginning of the end of the "modern world system" as a logical consequence.

But, there is almost no deeper analysis of the causes of this extraordinary situation or the dynamics that seem to exclude any alternative. There is no real, no deeper explanation of the world's dilemma and its causes (Werlhof 2007). For example, is the profit motive alone sufficient as an explanation? Why do most people believe that human nature is nothing but ego-centric? What about control and domination of nature? In what is it rooted?

I suggest the reason why most people do not really know why the crisis is happening is due to the fact that the left as well as the right, and the sciences in general, have never really analyzed patriarchy. And not having analyzed patriarchy also means not really understanding capitalism, because the two not only share a time of being together on this earth for 500 years now, but are deeply related to each other in a way that has not been understood by most people, even feminists. Therefore, it is time to take the necessary step of analyzing capitalist patriarchy from its roots and as a theoretical concept for the subsequent analysis of society. Only then can it be seen that patriarchy is much more than just a word for polemical purposes. It can instead be understood as a concept that explains the character of the entire social order in which we are living today, socialism included.

Capitalism: the Latest Stage of Patriarchy

Having defined patriarchy, what does this mean for defining capitalism? From my analysis of patriarchy it follows that capitalism and modernity, including so-called socialism, far from being or becoming independent from patriarchy, is the latest stage of patriarchy. My hypothesis is that patriarchy crystallizes into capitalism. Capitalism is the period in which patriarchy becomes really serious. *Homo faber* is supposed to be finally replaced by "homo creator", a sort of secularized God.

This means that with capitalism there is a break as well as a continuation in patriarchy. But both tend in the same direction, namely fostering patriarchy. The logics of patriarchy led straight to the modern epoch, because capitalism is the promise to finally realize the futuristic Gnostic utopia materially and on earth. It consists of the intent to produce a purely patriarchal society, "cleaned" of all its matriarchal vestiges, and propagated as a male-created second paradise.

Gnostic metaphysics are to become the new physics. This is the propaganda of modern society as a whole, its politics, economy, religion and technology.

Gnosticism becomes secularized. The content is the same, but the program has become one of action. The times of mere contemplation are fading away and the *vita contemplativa* is followed by a new kind of *vita activa* (Arendt 1987).

Since the Renaissance, the always increasing numbers of inventors and colonizers, scientists and soldiers, entrepreneurs and explorers, settlers and missionaries, merchants and money lenders are the modern activists on their way to the proposed, second, man-made and eternal paradise on earth (Rifkin 1998).

This is the beginning of the "Great Transformation" (Polanyi 1978) for which modern Europe became so famous. The new epoch was for the most part *not* seen as a continuation of an earlier one. It seemed, instead, to be the birth hour of a totally new society, not bound to history any more, a society that would be able to solve all the problems of mankind (indeed, not of womankind) for ever.

From the point of view of patriarchy, capitalism is the epoch in which women, nature, and life in general are finally successfully replaced by the artificial products of industry: gifts by exchange; subsistence goods by commodities; local markets by a world market; foreign cultures by western culture; concrete wealth and gifts by money, machinery, and capital, the new abstract wealth; living labor by machines; the brain/rational thinking by "artificial intelligence"; women by sex-machines and "cyber-sex"; real mothers and/or their wombs by "mother-machines"; life energy by nuclear energy, chemistry, and bio-industry; and life in general by "artificial life" like genetically modified organisms (GMOs). The only problem that remains today consists in how to "replace" the elements and the globe itself (see Introduction and part D.).

Therefore, technological progress – via the development of modern sciences and the invention of the machine as a totally new technological system – is the logical backbone of the modern patriarchal epoch. Patriarchy itself is progress, and all *"progress" today is patriarchal*. It serves the project of a materialization of metaphysical images via an industrial "life"-production which I call the *"alchemical system"* in development, because the idea behind it is as old as patriarchy and its first attempts to progress used the methods of a patriarchally-modified "alchemy" (Werlhof 2001).

The invention of profit that could be drawn from this adventure of the whole world's transformation convinced always more people, mostly men. But many people, especially women, had to be violently forced to participate in the new game. The political means consisted in processes of "original accumulation" which deprived the peasants of their means of production and the women even of the disposal over their bodies – through the so called "witch-hunt" – by leaving nearly no way to survive beyond capitalism (Federici 2004).

Through "progress" Mother Earth will be more and more destroyed. Some of these fast growing destructions are already irreversible, especially those due to nuclear and genetic modifications (Anders 1995; Chargaff 1988; cf. introduction and part D.). Artificial death and artificial wealth – the violent "nothing" – a lot of money, is all that is left. The earth is on the way to being transformed into dead "capital," full of empty holes on the one side, and trash-hills for the next billion years on the other side.

That all this is possible shows that most people believe in the *violent nihilism of patriarchy* and its dangerous delusion that has become "real". This astonishing fact can only be understood when one considers that the "alchemical wonders" patriarchy is promising, do not stem just from modern times, but are prophecies already 5.000 years old. Therefore, the destruction and desertification of the global ecology, including the human one, has not led to a general panic. On the contrary, it seems that, at least in the West, it is believed that only when the natural world has gone, can the patriarchal one finally be constructed, in all its glory, instead.

Capitalism – as well as socialism – with its activism, optimism, positivism, rationality, and its irrational belief in patriarchy, world domination, money, science, technology, and violence, is not just capitalism, but has to be defined as "capitalist patriarchy" (and, by the way, not as "patriarchal capitalism" because there is no non-patriarchal capitalism). This epoch is still on the march because it has not yet reached its destination. Therefore, there is no post-capitalist, post-industrial, post-modern or post-materialist epoch in sight – unless capitalist patriarchy is stopped by a breakdown of its resources, technologies, markets, and money systems, by huge natural and or social catastrophes, or by an upheaval of the people who do not want to lose their lives, their planet, and the future of their children. If the "matter" of capitalism, its *mater*, its mothers, its women, and its matriarchal remains do not "obey" any more, and if nature fails to as well, only then will capitalist patriarchy disappear. And as capitalist patriarchy is obviously not a society for eternity, all this may well be happening today already.

The "Deep" Alternative: Re-Emergencce of Matriarchy

What has to be recognized

The alternative to capitalist patriarchy has to be a "deep" one, or it will fail. First of all, the "roots" of this war system will have to be recognized at all levels of society, individual life, history, and the globe. This will occur like a huge transdisciplinary research-project of and for the people. Out of this experience, the alternative will be a systematically non-capitalist and non-patriarchal one. It will be based on the remains of the "second culture" of matriarchy and of the gift-paradigm within patriarchal society, because they offer a body of concrete experiences people have been familiar with ever since humankind began on earth.

Even though these have been underestimated, hidden and made invisible to most of us, they can be made conscious again, and this is happening already in many parts of the world (see Bennholdt-Thomsen, von Werlhof and Faraclas 2001).

Even if it appears overwhelming to overcome not only 500 years of modernity, but 5.000 years of patriarchal traditions, this is actually very little in comparison to the hundreds of thousands of years of human experiences outside patriarchy that we have to draw upon.

On the other hand, partial change/reform that maintains features of capitalist patriarchy will most probably, and quickly, lead back to the system that must to be overcome if we want to continue life on earth. Whether the alternative/s that can be found on this basis will again be matriarchal ones or not, cannot be foreseen. At least they will be *post-patriarchal*. At the moment it is historically open if matriarchy can be re-invented, and/or what a matriarchal society and a gift-economy would mean today.

What has to be done

What is needed is a re-version of a perverted parasitic society and (wo)mankind. The patriarchal "mother-father" as a "cyborg," which is the alchemical materialization of a metaphysical fiction has to fade away as soon as possible. We can accomplish this in a number of ways, mainly:
- de-constructing patriarchal institutions, policies, economies, technologies, and ideologies;
- making visible matriarchy as the second culture, the subsistence perspective and the gift paradigm and recognizing their importance in every day life;
- giving up the metaphysical Gnostic worldview, including the belief in patriarchal religions and the patriarchal philosophy of idealism-materialism;
- re-gaining a matriarchal spirituality that leads again to a recognition of the interconnectedness of all life;
- not defining technology/progress any longer as having to produce a substitute for life, women, and nature in general;
- not defining economy any longer as having to produce a "value" and a profit;
- recognizing that the paradise which is supposed to be invented, is already here: It is the earth as the only planet in the known universe that is full of life and the only one on which human beings can survive;
- taking action to save the earth from further human destruction (see part D.);
- liberating ourselves from the idea that "material" [physical] life on earth is unimportant, sinful, humble, and something that has to be overcome;
- liberating ourselves from the delusion and the hubris that there can ever be a substitute for life and nature on earth and Mother Earth herself;

- learning the lessons of nature again, recognizing that the destruction of nature for the purpose of its transformation does not lead to a better world, but to its destruction;
- giving up war, believing in violence, and seeking to rule over others; learning instead to live in commonality and organizing around egalitarian principles;
- taking seriously what we are doing in and to the world, and accepting our responsibility for the maintenance of life on the planet – and the latter one as well;
- learning to rehabilitate and love life, including our own, and the life of the earth;
- seeking creative ways for the maintenance and culture of life on the earth; acting in favor of and not in contradiction to them;
- giving up "masculation" (Vaughan 1997), "egotism" as the search for competitive "identity," and identifying instead with gift-giving, subsistence and the traditions of men and women in matriarchal cultures;
- learning that women can teach us a lot;
- and, finally, we have to give up the belief in patriarchy and to join with others in order to stop it, listening instead to the song of Mother Earth.

We need to be able to perceive an alternative to capitalist patriarchy and see that this alternative is already in the making. Soon we will not be able to understand any more how men and women supported and even admired such a destructive delusion for such a long time!

The Struggle

Many alternative movements in the whole world are *already* in this process, for historical reasons most of them initiated in the global South (Kumar 2007) and most of them *guided by women*. This is the case because the South and women have and had to bear most of the negative consequences of patriarchy and especially capitalist patriarchy. This is why they are at the forefront of the new movements. Additionally, for women it is still much easier to remember matriarchal society and culture, subsistence and gift giving, because the remains of matriarchal culture and practices have for the most part been maintained by them. The way into a post-patriarchal society, therefore, is much more logical and visible for women than for men. The thinking, acting, and feeling of women, especially of poor women in the South, often shows a high level of dissonance with western globalization and culture. They defend life on the "two fronts" of the conflict: against the war system of capitalist patriarchy and in favor of a new society (Bennholdt-Thomsen, Werlhof and Faraclas 2001; Werlhof 1985, 1991, 1996).

Movements that are active on only one of the "two fronts" we are facing today, or movements that do not address the most important aspects and dimensions of life under patriarchal attack, will find themselves in crisis, sooner or later. This is the case with many movements in the North and of those traditionally guided by men (Werlhof 2007).

It seems as if a larger and deeper movement in the North will only be possible when the illusions of moving upward within the system have been lost and the daily conditions of life have worsened further. But, in the meantime, extremists of the far right and religious "fundamentalists" everywhere are preparing their field of action, too.

Nobody knows what will be left of alternative movements and "deep feminism" in North and South when the patriarchal system and order of society is imploding and dissolving, and when the conflicts within it become increasingly violent. But if anybody has a chance to move in the right direction, it is the truly alternative *post-patriarchal* groups, communities, and movements worldwide.

Bibliography

Anders, Günther. 1995 [1956]. *Die Antiquiertheit des Menschen*. München: Beck.
Arendt, Hannah. 1987 [1967]. *Vita Activa. Oder Vom tätigen Leben*. München: Piper.
Chargaff, Erwin. 1988. *Unbegreifliches Geheimnis. Wissenschaft als Kampf für und gegen die Natur*. Stuttgart: Klett Cotta.
Chossudovsky, Michel. 1996. *The Globalization of Poverty*. London: Zed Books.
Frank. André Gunder. 1978. *Dependent Accumulation and Underdevelopment*. London: Basigstoke.
Klare, Michael. 2001. *Resource Wars. The New Landscape of Global Conflict*. New York: Henry Holt and Company
Kumar, Corinne, Ed. 2007. *Asking, we walk. The South as new political imaginary*, 2 volumes, Bangalore: Sstreelekha
Mies, Maria / von Werlhof, Claudia. Eds. 2003 [1998]. *Lizenz zum Plündern. Das Multilaterale Abkommen über Investitionen – MAI – Globalisierung der Konzernherrschaft und was wir dagegen tun können*. Hamburg: Rotbuch/EVA
Polanyi, Karl. 1978 [1944]. *The Great Transformation. Politische und ökonomische Ursprünge von Gesellschaften und Wirtschaftssystemen*. Frankfurt: Suhrkamp
Rifkin, Jeremy. 1998. *The Biotech Century*. New York: Tarcher/Putnam.
Wallerstein, Immanuel. 1974. "The Rise und Future Demise of the World Capitalist System. Concepts for Comparative Analysis." *Comparative Studies in Society and History* 16 (4): 387-415.
Wallerstein, Immanuel. 2004. Interview at the World Social Forum, Mumbai 2004. *Netzwerk gegen Konzernherrschaft und neoliberale Politik*. Info brief Nr. 15. March 2004. Köln: Demokratie von unten statt Post-Demokratie. 8-10.
Werlhof, Claudia von. 1985. *Wenn die Bauern wiederkommen. Frauen, Arbeit und Agrobusiness in Venezuela*. Bremen: Peripheria/CON.
Werlhof, Claudia von. 1988. "Women's Work: The Blind Spot in the Critique of Political Economy." *The Last Colony: Women*. Eds. Maria Mies, Veronika Bennholdt-Thomsen, Claudia von Werlhof. London: Zed Books. 13-26.
Werlhof, Claudia von. 1991. *Was haben die Hühner mit dem Dollar zu tun? Frauen und Ökonomie*. München: Frauenoffensive.

Werlhof, Claudia von. 1996. Subsistenz. Abschied vom ökonomischen Kalkül?. *Herren-Los. Herrschaft-Erkenntnis-Lebensform.* Eds. Claudia von Werlhof, Annemarie Schweighofer and Werner Ernst. Frankfurt: Peter Lang. 364-393.

Werlhof, Claudia von. 2000. "'Globalization' and the 'Permanent' Process of 'Primitive Accumulation' - The Example of the Multilateral Agreement on Investment (MAI)." *Journal of World-Systems Research* 6 (3) (Fall/Winter): 728-747.

Werlhof, Claudia von. 2001. Losing Faith in Progress: Capitalist Patriarchy as an 'Alchemical System'". *Subsistence and Worldwide Resistance to Corporate Globalization: There is an Alternative.* Eds. Veronika Bennholdt-Thomsen, Nicholas Faraclas, Claudia von Werlhof. London: Zed Books, 15-40.

11. Upheaval from the Depth. The "Zapatistas", the Indigenous Civilization, the Question of Matriarchy, and the West

Partly published as "Questions to Ramona" in: Corinne Kumar (ed.): Asking we walk. The south as new political imaginary, Vol. 2, Bangalore (Streelekha) 2007, pp 249-268; as "Questions for Ramona: Zapatismo and Feminism", in: Midnight Notes: Auroras of the Zapatistas. Local and Global Struggles of the Fourth World War, New York (Autonomedia) 2001, pp 145-160; total version in International Journal of Comparative Sociology, IJCS, Leiden (Brill) 1997, pp 106-130.

Preliminary remark 2010

This article was written shortly after the beginnings of the Zapatista movement. At this moment in time it was already evident how important this movement would become – not only for Mexico, but also for the whole world and especially for the social movements that criticized the process of "globalization". Today, after more than a decade, this becomes even clearer:
- The social movements which work against the "globalization" of multinational capital did not start in the global North, but they started in the global South – four years earlier – namely with the Zapatista movement.
- The Zapatista movement made an analysis of "neo-liberal" globalization that was far more radical than the one made in the social movements in the North, because:
- it defined globalization as the "fourth world war" which is waged by financial capital;
- it noted that the process of globalization is going on in the whole world;
- it criticized modern civilization as such, including socialism as part of the modern epoch and its "world system";
- it called for an alternative for capitalism as a world system – and instead of calling for socialism as an alternative (as mostly done in the North) – it proposed the realization of an "indigenous" alternative, not only in Mexico, but worldwide;
- it foresaw the "necessary" failure of the neo-liberal policy of the multinational corporations long before the financial crash in 2008 and the economic crisis which has manifested itself especially in Mexico in the meantime.

This is the reason why the "Zapatismo" has become a general provocation, especially for many of the already existing social movements, as its aims are neither related to technical "progress", and to the economic exploitation of nature, nor to the political or military seizure of state power and the establishment of hierarchical social "systems" that include the subjugation of women. This was expressed in the "Sixth Declaration of the Lacandona Jungle" in 2005, which also contained the seed for the emergence of the "Other Campaign" of the Zapatistas. In this other campaign the people were mobilized politically, but did not support the electoral process and the candidate of the Left.

Instead of taking the path of "development", the Zapatistas are relying on everything that the indigenous world had continued to cultivate because of their history: the love for the earth, the universe and life, the egalitarian treatment of everybody, direct democracy and the subsistence economy, which is characterized as not being dependent on the establishment of "colonies". In one word, the Zapatistas re-introduced the respect for the "dignity" of everything existing, including the things or beings which existed before and the things or beings which will (or would) exist in the future.

The Zapatistas do not want to be like us. They prefer "asking when walking", and this walk will not take them to a better modernity but to fields completely alien to modernity. I call it a "non-western civilization". And they are provocating western people because they claim that also we, the Europeans, should choose the way that leads to another, "non western", civilization. This is the reason why the question arose: Which civilization has been and which one can be an "indigenous" European civilization?

The Zapatistas have been suffering from an enormous number and magnitude of attacks. The Mexican government has tried to ridicule it, it has threatened, persecuted and criminalized it; it has betrayed it, as the results of the agreement of "San Andrés" show; it has attacked it by military means with thousands of soldiers and para-military forces, it has killed 45 of its members in the "massacre of Acteal"; it has offered "development" and money; it has tried to divide it and it has tried to separate it from other indigenous communities. But nothing was able to destroy the Zapatista movement yet. It was decided that it should organize itself "horizontally", instead of vertically by means of the "groups for good government" and by means of the "Caracoles", 5 regional administration centres for dozens of "autonomous" communities which have in the meantime begun to use their own "indigenous law" since 2003. In several neighbour states within Mexico similar structures have been emerging and the APPA-movement of teachers and indigenous peasants in Oaxaca are struggling for their "independence" within Mexico since 2006.

Introduction

With this article I neither want to participate in a specifically "Mexican" debate of social scientists, nor in the discussion of "Subcommandante Marcos'" personality. My "questions to Ramona," the Zapatistan leader, stem instead from my experiences during 30 years of research and theoretical efforts on the so-called "Third World", especially Latin America, on capitalism as a "one-world" system, on peasants' and women's issues; and they stem from the search for a society and culture that would no longer exploit and destroy people and nature (Wallerstein, Evers, and Smith, 1984; Werlhof, 1983, 1984).

The respective findings that Maria Mies, Veronika Bennholdt-Thomsen, and I have been publishing for many years and in different countries, including Mexico and the United States (see Mies, Bennholdt-Thomsen, and Werlhof, 1983, 1988, 1995; compare also Werlhof and Neuhoff, 1982; Werlhof, 1985a, 1985b, 1985c, 1985d, 1986a), center mostly around:

- the "housewifeization" of labor as the real "model" of capitalistic exploitation in contrast to "normal" ("proletarian") wage labor,
- the "colonization" of all spheres of life and nature, which takes place as a politics of "divide and rule," externally as well as internally,
- the "continuing " process of "primitive accumulation" that shows the real face of capitalism as a "necessarily" violent economic and political process that is rooted in the inclusion of all forms of commodity production (including the ones that are not organized in the form of wage labor), and of "subsistence production" (being without a wage) so that part-time wage laborers, peasants, the "marginalized mass," and the housewives as "producers" of labor power can be seen as integrated into the process of capital accumulation,
- the "subsistence perspective" as the only possible way out of the dilemma of exploitation and destruction – as it is expressed in the activities and debates of a growing number of social movements around the world, getting organized at the "periphery of the periphery" (see Bennholdt-Thomsen, 1977, 1980a, 1980b, 1981, 1982, 1984, 1988, Mies, 1991; Mies and Shiva, 1993; Werlhof, 1985e, 1991, 1996).

The processes of "globalization" and the application of neoliberal politics in all parts of the world are producing results that must be interpreted as the "best proof" of our findings. It is not housewives and peasants who are "disappearing" from the Capitalist World System (Werlhof, 1986c), but "proletarian" wage labor as the socially declared "model of reproduction" and supposed fundament of accumulation and exploitation.

Seen from this reality it is no longer surprising that the most radical struggles against capitalism and for a new society are coming from "below" the wage labor's sphere, and are those struggles that the left could never accept as "class struggles." And, indeed, in these struggles people do not want to seize power over capital and/or the state anymore, but develop a perspective that is totally "dissident" with the economic and political system as a whole. Therefore, the "dissidence" of the people, be it with "development", be it with commodity production, be it with all forms of coercion, violence, social hierarchies, and forms of domination in general, has become another major theme in my work (Werlhof, 1996; Werlhof, Schweighofer, and Ernst, 1996; Werlhof, ed., 1996). Moreover, I wondered whether the Zapatistas – as vanguards of a worldwide dialogue on "dissidence" in modern society – had also considered the question of "patriarchy" in their struggle against domination.

The Power of the State and the Power of the People as Their "Dignity"

When in January 1994 I heard for the first time about the rebellion of a socalled "Zapatista-movement" in the Mexican State of Chiapas, and when I saw the pictures of armed men with masks, I thought: "No, please not again!" After having experienced the politics of armed men in the sixties and seventies in Latin America, especially in El Salvador, I belong to those who react allergically to all forms of violence (see Werlhof, 1975: Topitas, 1994) Didn't the guerila, the "armed struggle", and generally the intent to overcome the system by using its own means fail everywhere, and didn't it only double the existing violence (see Debray 1975)? But Veronika Bennholdt-Thomsen, who had done research on Chiapas for years, told me that the case was different this time, the rebellion being an indigenous upheaval "from below", and not politics "from above", like the guerila activities initiated by urban intellectuals. In addition, I noted that the rebels included many women, namley about 30% (see Gorman, 1995).

Is the Zapatista-rebellion, which already has been described as the "first insurrection of the 21st century" (see Topitas, 1994, p. 14), the "social quake" after the earthquake of Mexico City in 1985 (see Werlhof, 1986b)? And why did it start in the countryside, where already the first insurrection of the 20th century, the Mexican Revolution, had started too? And what does it mean that both upheavals are connected with Emiliano Zapata, the leader of the Mexican Revolution, who still seems to be alive in the minds of the people, at least in the South East of Mexico today? (Zapata, the "campesino", wanted Mexico to be a free country of free peasants without private property and without a central state power.) And wasn't the Ejido-system a success of the Mexican Revolution, being at least a guarantee for the peasants' access to the land in many parts of Mexico since that time? In Chiapas this reform has not yet occurred; indeed, here one would still need a Zapata. The actual reform of Article 27 of the Mexican Constitution has cancelled the old agrarian reform resulting from the revolution. "By law we are not supposed to have access to the land anymore", the peasants say (see Gonzalez Esponda and Polito Barrios, 1994, p. 240). This is due to the fact that the Mexican land is left to the new "partners" of the North: it is Mexico's present to the United States and Canada who are now accepting Mexico as a member of the "First World", inserting it into the North American Free Trade Agreement (NAFTA). Thus, the insurrection of the Zapatistas started on the same day that the Mexican government capitulated to the North. On the first of January 1994, the day that was heralded to the Mexican people as the day of their biggest triumph, was the moment that the rebels cried out "Now it's enough'" ("Ya basta!"). It is, indeed, the first rebellion against "neoliberal" politics and its globalization – a politics that is doing away with the last remains of the sovereignty of the single nation-states (see Bennholdt-Thomsen. 1994, p. 260).

Upon reading the speeches of "Subcommandante Marcos", I noted that he had changed sides: he not only knows what he is criticizing, but also where he wants to go. And from this place he already is looking-back on modernity. Consequently he is not striving towards "height", but is rooting in "depth" (Guillermo Bonfil Batalla's "Deep Mexico: A Denied Civilization" [1989] seems to have foreseen much of the Zapatista Movement). Marcos not only expresses what he himself is thinking, but also what the indigenous peasants and women are thinking, to whom he is lending his voice – he, who in reality would belong more to the whites, the urban people and the intellectuals. Marcos, the "indianized" mestizo, is speaking in all languages, the white one, the indigenous one, and his own. But he is always telling the same story, so that it can be heard and understood in all parts of Mexico and in the whole world: "The prophecy of the South-East is valid for the whole country" (see Secret Revolutionary Indigenous Committee, 1994, p. 121). As an intellectual Marcos is reaching the minds, and as a poet he is reaching the souls of the people. The internal sovereignty he is expressing indicates that the government may still seem to be leading the situation militarily, but no longer spiritually. The rebels are much superior in the latter, and the state's power appears unworthy of belief, if not ridiculous (see Esteva, 1995).

Without any wrong compromise Marcos is showing what could be thought around the world, and full of compassion and love he is showing, too, what could be felt and done around the world. The rulers do not know this sort of veracity – the humor, the self-irony and the readiness even to die for a life in "dignity" – and all this combined with the renunciation of taking over state power, political power – the power that comes from outside, from above, from the "height", from the armed one, from the "foreign" power (foreign to the people), even from the power that one's self could possibly exercise. "Does (political) power not attract you?" a journalist asks Marcos. His answer: "It is frightening me" (see Marcos, 1995). But the people of the movement would not renounce their own power, the power of the living, their acting and thinking full of "dignity", as they say. Dignity stems from the connection with the depth, the roots. "We do not want charity, nor presents, but the right to live with the dignity of human beings, with the wisdom and justice of our old people and our ancestors" (see Dietrich, 1994, p. 130). And so, we in the West "staring at the 'unworthy poverty' of others ... did not pose the question of our own dignity anymore for a long time... This way we are thrown back to our own reality by them, ... in order to find the place of our own dignity again" (Dietrich, 1994, p. 142). "Dignity" is the central concept of the Zapatista movement. With their call for dignity they have obtained a spiritual victory that is recognized everywhere in Mexico and elsewhere.

In Mexico, the political power is not only put into question through neoliberalism, but also through another power, the one of the "words" (Esteva, 1995). At least, the few guns of the Zapatista "army" could not have split the "Party of the Institutionalized Revolution" (PRI) that has been ruling monolithically since the Mexican revolution. And there is also no other explanation for the fact that millions of Mexicans are actively sympathizing with the rebels, though they neither want to be a political party, nor to attain power. Marcos said: "We don't strive for duties, neither for glory, nor honour. We only want to be the frontage to a new world; a new world and a new form, to make politics, a new form of politics in which the people are the government, a politics of men and women who obey to the orders of the people" (see Esteva, 1995, p. 206). Did the people want their politics to consist of laying their destiny in the hands of international financial capital and the drug mafia? From the pint of view of the Zapatistas this is exactly what is happening by uniting Mexico with the "first world". Didn't the Mexican state in this way freely or consciously give up its political power? Consequently a new power is emerging, the proper power of the people themselves. Those who still think that social movements have only "demands" cannot imagine what all this means. For most people it is still unthinkable that striving for money, political power, rights, or general participation in progress and development does not contribute to solve the real problems. Rather the contrary is true, and therefore these are not demands of the Zapatistas.

Marcos said: "Call upon all people to resist, so that nobody will take from those who give by ordering. Write on your banners that you are not selling yourself.... That all the alms coming from the ruling are sent back.... Don't give up! These were the words coming out of the hearts of our deads, since always. We saw that truth and dignity were in their words.... We are not going to accept anything.... Even when we see that others sell themselves to the fist which is oppressing them.... Democracy! Freedom! Justice!" (s. Secret Revolutionary Indigenous Committee, 1994, pp. 123-124). The Mexican government tried to prove to the international public that the conflict would be solved by using money and/or violence (see Gonzalez Esponda and Polito Barrios, 1994, p. 244). In the meantime it is obvious that none of it works: "If the dignity of the Mexicans has no price, then what about the power of the ruling?" (see "Secret Revolutionary Indigenous Committee", 1994, p. 124.)

Why, then, "democracy, freedom and justice", knowing how used up, neglected and mendacious they have become (not only) in Mexico? "Are the Zapatistas naive?" many observers were asking. And in this way they were confessing that they knew that the Western system in the form of the "modem" Mexico as the "fictitious" one (see Bonfil Batalla, 1989) has finally reached the end of its possibilities. What is it then that the Zapatistas want?

Questions to Ramona

In 1995 I went to Mexico and Chiapas to better understand the Zapatista movement. I visited many people, men and women, from and around the movement, and discussed with them the questions treated in this article. I am formulating them as hypotetical "questions to Ramona". Ramona is one of the leading heads of the Zapatista movement and is representing the "Women's Committee" of the indigenous communities. My questions to Ramona are rhetorical questions about the "word", the language used by the Zapatistas, their concepts and pictures. I want to know how she is understanding the situation and what it means for the women, for the indigenous communities of today, for the indigenous patriarchy and possibly also matriarchy (the "deep" Mexico) and, last not least, for our situation in the West.

Politics

Ramona, what do you understand by politics? You are saying that the politician should be a "servant" of the community. He should not govern by ordering, but by obeying (see Esteva, 1995, p. 106; Topitas, 1994, p. 14). For you "political participation", therefore, is more than just electing politicians who are then "free" to practice politics as "a confrontation between the political organizations", without taking into consideration the political "proposals" from the people themselves (see "Secret Revolutionary Indigenous Committee", 1994, p. 120). Does being elected then mean that you neither want to elect a dominating group, nor desire that the people themselves be dominating ("democracy")? Isn't it more likely that you want "politicians" who are "only" exercising what the people really want and who therefore precisely have no political "power"? If the politician is "not good", he has to be "dismissable" (see Marcos, 1994, p. 38). Do you mean by this the old concept of politics – that cannot be expressed by the Greek concept of "polis" anymore – that normally is attributed to presumably "primitive" premodern and even pre-patriarchal societies (see Canetti, 1986; Clastres, 1976)? In these cases politics and communities had not yet been divided, the public sphere had not yet been dissolved from the private one, no social classes did exist, over which one would have to have dominated, and which consequently could not have been allowed to determine common politics.

Do you think that your so-called "authority", the elected politician of the community, can be compared to the "hero" ("heros") of the matriarchal community, its "king" or mediator to the "rest of the world" (see Göttner-Abendroth, 1980)? Do you think that the political proposals of the people should also stem from the community of women and children, whose acceptance would also be needed to make politics "possible"? Would it, from your point of view, be up to the women to define the contents of politics, whereas its practical exercise, especially the mediation between internal and external groups, would generally be the task of the men (Illich, 1982, 1983)? And how could you – how could we – reach this goal, knowing that reality, in your communities, too, is partly or totally different from what you yourself are proposing?

The Government

You say that the government that is elected should be like "the shadow of a tree" (see Esteva, 1994a, p. 77). For me this is a wonderful picture. If you want, you move to the protecting shadow of a tree. Isn't it a motherly picture? The tree is spreading its coat around all those who are sitting under its boughs and at its feet. The tree is more giving than taking. She reminds us of the tree of life, the tree of love and recognition, the family tree, the common ancestress. It is true, one is sitting at its feet, and it is elevated above us, but nevertheless there is no hierarchy in the sense of domination, control, the right to use violence. Here, nothing is going to be manipulated, but everything welcomes "conviviality" (see Illich, 1978), and not mutual rivalry and competition. Those gathering under the tree are like "relatives" to each other. Therefore they would neither plunder the tree nor cut themselves off from the tree. The tree is central for the community, it can be found in its middle, it is the place where everybody likes to be, where there is home and safety. Is the tree like the pasture-ground of the animals, a word that was basic to our concept of ethics, customs, and morals? This would be, not doubt, the "good" in contrast to the "bad" government, as you say. It is the government of the mother "over" her children, the people, but in a completely nonpatriarchal, nondominating sense (see Vegetti-Finzi, 1992). Do you agree with me?

Democracy

"Politics" and the "government" express what you understand by "democracy". As you are always stressing, you really want a democracy, though the word "kratos", domination, is included in it. Do you want the domination, too? I cannot imagine so, because you seem to think of a direct democracy from below that is also staying below and does not get separated from the base in order to be independent from it within a special sphere, the so-called public sphere. Political power and domination as a result of the "abstraction" of power from the single individuals and their own power as such, as we experience it in modern democracy (Werlhof, 1996, pp. 12-26), is not what you mean. Isn't it that you say that the "democracy, of which the president of Mexico is speaking, is a disdain in our eyes" (see "Political Direction," 1994, p. 156)? You are criticizing how power and money are concentrated, and debts and poverty distributed, in the ruling democracies of today. You are saying that this would be a dictatorship of power and money, as is typical for "party democracy", and in this way the promises of democracy could never be fulfilled. And it would be impossible, too, to transform the representative democracy (again) into a direct one, the way you understand it. A communal conviviality would, in any case, be impossible with the actual democracy – that, paradoxically, always appears as a condition for the former. You are saying that there is a growing tendency for the transformation of democracy into dictatorship, instead of dictatorships being just the opposite of democracy, as we all are normally told. And therefore you are saying that the people finally should decide for democracy, but the one, of course, that cannot lead into dictatorship. Which are the "democratic" experiences in history or from today that you have in mind?

Power

"Power" in your language is "a flower which is walking in the hands of the people" (see Esteva, 1995). This picture, again, is rather female, similar to that of the tree, taken from life in and with nature. Power as a flower is again not frightening. On the contrary, this power is decorating the people, it belongs to them, it brings them together and it unites them with the world. Your picture is expressing what I call the proper power of the living beings themselves. It is exactly the power that modern politics is extracting (abstracting) from the people to get them under control, directing their proper power, transformed into "political power", that is turned against them afterwards (see Werlhof, 1996, p. 126-144). "Power", then, is not a living power anymore, but a dead one, a killing one. So you too are refusing such an abstract, political "power", as one that is detrimental to conviviality, and that is separating the people and staying external to them. Don't you think, too, that such a power does not help solving the problems, because no real help or salvation can ever come from outside, but only from inside and from below, from the locality? There is no need of a central power – this is what you, like Zapata and Pancho Villa, have in mind. It seems to me that you are trying to avoid the repetition of experiences that you have had, when external and foreign interests have been carried through within the communities. Therefore you are now proposing a change in the election law, so that the propositions of the communities have to be recognized, even if they have not gone through the "political power", namely elections and political parties. How are you going to take care that the power remains a flower in the hands of the people, especially the women, given the realities of politics?

Autonomy

"Autonomy" is one of the words you like most (see "Peasant Communities", 1994, p. 245). But in your language autonomy means something totally different than in our language. In our language autonomy means independence from others as an individual who strives for living without any bonds with other individuals or groups. Such an "ego-logics" presumably is completely alien to you (see Keller, 1986; Ernst, 1996). It is an autonomy that stems from the machine-model of a society, in which the individual is just an interchangeable spare part (see Bammé et al., 1983). Whereas we understand by autonomy individual independence from nature and society, you mean by autonomy the economic independence of communities from the central state, as self-suppliers, and political self-determination (see Bennholdt-Thomsen, 1994, pp. 264-265). This means that you are organizing your economy in form of subsistence agriculture, or you would need the latter as a basis at least. But you do not speak about that. And the question for me is: Who would provide the economic basis for autonomy in your sense? Would this be done by all the members of the community together, or would it rest upon the women again and as always, without even being recognized (Bennholdt-Thomsen, 1994, pp. 267-268)? If you are denying the meaningfulness and "fertility" of women's work, taking it automatically for granted, your "autonomy" then would be built again on the patriarchal sexual division of labor of the "white man". Thus, where you are trying to get rid of all forms of colonialism, you would, paradoxically, keep its "internal basis". If the women remain "the last colony" (see Mies, Bennholdt-Thomsen, and Werlhof, 1988), you would retain a sort of "Trojan-horse", being a permanent threat to your autonomy and the rest of your further achievements.

Do you agree with me? I know that the discussion about the autonomy of the indigenous communities in the meanwhile has been extended to all parts of Mexico (see Esteva, 1994a). This shows how far the decay of the Mexican political system and its institutions has already gone. But nowhere have I read of a discussion about the basis of your "autonomy".

Law and Rights

In the negotiations with the government you are concentrating on carrying through your own legal order. You think of a local legal system, which does not necessarily have much to do with the universal, abstract law system of the West. In contrast to this you want to reintroduce and exercise your own local indigenous rights. Indeed, rights are not just an invention of the West or modern times. Indigenous ideas about rights that presuppose neither abstract legal norms, nor the formal "posing" of positive rights (see Ernst, 1993; Göttner-Abendroth, 1988), are also discussed in the West (see Lauderdale, 1993, 1996). Like the concept of a matriarchal society your legal order does not know imprisonment and it needs no legal apparatus and especially no police or military force. Gustavo Esteva told me that a man who would kill another man would in your community not be put in jail, but would have to take care of the family of the killed person for the rest of his life – the idea being that the perpetrator would be made responsible for the consequences of his act, and thus one would no longer need a criminal law.

But there are many people who feel that the concrete legal practice within the communities could eventually lead to hurt the so-called "human rights" (see Esteva, 1995). And indeed, in many indigenous communities patriarchal social relations under certain conditions allow the men, for example, to rape women of the community, to marry them against their will, to keep them in economic dependence, and to exploit them as a labor force. Therefore you have formulated the "revolutionary women's rights" from 1993 that have been called the "first upheaval" before the "general upheaval" (see Topitas, 1994, pp. 82, 93, 103). Now, the question is, does this proposal contradict the men's concept of law and rights?

On the other hand, it has to be asked whether something like equality, emancipation and "human rights for women" are enough, or can help at all. We women from the West can tell you that this needs to be doubted. Violence against women occurs despite the formal acceptance of so-called human rights that expressly include women. Never have the law or rights protected women effectively against violence. This is because the so-called human or "natural" rights are fundamentally perceived as men's rights over women and nature (see Bloch, 1991; Gerhard et al., 1990). So the claim for the Western human rights will be a disappointing experience for women, if not a boomerang. Therefore, I think the solution of the problem has to be found within the communities themselves. Violence against women can never be legitimate, if you think about democracy, power, and politics, the way you do. From your point of view there can be no justification of the violence against women, be it in indigenous law or be it in Western law.

Law and rights have had too much to do with patriarchy since its inception (see Werlhof, 1996, pp. 27-60). Therefore one has to dig deeper into the question. One would have to recognize women's rights and especially mother-rights the way they are in societies without patriarchal social relations of domination (see Werlhof, Schweighofer, and Ernst, 1996). So, especially with respect to the question of law and rights, you would have to profoundly criticize your own indigenous understanding of them. If not, it is likely that you would simply reintroduce a new structure of domination in the communities, or to confirm the old one. In any case, the right of women to have access to the land (see Topitas, 1994, p. 95) is an appropriate and very important one to start with, because in patriarchy it has typically been denied to them (see Mies, Bennholdt-Thomsen, and Werlhof, 1988).

Justice

"Democracy! Freedom! Justice!" These are your central and often-repeated political concepts. Justice has, of course, much to do with law and rights. By justice you understand veracity, credibility and honesty. Bishop Samuel Ruiz, who loves you so much, expressed it in the following way: "There is no justice between poverty and wealth.... There is a world of domination and of subjection, and ... the one doesn't exist without the other.... As long as we thought that we would have to treat equal spheres, we thought that we had to help on one side.... But, since we found out, that it is a question of justice, we have to take a decision. One cannot be with the people who are below, without telling the dominant people very clearly, that they have to come down.... The mighty have to get down from their throne, and the powerless have to raise themselves" (see Ruiz, 1994, p. 192). This shows that "your" Bishop does not think about justice anymore the way the West is doing it. Since Roman law, the West defines justice as "suum cuique", which essentially means to give the rich what "belongs to them", and the poor what belongs to them (namely nothing). In this concept of justice the equality or comparability of social relations is presupposed, as if they were independent from one another. Under these conditions justice starts from a status quo of relations of domination, and confirms what from your point of view is injustice. If I understand you well, you finally want to stop the injustice of equality between the dominating and the dominated by revealing the fact of domination itself as untruthful, unworthy of belief, and dishonest, so that it will have to disappear before something like a real justice could come into being.

I like this very much, but I think the same has to be applied to the relationship of dominance of men over women. Justice as equality of men and women does not help as long as women are the dominated. If there is to be justice for women, then men have to step down from their throne of power over women, and the women have to rise up – not on the throne, but simply to (be) themselves.

Freedom

Your idea of freedom means "to be free like the wind" (see Esteva, 1994b, p. 76). Freedom cannot be limited by fences and orders. It is the freedom to move, the inner freedom, the freedom of the spirit (wind, air, bird).

What a difference to our Western definition of freedom! Our freedom is the freedom of private property: with private property we can do what we want. This freedom is unlimited, too, but its foundation and consequences are different. They consist in their own opposite: the unfreedom of the owned and the impossibility to stop the liberty of destruction. You can see this most clearly with respect to the question of ecology. When land is private property, it can also be destroyed, and often enough it is not possible to limit this destruction by law. The same is valid for the question of private property of living people. In our case they are not called slaves anymore, but wives (see Reddock, 1995). Though the wife formally has a right to her physical integrity, this right is simply not observed in most cases (see Werlhof, 1996, pp. 27-60). The unfreedom of the one is seen as the basis for the "freedom" of the other one. The person who is "posed" or set un-free, cannot successfully claim the same freedom for him – or herself. This would be illogical. The only possibility to become free would consist in building his/her freedom on the basis of the unfreedom of others again. Therefore, Western freedom cannot be something good for women (nor men, nor nature), and I ask myself why men are still so proud of this freedom, be it in the West, be it in Mexico. Your freedom, the one of the wind, is not conceivable in the West. The beautiful thing about it is that the freedom of the wind can never become unfreedom for others, because it is a spiritual form of freedom, a mental freedom that exists by nature and cannot really harm anybody – even if it is a little bit stormy. This freedom can be taken by everybody without any permission, it is always there. There is – on the other hand – also no coercion to be free, and no one has to be liberated from unfreedom.

To find your freedom, we in the West would first have to get rid of our freedom of private property. Only then the respect for the freedom of others and the world would have a chance to come into being without having to be produced or to be fought for. This freedom could exist without having to put rules on anybody, and without having to be regulated by anybody. What about the state of freedom in your communities today?

The Land

"Land and freedom!" This is what you wanted all the time since colonialism (see Bennholdt-Thomsen, 1994, p. 264). Indigenous people belong to the land, and the land belongs to them. It is their basis. You will get what you need for your "autonomy" by producing yourself what you need. Some feminist colleagues and I call this subsistence production (see Mies, 1991; Werlhof. 1985e). Therefore, the land is nothing external to you, but it is the place where you are rooted, the depth from which you have emerged. You call the land "your mother". It is the mother of all human beings, animals and plants. She has birthed them. She is nursing them; she is body, spirit and soul in one. From this point of view the privatization of land, especially now in the neoliberal economical system (see Topitas, 1994, p. 241), can never be accepted by you. How can your mother be divided, sold, and transformed into the private property of people who are not even there (see Delona, 1973)? Therefore you are proposing that land is not a commodity but it is a "commonality", communally owned by all the indigenous peoples and peasants in general.

"Land or death!" This is again the question for you, in contrast to us in the West, who believe that this question will never be important for us again. How silly we are! We too knew the communal land, the "Allmende" as we called it – or the "commons" (see lllich, 1982; Boehme, 1988). To remember this tradition may be seen as the only possibility, to return to a situation where the land is not destroyed anymore. Only when you depend on the land on which you live would you bother about its well-being and an "ecological" way of life, in which a subsistence production and a politics of "regionalization" as an alternative to the global capitalistic economy are viable (see Bennholdt-Thomsen. 1994). How could "autonomous" self-supplied communities remain subjugated in the long run? Freedom through the land is an inexpressible taboo for those interested in domination. Land doesn't need domination: to the contrary, it dissolves it. But we in the West think that there is no life in freedom without dominating the land (including the peasants, the women, and the colonies worldwide). What a long way we in the West still have to go to get to our roots.

Community

You say that where there is community, there is the "good life". No good life without community. Community means living together, respecting one another, sharing things, not having to be sad because of loneliness and living without real troubles, because there is always someone who would help in case of necessity. "Community" is one of the heart and the soul. It is even a "cosmic" community where the relationship with nature is reappearing as human culture (see Klingler-Clavigo, 1995). This is the community of the "deep" Mexico, as Guillermo Bonfil Batalla is describing it.

We know, of course, that the indigenous communities of today have been reorganized by the Catholic church in colonial times and after, and that they, even on the basis of the ejido, do not represent this lovely picture anymore. The subjection of women especially has been responsible for this decay of the community. But you still know, at least, what you mean by community. In the West this is not the case anymore. In the meantime, we have destroyed practically all forms of community, and in the end we are dissolving the nuclear family, too. Whereas we have been forced to live as individuals and "egos", you have maintained a concept of "the indigenous" as "communal man" (and woman?), who lives in a community and not in a general competition of each against each (see Illich, 1982). In comparison with you, we have lost our roots and our community and do no longer know what a life of dignity and truth would feel like. And many people don't even want to know this anymore. But soon we will again need the community more than anything else in the world. And this is when our individualistic model of life will have come to an end. It is already becoming too expensive...

Your concept of community is, again, very female. Wouldn't it have to be central to every community to care about the next generation – and this means to look from the perspective of the mothers and children in the community, and not from the perspective of a male public sphere that is defined independently from the "private" one? So, the question remains how to build a community that would not be based on the subjugation of women and children but would in contrast be centered (positively) around them.

The Dead

If "culture is the way how humans are human" (Ruiz 1994, p. 190) then culture is also the way how the dead are dead. In your case the dead belong to the living. You say: "We are the dead of all the times" (see Dietrich 1994, p. 134). You feel connected-with the people beyond their time on earth. You remember what they lived for. And you even take this as a legacy for your actual life. If the people have to make a decision, Marcos says. "They turn to the mountains and to the places where the dead are living. And they ask their dead, if they would have died for the construction of a hospital, for a road or for credits with which their votes are bought, or if they would have raised themselves for freedom, democracy and justice the 1st of January" (Dietrich, 1994, p. 135). So, you are asking your dead, whether the living should fight for the goals for which they, the dead, have died: from hunger, killed by the landowners, tortured by the military, wasted away by pain and misery. And the dead have told the living that they should lead a life of dignity, because otherwise their death would have been in vain. The dead said that the living should not simply die, but fight for their lives, and this would be their responsibility to those who had already died (Marcos, 1994). And now, as the government is going to practically uproot you by taking your land away (because in the new liberal economic order it seems to be cheaper that you die than continue to live), here is your responsibility with the dead. You, finally, have to start to fight.

When the dead are speaking to the living as if they were still alive – like for example Zapata himself, who is not dead for you – it is also possible to say, viceversa, that you the living call yourselves "the already dead". For there is a continual relationship between the living and the dead, between life and death. So if you are the dead who have returned from memory, then there is nothing that still can be given to you, nobody can buy you, nothing is important for you – besides the subsequent reestablishment of your (that is, the dead's) dignity. Therefore you are strong enough to resist wrong promises and offers, and you have a measure for the veracity of your acting. The dead belong to your roots and to your dignity, which nobody can take away from you. And, as you have died already, you are invulnerable and have left behind all fear, greediness, and selfishness: "All for all, nothing for ourselves".

It is this culture of not allowing one to be divided from one's own experiences – your historical consciousness (sec Topitas, 1994, p. 184), the culture of the memory passing over times and distances (see Assmann, 1992), this not being cut off of past or of future generations, a sort of magical consciousness of the connectedness of all life and of life and death – that gives you such a spiritual superiority over Western thinking. When culture is the maintenance of this connectedness instead of using the principle of "divide and rule", like in the West, then it is we in the West, who with our resulting fear of death and life equally, have no culture anymore. Western progress on the one road of evolution has lost its culture. And if you don't think only of your dead, but also act in coincidence with your thinking – because the word has to become acting, as your concept of "k'op" says (García de Leon, 1994, p. 148) – then the connectedness is maintained in this way as well. The proper power of the living, the dignity of each and the capacity to cooperate with others, to build community, thus comes full circle. If you, in contrast to us, favor the connectedness of thinking, acting, and feeling, and if you do not experience them as contradicting each other, but as one proper and common power that has different sides, then it is exactly this connectedness that people feel when your people are speaking. Because then you are already proving by your words that the belief in an external political power (which is directed against the people) is silly, and that it is not even necessary to offer a sort of "counter-power". It now becomes clear why you, like Zapata and Pancho Villa, really do not want to seize power: As you have maintained your culture you don't need it – contrary to left movements and the guerillas.

And again, this rather immediate relationship with death and the dead appears to be very female, because in a cyclical movement one is returning to those from whom one has emerged, or they return to us. It is this cyclical, "hamaca"- or textile-like metaphorical understanding of the world that is so typical for non-Western or premodern societies (Meier-Seethaler. 1993).

The Prophecy of the Upheaval

In this sense your insurrection has its own logic and is a real upheaval from "the depth" of your culture. You are doing what the dead were saying. But at which point does cultural resistance transform into rebellion and even an upheaval? Finally, the prehistory of your rebellion embraces not only the last ten years of this century, but 500 years of colonization. "Maintaining the memory of the precolonial epoch as a part of one's own history which is reaching up to the present, colonization is becoming relative. It is perceived as a moment within this history which has a beginning and will have an end. This way, colonialization is obtaining a transitory historical dimension; it ceases to be an unrevertable and eternal natural destiny. It is becoming just a further chapter, which only has to be finished in order to be able to turn a new page" (see Bonfil Batalla, 1994, pp. 173-174). "All the colonialized people are conscious that the true history has been proscribed by the colonialist.... But in spite of all this, they know that their history exists and their presence as a people is the obvious proof for it. One's own history is not only necessary to explain the presence, but also to lay the ground for the future. Future means first of all liberation, regaining the right of self-determination" (p. 172).

This explains why the Mexican revolution did not mean the end of colonization for you. A new insurrection was unavoidable. In 1982, when the volcano Chichonal in Chiapas erupted, your historian Antonio García de Leon was already prophesying the rebellion: "The eruption occurred in order to range as a further announcement within the parts of this immense puzzle in the landscape of this slow battle of movements, of this apparently immovable chronology which can only be measured by centuries. Its tremendous shake... did only announce the impatience of the original and subterranean forces which where pushing to get again to the surface" (see García de León. 1994, p. 128). The oldest prophecies of your upheaval are said to go back to the Mayan calendar. Only we in the West who understand history as nothing else than a past that will never come back, and a future that is simply an extension of today, only we "evolutionists" could be surprised. I wonder: Which is the heritage that we in the West would finally have to remember (see Ganser, 1996)?

The "Army"

For Marcos the Zapatista Liberation Army is "the heart of the movement" (see Esteva, 1995, p. 208). I don't know any other army that would speak of itself as a "heart". "To follow one's heart" means, as you say, to find one's own dignity. So is your army the first in the world that wants to lead the people to their dignity? Or are you an army at all? "We are the product of 500 years of struggle. ... We are the heirs of the real founders of our nation, we, the ones without possessions... invite all of you to join this call as the only way not to starve in the face of the insatiable thirst for power of a dictatorship which lasts more than 70 years... of sellers of the fatherland... who are taking away from us everything, absolutely everything..." (s. General Command of the Zapatista Liberation Army, 1994, p. 20). And again Marcos, who has set up this army with years of work: "The question is, that they want to kill us.... On the 1st of

January we did not march out for a war to kill or to be killed. We left to be heard instead.... - it was neither suicide nor adventure" (Marcos, 1994, p. 27). And: "We believe that our war can serve those ... who suffer like we..." (s. Topitas, 1994, p. 156). The army as guardian and servant: It wants to serve like "politics"?

The paradox of this "army" can only be understood if one knows from where it stems, and the circumstances under which it came into being. "It was the people themselves who said: Let's start now! We don't want to wait any longer, because we are all starving.... so the struggle started" (Topitas, 1994, p. 159). The whole people had been asked before and the communities themselves proposed the insurrection. The army is well accepted in the civil population. They know that the rulers fear the union between the armed and the civil population. The armed people say: "We are peaceful people. We have a lot of patience. If not we would have started with our rebellion a long time ago" (see Topitas, 1994, p. 156). Behind this you find the concept of "k'op" again. You cannot decide to start an insurrection and not realize it afterwards. This would be "illogical" (p. 183). And you saw "that it is bad to die without having fought" (p. 36). It was the last alternative; everything else had already been tried.

Is there anything like a "symbolic" army, an army that is expressing the wish and the will for resistance, but that is not "really" an army in the sense of the military concept? If you equate "army" and "war" with struggle, only then are you able to explain the paradox of "an armed liberation army which has invented a resistance which is strictly free from violence and has eliminated the traditional guerilla with its violent concept of power from the project" (see Dietrich, 1994, p. 137). Today our problem is that – after such a long militaristic history full of wars – we think that struggle is always the same as war, violence, and militarism. We do not know a struggle anymore that would not contain militaristic forms of conflict. And this means that we have left to the state and to the military the responsibility to deal with conflicts, and we behave as if in this way we will have been liberated from conflicts altogether. We behave as if the (so-called "legal") violence that the state/military uses would be justified and "necessary" on the one hand, and as if we, on the other hand, would have nothing to do with it. This way, we fancy being peaceful, because we have left violence to others.

Maybe it makes sense to characterize your army this way. It wants to bother about something that can neither be delegated nor displaced. We could distinguish between the institutionalized army of the state (which can also be directed against the proper people – that is to say an abstract apparatus that does not stem from below, but from above) on one hand, and the "guerilla" that wants to seize power, on the other hand, and finally the so-called "popular resistance" as a third possibility (see Virilio and Lothringer, 1984, pp. 110-111). Distinguishing between the regular army and the guerilla, including terrorist groups, on one side and popular resistance on the other side, the Liberation Army would undoubtedly belong to the tradition of popular resistance (compare Virilio and Lothringer, 1984). It doesn't omit the question of death, it stems from its own milieu, and it is using no special means besides several guns, which is not very special if one thinks about the norms of modern military equipment. Furthermore it has to do more with civil disobedience and peaceful resistance than with a so-called "armed struggle" (see Ebert, 1983). Its members are not socially atomized and "deterritorialized" urban individuals, but "are able to do something" independent from "technocratic situations", where only terror is possible. You do not use terrorist strategies. You try to avoid situations of violence, but you have arms in order to show that you are going to defend yourself. Marcos is repeating again and again, that it is his aim to make the army superfluous and to abolish it, when the threat has ceased to exist. This struggle would never be won through gunshots.

Nevertheles, there remains an ambivalence. It is so difficult to avoid a further "patriarchalization", especially in the case of crisis, and every fighting party is in a crisis. Where there are arms, "male bonding" is to be expected, which has the tendency to become independent and to produce the legitimation for its continuation (see Volger and Weick, 1990). This has been the case in indigenous movements, too (see Münzel, 1978).

The participation of women in armed conflicts is a special problem. Indeed, it belongs to the oldest traditions of humankind, that women are actively defending their communities, especially the life of their children, without hesitating. They have even been feared because of this attitude (see Eisler, 1987: Aliti, 1993; Loraux, 1992). But under the conditions of today one has always to take into account that the 'equality' of women in the army, from which Marcos is speaking, could in the end also be a step in the opposite direction. Does the struggle-experience of the women contribute to a new, modernized form of patriarchalization? Or does it improve the conditions for the re-invention of even matriarchal relationships in the community – as would be more likely in the case of a people's resistance? Isn't it that nearly all popular upheavals in history, including the ones that lead to the big revolutions, have been started and in their beginning even guided by women (see Mies and Reddock, 1978)? Will the experience of women in the Zapatista Liberation Army result in greater awareness, so that women could begin to bother about the huge problems in the community more actively and without any fear of conflicts? Or will they only have learned to subject themselves in a new way and to obey – even if they may have commanded in the army, too? Could the popular resistance in the end be transformed into a new model of domination, and will it then only have contributed to its training (see Topitas, 1994, pp. 47, 163)? On the other hand, what was the alternative?

The Question of Matriarchy and the West: What Is a "Civilization"?

My last two major questions have, to my knowledge, not been discussed much in Mexico yet. One question refers to a so-called "matriarchy" in Mexico, and the other to the issue of "Western civilization". The question of matriarchy is the question of the character of the Central American "civilization", which in the form of the "deep Mexico" seems to have become a social vision again. Has this civilization or culture been an essentially "female" or nonpatriarchal one? Guillermo Bonfil did not pose this question. He did not even realize it. So should the "beautiful indigenous cause" only end up in a local "post"-capitalistic neopatriarchy? Does one want to miss the chance to overcome relationships of dominance and violence at the "lowest" level, too? To avoid this, these relationships have to be discussed (see Bennholdt-Thomsen, 1994). Or has even the "deep" Mexico been organized in a patriarchal way, and were even the Mayas at the time, when the West knew their societies no longer matriarchal (compare Popol Vuh, 1993)? Would a "matriarchal" society in Central America still have to be "discovered"?

In your language, Ramona, your thinking and acting, I could not find a patriarchal tradition. Your pictures and concepts seem to me much more "matriarchal": they do not claim domination of any kind. Your language remains bound to concrete experience and thus is not abstract. It speaks of "general" problems and conflicts in life, but it is never "universalistic". It is a language that could be valid for the world in its totality, without being "totalitarian" at all. It remains rooted in the "depth" and from there it directs itself against the ruling and the mighty, without wanting to replace them, and it points in the direction of a (worldwide possible) culture, free from domination. Your language is friendly, positively related to life and nature, it is erotic and tender, motherly and very near to the earth, full of love and soul, and last not least, supported by a tremendous spiritual freedom. This language does not stem from the darkness of historical patriarchies, including the modern capitalistic ones. But patriarchy – in the form of capitalism – is the reality today, in your indigenous communities as well (see Bennholdt-Thomsen. 1988: Gunn Alien, 1986). And might not a new "deep", but patriarchal Mexico finally attract everything you have wanted to do away with since colonial times?

Guillermo Bonfil spoke of the existence of two different civilizations, the Western and the Central American, as if they could he analyzed independently from one another. He said that the latter had been subjugated by the former. But what if the subjugated (part of a) civilization is really going to liberate itself from the subjugating one? What kind of civilization will be the result? And what will then happen to the subjugating civilization? If (part of a) civilization is able to exist independently from the other one, then the question arises, whether the subjugating (part of the) civilization would be capable of independence from the subjugated one or not. Why did it subjugate another civilization? If it did it because it could not develop on its own, it is not deserving the name "civilization" as such. How can something that is not (or does not want to be) self-sufficient – the subjugating civilization – carry the same name as something that has been self-sufficient – the subjugated civilization? In case your indigenous civilization should again emerge as an independent one in Mexico, the actual situation would suddenly be completely per- (or better) reverted: The indigenous civilization would be recognizable as the independent, the Western as the dependent one! It was the West that needed colonialism – cheap raw materials, labor power and international markets – to become a "Western civilization" (see Mies, Bennholdt-Thomsen and Werlhof, 1988). What will happen to "Western civilization" if the colonial situation that it is based upon broke down not only in Mexico but elsewhere, too? Does Western civilization break down when there are no colonies anymore? Does "Western civilization" mean to have colonies? Is "Western civilization" defined by the fact that it has subjugated other civilizations and is nourishing itself from them? Or would the West become a real civilization only if there are no colonies anymore? And would this civilization then be still a "Western" one?

What we define as "Western civilization" is a product of modern times and colonialism. By "Western civilization" we do not refer to the middle ages or an old, European-type, even matriarcal civilization that no longer exists (see Gimbutas, 1982). Whereas you will be able to relate to your own traditions, we in the West are standing empty-handed. We invented so many heights, but have lost our "depth". Where are our own roots and forces, the heritage of our culture and former civilizations that might not have been parasitic and maybe not patriarchal (nor capitalistic, of course), either?

The decay of Western power in Mexico (the end of the "fictitious" Mexico, as G. Bonfil says) also means the decay of power and civilization in the West. Therefore, we in the West have to ask the same questions as you. The difference is: That we do not know how to do this without subjugating others. But whereas we are not even really asking these questions, you are already preoccupied with the answers. With your upheaval – which is not only an insurrection – and with the perspectives it has in relation to the global economic crisis and neoliberalism as a form to globalize this crisis, the relations suddenly appear to be turned upside down. Now it is the West that is weak. Does it destroy non-Western or your civilization completely? Is it going to decay because it is losing its basis? Does it let the non-Western civilization be independent, to also decay? There is only one solution: The reconstruction of a non-Western civilization in the West and all over the planet. And this cannot mean replacing the external colony by an "internal" one (or maintaining it). When women remain to be treated as "the last colony," it would only repeat internally what had just perished externally.

Bibliography

ALITI, Angelika 1993 Die wilde Frau. Rückkehr zu den Quellen weiblicher Macht und Energie. Hamburg: Hoffmann & Campe.
ASSMANN, Jan 1992 Das kulturelle Gedächtnis. München: C.H. Beck.
BAMMÉ, Arno, Renate GENTH, Guenther KEMPIN, and Guenter FEUERSTEIN 1983 Maschinen-Menschen, Mensch-Maschinen. Reinbek: Rowohlt.
BENNHOLDT-THOMSEN, Veronika 1977 "La Conciencia Campesina Derivada del Desarrollo Capitalista en México". Revista del México Agrario 10(3): 11-26.
BENNHOLDT-THOMSEN, Veronika 1980[a] "Investment in the Poor: Analysis of World Bank Policy". Part 1 and 2. Social Scientist. 8 (7): 1227-1243; 8 (8): 2012-2027.
BENNHOLDT-THOMSEN, Veronika 1980[b] "Towards a Class Analysis of Agrarian Sectors: Mexico." Latin American Perspectives. 7 (4): 100-114.
BENNHOLDT-THOMSEN, Veronika 1981 "Marginalidad en América Latina Una Crítica de la Teoría." Revista Mexicana de Sociología 43 (4): 1505-1546.
BENNHOLDT-THOMSEN, Veronika 1982 "Subsistence Production and Extended Reproduction: A Contribution to the Discussion about Modes of Production." In: Journal of Peasant Studies 9 (4): 241-254.
BENNHOLDT-THOMSEN, Veronika 1984 "The Sexual Division of Labour in Capitalism." pp. 252-271 in: Households and the World Economy, edited by Immanuel Wallerstein, Hans-Dieter Evers. Joan Smith. New York: Sage.
BENNHOLDT-THOMSEN, Veronika 1988 Campesinos: Entre Producción de Subsistencia y de Mercado. Mexico: UNAM/CRIM
BENNHOLDT-THOMSEN, Veronika 1994 "Die Zapatistas und Wir". pp. 257-268 in: Ya Basta! Der Aufstand der Zapatistas, edited by Topitas. Hamburg: Libertäre Assoziation.

BENNHOLDT-THOMSEN, Veronika, ed. Juchitán. la Ciudad de las Mujeres. Oaxaca (Mexico): Institute Oaxaqueno de las Culturas.
BOEHME, Hartmut 1988 Natur und Subjekt. Frankfurt: Suhrkamp.
BLOCH, Ernst 1991 Naturrecht und menschliche Würde. Frankfurt: Suhrkamp.
BONFIL BATALLA, Guillermo 1989 Mexico Profundo: Una Civilización Negada. Mexico: Grijalbo.
BONFIL BATALLA, Guillermo 1994 "Geschichten, die noch nicht Geschichte sind." pp. 169-174 in: Ya Basta! Der Aufstand der Zapatistas, edited by Topitas. Hamburg: Verlag Libertäre Assoziation.
CANETTI, Elias 1986 Masse und Macht. Frankfurt: Fischer.
CLASTRES, Pierre 1976 Staatsfeinde: Studien zur Politischen Anthropologie. Frankfurt: Suhrkamp.
DEBRAY, Regis 1975 Kritik der Waffen. Wohin geht die Revolution in Lateinamerika? Reinbek: Rowohlt.
DELORIA, Vine, Jr. 1973 God Is Red. New York: Gosset and Dunlop.
DIETRICH, Wolfgang 1994 "Die wütende Erde Mexikos". pp. 125-143 in: Ya Basta! Der Aufstand der Zapatistas, edited by Topitas. Hamburg: Verlag Libertäre Assoziation.
EBERT, Theodor 1983 Gewaltfreier Aufstand. Frankfurt: Waldkircher Verlagsgesellschaft.
EISLER, Riane 1987 The Chalice and the Blade. San Francisco: Harper and Row.
ERNST, Werner 1993 "Formale Form als Rechtsgewalt". in: Ethica: Wissenschaft und Verantwortung I (2) pp. 163-184.
ERNST, Werner 1996 "Metapsychologie und egologisches Subjekt". pp. 80-110 in: Herren-los. Herrschaft-Erkenntnis-Lebensform. edited by Claudia von Werlhof, Annemarie Schweighofer, and Werner Ernst., Paris, New York: Peter Lang.
ESTEVA, Gustavo 1994[a] "Basta!" pp. 65-78 in: Ya Basta! Der Aufstand der Zapatistas. edited by Topitas, Hamburg: Verlag Libertäre Assoziation
ESTEVA, Gustavo 1994[b] Crónica del Fin de una Era. Mexico: Editorial Posada
ESTEVA, Gustavo 1995 Fiesta: Jenseits von Entwicklung, Hilfe und Politik. 2nd ed. Frankfurt/Wien: Südwind.
GANSER, Renate 1996 "Der Springende Punkt: Vom natürlichen zum künstlichen Gedächtnis; Erinnerung zwischen Herschaft und Widerstand." pp. 111-132 in: Herren-los: Herrschaft-Erkenntnis-Lebensform. edited by Claudia von Werlhof, Annemarie Schweighofer, and Werner Ernst. Frankfurt, Paris, New York: Peter Lang.
GARCÍA DE LEÓN. Antonio 1994 "Aspekte der Vorgeschichte der Zapatista-Bewegung." pp 148-150 in: Ya Basta! Der Aufstand der Zapatistas, edited by

Topitas. Hamburg: Verlag Libertäre Assoziation.
GENERAL COMMAND OF THE ZAPATISTA LIBERATION ARMY 1994 "Erklärung aus der 'Selva Lacandona'". pp. 20-22 in: Ya Basta! Der Aufstand der Zapatistas, edited by Topitas. Hamburg: Libertäre Assoziation.
GERHARD, Ute, Mechtild JANSEN, Andrea MAIHOFER, Pia SCHMID, and Irmgard SCHULTZ, Eds. 1990 Differenz und Gleichheit: Menschenrechte haben (k)ein Geschlecht. Frankfurt: Ulrike Helmer.
GIMBUTAS, Marija 1982. The Goddesses and Gods of Old Europe. Berkeley: University of California Press.
GONZALES ESPONDA, Juan, and Elizabeth POLITO BARRIOS 1994 "Bauernbewegungen in Chiapas." pp. 230-244 in: Ya Basta! Der Aufstand der Zapatistas, ed. Topitas. Hamburg: Libertäre Assoziation.
GORMAN, John 1995 "Understanding the Uprising: Two on Chiapas." Native Americas (fall): pp.62-63.
GOTTNER-ABENDROTH, Heide 1980. Die Göttin und ihr Heros. München: Frauenoffensive.
GOTTNER-ABENDROTH, Heide 1988 Das Matriarchat I: Geschichte seiner Erforschung. Stuttgart, Berlin, Köln: Kohlhammer.
GUNN ALLEN, Paula 1986 The Sacred Hoop - Recovering the Feminine in American Indian Tradition. Boston: Beacon Press.
ILLICH, Ivan 1978 Fortschrittsmythen. Reinbek: Rowohlt.
ILLICH, Ivan 1982 Vom Recht auf Gemeinheit. Reinbek: Rowohlt.
ILLICH, Ivan 1983 Gender. New York: Pantheon Books.
ILLICH, Ivan, Sigmar GROENVELD, Lee HOINACKI, Bernhard HEINDL 1993 The Hebenshausen Declaration on Soil. Man.: Hebenshausen.
KELLER, Catherine 1986 From a Broken Web: Separation, Sexism and Self. Boston: Beacon Press.
KLINGLER-CLAVIGO, Margit 1995. Kosmovision in Konflikt. Interview, 22 November. Frankfurt: He.ssischer Rundfunk.
LAUDERDALE, Pat 1993 "Alternativas al Castigo: Una Percepcion Indígena del Derecho." Opcioncs 20: 9-17.
LAUDERDALE, Pat 1996 "Indigene Nordamerikanische Alternative zur Vorstellung von Recht und Strafe in der Moderne: Was die Natur uns lehrt." pp. 133-156 in: Herren-los: Herrschaftl-Erkenntnis-Lebensform. edited by Claudia von Werlhof, Annemarie Schweighofer, and Werner Ernst. Frankfurt, Paris, New York: Peter Lang
LORAUX, Nicole 1992 Die Trauer der Mütter: Weibliche Leidenschaft und die Gesetze der Politik. Frankfurt: Campus
MARCOS, Subcommandante 1994 "Marcos zur 'Moderne'". pp. 27-38 in: Ya Basta! Der Aufstand der Zapatistas, edited by Topitas. Hamburg: Libertäre

Assoziation.

MARCOS, Subcommandante 1995 "Interview" (of Subcommandante Marcos) Focus 41: 351

MEIER-SEETHALER, Carola 1993 Von der göttlinchen Löwin zum Wahrzeichen männlicher Macht: Ursprung und Wandel grosser Symbole. Zürich: Kreuz

MIES, Maria 1991 Patriarchy and Accumulation on a World Scale: Women in the International Division of Labor. 4th ed. London: Zed Books.

MIES, Maria, SHIVA ,Vandana 1993 Ecofeminism. London: Zed Books.

MIES, Maria, Veronika BENNHOLDT-THOMSEN, Claudia von WERLHOF 1983 Frauen. die Letzte Kolonie. Reinbek: Rowohlt

MIES, Maria, Veronika BENNHOLDT-THOMSEN, Claudia von WERLHOF 1988 Women, the Last Colony. London, New Delhi: Zed Books

MIES, Maria, Veronika BENNHOLDT-THOMSEN, Claudia von WERLHOF 1995 Women and the World System (in Japanese). Tokyo: Fujiwara

MIES, Maria, REDDOCK, Rhoda Eds 1978 National Liberation and Women's Liberation. The Hague: Institute of Social Studies.

MÜNZEL, Mark 1978 Die indianische Verweigerung. Lateinamerikas Ureinwohner zwischen Ausrottung und Selbstbestimmung. Reinbek: Rowohlt.

PEASANT COMMUNITIES OF THE SELVA LACANDONA 1994 pp. 245-250 in: Ya Basta! Der Aufstand der Zapanstas, edited by Topitas. Hamburg: Libertäre Assoziation.

POLITICAL DIRECTION OF THE ZAPATISTA LIBERATION ARMY 1994 pp. 156-162 in: Ya basta! Der Aufstand der Zapatistas, edited by Topitas. Hamburg: Libertäre Assoziation.

POPOL VUH 1993 Das Buch des Rates. München: Eugen Diederichs

REDDOCK, Rhoda 1995 Women, Labour, and Politics in Trinidad and Tobago: A History. London: Zed Books.

RUIZ, Samuel 1994 "lnterview mit Bischof Samuel Ruiz". pp. 187-192 in: Ya Basta! Der Aufstand der Zapatistas, edited by Topitas. Hamburg: Linertäre Assoziation

SECRET REVOLUTIONARY INDIGENOUS COMMITTEE 1994 "Interview". pp. 119-124 in: Ya Basta! Der Aufstand der Zapatistas. edited by Topitas Hamburg: Libertare Assoziation.

TOPITAS (Angela HABERSETZER, Anette MASSMAN, Beate ZIMMERMANN, Danuta SACHER, Gaby SCHULTEN, Herby SACHS, Theo BRUNS, and Ulrich MERKER) Eds. 1994 Ya Basta! Der Aufstand der Zapatistas. Hamburg: Lilbertäre Assoziation

VEGETTI-FINZI, Silvia 1992 Mondkind: Psychologie von Frauen-phantasien und Mutterträumen. Reinbek: Rowolhlt

VIRILIO, Paul, and Sylvére LOTHRINGER 1984 Der reine Krieg. Berlin: Merve.

VOLGER, Gisela. and Karin von WELCK, Eds 1990 Männerbande. Männerbünde. Zur Rolle des Mannes im Kulturvergleich, 2 vols. Köln: Rautenstrauch-Joest-Museum.

WALLERSTEIN, Immanuel, Hans-Dieter EVERS, Joan SMITH, Eds 1984 Households and the World Economy. New York: Sage.

WERLHOF, Claudia von 1975 Prozesse der Unterentwicklung in El Salvador und Costa Rica (Processes of Underdevelopment in El Salvador and Costa Rica). Saarbrücken: Breitenbach.

WERLHOF, Claudia von 1983 "Production Relations without Wage Labor and Labor Division by Sex: Collective Cooperatives in New Irrigated Farming Systems in Venezuela." in: Review (The Household and the Large Agricultural Unit, New York: State University, Fernand Braudel Center) 7 (2): 315-359.

WERLHOF, Claudia von 1984. "The Proletarian is dead. Long Live the Housewife? The Economic Crisis and War Danger as Problems of a Restructing of the International and Sexual Division of Labor." pp. 131-147 in: Households and the World Economy, edited by Immanuel Wallerstein, Hans-Dieter Evers, and Joan Smith. New York: Sage.

WERLHOF, Claudia von 1985[a] "El Desarollo Agroindustrial y el Nuevo Movimiento Campesino en Venezuela." Boletin de Estudios Latinoamericanos y del Caribe 39 (Amsterdam): 3-43.

WERLHOF, Claudia von 1985[b] "El Proletario ha muerto. Viva el Ama de Casa?" El Gallo Ilustrado (weekly supplement of "El Día", Mexico D.F.) (18 August): 12-17.

WERLHOF, Claudia von 1985[c] "La Mujer y la Economía Política." El Gallo llustrado (1 December): 16-20.

WERLHOF, Claudia von 1985[d] "Vía Campesina en Venezuela: La Teoría y la Práctica de un Nuevo Movimiento Social en las Zonas Rurales de un País Petrolero." El Gallo llustrado (10 November): 7-10.

WERLHOF, Claudia von 1985[e] Wenn die Bauern wieder kommen. Frauen, Arbeit und Agrobusiness in Venezuela. Bremen: Peripheria-Verlag/Edition CON.

WERLHOF, Claudia von 1986[a] "El Proletario ha muerto. Viva el Ama de Casa?" Homines, Revista de Ciencias Sociales 10 (1) (Universidad Interamericana de Puerto Rico, San Juan): 2245-2258.

WERLHOF, Claudia von 1986[b] "La Burla del Progreso." El Gallo llustrado (22 June): 3-4.

WERLHOF, Claudia von 1986[c] "Porqué los Campesinos y las Amas de Casa no Desaparecen en el Sistema Capitalista Mundial" (Why peasants and housewives do not disappear in the capitalist world system, Washington: Meeting of the American Ssociological Association). El Gallo llustrado (9 February): 2-10

WERLHOF, Claudia von 1991 Was haben die Hühner mit dem Dollar zu tun? Frauen und Okonomie (What does the Chicken have to do with the Dollar? Women and Economy) München: Frauenoffensive

WERLHOF, Claudia von 1996 Mutter-Los. Frauen im Patriarchat zwischen Angleichung und Dissidenz. (Mutter-Los: Women in Patriarchy between Alignment and Dissidence). München: Frauenoffensive.

WERLHOF, Claudia von and Hans-Peter NEUHOFF 1982 "The Combination of Different Production Relations on the Basis of Non-Proletarianization: Agrarian Production in Yaracuy, Venezuela." Latin American Perspectives 34: 79-103.

WERLHOF, Claudia von ed. 1996 Beiträge zur Dissidenz (Contributions to Dissidence). Frankfurt, Paris, New York: Peter Lang.

WERLHOF, Claudia von, Annemarie SCHWEIGHOFER and Werner ERNST Eds. 1996 Herren-los: Herrschaft-Erkenntnis-Lebensform. Frankfurt, Paris, New York: Peter Lang.

12. The Interconnectedness of All Being: A New Spirituality for a New Civilization

in Kumar, Corinne (Ed.): Asking, we walk. The south as new political imaginary, Bangalore 2007, Vol. 2 (Streelekha), pp 379-386

When I had become an activist against globalization in 1998, a colleague of mine told me that if I was going to try to fight globalization I was only going to make a fool out of myself. I was very surprised. I did not understand. He said: "You cannot fight the multinationals. Trying to do that is absurd. You cannot actually achieve anything struggling against these people".

Shortly after this conversation, however, the MAI treaty – the Multilateral Agreement on Investment of the OECD-WTO – did not get signed because of the emergence of a huge worldwide anti-globalization movement in 1998 which caused the French government to withdraw from the treaty (Mies, Werlhof 2003). In the meantime even the WTO itself has been at the brink of failing, too, because the worldwide movement succeeded twice in blocking its summits (Seattle, Cancún). The next step was the struggle against GATS, the General Agreement on Trade in Services, of the WTO which is still on the table (Barlow 2001).

What seems undeniable is that the paradoxical politics of *profitable destruction* (Chossudovsky 1996) these treaties are an expression of have by now produced its own boomerang, in other words: the consequences of the destruction are coming back to haunt us, as shown, for example, by the various natural disasters we have recently been witnessing. At this point it will not suffice to think about what to do in the future, once everything has collapsed and vanished. We need to think about how to oppose the destruction that is happening here and today. There is no alternative to the search for an alternative. We need a vision what to do now and how to do it.

In this context, Renate Genth (2002) says that we need a new "politics of civilization", since we are experiencing a "civilization crisis". This new politics of civilization has to focus on a new relationship to nature, a new relationship between the sexes, a new relationship between the generations, and a new relationship to "the transcendent". The transcendent generally means religious needs and our relationship to death. I would say that the relationship to the transcendent is the relationship to *earth spirituality*.

The goals of this new politics of civilization, according to Genth, are based on the "five political senses", the sense for community, the sense for justice, the sense for equality (as in: material equality – not spiritual or emotional equality), the sense for freedom, and the sense for responsibility. This implies that diversity is possible – yet there exists a common base.

From this point of view each living being is born free and equal by nature. The first "natural right" is defined as the old mother right that is based on the understanding that everything that has come to life has an innate right to live. Mutual respect is the foundation of all. Society always has to be accountable for what it does.

But, how do we get there? And what all is in our way?

As dreadful as globalization is, it is at least making clear what is actually happening. It seems to have become impossible to ignore what is at stake here. It is now more obvious than ever. Still, next to deep- rooted concepts like Genth's, we hear suggestions about trying to help "shaping" globalization rather than opposing it. Me, however, I am an uncompromising opponent to globalization because what is happening under its banner can never be reconciled with a notion of a world of justice, freedom or equality. That is why I regard the somewhat pretentious notion of "participation in shaping the course of globalization" (Attac) as inappropriate. This notion will lead and has already led to a split in the anti-globalization movement.

What we need is truly radical opposition, meaning: an opposition that targets the roots of the problem and embarks on a fundamentally different path of thinking and feeling. Which leads me again to my main question: How will this be possible?

As long as we keep on believing that our civilization, and what it has brought to us, is in any way superior to other civilizations, or that our culture is in any way superior to other cultures (past or present), as long as we keep on believing this – and many people generally critical of globalization still do – we can not find common ground. We have to realize that we are indeed facing a crisis of western civilization and that this concerns not only capitalism and modernity, but the entire patriarchal endeavour – in other words: the socio-political order with which the whole problem began (Werlhof 2007).

Since I have been actively involved in the anti-globalization movement for some time now, the search for the "what to do?" equalled a personal crisis that was not bereft of pain. What is, in fact, the key to an effective movement against this global madness?

I have been part of many movements, and already in the 1970s, some feminist friends and I developed the "subsistence perspective" through our own experiences in the periphery, where people had already been reflecting on the unsatisfying state of the world – or the part of the world they live in – for decades (Mies, Bennholdt-Thomsen, Werlhof 1988, Bennholdt-Thomsen, Mies

1999). The subsistence perspective means a notion of community that is based on local involvement and engagement, and a related notion of an economy that is based on the forces (both materially and non-materially) and natural potentials of a specific place without trying to exploit them. Meanwhile, different terms have been coined to describe this perspective: Helena Norberg-Hodge calls it "localization", Vandana Shiva speaks of a "living democracy", and people in Porto Alegre (where the worldwide anti-globalization movement began to gather annually as the "World Social Forum") speak of an "economy of solidarity" (Bennholdt-Thomsen, Faraclas, Werlhof 2001).

There is also the term "sustainability", but this term remains within the logic of the system. It does not fully recognize that we really do need a different form of civilization, not just an economic reform. We need a different culture, because *cultura* means nurturing. The question always is, of course, what are we nurturing? Right now, we nurture machines rather than community. We nurture violence rather than love. This renders our culture useless. It needs to be changed (which, of course, does not exclude saving certain aspects we might recognize as useful).

We need far-reaching, global, perhaps even further extending notions and terms that are tied into a way of thinking, acting and feeling that is able to confront globalization with the possibility of success. Yet, success ought not to be *expected*, since this would instantly lead us back into a modern, rationalizing, calculating way of thought. When it comes to calculation, we are inferior to "them". In the same vein, we can not "*participate*" in anything. The gender movement is wrong in the assumption that women's future is determined by the logics of becoming sex-less, male or patriarchal. Under conditions of globalization such theories have all become irrelevant and lead nowhere. Christina von Braun (2000), for example, says that there is no possibility for transformation at all anymore because she assumes that we have already been so alienated from ourselves by patriarchal conditioning that is has become impossible to return (or progress) to non-patriarchal forms of community. This kind of pessimism is also prevalent in the gender movement, and translates into the quasi-optimistic notion that we can at least still go somewhere *within* the system of capitalist patriarchy. It is always this *failure to leave* the confines of the system that divides all social movements. In other words, making compromises with the system by taking it for granted will always lead us back into it.

In patriarchy, everything is separated: the material from the spiritual, men from women, the lower from the higher, etc. This becomes expressed, on the one hand, in the form of a materialism that regards matter as spiritless, and on the other hand, in the form of an idealism that regards matter as not important.

When comparing to this the notion of *subsistence* I realized that the reason why so many people still do not understand subsistence must also lie in the fact that we, who propose subsistence as an alternative, have forgotten something or have not thought it all the way through. That is exactly the point.

What needs to happen is that our notion of subsistence which is materialistic in the sense of focusing on what materially shapes our existence, has to be explicitly complemented – not by idealism, but by an explanation of how the material relates to the non-material, to mind and soul, to the spiritual. In other words: we also have to explain mind and soul, the spiritual, through our notion of subsistence. The connections exist anyway – the separation is always but a fictitious and imagined one. All things are connected. This has to be made explicit. This is why I speak of "earth spirituality".

As a next step, I concluded that it is not enough to call for a relationship to nature that is simply not antagonistic anymore but caring, or that is also spiritual and not only material, etc. It is also not enough to say that we want to "cooperate" with nature or that we want to "be part of a network". These are all "*cold*" *terms*. They are rationalistic terms that always miss something. When we speak of co-operation we have a guideline for action – since co-operating means acting with – but we do not address any emotional or spiritual dimension. The biggest problem with rationalism is that it tries to extinguish our feelings, or tries to turn them into their opposites: for example, love into hate. I believe this is the main problem of our rationalistic society. The problem is amplified by the history of National Socialism that has abused our feelings violently and still leaves the question: how can we rehabilitate our emotions without arousing suspicion of becoming susceptible to a new form of Nazism or fashism?

But we cannot shun the problem because as humans we are sentient beings. If we do not feel, we can not think. Thinking and acting and feeling are intrinsically linked. In our society, we have separated the three. We think differently to how we feel and act. Native Americans know the term K'OP – a term that expresses the understanding that acting, thinking and feeling belong together and correspond. We have lost this understanding through the permanent processes of separation.

I then reflected on "*wilderness*". What is wilderness? I have always been looking for a term to substitute "nature" with. The term "nature" has been abused and become abstract. I realized, while reflecting on wilderness as the original and first expression of nature, that we need a notion of a "spirituality" that is linked to the wild!

Basically, spirituality is a notion that is always related to wild nature, and that does not see nature as exclusively material, but also as mind and soul – we could also say: as *alive*. Spirituality is embedded in the vitality of nature. This is my notion of spirituality, hence "earth spirituality". But how can we express this without championing just another "cold" term on the one hand, or, on the other, without reproducing a notion of spirituality that is purely idealistic and knows of no relationship to matter, leave alone of political reflection and activism?

Eventually, I did find the answer.

We need a term that is not just cold, but that expresses the *affection* that is inherent in life. The term is: "*interconnectedness of all being*"! This has become my central term in the search for what it actually is that we need to be based on in order to confront the madness of globalization and to get a sense for where to actually go.

When I speak of the interconnectedness of all being, I am not only talking about connectedness as an opposition to separation, but about intrinsic links between everything there is. Everything is tied together. Everything is connected with each other. We are not in the world as human beings alone.

Systems of ethics do not suffice to explain what that means, however. They mostly negate the relationship to nature (Jonas 1979). Religion does not work as a term either, because it does not want to reconnect us with the wild and is based on the separation that has occurred.

My point is: There is no separation – it is purely fictitious. That is how I came to the notion of interconnectedness as the truth about our reality, if we want it or not.

The notion of interconnectedness of all being is a notion that is very comprehensive – a notion that guides us back to the unity that truly exists underneath all. The notion of interconnectedness is a notion in which *love and knowledge belong together.* Contrary to rationalism which distances itself from nature – particularly evident in the machine-logics of a computerized rationality that systematically eradicates all feelings of love and belonging – the notion of interconnectedness embraces everything.

Interconnectedness means that we are connected and feel mutually bound in solidarity in a decisively caring environment to which we belong. In English we have the terms "solidarity", "bonds" and "ties", in Spanish "*apego*", a term expressing closeness: the child who discovers the world still attached to its mother, or "lazo", which translates as connection and bond. In German I call it "*die Verbundenheit alles Seienden*". These terms are rather poetic than analytical. I find them very useful to provide some kind of an orientation within the diversity of being, including the diversity of social movements. Because when one feels connected to all being – and I mean really from the leaves of grass to the universe – there is no end to this feeling. And it is precisely then when one will actually find solid ground under one's feet.

With the concept sketched above, we will have a point of reference which will tell us what it is that we do, what it is that we shall and can do, and what it is that we can not do. And it is by way of this that we will find a holistic way of thought that does not omit anything: not the animals, not the elements, not the planet. We will find a holistic way of thought that will not allow for gaps, since true interconnectedness knows no gaps either. *Nature has no gaps.*

Furthermore, the concept requires a call for action, namely to take a stand for the defence of all being and its interconnectedness, and I mean on all levels. Only through this will we be able to feel and take on responsibility. With the return of the emotional, the passion to defend that which is alive will return as well. Our feelings will regain their place. They will be able to flourish again without being abused, because on the basis of the notion of the interconnectedness of all being, it is impossible to be corrupted or seduced or confused.

At any rate this is my thesis.

Because if nature is alive and not just machine or resource, or whatever these patriarchal terms replacing nature are, then she is neither merely object nor no object at all, but subject, meaning: she is telling us something, she speaks to us, she communicates with us, she is sending us messages, and we can turn to her, *we can ask her what we shall do*. We can ask where it was that we have erred and where to go from here.

We not only have to regain our senses and our sensitivity, but we have to expand them, also in the terms of Günther Anders (1987) who always demanded that. In order to expand our senses, to let them grow above us, we have to "deploy" antennas of perception and realization of the interconnectedness, but not in any super-sensual terms (*übersinnlich*: that which goes beyond the senses), but in *trans-sensual or cross-sensual* terms (*transsinnlich* and *quersinnlich*), which will allow us to also perceive the senses of others, not only our own. My energies are not only isolated and ego-logical ones, exclusively focused on me, but they are connected to other energies and forces that support me, just as I support them.

I know that this is the way it is. I have experienced it. If we open ourselves to the interconnectedness of all being, then all energies are with and behind us, and they will guide us, and we will be their advocates and voices.

We have a calling in this world, namely to prevent the destruction from continuing. This also leads us close to Gandhi's notion of *ahimsa*, which is always translated as non-violence, but which also means *innocence*. Ahimsa is a way of action that does not follow self-centred goals and the interest to *be personally successful*, but that follows the bonds of life and that thereby offers new possibilities of acting and resisting and creating alternative ways of living.

This way we can finally leave ego-centrism behind us and become channels of and for mother earth.

Only such a way of feeling, thinking and behaving makes it possible to act without rational calculation and unnecessary compromises. *Compromises will be made, but not with society.* We will gain a truthfulness of action, and even though the web in which we act will be large, it will always be possible to have an orientation and to act very concretely in each specific case. This is an outstanding experience since so far we have not had many possibilities (and were prohibited from having them) to unite theory and practice in such a way.

Acting, thinking and feeling along the lines of the interconnectedness of all being also creates a *"mimetic sphere"*, meaning: a mimesis which allows for the extended and conscious exchange of energies with other living beings, since we will establish always more contacts with them and will thereby also create common ground and orientation.

For me all this means the possibility to escape the one-step-at-a-time character of the alleged alternatives offered – from above, from the west, from the left – so far, their temporality and weakness, their incompleteness, and their lack of vision and orientation. But this happens without needing a "political program" or "technological project", not to speak of new forms of domination.

What we have instead is a way of perceiving and thinking that follows the interconnectedness of all being and that knows as its base the depth of this interconnectedness – I call it *"deep feminism"*.

There will also be no more separations in action and thought. There will be no *nihilism* that denies life, any more. The interconnectedness of all being teaches us that there are no ruptures and gaps, but that there is always a connecting *rope* that guides us and that we can hold onto.

The main challenge that remains probably is: how can we turn this awareness into appropriate action *in each specific case*? How can we exchange the experiences we are making on this path? How can we know that we do the right things in order to defend mother earth? And how do we know that we are really on the way to another civilization?

I consider the development of a spiritual understanding in the way outlined above for absolutely necessary and, in the end, I consider it to be the only possible way to find an adequate response to globalization and to develop alternatives to it that will not lead us astray once again.

Bibliography

Anders, Günther, 1979, Die Antiquiertheit des Menschen, München

Barlow, Maude, 2001, The Last Frontier, in: The Ecologist, February, London

Bennholdt-Thomsen, Veronika, Faraclas, Nicholas, Werlhof, Claudia von (Eds.) 2001, There is an Alternative. Subsistence and Worldwide Resistance to Corporate Globalization, London

Bennholdt-Thomsen, Veronika, Mies, Maria, 1999, The Subsistence Perspective: Beyond the Globalized Economy, London

Braun, Christina von, 2000, Gender, Geschlecht und Geschichte, in: Braun/Stephan (Eds.), Gender Studien. Eine Einführung, Stuttgart-Weimar

Chossudovsky, Michel, 1996, The Globalization of Poverty, London

Genth, Renate, 2002, Über Maschinisierung und Mimesis. Erfindungsgeist und mimetische Begabung im Widerstreit und ihre Bedeutung für das Mensch-Maschine-Verhältnis, Frankfurt- New York

Jonas, Hans, 1979, Das Prinzip Verantwortung, Frankfurt

Mies, Maria, Bennholdt-Thomsen, Veronika, Werlhof, Claudia von, 1988, Women, the Last Colony, London

Mies, Maria, Werlhof, Claudia von (Eds.), 2003, Lizenz zum Plündern. Das Multilaterale Abkommen über Investitionen, MAI – Globalisierung der Konzernherrschaft und was wir dagegen tun können, Hamburg

Werlhof, Claudia von, 2007, Capitalist Patriarchy and the Negation of Matriarchy. The Struggle for a „Deep"Alternative, in: Vaughan, Genevieve (Ed.), Women and the Gift Economy. A Radically Different World View is Possible. The Gift-Economy inside and outside Patriarchal Capitalism, Toronto: Inanna, pp 143-157

D

The Latest Challenge: "Military Alchemy" as a Dystopia for Planet Earth

13. Call for a "Planetary Movement for Mother Earth"[*]

Preliminary remark 2010

As we have mentioned in the Introduction to this book already, we learned about an incredibly huge challenge: the secret military experiments with the electromagnetic systems of the planet itself. These experiments have been developed during the last centuries after World War 2 – first in the East, then in the West. The application of these new weapons manifests itself as natural catastrophes, climate change, and terrible "accidents". They are phenomena caused by "plasma weapons, weather wars and geo-engineering", as one of the most thorough researchers of these developments, scientist Dr. Rosalie Bertell, defines them. People who dare to speak about them are nearly always labeled as "conspiracy theorists" and this is generally agreed upon, especially by the public, as these technologies appear to be unbelievably powerful, futuristic and science fiction-like. Things are worsened because these new military technologies do not relate to the usual "mechanistic" sciences any more, but to the concepts of inventor Nicola Tesla which describe the natural world as electromagnetic and scalar "fields" and "waves". This worldview is so unusual that the consequences of its application in the sciences and for warfare are not yet understood by "normal" scientists and the public in general.

The development of our approach to this latest, horrible challenge – which could not even have been imagined some years ago – was only possible because we had the theoretical basis in the form of our "Critical Theory of Patriarchy". This theory is based on another concept of nature than the usual modern, mechanistic one and on a concept of "alchemy" that criticizes patriarchal technologies as "creation by destruction" (or destruction by "creation"). This, on the one hand, allows us to directly see the connection between the utopian logic of (modern) patriarchy and the military and on the other hand, the dystopian character of its latest technologies, even if we are not natural scientists or Tesla-experts (yet).

Therefore, we urgently call for a "Planetary Movement for Mother Earth" as we cannot act differently than to oppose the creation of dangers that are able to not only destroy life on earth but even our planet as such.

---

[*] Translation from German by Tadzio Müller

International Goddess-Conference "Politics and Spirituality"
Castle Hambach, Germany, 29th May 2010, www.pbme-online.org

We are gathered here at a special location, one that has always been about freedom, and where we came together ten years ago to proclaim the "women's millennium". Today we live in an age such as the one invoked by Annette Rath-Beckmann, when she cited an inscription that was made in Bucharest some 4.300 years ago: "When the silver-winged birds fly, when the houses touch the sky; when the lions disappear and the frogs silently peer, then the goddess will return."

Indeed, we now live in such times, and of this, I will speak here.

The women's millennium has gotten off to a rather difficult start, which is why I will not speak, as I had planned, "on loving the grass near the highway".[1] Rather, current events force me to speak of the patriarchal hatred of Mother Earth, our wonderful planet, and what we can do about it.

I have come to make a terrible accusation!

Because: Not only has life on Earth come to be threatened with extinction. No, the planet itself is under a permanent attack that goes to its very foundation. What is at stake is the *ultimate matricide*, murdering the Earth herself – the conceivably, inconceivably, unimaginably greatest crime of all times.

I am thus here in good company. For I have – albeit only symbolically – brought with me a few of the children of our beautiful and strong Mother Earth, whom I will now call upon:
- the whisper of the trees
- the murmur of the streams
- the flickering of the light
- the black panther of the night
- the eternal serpent and
- the elder mothers in the form of the dinosaurs, whom I want to once again awaken – my life's task as long ago imparted to me by my son Götz.

All this wonderful life, this beauty and variety, this strength and power of Mother Earth, our planet, are in danger today, because the planet itself is heavily threatened. There is agitation about and Earth calls upon us, to stand by her side. That means: *We have to change sides.* We stand with Mother Earth, not with human society! "Pachamama o Muerte!" – Mother Earth or Death! This said

---

1 Cf. e.g. Werlhof: Über die Liebe zum Gras an der Autobahn. Analysen, Polemiken und Erfahrungen in der ‚Zeit des Bumerang', Rüsselsheim 2010, Christel Göttert

Evo Morales, the indigenous president of Bolivia, at the great climate tribunal and conference on the rights of Mother Earth in Cochabamba, Bolivia, in April 2010.[2]

He didn't know then, however, that what is at stake is no longer simply a conflict between "capitalism", as it is generally understood, and Mother Earth. This is about far more than mere economics: it is about new technologies that have been developed over the past decades and which are being put to ever more dangerous uses – be it for experiments, be it in targeted actions – technologies of planetary destruction *by way of* the planet itself.

Planet Earth has thus been self-retooled to become a weapon of mass destruction, the very same "bad nature" that it had supposedly always been. This new type of destruction now occurs through *seemingly natural catastrophes*.

This development over the last decades has remained hidden from nearly everyone because it has been systematically kept secret. For it is of a military nature, and both the West and the East, the US, Europe and the Soviet Union/Russia have been driving it forward simultaneously. While the peace movement is currently busy looking at "nuclear weapons negotiations... the military (has) moved to plasma-weapons, weather wars, and geo-engineering". Thus Rosalie Bertell[3], virtually the only civilian scientist on the planet to have tracked the invention of these non-nuclear weapons of mass destruction in her profoundly upsetting book: "Planet Earth - The Latest Weapon of War".[4] Bertell continues: "There is a profound ignorance of the general public and even academics of the weather modifications and military plans to use the whole earth system as a weapon, which has fuelled military research since WW II."[5]

So while we are here celebrating Mother Earth and/as "the Goddess", we are not even aware of the fact that, behind our backs, *she is being tortured* as some kind of mega-witch. Every year more of her bones are broken; every year the depth of her innards is being penetrated, x-rayed and shaken up; her aura is being dissected and perforated; her breath is being taken away and heated unbearably; she is being forced to destroy herself through droughts and floods, through tornados and even volcanic eruptions. Thus, her cycles and patterns that have lasted millions or even billions of years, her currents of air and water, as well as their connections and compositions are distorted and perverted, grotesquely amplified and manipulated, or eroded beyond recognition by alien

---

2 Cf. Greenhouse Infopool, greenhouse@jpberlin.de, 23/04/2010, Klima der Gerechtigkeit, http://klima-der-gerechtigkeit.de/2010/04/23
3 R. Bertell, email to C. v. Werlhof 20/05/2010
4 Rosalie Bertell: Planet Earth. The Latest Weapon of War, London 2000, The Women's Press
5 R. Bertell, email to C. v. Werlhof 29/03/2010

substances and toxins. Mother Earth has been *appallingly humiliated*, she has fallen ill, she can no longer stick to her own rules. She is being maltreated and mocked at, she is forced into artificial vibrations as though under electric shocks. She can no longer calm down, recuperate, find back to her own dynamic equilibrium. And she has no chance to escape these attacks, for she cannot fly away like a bird.

What has happened? What is happening? What is this unbelievably monstrous, unspeakable crime, a crime that has hitherto seemed entirely unthinkable, unimaginable, indeed, impossible?

The end of the naivety and rose-tinted blindness in which I, like 99% of the human population, was living, came to me during a debate about whether the great earthquake in *Haiti* in January 2010, which claimed more than 200.000 lives, might have been artificially produced. I mentioned this monstrous hypothesis from the international debate in an interview with an Austrian newspaper, to which I had been invited in February because of a discussion about the general crisis.[6]

This led to two campaigns being waged against me: one by my university department, which declared publicly that I had "damaged" the department; and a second three weeks later, when the entire Austrian print-media personally attacked me, and called for my discrediting as scientist, university teacher, researcher and human being. Their gist was: she is a "scandal", she spreads conspiracy theories, is mentally ill, and has to be removed from the public sphere. Many of you know this because you worked to get a global campaign of solidarity started: In Germany, Mexico, the US and Austria, with petitions and letters from all around the world that deeply moved me, that gave me joy and excitement. *Today, I publicly thank you for your efforts!*

After all: rather than investigate the Haiti-thesis, so-called public opinion tried to label it a "conspiracy theory", and thus to destroy and consign it back to the underworld!

Then I understood: This had not been about me, but about the attacks on Mother Earth! It had been about turning me into a modern "witch", a monster, in order to hide something behind that. It was Rosalie Bertell, whom I have just cited, who revealed to me what was supposed to be hidden there. For it was during my quest to find out what had really happened in Haiti that I met her. Ten years ago, at the beginning of the women's millennium, she wrote the book "Planet Earth", which I already mentioned above. The only reason it failed to reach a wide audience was that its publisher went bankrupt and did not distribute the book. Virtually no one was thus aware of Bertell's seminal investigation into

---

6   C.v. Werlhof: Kapitalismus, ein Zerstörungsprojekt, *Der Standard*, Vienna, 13/14/02/2010

the emergence of weapons of planetary destruction. And suddenly, I had arrived at the source, holding her book in my hands, which she had immediately sent to me. Rosalie, who has since become a good friend – a friendship that I am proud of –, is both a natural scientist and a nun. Already in the 1980s, she had become known as a biologist, radiologist and eco-feminist through her analyses of the health consequences of nuclear contamination. In 1986, she was awarded the *Right Livelihood Award* or alternative Nobel Prize. Her book on the subject, "No Immediate Danger?"[7], achieved global fame. But of her second great book, "Planet Earth", only the first part of the title became known, obfuscating the content that is only revealed in the second part of the title. In this book she describes what I have come to call "HAARP-Alchemy" and the development that has taken us there.

Presentation of "Planet Earth. The Latest Weapon of War"

For decades, the Soviet/Russian as well as the US military have conducted secret experiments, including detonating powerful nuclear devices. These experiments can destroy those vital layers of the atmosphere that protect us against lethal solar and cosmic radiation. Moreover, they have been, and continue to be, conducted without any civilian experts being consulted. The risks to those layers of the atmosphere that maintain life on this planet are not taken into account. The author assumes that accelerated global warming, increased incidence of earthquakes as well as extreme weather conditions are at least partly caused by these experiments. After all, they rely on a systematic "heating up" of, in particular, the ionosphere by way of artificially generated electromagnetic waves, which the many transmitters of the HAARP-installation(s) in the east and west can send up into the skies, and from there to any point on the planet, by using the air that has been thus condensed by the "heat" and curved to form one giant reflector.

More specifically:

No later than in July 1962, the US space agency NASA announced that nuclear weapons tests in higher atmospheric strata had created a new radiation belt stretching some 750 miles wide around the planet – in the creation of which, to be sure, the USSR was equally active. According to Bertell, US scientists found out that it would take hundreds of years for the Earth's protective Van Allen Belts to recover from this. The ozone layer, too, was already damaged back then.

---

[7] Rosalie Bertell: No Immediate Danger?: Prognosis for a Radioactive Earth, London 1986, The Women's Press

The effects of such assaults would, quite possibly, not remain limited to the atmosphere. Another story told by Bertell is that of a nuclear experiment, which created new electromagnetic belts in the atmosphere, and after which the Caribous, for the first time in 3.000 years, did not migrate. It is possible that other animals, fish or birds might also react to disturbances in electromagnetic fields, including human beings.

In spite of opposition from within the International Astronomers' Union, the US military had shot the incredible amount of 350.000 million copper needles into orbit around the Earth as early as 1961. The result of this action is unknown. It may have resulted in a disturbance of the Earth's magnetic field, which in turn led to the 8.5-strong earthquake in Alaska, and to Chile losing part of its coast.

These programmes are primarily about waging war from space (SDI/"Star Wars") and to affect the Earth. This includes programmes to produce "heat weapons" with solar energy that can burn people and buildings the same way a microwave-oven does; or start fires on the ground, for example in forests or fuel-depots, by way of ultraviolet radiation. This kind of technology, according to the author, was tested during the last Gulf War, among others.

Laser technology – that is, the concentration of light to a single wavelength and its subsequent rhythmic resonance rise – is also playing an ever more important role, as it can be used to build "smart bombs", to cut metal or atmospheric layers, and to fly to the moon.

The point of all this, according to the author, is to invent and develop the weapons and communications systems for the coming wars.

The HAARP-Technologies:

Construction on the HAARP-installation (HAARP: the US's High-Frequency Active Auroral Research Program) began in Alaska in the early 1990s. It was supposed to "transform the capacity of communications- and surveillance-systems". Harmless though this may sound, there are today some 180 aerial-transmission-towers that fire electromagnetic waves, which are in turn powered by large oil- and gas-fields and/or nuclear power plants, and their number is projected to increase to 360 or even 720 transmitters[8]. Financing for all this comes from the military and the "Star Wars"-defence-network. The military views HAARP and its associated projects as "ionosphere-modification-installations". For HAARP is meant to initiate and control natural processes in the lower ionosphere – the transmitters reach up to about 150-200 km – in such a way that they can be "put to use in pursuit of the goals of the defence department". Put differently, the ionosphere, which protects the Earth, is to be

---

8 Cf. "HAARP verändert die Welt", *Der Soldat*, Vienna, 10/02/2010

used as, so to speak, the barrel of a gun. The technology on display in the HAARP-installations is built on the inventions of Croat scientist Nikola Tesla (1856-1943), who wrote treatises on alternating currents, high-voltage electricity, as well as wireless communication, and who developed plans for the construction of new weapons employing electromagnetic energy. The Russians, too, were supposedly working with Tesla's inventions since the 1960s, and there has been speculation about the invention of super-weapons, including an earthquake-weapon, since the 1980s.

According to Bertell, in one of the experiments the transmission towers would all together emit a giant beam, which is so strong that, in an eruption lasting several minutes, it slices through the ionosphere "like a microwave-knife", leaving a long cut in this vital layer of the atmosphere. These experiments have to do with rocket-, satellite- and space-technology. They make it possible to push through the atmospheric layers above the Earth.

However, the most important goal of HAARP, as Bertell reminds us, is the above-mentioned "heating up" of areas of the ionosphere to the point where they become an overheated plasma, as a result of which they turn into a sort of curved "lens". This, like a mirror, can reflect the enormous energy-radiation coming from the HAARP-aerials and retransmit them back down to Earth as artificial lightning or energy waves. They appear as light effects, which, because of the warming of the particles in the atmospheric layers, look rather like northern lights – auroras – or parts of rainbows. These electromagnetic currents can be steered through these artificial lenses to reach and destroy any target on the ground, possibly without leaving even a trace of the cause of this destruction.

The author reminds us that we know so little of the layers in our atmosphere that nobody could fully grasp the effect of cutting open the ionosphere, or of condensing and bending it into a lens, or of vibrating the entire Earth through these experiments. The military's goal is *"rather than accepting the limitations imposed on operational systems by the natural ionosphere, it envisions seizing control of the propagation medium and shaping it to insure that the desired system capability can be achieved"* (to gain "control over the medium of the ionosphere, and to mould it in such a way as to achieve the desired *systemic capacities."*) (p. 125)

This means that the Earth is supposed to be transformed into a "system" that can be steered, into a machine or some kind of apparatus!

HAARP and other, similar installations in Russia near Nizhni Novgorod – in which the US have participated – can also emit pulsating, extremely low frequencies as waves (ELF), which are aimed deep into the Earth. These waves are capable of tearing apart the precariously balanced tectonic plates of the

Earth's crust. The investigations into the subterranean world that thus become possible are also called "deep earth-" or "earth-penetrating tomography". According to Bertell, however, we know very little indeed about the interplay of tectonic plates, volcanoes and the Earth's molten core.

For example, a Soviet experiment in the ionosphere was conducted shortly before an earthquake in China 1967, which claimed 650.000 lives. In the US, ELF-waves were detected just before the 1989 earthquake in San Francisco, and similar unnatural and inexplicable waves appeared before the earthquakes in Japan in 1989, as well as the one in Los Angeles in 1994.

One thing that is certain, as Bertell demonstrates, is that the global incidence of earthquakes is more than twice as high since the military began experiments affecting the atmosphere and the Earth itself. But there is more evidence that something unusual is afoot. An earthquake in Bolivia, in 1994, came from 600 km below the surface of the Earth, 24 times as deep as it normally would.

Between mid-January 2010, until April, there were at least 9 partly very severe earthquakes worldwide.

But ELF-waves not only match the Earth's resonance frequency, but also that of the human brain, and can therefore be used for the manipulation of living beings. They can, for example, be superimposed upon brain waves for the purpose of mental manipulation.

Scientists have now warned that the energies emitted by HAARP might overlap with or amplify natural electromagnetic wave frequencies, leading to results that might be disproportional to the original input and destroy the harmony between life forms on Earth and the planetary order that sustains them. More generally, we are seeing accidents happen as a result of such "interference" of waves coming from electromagnetic installations. They can lead to airplane crashes, or "friendly fire" incidents.[9] After all, one aim, among others, is to develop methods of control and use of information technology as a weapon.

---

9   Cf. Joseph Weizenbaum: Kurs auf den Eisberg. Oder nur das Wunder wird uns retten, Zürich 1987, Piper. Weizenbaum taught computer science at the MIT in Cambridge, USA, and was a globally renowned expert in the field of computer technology. In this book, he explained how he, slowly but surely, changed from an initially enthusiastic natural scientist and devoted "fan" of his discipline into a sharp critic of his science and the threat of a dictatorship of technology emanating from there. The conversation ends with Weizmann's blazing attack on the naïve neutrality of natural scientists who fail to think through the consequences of their actions, and with his inspiring call for individual courage and responsibility – which, for him, is the only grounds for hope given a global situation that he views rather negatively.

We can thus not exclude the possibility that HAARP and its "brothers" might trigger catastrophic changes for humans, the environment, or, indeed, the planet. For, as Bertell reminds us, everything is connected to everything else, everything in our universe exists in a dynamic equilibrium, and HAARP might just destabilise a system that was built up over millions, possibly billions of years, and which has since then maintained its own internal circulation.

Bertell shows that the incidence of natural disasters has increased ten-fold from the 1960s to the 1990s.

She tells us of an expanding network of surprisingly large and potentially interactive military installations that use different types of electromagnetic fields and wavelengths, each equipped with a different kind of capability to influence the Earth or its atmosphere. The installation in Alaska, for example, will be – or is already – equipped with a magnetic field that is 60.000 times stronger than that of the Earth itself. The risks posed by these installations are therefore obvious, though they remain largely hidden and un-discussed. After all: the Earth's magnetic field is the result of electric currents within the Earth's liquid core interacting with the atmosphere's Van Allen-belts in ways that we do not yet understand. Hence, it is impossible to judge what effect a magnetic field might have on the Earth's interior or the atmosphere that is some 60.000 times stronger than that of the Earth. Bertell assumes that military experiments have already destabilised the Earth's balance and caused it to wobble.

According to Bertell, IT is logically conceivable that all these experiments with heating up the atmosphere could have contributed to global warming – adding to the massive depletion of the ozone layer which had already started earlier. And if the ozone layer were, as a result of this "shooting holes in the sky", to grow to twice the size it is today, it could in fact make it impossible for plant life to flourish on Earth.

Would that be the end of the "green" planet?

A number of unusual weather conditions and "natural" catastrophes may also have been directly caused by experimenting with installations such a HAARP. In the US, the task of influencing the weather is located with the Air Force, while the Russians reported in 1992 that they had already mastered the technique. Bertell demonstrates how the "El Niño"-phenomenon has changed its cycle since the beginning of the "Star Wars" experiments, and how it has become far more severe and destructive. For example, the so-called GWEN-effect, a kind of short-circuit between atmospheric layers and the Earth's surface, can amplify the effect of attempts to influence the weather – in the case of storms and rainfalls, for instance – making them much, much stronger than normal, and thus also increase associated risks beyond all bounds.

Rosalie Bertell also advises strongly against so-called geo-engineering technologies, which only benefit the military, while being sold as means of mitigating climate change (e.g. the use of "chemtrails"[10]). She argues that these techniques form part of a broader attempt to control the world as a whole, and to further expand the experiments with different parts of the atmosphere.

Weapons and/or experiments, that affect and transform the atmosphere in a hostile intent, however, are in violation of the UN's 1977 Environmental Modification Convention (ENMOD). The US signed this document, but, as Bertell points out, the White House neglected to enforce the requirement contained therein to assess the Pentagon's actions with regard to their environmental impacts.

Furthermore, we may add that the topic of ENMOD and climate change was excluded from the agenda of the 2009 climate summit in Copenhagen.[11] *Nor was the issue of the military discussed at the Earth Summit in Rio, in 1992.*

To be sure: the US and Russia are not the only countries to possess such weapons. According to Bertell, revelations from 30 years of military innovation show that the UK, Germany and NATO were all involved in military developments that demonstrate an almost criminal disregard for life on Earth. Apart from Siberia, one can also find HAARP-type installations in Tromsö, Northern Norway, operated by the German Max-Planck-Institute, but also in Sweden and Puerto Rico.[12]

The author points out that, beyond all this, there is still the possibility that accidents, miscalculations, acts of madmen, or (faulty) political decisions may produce one final global catastrophe. A US empire that dominates the world, together with the vision of divinely caused Armageddon if this were to fail, cause the self-appointed players to believe that their game is worth the attempt. They accept every risk, and then deny that there is, in fact, any risk. But just like the war criminals of old, they will always claim that their crimes aren't crimes at all, but rather steps towards their allegedly "reasonable" goals.

Nothing is holy anymore!

The deliberate exclusion of civilian scientists also makes it impossible for them to issue early warnings or course corrections. According to Bertell, *there have so far not been any serious investigations into the HAARP-installations.* Whoever made such attempts was ridiculed, had their scientific reputation

---

10 On the same weekend this talk was given, a meeting of the Belfort Group, a Greco-Belgian environmental organisation, took place in Ghent, Belgium. For more information, contact info@belfort-group.eu.

11 Cf. Michel Chossudovsky in Global Research, ca. 27/03/2010.

12 Cf. „HAARP verändert die Welt. Ein Forschungsprogramm mit apokalyptischer Perspektive", in: *Der Soldat*, Vienna, Wien, No. 3, 10/02/2010

ruined, or got cut off from research funding. *Something very similar just happened to me!*

These military experiments are also conducted in what is euphemistically called 'peacetime'. Because of these technologies we find ourselves in a permanent state of war, without being conscious of this fact: military research today has become a war against life and the planet as a whole. *The stability of life on Earth and the Earth as a living being is thus in danger.*

Bertell concludes: "I hope this book has given readers some inspiration as to how they might become involved in helping this peaceful planet evolve to its full potential. Despite years of abuse, it is still an amazing and beautiful creation. It deserves our best efforts. Enjoy it, love it, and save it" (p. 223).

Bertell and the "critical theory of patriarchy"

Bertell's book was largely ignored both within eco-feminism and military- and peace-studies circles; neither was it read by those who engage in the critical study of technology, nor by women's studies. Maybe this is due to the fact that we often do not understand enough of technology and natural science, and that we are not terribly interested in these issues, let alone in developing a critique of them. Nor have the alter-globalisation movements discovered her. On the other hand, Bertell is a natural scientist, not a social or political scientist, and her arguments appear fairly naïve with regard to the possibility of changing or even abolishing these military projects. The approach that is currently able of integrating Bertell's work is obviously the "critical theory of patriarchy" that has been emerging here in Innsbruck over the last two decades, especially because of the critique of technology, that lies at its core – more specifically, the critique of "alchemy".[13]

"*HAARP-alchemy*": reading Bertell, the first thing that catches the eye about the way that the military conduct their research and the basic ideas they seem to be pursuing, is their patriarchal character. One might say that their goal is to subordinate the entire planet like a woman, to take hold, to rape, to subject to male control, and to transform it into something that no longer has any real autonomy or power. In the critical theory of patriarchy we call this process "creation from destruction". In this case, the intention is to, first, "kill" the Earth

---

13 Cf. C. v. Werlhof: West-End. Das Scheitern der Moderne als "kapitalistisches Patriarchat" und die Logik der Alternativen, Köln 2010, PapyRossa/same, dies.: Vom Diesseits der Utopie zum Jenseits der Gewalt, Freiburg 2010, Centaurus/Projektgruppe „Zivilisationspolitik": Aufbruch aus dem Patriarchat – Wege in eine neue Zivilisation?, Frankfurt a. M. 2006, Peter Lang

as a planet and alleged chaos together with its order, or, in the language of alchemy: to "mortify" it. Finally, in a "Magnum Opus" it is to be re-created as a supposedly more valuable, fantastic machine-like system that can be freely manipulated, employed, switched on and off. This is what the military research cited above referred to as the Earth's "system capabilities"! It is what I call typically "alchemical", for the thought behind all patriarchal alchemy/ies since ancient times has always been that so-called "fathers" can wantonly create new and allegedly "higher" forms of matter and life. These "fathers" hope to usurp the place of the mother, and justify this by promising to bring forth a better creation by helping nature to realise the higher development that she supposedly desires herself. The goal is obedience![14] Throughout the ages, this thought has justified any and all violence against women and nature. There cannot be a greater crime: to destroy Mother Earth through the military-industrial complex's planetary system of war that is currently under construction; to commit the ultimate matricide! This level of "progress" of the natural sciences and technology represented by the HAARP-technologies, as described by Bertell, appears as the last step on a long path towards an intentional creation from destruction. Life on, within and above the planet Earth have already come under the sway of modern technology and its alchemical projects of transformation. It is, therefore, only fitting that it is now the turn of the planet itself. Today, it is literally everything that is at stake.

Presumably, the rational, that is, supposedly reasonable goal of all this is to get a comprehensive grip on the Earth as macrocosm – as the "life sciences" do to the microcosm; to grasp her through the antennae's electromagnetic waves, to reach her from all sides, from above and the outside just as much as from below and within. In this, all of her own forces are employed; not just material, but also ethereal ones, which now appear as targets of manipulation. They can be amplified and minimised, directed at will, and deployed everywhere, even against the planet itself. This would be the newest "philosophers' stone"! The lords of the planet now have a method to use the latter as they see fit! And, grotesquely, this is occurring on the basis of what is basically an "alternative" technology, namely that developed by Tesla. Unlike traditional physics, he clearly also worked with the Earth's more ethereal layers: the electromagnetic waves, which have to be seen as expressions of the mobility and vitality of the Earth as planet. This takes us to new heights of perversion: as soon as the not immediately materially perceptible forces of the Earth, which are, after all, proof

---

14 Cf. Craig Venter on his recent "creation" of artificial bacteria: "They're doing what we want!" Cf. Jim Taylor: The Implications of Synthetic Life, 30/05/2010, http://www.papercut.biz/emailStripper.htm

of her vitality that it is usually denied, are de facto recognised by experiments, they are then once again turned *against* the Earth, and thus immediately denied once more! What a Paradox!

In fact, this completely negates the living connection of the Earth to the solar system and the universe in general. The in-between, the living substance that was once called "ether", but was later denied, the "5th" element, is being attacked by missiles, satellites and space travel. As a result, it may at some point no longer exist, making its existence impossible to prove. A self-fulfilling prophecy: the utopia becomes real! Maybe at some point the planet will in fact be dead and race through an equally dead universe, just as modern natural science (both military and civilian) had always imagined. Only then we'll all be dead, too. Thus the image of geo-engineering and the planetary "engineer" corresponds perfectly to the no longer geo- but helio-centric perspective of the 16th century, which looked at the world from the outside, from an "Archimedean" point in space[15]. At least that's what it looks like to the makers and divine fathers of a new Earth and a new heaven, just as religion and esotericism had prophesied.

Alchemy is to act like a God, *to be as God*, to in the end become God. The basis for this is the faith in technology. This is almost certainly what the military men feel like: literally omnipotent! From their perspective, they are already lording it over the largest of all living beings: the planet itself.

Call for the creation of the "Planetary Movement for Mother Earth"

For all these reason we must create the "Planetary Movement for Mother Earth", and Bertell's book must become the book of the movement![16]

The military-industrial complex's project can only fail, i.e., destroy the planet without any alternative. The contradiction between the envisaged "system capability", that is, between the machine-like condition of the Earth and its denied vitality cannot be overcome. It is not envisaged that the Earth might react, or even resist, to the experiments conducted upon her as a living creature.

We, however, who belong to the planetary movement for Mother Earth:
We are already resisting!

---

15 Cf. Renate Genth: Über Maschiniserung und Mimesis: Erfindungsgeist und mimetische Begabung im Widerstreit und ihre Bedeutung für das Mensch-Maschine-Verhältnis, Frankfurt a. M. 2002, Peter Lang. S. 211f
16 Bertell's "Planet Earth" is currently being translated into German. We are still looking for a publisher.

Together with animals, plants, landscapes and elements, we, the children of our Mother Earth, rise to protect her, the basis of our lives; to protect her as the most beautiful, amazing, strongest and most powerful of all living creatures. We will celebrate Her, show her in her beauty *and* vulnerability, in her power *and* humiliation.

We join her side against this society!

We recognise her dignity before any so-called human dignity, as long as the latter consists of the ever further "domination of nature". Humans have to be denied the right to "subdue the Earth", to feel themselves the "pride of creation" while at the same time abusing, indeed, destroying it! We are thus no longer fighting for granting dignity to the Earth, *too*. This would be the viewpoint of the liberation theologian and co-founder of the "Earth-Charter" Leonardo Boff and others who asmbivalently remain stuck within the framework of patriarchal spirituality and for whom true rights and true dignity ultimately always have belonged to humans alone.[17]

No, we follow the indigenous and matriarchal spirituality of the Earth itself as the Great Mother, to whom we all belong. We are not merely a "part" of her, but we are *connected* to her as her creatures, in love, curiosity and tenderness.

We rise up for her!

We are developing the outlines of a different way of human existence on this planet, of another science and a militant art, and of a different society, or indeed, civilisation, which is based on Mother Earth coming first, not last; on her and her order becoming the *measure* of our actions, thoughts and feelings; on her being the measure whose reality we follow, whose beauty, strength and multiplicity guide us. Mother Earth as primal, as wilderness, is the most precious expression of the cosmic creative force and the love of the universe. The Goddess is primal nature. She must not be sacrificed to the patriarchs' mania of pragmatism, destruction and domination!

Thus we rise up!

Worldwide, everywhere, global, planetary… For patriarchy has not disappeared. In fact, it is preparing its final, decisive and destructive blow! We cannot look away or merely look upon. Today, as the entire planet is under threat from the patriarchs' *alchemical hellfire*, we also see the interconnections between this and all other threats and crises, be they economic or social, political or psychological. We become aware of how they are all connected, that

---

[17] Vgl. Leonardo Boff: Würde und Rechte der Mutter Erde, Greenhouse-Infopool, greenhouse@jpberlin.de v. 23.5.2010, www.npla.de/de/poonal/2832-wuerde-und-rechte-der-mutter-erde, sowie ders./same: Die Erde ist uns anvertraut. Eine ökologische Spiritualität, Kevelaer 2010, Butzon & Bercker GmbH

what is at stake is a single, enormous project of destruction: a masculine-patriarchal creation from destruction that is being sold to us as progress.

Against this, we rise up!

For if the Earth falls ill and dies, then everything else, too, will fall ill and die. Today, we can finally see things clearly, and we will show them to others: in writing and in speech, in theatre, drama and celebration, in caricature and cabaret, in song and music, in dance and in scream! For this is what the patriarchs fear most: us, the women, us, the civilians, us and the general public, us and our lack of fear.

We will act everywhere: Locally and internationally, in small groups and at large gatherings. No social movement has yet realised the importance of this issue. Now is the time!

TOGETHER WITH YOU, I HEREBY DECLARE THE FOUNDATION OF THE "PLANETARY MOVEMENT FOR MOTHER EARTH"!

And now we sound the first song that was dedicated and given as a present to the movement by a man, a supporter and an ally from the very beginning: the composer, musician, singer and songwriter *Konstantin Wecker* from Munich!

The song is called "...*let us live only for this!*" ("... nur dafür lasst uns leben"). The chorus line goes:

To us, dear Earth,
have given so much.
That this world may never end,
That this world may never end,
Let us live only for this!

14. What is Man Doing – what Mother Nature?
Planet Earth in Growing Distress…*

Introduction

„Much of what people think is "climate change" comes from this deliberate experimentation with the electromagnetic system that holds the earth, moon and sun in place."

(Rosalie Bertell, Russia: Joint US/Soviet Involvement/A Grave Danger to Earth, email 23.7.2010. p.3.)

„Historically, the military have not reused the weapon they introduced in one war in the next war…(In fact) the military has moved on and no longer depends on the nuclear except to…keep the peace people busy."

(Rosalie Bertell, email 17.6. 2010)

a) Planetary military dictatorship by ways of "Geo-Engineering" or actually the destruction of the planet itself?

"The sky is blue", says somebody. And the inmate of the concentration camp responds: "Could be", after all he cannot see the sky (cf. same titled book ed. by L. Trallori, 1985). The sky has become visible again for the concentration camps have been cleared. Its blue color however, cannot always be seen. "Chemtrails", which are artificial clouds created by civil and military aircrafts flying at a high altitude dispersing chemicals and nano-particles containing Barium, Aluminum, and Strontium, pollute the skies around the globe more and more frequently, leaving behind a trail that spreads to a milky white veil within a few hours following the "operation". The golden sunrays and the blue reflection of the atmosphere can no longer be seen. Subsequently these billions of particles sink to the ground, are inhaled by us, and can be found on plants, in the water, snow, and soil. The result is illness. Our soil, the plants, and the bodies of water get poisoned; light only reaches us through a haze of fine particulates. As the other

---

* Translation from German by Pamela Oberoi

elements before, the element of air has now also become subject to a systematic and technological attack. Breathing protection will not help those affected. Nano-particles reach everywhere, the inner organs, the blood, the brain, and the heart. After all we do not have an alternative to breathing (cf. M. Murphy 2010). *What does being forced to breathe toxic substances that have been dispersed in the atmosphere around the globe mean for us?*

Chemtrails are experiments and "operations" on the way to "*Geo-Engineering*", an attempt to subjugate the planet earth as a whole bringing it under mechanical control from the interior, the exterior, and from above (cf. C. Hamilton 2010). This is not being admitted, it is actually being officially denied. (In the meantime genetically modified organisms have been patented in the US, which are immune to the effects of Aluminum, cf. M. Murphy).

"Geo-Engineering" as such is a topic that is actually being discussed in the meanwhile, although not in the light of military projects; on the contrary, the vision of the largest environmental project that would supposedly save the planet from climate change, in particular from global warming, has been created (cf. Politische Ökologie 2010). This has been discussed at the failed climate summit in Copenhagen 2009 and will be officially addressed at the renowned "Royal Society" of London in November 2010.

"Albedo" is one of the measures being publicly discussed in the scope of Geo-Engineering. This term means the whitening of the planet on the ground and especially as a reflecting protective shield far above the earth in order to ward off solar radiation and create a cooling effect ("solar radiation management"). This model includes the artificially created effects of volcanic eruptions that have the potential of cooling off the atmosphere for years as well as the idea of "fertilizing" the oceans in order to combat CO^2 by producing more algae for the absorption of carbon dioxide.

Contrary to comments stating that until now these are mere ideas, parts of these projects have entered an experimental phase that has begun years ago. Nothing is being admitted, nor are those who are impacted by these experiments being asked. This is especially true for the experiments with Chemtrails (cf. C. Haderer/P. Hiess 2005).

"Land or death" ... the peasants say, "Tierra o muerte!" And now: "Heaven or death", "*Cielo o muerte!*"?

„O Capitalismo o Pachamama!", says Evo Morales, Bolivia's president at a large conference about climate change and the rights of mother earth in 2010: "Either capitalism or mother earth!" And now he can add: "O Geo-Ingeneria o Panchamama". Either – or....

For, there are other technologies that tamper with the skies as well as with the interior of the earth. Until now however, this has not been a topic for most of the movements against Chemtrails and Geo-Engineering. Artificially created extremely low frequency waves, referred to as ELF waves by HAARP (cf. C. v. Werlhof 2010a), much as those of its Russian counterpart, the "Woodpecker" project, and the American "GWEN-Tower VLF waves" (Bertell 2010, p. 7f) can be pulsed, combining vibrations with the correct resonance of the earth itself which could lead to gigantic *"Plasma- and Weather Wars"* on the surface of the earth. Not only that, these pulsed waves can be directed deep into the earth, penetrating it, until the vibrations cause gigantic earthquakes, much in the way the effects of telegeodynamics were described by Tesla (Tesla 1935, cit. in Bertell 2010, p.5); as if that was not bad enough, the effect could be strong enough to break open the earth's mantle, "practically destroying civilization" (Bertell a.a.O., p.4f). *"Global electromagnetic weapons"* (p.6) could disrupt the electromagnetic field of the earth, responsible for keeping the earth in balance with the sun and the moon. Damage to this balance and to the electromagnetic field could theoretically even result in the earth being sent into the sun or catapulted into space!

Planet earth, a giant laboratory for uncontrollable mega experiments conducted by a group of "Military Alchemists" (and governments cf. Belfort-Group 2010) *trying to "censor", "industrialize", yes, take from us the sweet- and the saltwater, the sea, the air, the sunlight, and the heavens after already having done this with the land; that think themselves to be omnipotent, as from their perspective only their "godfather" is? In accordance with John's biblical apocalypse they want to now bestow upon us "a new heaven and a new earth", not meaning a better heaven or a better earth, but rather a destructed heaven and a destructed earth!*

So "earth-ionospheric zapping system" essentially means an *Earth-Ionospheric-eradication system*! (Bertell 2010, p.3) This is what I call "*Military-Alchemy*": the supposed possibility of a new creation resulting from destruction! This time it is our atmosphere, and even the planet as a whole…

Unprecedented dreads, the likes of which have never been experienced on earth before…what are we going to call it? How are we going to feel about knowing that the clouds in the skies, severe weather or even an earthquake, a storm or drought, heat or coldness could be manmade? *What would it be like, not being able to rely on the knowledge any more that unusual events as well as those that are normal, occur naturally?*

The earth's electromagnetic system, its "order of life", is being interfered with since the 1970ies by taking influence on it from inside as well as from outside. As a result the earth's rotation has slowed down causing a wobble of its spin (p.8). These circumstances have made the earth more vulnerable to outside astronomical influences and have increased the chances of an asteroid or a meteorite hitting its surface, setting off a destructive resonance with the potential of even splitting the planet, as predicted by Tesla (ibid.).

The resonance between the earth, sun, and moon could lead to a surge in the sun's electromagnetic energy, suddenly and violently erupting, destroying life on earth in the process (p.9). Ionospheric heating causes the planet's protective shield damage and weakness, perforating and intersecting it and therefore disabling it from protecting itself against solar and cosmic radiation, and even destroying it (e.g. the hole in the ozone layer that has not been caused by sprays rather than through nuclear experiments in the atmosphere, by supersonic flights and by aerospace). However, even without disrupting the balance within the solar system the destruction of the earth itself becomes possible, just through the use of huge scalar electromagnetic weapons that will cause disruptions in the electromagnetic fields of the earth as for example the nuclear bomb blasts did, which interfered with the protective magnetic Van Allen Belts around the earth.

Finally an electro-gravitational pulse that happens to disrupt the sun's and moon's natural scalar electromagnetic feedback loops could lead to convulsions on earth resulting in a drastic increase in the temperature of the earth's molten core, leading to the eruption of the core itself that breaking through the earth's mantle would cause a planetary volcanic eruption (p.10).

Is it impossible for traditional Geophysics to recognize the huge dangers we face because of ignoring the "alternate" work of Tesla science concerning natural and artificial electromagnetic vibrations?

b) Reasons for Global Warming

Public policy measures to combat global warming downplay the role of Geo-engineering. Especially in the light of the failed Climate Change Conference in Copenhagen 2009, the progression of climate change and global warming are being discussed without considering the causes of it. One of the main reasons for this development is seen in an increase of CO^2 emissions by the industrial world. Other causes are not being considered, let alone dealt with. Since it doesn't seem politically possible to agree on measures that would lead to a drastic decrease in CO^2 emissions and achieving this is obviously not attainable by negotiation, other counter measures need to be taken. The idea of controlling and dimming the sun's radiation and therefore preventing or minimizing the warming up of the earth was born. Instead of solving the main cause of the problem a bundle of politically viable and "cost effective" technologies was introduced, first of all satisfying the carbon dioxide producers, who this way need not curb their production.

Nobody can be sure though, that these new technologies will work, what risks and side effects they bear, how large the "collateral damage" will be – e.g. in the agrarian sector, for the health and wellbeing of all living creatures, or for planet as a whole. We do not know how they might interfere with the delicate balance that exists on the planet and what possibly dramatic effects an imbalance might have. Until now none of these concerns and questions has been answered with certainty. The only thing that seems to be sure is that once again it will be the global south suffering the most from the effects of Geo-Engineering, as has publically been discussed; there is an even greater risk of drought. The plan however is, to take Geo-Engineering to new heights, making its existence a permanent state on earth without another alternative, to be stopped solely through the punishment of instantaneous heat stroke.

What would a military dictatorship mean, that tried to systematically take control of the whole planet, without an alternative and hence for eternity? How would the planet react?

So far, - so bad. And then Rosalie Bertell comes our way with her book "Planet Earth – The Latest Weapon of War". She writes about the reasons for climate change and global warming through the use of Tesla technology that produces artificial electromagnetic waves which systematically heat up the ionosphere. So there are these other causes of global warming, the ionospheric heaters, positioned by the military like HAARP in Alaska, the installation in Puerto Rico, the ones in Russia and northern Europe, and meanwhile possibly also in Australia, China and Japan…In the meanwhile there seem to be more than a dozen of these facilities around the globe. These facilities have been active on a small scale since the 1970ies, have grown and have started collaboration. Officially civilians know little to nothing about these installations. The growing grids of antennas, as Bertell states, systematically heat the ionosphere, a component of the earth's middle to upper atmosphere. Heating or zapping this part of the atmosphere at an altitude of about 200 km is the main aim of these installations. As in the case of HAARP the buildup takes place with 3.6 million watts (Bertell 2000, p.121), followed by an increase to 10 million watts, so 10 mega watts, later the antenna array has been expanded to radiate power of 1.7 Giga-watts (billions of watts) (Bertell 2010, cf. p.3f). The giant beams emitted with such power have the potential to slice through the ionosphere producing long incisions. The main aim however, is to heat the sections of the ionosphere until they bulge to form a "lens" which can reflect the beams back down to earth, directed to destroy a selected target. Freak weather, tsunamis, earthquakes, tornados, blazes, as well as the disruption of communications all over the world could be the effect, causing the crash of airplanes or "friendly fire".

So the question becomes: *How much do HAARP and similar installations around the globe contribute to global warming?*

Further: There cannot be more artificial and intensified entropy given the release of such tremendous amounts of energy into the atmosphere!

It cannot be a coincidence that Alaska, where HAARP is located, has the highest rate of global warming, a plus of 7 degrees Celsius. The fact that certain areas, especially those located around the North Pole, show a higher degree of warming has kept climatologists busy. The emission of carbon dioxide cannot be the reason, on the contrary.

There has not been an answer to this question; in fact, it has not been posed by anyone before Bertell. The growing Anti-Chemtrail and Anti-Geo-Engineering movements have not shown any signs of connecting their criticism to these questions. A fact is that the experiments in these installations as well as the connectedness amongst them have increased drastically during the last decade. There must be a visible outcome of the effects from these experiments, as seen in the melting of the arctic ice. In fact Bertell states: *...starting in the late 1960's, US and Soviet scientists began a series of joint efforts to warm up the Arctic.* By the late 1970's, the US joined in its own weather-modifying ELF signals! (cf. p.1) The *Vladivostok Summit 1974* had lead to a joint and secret US-SU agreement about weather engineering operations (L. Ponte 1976, cf. Bertell 2010, p.6).

The objective is to access the natural resources below the Arctic Ocean. The reason is twofold, one being of purely speculative nature and the other the gain of wealth.

These people are therefore gamblers and addicts! They do not stop on their own and their failed attempts do not bring about a change of thinking in them. We can prepare for further catastrophes like the most recent one in the Gulf of Mexico. Yes, Mother Earth and life on her is being sacrificed, just one example are the polar bears.

The mega crime of melting down the North Pole makes Bertell fear a reversing of the Gulf Stream which would inevitably lead to the glaciation of Europe, major flooding of coastal areas and islands, and could even create a polar shift or a total polar reversal (Bertell, 21.6.2010, email).

A global catastrophe of this dimension would probably mean the end of us all. So why do we allow certain people – not meaning "Man" in a general sense – to indulge in such an uncalculated risk, after all there is nothing less at stake than the whole spectrum of life on earth?

On the other hand it is not only about resources, it is also about power. The new technologies hold the promise of unlimited power for those making the decision about their operational application. In case of a global warming this question needs be answered. It is a plenitude of power on a planetary scale, like nothing mankind has faced before. A seduction the influential circles will probably not be able to resist!

So, knowing about the impact installations like HAARP have and what the violent outcomes of their operations could be means that they obviously need to be *shut down*! For this exact reason and in order to avoid having to take these actions, secret mongering about these installations goes as far as to discredit those demanding more information or even an end to these experiments. Any information that is talked about is being treated as a conspiracy theory and those talking about it are called insane (cf. C. v. Werlhof 2010b). A civilian scientific inquiry about the nature of the installations has not been made until this day.

Bertell's book, however, *is* the scientific inquiry which was not supposed to progress further. She proves how the existing non nuclear weapons of mass destruction were developed and how they function. Not even today's eco-social movements know about this, let alone the people these technologies will impact! Probably the warming of the planet and the ionosphere, caused by the operation of HAARP and similar facilities, is greater by a percentage X – and on top of it variable in its shaping – than through the emission of carbon dioxide alone.

Quantifying the coherences one could probably find good reasons to reject all the attacks coming from the supporters of military Geo-Engineering and that are masked as being measure supporting the environment.

An interesting fact seems to be that even those who don't assume that climate change is due to emission of carbon dioxide – the military does not talk about global warming anyway – still argue the case of Geo-Engineering (C. Hamilton 2010)! This supports my Alchemy-hypothesis, which is about the goal of achieving divine power through a new, utopian dimension, a technological transformation of the planet: its assumed possible recreation through its prior destruction!

Why has nobody made an appeal so far to shut down the military facilities and put an end to the ionosphere zapping experiment? In this way it would be possible to soon realize what the actual cause of global warming is, who or which factors contribute the most. All this without large studies, which today's civilian science is not capable of anyway.

The military itself seems to be taboo. No movement, not even the peace movement, has tangled with it. It is excluded from debate officially as well as unofficially. Should this status quo be maintained even when it can cost us – and now even the planet as a whole is affected – our lives?

Do we all find ourselves to be in a madhouse meanwhile?

c) *Where do we belong: On the side of the so called dominators of nature or on that of nature, on the side of wannabe masters over the planet or on that of the planet, our vital "Mother Earth", itself?*

First of all there is a need for a few questions:

Was does it mean for us, if the general assumption of a natural order doesn't apply to all phenomena anymore and it becomes obvious that the normality of this order is breaking down, so that we cannot rely, as we have done so far, on nature, and we cannot be at home in nature's bosom any more? What kind of a deep shock would this be, one never experienced before by mankind on a global scale? What unfathomable horror, what great despair, fear and bewilderment, what great distrust, anger and hatred would be triggered? And: Whose interest would such a gigantic *psychological crisis* of mankind serve?

There are 3 ways of dealing with these new and always more emerging small and large scale, as well as the catastrophic, alleged natural phenomena around us:

- One puts up a brave face thinking that this is a natural reaction that needs to be accepted, since, after all, it has been us causing the damage through the emission of too much carbon dioxide. It was clear that we were to expect this answer. There really is no point in blaming this on nature (e.g.: the volcanic eruption in Iceland, the heat wave during the summer of 2010).
- One believes that the earth is evolving to a higher level naturally and there is the need to attain a higher level of consciousness oneself in order to survive the new challenges. (The esoteric variation that has been introduced into the debate for some time already, as if there were a kind of "auto-alchemy" of the earth, as in a part of the Mayan 2012 prophecy).
- One believes in the necessity to slowly begin *implementing new ways to dominate nature* to finally protect ourselves from "evil" nature, even when we see ourselves as being responsible for the disaster. We cannot or don't want to limit our influence, be it politically or technologically, be it short term or long term, let alone reverse it. This is probably the longstanding consequence of a) and b). This is the reaction the Geo-Engineering circles, namely the military, have been waiting for. It recommends itself as being the solution for a problem in which the root cause will not be eliminated, like exorcising the devil with the devil. It suggests the arrival of the "age of man", an era in which mankind will supposedly dominate the whole planet by technically mastering it, as if it were transformable into a device (Schwägerl 2010) – *Gaia as a controllable machine?*

So how, if the causes for the changes in nature and on the planet are totally different than the ones assumed normally?

What if nature, our planet, isn't changing on its own and is also not reacting to the general consequences of industrialization (carbon dioxide etc.), as we think, but rather being violently forced into change *more and more in a very different manner?*

What if the so called "age of man" is neither a whole era nor a time that will be dominated by mankind at all, but rather a short (end-)phase of human hybris on this planet, determined by a small group of omnipotent megalomaniacs that have declared themselves to be *"gods in uniforms"* who nobody dares question?

So what, if now was the time for a new *"planetary consciousness"* and a new sense of and willingness to take action, a time for the awareness about our planetary existence as a whole, the consciousness about our dependence on this vital earth, without having another choice? All of this embedded in a positive connectedness to the earth, yes, in a profound feeling of belonging and the knowledge of kinship with her. This kind of consciousness would be totally different than one intending to be divided from the planet trying to dominate her, wanting to overcome and to substitute Mother Earth as is characteristic for our modern age. It is more about the consciousness and feeling about the rediscovery of *deep love for nature and Mother Earth*, as opposed to an alienation from her. It is about being resolute in standing up for our planet in the knowledge that this is our basis of life, a Mother Earth that is not evading us, but that it is rather us who have turned away or allowed her to be withdrawn from us.

So what, if the earth turns out to have been subjugated and forced, and isn't the evil "step mother" we have been made to believe in modern times? What if she is our Mother Earth, loving us and nourishing us, but being massively prevented from doing so? In this case our attitude towards her and towards what needs to be accomplished will have to be a totally different one!

Instead of seeking shelter from her, we need to shelter her!
Instead of fearing her, we need to love her!
Instead of allowing her to be taken from us, we need to fight for a reunion with her!

It is precisely not nature and the earth that are our "enemies" but rather those, who try to convince us that it is so. They do so in order to be able to exert and extend their power without a question, jeopardizing our lives and the planet in doing so.

Where should we turn to, what do we have to learn to feel again, to see and to know, what conclusions can we draw, and can we reunite? *How do we stand by her side again?*

And what does that mean? What will it look like for her, for us, for the others, for everyone and all? How are we going to think, speak, and take action then? How will this recognition, this feeling, and this action connect to each other? What will we need, search for, and invent then?

Soon there will not be the possibility anymore of compliancy, denial of assistance, cowardice, of turning a blind eye or not listening, of keeping quiet or suppressing. The effects of our bad treatment of the planet are spreading rapidly. They concern everyone now, including the culprits of this ultimate phase of crime by patriarchy. If now finally it becomes transparent that there is a *"Project of Destruction"* for the earth and all life on it, that masquerades itself as a project of salvation while in reality the aim is to gain total control over and against life on the planet, then the outrage will find an expression that forges ahead. It will not be possible anymore to sweep this awareness under a rug because all the strength and energy will be on our side, addressing the most important instinct in us: our survival instinct.

We are whistleblowers! Those who warn about existing or nearing danger, feeling committed to nothing else than the ethics of life.

Therefore there is *no alternative to a Planetary Movement for Mother Earth*, its existence is essential, no matter what its success may be. It is the logical consequence and answer to and against what is really happening: an appeal to all, including the existing social movements, to join together and *return to life and to earth, to rediscover the love of life and for the planet, to re-establish the best traditions of human culture*, in opposition to the holders of power – operating and taking action without calculating gains, without having strategies, tactics or being deliberate, by just being here. It is as Gandhi said: "Violence is always a lie", and to practice "ahimsa", taking action without violence and in "innocence", is the right thing to do. What a great and spiritual task to accomplish! This is what we need to work on, to attain clarity. This is a task we need to define, try out, and recognize even in conflict and practice daily.

The journey is its own reward, *as we walk by asking questions*, the Zapatistas say…

Bibliography

Belfort Group, info@belfort-group.eu, 2010

Bertell, Rosalie: Planet Earth. The Latest Weapon of War, London 2000 (The Womens Press)

Bertell, Rosalie: Joint US/Soviet Involvement, 21.6.2010-10-08 email

Haderer, Chris and Hiess, Peter: Chemtrails. Verschwörung am Himmel? Wettermanipulation unter den Augen der Öffentlichkeit, Graz 2005 (V F Sammler)

Hamilton, Clive: The Return of Dr. Strangelove. The politics of climate engineering as a response to global warming, en el mismo: Requiem for a Species: Why we resist the truth about climate change, London y Sydney 2010 (Earthscan y Allen & Unwin)

Murphy, Michael J.: What in the World Are They Spraying? Part II. Could Aluminum, Barium and Other Substances From Stratospheric Aerosol Geo-Engineering Programs be Destroying Eco-Systems around the World? A Closer Look, 2010 www.truthmediaproductions.com y nueva película: Edward Griffin http://www.infowars.com/what-in-the-world-are-they-spraying-2/

Politische Ökologie, 120: Geo-Engineering. Notwendiger Plan B gegen den Klimawandel? München 2010 (oekom)

Ponte, Lowell: The Cooling: Has the Next Ice Age Already Begun? Englewood-Cliffs 1976. (Prentice-Hall)

Schwägerl, Christian: Menschenzeit. Zerstören oder gestalten? Die entscheidende Epoche unseres Planeten, München 2010 (Bertelsmann)

Trallori, Lisbeth (Ed.): „Der Himmel ist blau". Kann sein, Viena 1985 (Promedia)

Werlhof, Claudia von: Call for a "Planetary Movement for Mother Earth", International Goddess-Conference "Politics and Spirituality", Castle Hambach, Germany, 29th May 2010, see 1. Information Letter, Sept. 2010a – www.pbme-online.org

Werlhof, Claudia von: A Case of Organized „Hysteria": Claudia von Werlhof and the Viennese Thought Police, in: CNS Capitalism-Nature-Socialism, Nr. Sept 2010b, London/New York (Routledge), pp. 102-106

15. Public Appeal to Social Movements Worldwide

The "Planetary Movement for Mother Earth" has been founded

Professor Claudia von Werlhof called for the creation of the *"Planetary Movement for Mother Earth"*, May, 29th 2010 at the International Goddess-Congress "Spirituality and Politics" at the Castle Hambach, Germany. (1)

300 participants signed as the first members of the movement.

"We have discovered that the military in the east and west has developed new technologies which could attack the planet and transform it into a weapon itself! This technological process is by no means controlled by the public (2) and it is not even acknowledged by existing social movements. Moreover, these technologies can be used everywhere on the planet as "plasma weapons, weather war and geo-engineering" (R. Bertell). Not only do they multiply or enhance already existing atomic and other technological (cf. British Petrolium disaster in the Gulf of Mexico) dangers to an unimaginable extent, but their development and exercises also seem to be responsible for much of the observed climate changes and can endanger the existence of our Mother Earth as a whole!

We rise up against these new methods of making war even in peace times!

We must act now, if we and our children are to have a future worthy of the name. We demand that these technologies finally be discussed in public, examined by independent scientists and their use or the experimentation with them be forbidden as long as they are threatening life on Earth and the Earth itself (or are against the ENMOD Convention – adopted by the UN General Assembly 1977 – which prohibits modifications of the environment for hostile purposes). Until now a public discussion of these dangers has not occurred. On the contrary, any attempts of this kind have been actively impeded. If the activities of installations like HAARP (High-frequency Active Auroral Research Program) in Alaska, "Woodpecker" in the Ukraine, similar installations near Nishni Novgorod, in Norwegian Tromsö, in Puerto Rico and elsewhere are only harmless, why is no one allowed to know what they are really doing?

We want these technological developments exposed and examined everywhere, by climate and environmental conferences, by environmental organizations and in general by all social movements, by the scientific community and by politicians. Even the "World People's Conference on Climate

Change and the Rights of Mother Earth" in Cochabamba, Bolivia in April 2010 with 40.000 participants from all over the world did not have any discussion of the new military technologies on their agenda! It seems that up to now no one can or wants to make an estimate of the contribution of these military experiments to global warming, the climate crisis, apparently "natural" catastrophes and other already existing ecological damages.

As an eco-feminist and a researcher on matriarchy, a critic of capitalism, patriarchy and globalization (3), I came across the existence of these new technologies only through the international discussion of the thesis regarding some possible artificial triggers of the earthquake in Haiti in January 2010. When I mentioned this outrageous suspicion in an interview about "the crisis" in the Austrian daily "Der Standard" in February, a personal campaign against me was started by my own department at the university and practically by all Austrian print media. The aggressors claimed I supported an unscientific and absurd "conspiracy theory", and that I therefore was mentally disturbed (4). The topic in question was obviously not supposed to be discussed or even to be researched.

During the following turbulent weeks I continued my own research on the question of what had really happened in Haiti. I examined the research of the internationally highly praised American natural scientist, Dr. Rosalie Bertell (Laureate of the Right Livelihood Award, 1986), and her practically unknown second book (2). Upon reading her book I started to understand the whole dimension of the technological "innovations", mentioned above. Bertell has extensively and accurately traced the history of the development of new military technologies since the Second World War. They reach from atomic to non-atomic ways of mass destruction on the basis of the inventions of Nikola Tesla who died in 1943. Using Nikolas Tesla's ideas the military experimented with electromagnetic and scalar waves and their artificial creation. Furthermore the military used these waves in unnaturally high intensities. By an installation of huge antennas or transmission towers these waves are focused in different frequencies and "shot" into the layers of the ionosphere where they may cause "cuts" or "holes" in the atmosphere (which is not just "air", but a form of "matter" , a sort of thin "skin" that holds together protecting the Earth and the life on it). Another function of the "ionospheric heater" consists of heating the layers of the ionosphere, the "plasma", and compressing and curving it into "lenses" in order to use them like a mirror for projecting the waves back anywhere on the Earth and beneath its surface – i. e. in form of the so called "deep earth-penetrating-tomography" – thereby mapping the interior of the planet, and/or causing seemingly "natural" catastrophes. In addition to the already dangerously huge ozone hole, a product of nuclear tests, supersonic flight and rocket experiments, enormous thunder-storms, droughts, abnormal hurricanes, volcanic eruptions and giant earthquakes can be the destructive consequences of the application of these technologies, as Bertell noted. Furthermore there are related dangers because of the repercussions of intentional and unintentional interferences of waves, reactions of the magnetic field of the earth, like turbulences in the Van Allen belts around the planet, and the fluid magnetic core in the interior of the planet. What has been happening with regard to the new technologies within the last 10 years and what is planned for the future, we do not know from the original book. However, Bertell, whose book ends with the year 2000, is updating it now for the German edition and an English updated version to be released in the future.

Bertell's book is needed as a source of information for the "Planetary Movement for Mother Earth" and the public in general. This book contains the most serious possible research on this topic worldwide. We are still looking for a publisher of the German edition!

The "Military Alchemists" – as I call them – in east and west, in Russia, America, Europe and elsewhere must be stopped from going forward with their plans, doing whatever they want without any public control and consciously putting at risk the life on, below and above the surface of the planet and even the planet itself, without assuming any real responsibility, without being or feeling the least responsible, for ourselves as civilians, the animal and the plant world, the climate and our Mother Earth. On the one hand we do not know much about the delicate blue heaven above and the corresponding worlds on and below the surface of the Earth. On the other hand the military seems to believe that the whole planet and all its "parts" – as they perceive them – are or have to be under their control as if it could be managed like a machine, and as if they could act like "God" himself (as they imagine "him")!

Thus, we call for an alternative science, one which works with and for nature, the planet, the Goddess, Mother Earth and not against them. Even non-military natural science and related fields of science which orient themselves toward natural science are heading in the direction of methods of destruction instead of preservation, so that life on earth is more and more receding. The military represents just the tip of the iceberg, albeit a very new, hyper dangerous and outrageous iceberg, as it attempts to transform the planet itself into a giant weapon, or has already succeeded in doing so! These experiments are not carried out during wartime or in the laboratory only, no, we – literally the whole human, animal and plant race – have been in a very real everyday state of war for Decades already. And we did and do not even know about it! Should we know about it only when it is too late?

Worldwide we – women and men – are calling for action against this obvious threat. Our Planetary Movement for Mother Earth is an answer to this form of globalization of militarism, militarization of Earth, planetary means of destruction, and the related "war without borders" of neo-liberal globalization (3), neo-colonialism, and capitalist patriarchy in general (4). Our movement founded in the North completes the already existing and worldwide coming into being of indigenous movements for Mother Earth and reminds us of our own old-European indigenous origin. And our movement is linked to Decades of struggles to recognize and to practice alternatives to capitalist patriarchy in all parts of the world. We cannot want that our efforts are destroyed by destroying the planet!

The use and destruction of Planet Earth by military experiments have to be stopped immediately!

A new planetary civilization has to arise that respects and celebrates the diversity of life on this wonderful, beautiful and friendly planet (5). We say NO to the appropriation, transformation and destruction of life. Instead, we call for a deep understanding of our interconnectedness with our Mother Earth and all her creatures, which was our original relationship with Her and should be our normal attitude towards Her again. A loving relationship with Mother Earth is our only choice!

Consider again the impact of the grotesque, irresponsible and nihilistic illusion of our capitalist-patriarchal civilization. Those in power think that they have to or can "get rid" of Her by inventing a competing artificial "creation by destruction" in order to *substitute* Her with a supposedly "higher", "better" and "nobler" world, a world that is under their exclusive control. Today this *matricidal delusion* is rampant in the military-industrial complex, but also everywhere else. It has to be stopped as soon as possible!"

To sign: If you want to sign the Planetary Movement, write to: Prof. Dr. Claudia von Werlhof, mail: Claudia.Von-Werlhof@uibk.ac.at

Donation account: Claudia von Werlhof, Planet. Beweg. f. Mutter Erde
Bank account number 30053191867, bank code 57000 Hypo Tirol Bank, Innsbruck, IBAN: AT755700030053191867, BIC: HYPTAT22

Information: The MatriaVal-review will continuously report about the Movement. More Information in the MatriaVal, issue 12. For the future a special newsletter is schemed for all interested parties.
www.pbme-online.org
http://de.groups.yahoo.com/PlanetaryMovementForMotherEarth

Notes

(1) The speech of foundation by Prof. Claudia von Werlhof can be ordered at AVRecord, fax: 0531339145, tel. 0531-339157, mail: info@avrecord.de, keyword: Goddess-Congress, it is part by part also available on YouTube, 1. part http://www.youtube.com/watch?v=qYmw6CglyjA

(2) Bertell, Rosalie: Planet Earth. The Latest Weapon of War. London: 2000. (Since the publisher closed down, the book has nearly not been distributed). Dr. Bertell's other publications may be found at www.IICPH.org

(3) Mies, Maria: Krieg ohne Grenzen. Die neue Kolonisierung der Welt, Köln: PapyRossa, 2004

(4) Projektgruppe "Zivilisationskritik". Aufbruch aus dem Patriarchat. Wege in eine neue Zivilisation? Frankfurt a. M.: Peter Lang, 2009; Von Werlhof, Claudia: West-End. Köln: PapyRossa, 2010; Von Werlhof, Claudia: Vom Diesseits der Utopie zum Jenseits der Gewalt, Freiburg: Centaurus, 2010

(5) to check up on www.fipaz.at (Forschungsinstitut für Patriarchatskritik und alternative Zivilisationen, e.V. Innsbruck)

Beiträge zur Dissidenz

Herausgegeben von Claudia von Werlhof

Band 1 Renate Krammer: Frauenpolitik. 1996.

Band 2 Doris Miller: Über – Gänge. Ein Plädoyer gegen die gespaltene Existenz der Menschen und für eine abenteuerliche Reise in eine bewegte Welt. 1996.

Band 3 Alex Fohl: Gratwanderungen. Autonomie und Pathologie. 1996.

Band 4 Sibylle Hammer: Humankapital. Bildung zwischen Herrschaftswahn und Schöpfungsillusion. 1997.

Band 5 Doris Schober: Angst, Autismus und Moderne. 1998.

Band 6 Michael Stark: vom Grund. 1998.

Band 7 Gerhard Diem: Über die Melancholie. In der Spannung von Last und List, Apokalypse und Aufklärung. 1999.

Band 8 Renate Genth: Frauenpolitik und politisches Handeln von Frauen. Ein Versuch im Licht der Begrifflichkeit von Hannah Arendt. 2001.

Band 9 Michaela Moser: Drogen und Politik. Dionysische Welten und die gereinigte Gesellschaft. Überlegungen zur staatlichen Heroinabgabe anhand von Erfahrungen aus Tirol. 2001.

Band 10 Renate Genth: Über Maschinisierung und Mimesis. Erfindungsgeist und mimetische Begabung im Widerstreit und ihre Bedeutung für das Mensch-Maschine-Verhältnis. 2002.

Band 11 Jürgen Miksikk: Wider die Metaphysik. Patriarchale Leibes-, Lebens- und Liebesvorstellungen und ihre gesellschaftspolitische Wirksamkeit. 2002.

Band 12 Elisabeth Sorgo: Die Brüste der Frauen. Ein Symbol des Lebens oder des Todes? Brustkrebs als Ausdruck der "Kränkung" von Frauen im Patriarchat. 2003.

Band 13 Barbara Thaler: Biopiraterie und Indigener Widerstand. Mit Beispielen aus Mexiko. 2004.

Band 14 Irene Mariam Tazi-Preve: Mutterschaft im Patriarchat. Mutter(feind)schaft in politischer Ordnung und feministischer Theorie – Kritik und Ausweg. 2004.

Band 15 Markus Walder: Die Diskussion um erneuerbare Energien in der Politik. Ist die Nutzung erneuerbarer Energien nur noch eine Frage des politischen Willens? 2004.

Band 16 Johannes Eder: Die Villgrater Kulturwiese. Von der Schwierigkeit des *Anderssein-Wollens* im Dorf. 2004.

Band 17 Ines Caroline Zanella: Kolonialismus in Bildern. Bilder als herrschaftssicherndes Instrument mit Beispielen aus den Welt- und Kolonialausstellungen. 2004.

Band 18 Franco Ruault: Neuschöpfer des deutschen Volkes". Julius Streicher im Kampf gegen Rassenschande". 2006.

Band 19 Verena Oberhöller: WasserLos in Tirol. Gemein – öffentlich – privatisiert? 2006.

Band 20 Andrea Salzburger: Zurück in die Zukunft des Kapitalismus. Kommerz und Verelendung in Polen. 2006.

Band 21 Eva-Maria Loidl: Risiken und Nebenwirkungen von Gender Mainstreaming. Am Beispiel der *Offenen Jugendarbeit*. 2006.

Band 22 Sibylle Auer: „Heiliges Land Tirol"? Enteignung, Zerstörung und Umwandlung von alten Baum-, Stein- und Quellkulten. Sakrale Spuren in der Landschaft. 2009.

Band 23 Projektgruppe „Zivilisationspolitik" (Hrsg.): Aufbruch aus dem Patriarchat – Wege in eine neue Zivilisation? 2009.

Band 24 Claudia von Werlhof / Mathias Behmann: Teoría Crítica del Patriarcado. Hacia una Ciencia y un Mundo ya no Capitalistas ni Patriarcales. 2010.

Band 25 Christoph Furtschegger: Grüne Gentechnik als Krieg gegen Mensch und Natur. Zur Bedrohung von Ernährungsgrundlagen durch Konzerninteressen – und die Alternativen. 2011.

Band 26 Claudia von Werlhof: The Failure of Modern Civilization and the Struggle for a "Deep" Alternative. On "Critical Theory of Patriarchy" as a New Paradigm. 2011.

www.peterlang.de

Elżbieta Hałas

Towards the World Culture Society
Florian Znaniecki's Culturalism

Frankfurt am Main, Berlin, Bern, Bruxelles, New York, Oxford, Wien, 2010.
258 pp.
Studies in Sociology: Symbols, Theory and Society.
Edited by Elżbieta Hałas and Risto Heiskala. Vol. 6
ISBN 978-3-631-59946-4 · hardback € 41,80*

If the new cultural sociology is to gain firm grounds, it should rediscover the classic studies on cultural dynamics and cultural systems. This book contributes to a better understanding of Florian Znaniecki as an eminent culturologist and the lasting relevance of his theory of cultural becoming. Znaniecki opted for a humanistic approach that he called culturalism. Culturalism, founded on the principle of the humanistic coefficient, is applied also to the cultural person. The concept of social values makes this cultural approach an original one. The cultural logic and cultural ethos of Znaniecki's thought is inherent in the very principle of a creative evolution of culture, augmenting his vision of a new civilization of the future and a world culture society.

Content: Classical Cultural Sociology · Semiotic Interpretation of the Humanistic Coefficient · Constructing Social Values · Cultural Approach to Social Sentiments · Dialogical vs. Hegemonic Models of Interaction between National Culture Societies · Culture and Power · Possibilities and Responsibilities for the World Society

Frankfurt am Main · Berlin · Bern · Bruxelles · New York · Oxford · Wien
Distribution: Verlag Peter Lang AG
Moosstr. 1, CH-2542 Pieterlen
Telefax 00 41 (0) 32 / 376 17 27

*The €-price includes German tax rate
Prices are subject to change without notice
Homepage http://www.peterlang.de